"How clearly and emphatically Professc [...] thinkers of varying time periods, religi [...] understand Jewish virtues differently. With the diverse (and even quite troubling) primary textual sources he provides and clarifies, readers are bound to join the discourse and define their own Jewish understandings of virtues they hold as central in their own lives."
—Rabbi Vanessa Ochs, professor in the Department of Religious Studies, University of Virginia

"Casting a wide net in the Jewish ethical canon and offering his invariably lucid commentary, Claussen illuminates the diversity of modern Jewish moral thought. *Modern Musar* will be an invaluable resource for scholars and general readers alike."
—Elias Sacks, director of the Program in Jewish Studies, University of Colorado Boulder

"Geoffrey Claussen's *Modern Musar* is a major contribution to the contemporary literature of musar. Having assembled more than a simple anthology, Claussen takes excerpts from both the traditional and the most contemporary musar authors and places them in conversation with one another, guided by his own explanations and evaluations of the material. His willingness to broaden the conversation to include those who might not consider themselves musar writers is not only refreshing but also illuminating. It suggests the breadth of ethical writing within Judaic sources and invites the growing number of folks drawn to musar to take a similarly broader view of the field."
—Rabbi Ira F. Stone, Rosh Yeshiva, Center for Contemporary Mussar

"With this deeply learned study, Geoffrey Claussen opens an inspiring vista of Jewish ethical thinking through a series of debates and a range of diverse views. His lucid explanations make this book a fabulous introduction to Jewish ethics."
—Susannah Heschel, Eli M. Black Distinguished Professor of Jewish Studies, Dartmouth College

"A mind-expanding view of Jewish ethical character development and a pedagogic tour de force. In juxtaposing contrasting perspectives—rather than a single 'paradigmatically Jewish' view of moral virtue—on many ethical issues, Professor Claussen compels us to consider divergent views of qualities of soul. This work will become an indispensable text for students of mussar and of Jewish tradition in general."

—Rabbi Amy Eilberg, author of *From Enemy to Friend: Jewish Wisdom and the Pursuit of Peace* and senior faculty, the Mussar Institute

MODERN MUSAR

The Jewish Publication Society expresses its gratitude for the generosity of the sponsors of this book.

Dr. Jeffrey S. and Susan J. Aronowitz in loving memory of our son Jordan Adam Aronowitz (1995–2019) z"l

Alison B. Lukacsko in honor of Jordan Adam and his parents, Jeffrey S. and Susan J. Aronowitz, faithful and treasured *ḥavruta*, whose friendship and love lift my soul

The Lori and Eric Sklut Endowed Professorship in Jewish Studies at Elon University

JPS ANTHOLOGIES
OF JEWISH THOUGHT

UNIVERSITY OF NEBRASKA PRESS   LINCOLN

MODERN MUSAR

CONTESTED VIRTUES
IN JEWISH THOUGHT

Geoffrey D. Claussen

Foreword by Louis E. Newman

The Jewish Publication Society PHILADELPHIA

Acknowledgments for the use of copyrighted
material appear on pages 363–72, which
constitute an extension of the copyright page.

All rights reserved. Published by the University of
Nebraska Press as a Jewish Publication Society book.
Manufactured in the United States of America.

Library of Congress Cataloging-in-Publication Data
Names: Claussen, Geoffrey D., 1979– author.
Title: Modern musar: contested virtues
in Jewish thought / Geoffrey D. Claussen;
foreword by Louis E. Newman.
Description: Philadelphia, PA: Jewish
Publication Society; Lincoln, Nebraska:
University of Nebraska Press, [2022] | Series:
JPS anthologies of Jewish thought | Includes
bibliographical references and index.
Identifiers: LCCN 2021047913
ISBN 9780827613508 (paperback)
ISBN 9780827618879 (epub)
ISBN 9780827618886 (pdf)
Subjects: LCSH: Jewish ethics.
Classification: LCC BJ1285.2 .C55
2022 | DDC 296.3/6—dc23
LC record available at
https://lccn.loc.gov/2021047913

Set in Merope by Mikala R. Kolander.
Designed by N. Putens.

Contents

Foreword

Louis E. Newman

The past few decades have seen a marked revival of interest in the tradition of musar, variously translated as "moral discipline" or "pietistic ethics." Though its roots are in the world of medieval ethical treatises that focus on rigorous, even severe, moral self-examination, the contemporary reappropriation of this tradition has focused largely on the cultivation of certain moral virtues, or *middot*. This emphasis on virtue or character clearly appeals to contemporary Jewish sensibilities, which (outside of Orthodox communities) reject a more legal, rules-based approach to ethical issues. The renewed interest in musar can be seen in the emergence of the Mussar Institute, in the initiatives by all the non-Orthodox movements to offer intensive musar training to both rabbis and laypeople, and in the proliferation of books on musar written for general audiences.

The significance of these developments is multidimensional. Musar in its contemporary inflections reflects a resurgence of interest in personal moral development, as distinct from the focus on social and political ethics that dominated much of the Jewish ethical discourse in the late twentieth century. It also dovetails with the desire among large segments of the North American Jewish community to reconnect Jewish life with spiritual life, and with a quest for meaning that many felt had been eclipsed by the post-Holocaust emphasis on Jewish identity and continuity. Finally, the interest in musar is almost certainly at least partly a corrective to the contemporary culture's emphasis on materialism and status, as well as widespread corruption and a perceived decline in personal ethics among many highly public figures.

Against this background, Geoffrey Claussen's book offers important insights into the development, scope, and diversity of the musar tradition. As a scholar of Jewish ethics whose earlier work focused on a key figure in the nineteenth-century Musar movement that sought to revive this tradition, as well as someone sympathetic to the goals of the movement, Claussen is ideally situated to guide us through its contemporary expressions. His stated aim here is to demonstrate the diversity within this tradition and so to challenge simplistic presentations of Judaism as having monolithic views on complex topics like humility, courage, compassion, and righteousness. He does this by carefully juxtaposing diverse views on these and other key virtues in ways that highlight the controversies among these thinkers. If this were all that he achieved here, it would be a worthwhile volume and an important contribution to the growing literature on musar.

But Claussen's collection of contemporary musar texts is valuable in several other ways.

- By including a number of writers who do not explicitly identify themselves as "musar thinkers," Claussen expands the scope of this phenomenon. Many of these individuals are concerned with particular themes, among them war, interfaith dialogue, the environment, and family life, but nonetheless have much to say about the personal ethics and values that animate their approach. By highlighting the musar dimensions of their thought, Claussen shows us that this character-centered approach to Jewish ethics is far more widespread, and takes many more forms, than has been previously acknowledged.

- The selections themselves showcase the many ways in which contemporary Jewish thinkers have drawn on a wide range of philosophical traditions and ideologies, from feminism to nationalism to universalism. The richness of the musar tradition emerges from these pages with striking clarity. Modern musar, as Claussen presents it here, is no mere adaptation of classical thinkers like Baḥya ibn Pakuda or Moshe Ḥayyim Luzzatto. Rather, it is a dynamic tradition, very much in conversation with the intellectual movements and social trends that have shaped late twentieth- and early twenty-first-century life.

- Claussen has also brilliantly brought into conversation not only the thinkers who very much *were* in dialogue but also a range of thinkers who never met and, in all likelihood, would not have wanted to be in conversation even if they had. Creating this wide-ranging interchange of writers with widely disparate viewpoints and drawing out the implications of each contributor's views has the additional benefit of enabling us to see the distinctiveness of each position more fully. Like the anonymous redactor of the Talmud, Claussen has brought together the views of generations of important (and many lesser-known) thinkers so that we are drawn fully into the discourse and forced to consider what is really at stake in these debates.

- Finally, Claussen's selection of thinkers here is bold and challenging in itself. Many of these figures — Meir Kahane is a prime example — have been highly controversial within the Jewish community. Without endorsing any of the extreme positions represented here, Claussen challenges each of us to take seriously many views we might otherwise have dismissed out of hand. Importantly, he helps us to see that all of them have a place within our very wide-ranging tradition.

In all, this book is an expression of Claussen's own humility: his willingness to concede that he (and we) have something to learn even from views with which we strongly disagree. *Modern Musar* is an invitation to us to reconceive the boundaries and significance of this important religious-ethical tradition.

I cannot conclude this foreword without a brief personal acknowledgement. Twenty years ago, a young man showed up in my Introduction to Religion course at Carleton College, where I was then a professor of religion. Quiet and unassuming, he quickly distinguished himself as one of the most insightful and talented students I had the privilege of teaching there in more than thirty years on the faculty. He went on to take several other courses from me before he graduated and went on to rabbinical studies and then doctoral work in the field of Jewish ethics. That former student became a valued colleague and conversation partner as well as a personal friend. And now, with the publication of this and other works in this field, he has become an important teacher as well. For this I am profoundly grateful. That he has become a major scholar and interpreter of musar is something for which we can all be grateful.

Acknowledgments

It has been a pleasure to work with The Jewish Publication Society (JPS) and University of Nebraska Press (UNP) on this book. I am grateful to Rabbi Barry Schwartz, the JPS director, for inviting me to undertake this project and for all of his support and encouragement. I am very grateful to JPS managing editor Joy Weinberg for her expert editorial work that did so much to improve this volume. I thank Leif Milliken, Elizabeth Zaleski, and the rest of the UNP staff who assisted with its publication. And I thank Dr. Jeffrey S. and Susan J. Aronowitz as well as Alison B. Lukacsko for generous financial support that made this book possible.

This book was also made possible thanks to the support of Elon University, where I have taught since 2011. I am grateful to the university for the sabbatical during which I completed much of the work on this project and for subvention funds provided by the Office of the Provost, the Office of the Dean of the College of Arts and Sciences, and the Lori and Eric Sklut Endowed Professorship in Jewish Studies. I give special thanks to Lori and Eric Sklut for their incredible generosity and commitment to supporting Jewish Studies scholarship.

Many colleagues at Elon have provided encouragement and support for this project. I especially thank Religious Studies and Jewish Studies colleagues including Amy Allocco, Lynn Huber, Ariela Marcus-Sells, Andrew Monteith, Helen Orr, Sumeyye Pakdil, Brian Pennington, Rebecca Todd Peters, Jeffrey Pugh, L. D. Russell, Andrea Sinn, and Pamela Winfield;

librarians including Lynn Melchor and Patrick Rudd; and administrative leaders including Steven House, Tim Peeples, Jim Piatt, Gabie Smith, Jeff Stein, Aswani Volety, and Kirby Wahl.

Thank you to my Jewish Ethics students in 2019 and 2021 who engaged with drafts of this book and brought it to life through animated discussions and role-playing activities. And thank you to the Society of Jewish Ethics for the opportunity to present about my experience teaching with this book at the SJE annual meeting; to Benjamin Ricciardi for his response; and to the *Journal of Jewish Ethics* for publishing the article that emerged from that presentation ("Teaching Modern Jewish Ethics through Role Play," *Journal of Jewish Ethics* 6, no. 1).

Many mentors, colleagues, and friends offered their encouragement and feedback on this project. I am especially grateful to Louis Newman for his support and encouragement. I also give special thanks to Joshua Ben-Gideon, Rebecca Ben-Gideon, Yoni Brafman, Misha Clebaner, Emily Filler, Meir Goldstein, Alex Green, Shai Held, Sandra Lawson, Amanda Mbuvi, Andrew Mbuvi, Alan Mittleman, John T. Roberts, Elias Sacks, and Ira Stone. I thank William Templer for contributing an original translation to this volume. And I thank those who wrote original contributions or revised earlier works for inclusion in this volume: Amy Eilberg, Emily Filler, David Jaffe, Sandra Lawson, Amanda Mbuvi, and Shmuly Yanklowitz.

Finally, I am so grateful for the love and support of family. Thank you to Bruce and Jo Ann; Kevin, Arden, Caelen, Ewin, Lillien, and Durgin; Laura, Dmitri, Alex, Max, and Kate. Thank you to Hillary, J, Lahav, Abir, and Rayah. Thank you to Katy for love and support and for conversations about each of the chapters in this volume. Thank you to Eliana and Talya for endless love and joy and for inspiring me and teaching me so much, every day.

With particular gratitude, this book is dedicated to my mother, Eileen Claussen, who has provided unwavering love, support, and encouragement, who has been a role model, mentor, and inspiration, and who has taught me so much about virtues including justice, courage, honesty, and asking challenging questions.

Introduction

What kinds of people should we aspire to be? What characterizes human beings at their very best? Jews have often answered these questions in the same sort of way that members of other communities have answered them: by articulating moral qualities — virtues — that people ought to possess. Diverse Jews throughout history have often agreed on the importance of moral virtues such as honesty, humility, forgiveness, compassion, and justice. But their agreement that these virtues are important does not imply that they have agreed on the meaning of these virtues. Indeed, virtues that are important to communities are almost always the subject of fierce disagreement and debate.

Students of Jewish ethics may be misled by claims that suggest otherwise. It is not uncommon for contemporary books about Jewish ethics to describe, for example, "the Jewish view of forgiveness," "the uniquely Jewish view of compassion," or "the Jewish sense of justice."[1] Descriptions like these often reflect efforts to give authority to particular ethical views, implying that they are supported by some consensus or authentic line of tradition and casting doubt on the authentically Jewish character of dissenting opinions.

This book seeks to counter such efforts. The pages that follow introduce readers to the diversity of *musar* — broadly defined in this volume as Jewish discourse about virtue and character — without making claims about the authority or authenticity of any particular view. Approaching my task as a historian of modern Jewish ethics, I document how influential Jewish thinkers have developed diverse approaches to musar and how these thinkers have passionately disagreed with one another. While some have claimed that their views represent the authoritative and authentic "Jewish view," this book makes clear that when we look at the history of disagreement, debate, and dissent in Jewish ethics, it is impossible to identify "the Jewish view" of any particular virtue. This is especially clear when we focus on the modern era, a period that this book defines as beginning with the upheavals of the late eighteenth century.

Modern Jewish discourse about virtue has been highly contested. Amid massive political, economic, and cultural changes, and with the crumbling of traditional Jewish authority structures, modern Jews have had little agreement on what might constitute "Judaism" or "Jewish ethics." Over the past two and a half centuries, they have variously embraced, pushed back against, and argued about the merits of individualism, universalism, secularism, historicism, rationalism, romanticism, feminism, capitalism, socialism, communism, anarchism, and nationalism. They have spoken with very different perspectives on controversial questions regarding national identity, religion, and politics; questions regarding gender, sexuality, and family; questions regarding the existence and character of God; questions regarding the authority and meaning of the Torah's laws and narratives; questions regarding the ethics of war and violence; questions regarding the relationship between humans and nonhuman animals; questions regarding the relationship between Jews and non-Jews; and questions regarding the Holocaust, Zionism, and the establishment of the State of Israel. Amid debates on these topics and many others, they have articulated very different perspectives on virtues such as honesty, curiosity, humility, courage, self-restraint, gratitude, forgiveness, love, solidarity, and justice.

THE GENRE OF MUSAR

Jewish literature that discusses virtue and character is often known in Hebrew as *sifrut musar*—"musar literature," where the word *musar* (sometimes spelled *mussar*) may be translated as "moral discipline," "moral instruction," "moral correction," or simply "morality" or "ethics." This term is generally used to refer to writing that discusses character traits, especially writing that defines virtues, recommends their acquisition, and teaches how to acquire them. Musar literature is a form of *normative* ethical literature—literature that makes explicit claims about how human beings should think, feel, speak, or act. It may be distinguished from another prominent form of normative Jewish literature, *halakhic* literature, which defines rules and laws. While halakhic literature teaches norms for conduct, musar literature points to ideals of character—not just how people should act, but what people should be like.

Scholars have sometimes defined the "classical" form of musar literature as books organized around particular aspects of the ideal life, with sections of musar texts typically devoted to individual virtues treated one at a time.[2] For example, a popular medieval treatise in this form, Rabbi Bahya ibn Pakuda's eleventh-century *Book of Direction to the Duties of the Heart*, includes chapters devoted to humility, asceticism, and love of God, among other topics; an early modern classic of this genre, Rabbi Moshe Hayyim Luzzatto's *Path of the Upright* (1740), includes sections on watchfulness, zeal, and the fear of sin. But virtue-focused literature—that is, musar literature—in the medieval and early modern periods took a variety of other forms: ethical letters, treatises, monographs, homilies, commentaries on classical texts, and even stories and poems. Musar literature is appropriately defined not by a particular literary form but by its focus on virtue and character.[3]

In the modern era, musar literature has continued to be produced in the classical form of books that devote individual chapters to individual virtues. Some examples discussed in this volume include *The Book of Moral Accounting* (*Sefer Heshbon ha-Nefesh*, 1808) by Menahem Mendel Lefin, a leader of the Haskalah (Jewish Enlightenment) movement in Poland; *The Book of Character Traits* (*Sefer ha-Middot*, 1811) by the Hasidic rabbi Nahman of Bratslav, Ukraine; *Wondrous Adviser* (*Pele Yo'etz*, 1824) by the Bulgarian Sephardic rabbi Eliezer Papo; or, more recently, *The*

Jewish Moral Virtues (1999) by the American Reform movement's Rabbi Eugene Borowitz and Frances Schwartz.

Other modern musar literature discussed in this volume replicates other forms mentioned above—letters, treatises, monographs, homilies, and commentaries. And as new literary forms have emerged in recent centuries, musar literature has found expression in those forms as well. Thus, for example, when the Lithuanian rabbi Israel Salanter sought to found a mass movement focused on musar literature and the development of moral virtue in the mid-1800s—what came to be called the "Musar movement"—he wrote not only ethical letters and homilies but also journal articles, using a new literary form that could help him communicate his moral teachings.[4] When Jewish ethicists, philosophers, and theologians in contemporary academic settings have sought to communicate their ideas about virtues, they have also written journal articles, though these are guided by contemporary academic norms and so take a very different form from Salanter's. Other Jewish thinkers have laid out their conceptions of virtues in books, essays, articles, or (more recently) blog posts. Writings focused on virtues, in all of these forms, constitute important examples of modern musar. This volume features examples of modern musar writings that take diverse forms and illustrate the broad diversity of modern Jewish approaches to virtue.

ABOUT THIS BOOK

This volume is organized around ten particular virtues or closely related qualities, with each chapter devoted to a different virtue or set of related virtues: honesty and love of truth; curiosity and inquisitiveness; humility; courage and valor; self-restraint and temperance; gratitude; forgiveness; love, kindness, and compassion; solidarity and social responsibility; and justice and righteousness. As such, this volume itself would seem to take the form of a classical musar text. But this book is not a work of normative literature that makes claims about what kinds of people its readers should aspire to be and what characterizes human beings at their very best. Rather, it is a work of descriptive literature that demonstrates how diverse Jewish thinkers have made claims about what human beings should be like.

I have *not* chosen these ten qualities because I think they are the most important virtues for modern Jews to cultivate; rather, I have chosen them because they have been appreciated and thoroughly debated by a broad range of influential Jewish thinkers, from a wide range of perspectives, diverse geographic locations, and various time periods from the late eighteenth century to the present. These virtues have appealed to Jews who might be viewed as more "liberal" or "conservative" or "Orthodox"; Jews who might be viewed as "religious" or "secular"; and Jews of various genders, sexual orientations, and racial and ethnic backgrounds. In seeking virtues that would be embraced by a particularly broad range of Jews, I have excluded virtues, such as "love of God" or "fear of sin," that large groups of Jews have plainly rejected. The selected virtues are more broadly popular but are also, at the same time, fiercely contested.

Likewise, I have chosen the primary sources included in this volume because I believe they illustrate significant tensions or arguments — and *not* because I think they are the most compelling or inspirational texts. Some of the selected texts express views that I personally find problematic, disturbing, even horrifying, and readers are likely to judge certain selections negatively as well. Understanding the diversity of modern Jewish thought requires understanding both the modern Jewish thought that we judge positively and the modern Jewish thought we judge negatively.

That having been said, I hope that this volume may stimulate readers to think about how the virtues under discussion play out in their own lives, and to weigh and refine their own ethical perspectives. One of the most important reasons to study the history of ethics, with all of its warts and blemishes, is that the honest study of the past can help to inspire our ethics in the present. Studying the past may encourage us to learn from the past, and it may also help us to see how we might improve on or reject models from the past. And Jewish ethical approaches are improved when we are able to evaluate a broad range of sources and locate our own judgments within the wide terrain of modern Jewish thinking.

As such, I intend this volume not only for readers whose primary motivation is to understand modern Jewish thought from a distance but also for those whose primary motivation is to gain instruction from the history of modern Jewish thought. This volume encourages the critical study of modern Jewish ethics, but it may also encourage thinking critically about one's own ethical formation. Whether read in a classroom setting, an adult-education setting, a musar or other group, with a *havruta*, or on one's own, this volume invites us to consider our own moral ideals and moral character.[5]

Each chapter of this volume features the writing of approximately ten Jewish thinkers from diverse times, locations, and perspectives, generally presented chronologically. Each is a Jewish thinker who was (or is) in a position of relative influence in shaping the attitudes of other Jews. The seventy-eight Jewish thinkers featured in the volume (some appear in more than one chapter) are elite figures: most of them have either rabbinical ordination, a doctorate, a public profile as an author, or some combination of these. Rabbis who engage with classical Jewish texts are especially well represented — not because I am claiming that their perspectives are more authentic or that their positions best represent modern Jewish ethics, but because their disparate uses of shared texts illuminate how virtues have been contested.

These diverse Jewish thinkers have generally agreed that the virtue they are discussing is important but have disagreed about its character, its significance, and how it ought to be applied. Often the sources that I have selected focus on the same issue, employ similar language, or quote the same classical text — and are in disagreement or in tension. The juxtaposition of these sources allows us to see these tensions with particular clarity.

Many influential thinkers are included in this volume, though influence has not been the decisive criterion for inclusion and there are many influential Jewish thinkers whose writing does not appear here. The twenty-one thinkers discussed in more than one selection across chapters—Rebecca Alpert, Hannah Arendt, Shalom Arush, Shalom Noah Berezovsky, Eliyahu Eliezer Dessler, Amy Eilberg, Marc Ellis, Natan Tzevi Finkel, Emma Goldman, Abraham Joshua Heschel, Menaḥem Mendel Lefin, Emmanuel Levinas, Meir Kahane, Abraham Isaac Kook, Amanda Mbuvi, Naḥman of Bratslav, Judith Plaskow, Susan Schnur, Shneur Zalman of Liadi, Sherwin Wine, and Shmuly Yanklowitz—receive particular attention because their writings fit particularly well into the debates featured in this book.

Seeking to highlight disagreement, I have sometimes featured thinkers and sources that are particularly provocative, idiosyncratic, or radical. Some readers may wonder whether some of these sources should count as "Jewish," because their views seem too extreme or because they don't seem strongly connected to Jewish communities or traditions in the way that certain readers consider normative. But such thinkers and sources are part of the history of modern Jewish ethics, both in their own right and also because of the influence they have had (or have sought) in shaping the perspectives of other Jews. I have sought to include a wide range of thinkers who identify as Jewish and who have (for the most part) had interest or success in shaping Jewish identities, communities, or traditions, even if their writings quoted in this volume are not primarily directed at a Jewish audience. And while, to be sure, not all of the sources in this volume claim to represent authentic or authoritative musar, all of them represent perspectives that have been of interest to some groups of modern Jews, especially modern Jews considering how their Jewish identities might inform their moral lives.

The decision about which voices should be included in this volume has also been shaped by a desire to include figures from a range of modern Jewish movements. Particular attention has been given to those Ashkenazi Orthodox movements in Europe, the United States, and Israel among which the production of modern musar literature has especially flourished. As Joseph Dan, the leading contemporary scholar of musar literature, has noted, the Hasidic and Musar movements were particularly prolific in producing musar literature in the eighteenth, nineteenth, and early twentieth centuries; such literature was also produced by the Mitnagdic movement (non-Hasidic Lithuanian traditionalists, e.g., Ḥayyim of Volozhin), the Religious Zionist movement (e.g., the writings of Abraham Isaac Kook), and other Orthodox movements in the United States and Israel following the Holocaust.[6]

Dan's presentation of modern musar, however, neglects to note the flourishing of musar literature produced by non-Orthodox Jews. This volume adds to Dan's discussion by pointing out how prominent figures associated with the Reform movement, such as Hermann Cohen and Kaufmann Kohler, wrote about the virtues in the early twentieth century. So did secular Zionists including, for example, Mikhah Yosef Berdichevsky. Later in the twentieth century, musar writing was produced by rabbis associated with the Conservative movement such as Abraham Joshua Heschel, rabbis associated with the Reconstructionist movement such as Mordecai Kaplan, rabbis associated with the Reform movement such as Eugene Borowitz, and rabbis from Humanistic Judaism such as Sherwin Wine. Looking to more recent writing, this volume highlights the contributions of female rabbis such as Amy Eilberg and Danya Ruttenberg (Conservative), Sandra Lawson and Rebecca Alpert (Reconstructionist), Ruth Abusch-Magder and Karyn Kedar (Reform), and Lynn Gottlieb (Jewish Renewal).

That said, Jewish movements such as these include diverse ethical perspectives, and any particular text should not be taken as representative of that movement. Similarly, readers are cautioned not to judge a particular thinker's ethical perspective solely based on the selections featured in this volume. Since these texts were chosen because of the ways in which they contrast with other perspectives, and not because they epitomize the thought of any particular thinker, individual thinkers may not always be well represented by a given selection. I hope that readers interested in particular figures will be inspired to read more of their writings.

Nor should any particular text be taken as representative of Judaism or Jewish ethics. Many of the views presented here could be—or have been—portrayed as "the Jewish perspective," "the view of Jewish ethics," "the musar perspective," or "the view of the Torah," but this volume invites readers to challenge such claims. As you will see, there are many different Jewish perspectives, many different views of Jewish ethics, many different musar perspectives, and many different views of the Torah. Modern Jewish ethics in general, and modern musar in particular, has been complex, multivocal, dynamic, and highly contested.

MODERN MUSAR

1

Honesty and Love of Truth
(*Yosher/Ahavat ha-Emet*)

Must we always tell the truth? When might it be okay to lie? What does it mean to be appropriately honest or appropriately dedicated to truth? Ancient Jewish texts often condemn dishonesty, teaching that "lying speech is an abomination to the Lord" (Prov. 12:22). In the Babylonian Talmud (BT), Rabbi Jeremiah bar Abba lists liars as among those who "do not receive the Divine Presence" (BT *Sotah* 42a). Classical Rabbinic literature associates God with truth, as when Rabbi Hanina declares that "the seal of the Holy Blessed One is truth" (BT *Shabbat* 55a). Dedication to truth is also an important theme in medieval musar literature, and Maimonides singles out "love of truth" as one of the virtues required for every judge.[1]

But the Bible sometimes describes lying without condemning it, and classical Rabbinic interpretations sometimes justify dishonesty for a good cause. In the biblical book of Genesis, for example, the Patriarch Jacob steals the blessing that his father Isaac intends for his brother Esau. Jacob disguises himself as his brother and claims, "I am Esau, your first-born" (Gen. 27:19); Isaac later describes him as "coming in deceit" (27:35). While some ancient commentaries retell the story so that Jacob is not guilty of an outright lie, others justify Jacob's deception, explaining that he "came with the wisdom of his Torah."[2] From this latter perspective, wisdom may sometimes require deceit.

1

Other Rabbinic traditions are more explicit in affirming exceptions to traditional prohibitions against lying, especially when dishonesty may prevent negative consequences or ensure positive consequences. For example, the Talmud (BT *Shabbat* 153b) warns against revealing laws that may lead to further transgressions, invoking a biblical verse: "It is the glory of God to conceal a matter" (Prov. 25:2). BT *Yevamot* 65b teaches that truth may be altered "for the sake of peace." BT *Bava Met-zi'a* 23b–24a records that "the rabbis" deviate from the truth in three matters: "hospitality" (perhaps to ensure that hospitable people will not be identified and exploited), "a bed" (perhaps to ensure modesty about sexual behavior), and "a tractate" (seemingly to ensure modesty about one's learning).[3] And while some manuscripts of the Jerusalem Talmud (*Berachot* 14d) caution that "fictions [or: lies] concerning Torah are bad," other manuscript traditions say, quite to the contrary, that fictions or lies concerning Torah "are good."[4]

The modern sources excerpted in this chapter, arranged chronologically, present a number of Jewish perspectives on the virtues of honesty and love of truth, many of which draw on the premodern sources discussed above. As we will see, Jewish thinkers from diverse locations over the past two centuries have praised common ideals but come to different conclusions regarding honesty and love of truth. Some of these thinkers have even built their divergent ideas on common sources: two modern rabbis discussed below, for example, take guidance from the story of Jacob deceiving his father and stealing the blessing intended for his brother. In section 1.4, Eliyahu Eliezer Dessler argues that while Jacob appears to have deceived his father, he was justified because he was fulfilling God's will and thus acting for the sake of a higher truth. A love of God's ultimate truth, from this perspective, may sometimes necessitate being less than truthful with other people. In section 1.8, by contrast, Abigail Treu describes Jacob's deceit as a moral failure. For Treu, the story is teaching us to strive to be more honest than Jacob was in this instance.

This chapter pays particular attention to the virtue of *intellectual* honesty, the disposition to honestly and fairly acknowledge evidence, even when what is revealed might be disturbing or at odds with one's commitments. A number of selections below explore this theme with regard to the history of Jewish traditions themselves. Sections 1.3 and 1.5, for example, affirm the importance of honestly acknowledging unpopular ancient Rabbinic teachings, although the authors of each of these selections show limited openness to acknowledging traditions at odds with their beliefs. Section 1.6 shows a more complete embrace of standards of intellectual honesty affirmed in contemporary academic settings. Section 1.10 calls for acknowledging painful truth with the particularly radical honesty that is demanded when confronting disaster.

We will also see challenges to these sorts of standards of intellectual honesty. In section 1.2, one rabbi argues that preachers may deceive their audiences in order to communicate higher truths. In section 1.7, another rabbi criticizes honest discussions about the failures of one's country with students who have not yet developed a foundation of national pride. Section 1.9 notes a number of other reasons that have been used to justify rabbinical censorship, including protecting honor or promoting modesty, peace, and understanding.

Intellectual honesty may be a particularly important virtue for readers of this volume to grapple with, as we ourselves consider how to honestly study and present the diverse views that Jewish thinkers have taken on these subjects. Personally, I have tried my best in this chapter to honestly acknowledge that debates about honesty and love of truth have not been settled among modern Jews.

1.1. HONESTY IN EVERY RESPECT

Menaḥem Mendel Lefin (1749–1826) was a leader of the Haskalah (Jewish Enlightenment) movement in Poland. Lefin depicted himself as a moderate, opposed to the atheism and disregard for Jewish law that he saw among liberally inclined Jews as well as to the radicalism and irrationality he saw in Hasidism. As the historian Nancy Sinkoff has argued, Lefin's primary work of musar literature, the *Book of Moral Accounting* (*Sefer Ḥeshbon ha-Nefesh*), was above all intended to teach young Jewish men to resist the charisma and insincere arguments of Hasidic leaders.[5] Lefin was particularly outraged by the sermons of Hasidic preachers of his era that, in his view, often misrepresented tradition and were filled with lies designed to bolster the honor and power of the preacher. Hasidic preachers, Lefin contended, falsely claimed that they themselves could bring healing and salvation; they benefited financially from such lies, extracting monetary donations (*pidyonot*) from their followers (which they spent on luxuries for themselves) in exchange for assurances that their followers' prayers would be answered; and they claimed to possess virtues that they did not in fact possess.[6]

Lefin's polemic against Hasidism may misrepresent the motivations of Hasidic leaders who saw themselves as honest faith-healers or who viewed deception as ultimately justified for the sake of truth (see section 1.2). Lefin, however, also rejected the idea that falsehoods of these sorts could be justified.

The selection below, from Lefin's chapter on "Truth" in his *Book of Moral Accounting*, shows his uncompromising devotion to values of sincerity and honesty. Lefin insists that "even an offhand remark" must be true "in every respect," and "one must beware even of what only hints at being a lie, and of language that might be ambiguous, and even of falsehoods that are not explicitly stated but that may be implied or deduced." Lefin believed that any sort of deceit was disgraceful, and that one must speak honestly even when this will cause one to lose power, wealth, and money. Thus Lefin adjures his audience to value moral duty over a concern for consequences. At the same time, however, he assures readers that, in the long run, this approach to living will benefit them. The consequences of lying will be devastating, whereas honesty will ultimately lead to good outcomes.

Lefin's *Book of Moral Accounting* remains in print to this day, and its ethical perspectives continue to provide guidance and inspiration to a diverse range of Orthodox and non-Orthodox Jews.[7]

Menaḥem Mendel Lefin, *The Book of Moral Accounting* (1808)

Nothing should come out of your mouth, not even an offhand remark, unless your heart can attest to its truth in every respect.

Lying is a very disgraceful sickness of the soul. At first, it emerges when pursuing the permitted pleasures of money, honor, or being loved by one's fellows; it then [encourages] forbidden pleasures; and in the end one becomes conditioned to lies for their own sake. And when joined with the evil inclination [*yetzer ha-ra*] to engage in idle talk, it will even lead to a desire to swear false oaths, God forbid.

For example: a boastful man exerts himself to the greatest degree to flaunt virtues that he does not possess, and he strengthens himself so that he may deceive others with mountains of proofs and exaggerations that are empty and void, in the hopes that they may believe him. . . .

But in the end, "a lie has no legs,"[8] and even when [the liar] later speaks the truth, no one will believe him. Such is the punishment for those who are boastful, hypocritical, swindling, or deceitful: they are exposed, first to one person and then to another, until they are known by all [for their lies] and are despised, debased, and hated by all.

Therefore, when one first [finds oneself telling a lie] one must scrutinize oneself and search for the source of one's sickness, so that one may root it out by training oneself in the character traits of humility, justice, and silence; and afterward, one also needs training in the character trait of truthfulness, so that one may fulfill the distinct commandment of "loving truth," even when by doing so one will lose the pleasures of money or what seems like honor. . . .

And one must beware even of what only hints at being a lie, and of language that might be ambiguous, and even of falsehoods that are not explicitly stated but that may be implied or deduced, etc. — until one's eyes are opened and one sees the beauty of truth, and how beloved it is to the One-who-spoke-the-world-into-being, who is called the God of Truth.[9]

1.2. LIES CONCERNING TORAH

Shlomo ha-Kohen Rabinovich (1803–66) was a rabbi in the Polish town of Radomsk. After his appointment to his rabbinical post in 1834, he began to conduct himself as a Hasidic rebbe—a charismatic leader also known as a *tzaddik*, a "righteous man." Though Rabinovich was involved in disputes regarding his authority and income with non-Hasidic leaders in Radomsk, he emerged victorious thanks to the intervention of government authorities. Ultimately he became the founder of the influential Radomsk Hasidic dynasty. His teachings, like those of many other Hasidic leaders, often emphasize the authority of the *tzaddik*.[10]

In the selection below, Rabinovich displays a sort of Hasidic attitude toward truth that Menaḥem Mendel Lefin condemned. Rabinovich proposes that rabbinical preachers may in fact deceive their audiences regarding the veracity of a story when doing so can enable them to more effectively communicate their true insights into the Torah. He points out that there is good precedent for such an approach: past rabbis, after all, engaged in a similar sort of deceit when claiming that the story narrated in the biblical book of Job did in fact happen, even though the Babylonian Talmud admitted that the story was in fact only a fable. Rabinovich also references the traditional interpretation of a Talmudic dictum (BT *Bava Metzi'a* 23b–24a) that rabbis may deviate from the truth in certain situations, specifically in sharing about others' hospitality (to guard against their exploitation), in mentioning their own sexual behavior (for reasons of modesty), and in discussing one's studies (so as not to boast). As he notes, the *Penei Moshe* Talmudic commentary (by Rabbi Moshe Margolies, d. 1781) linked the permission to deceive others about one's studies with a statement found in some manuscripts of the Jerusalem Talmud (*Berachot* 14d): "All lies are bad, but lies concerning Torah are good." Building on these sources, Rabinovich asserts that rabbis may deceive others about matters of Torah, at least in certain ways, "in order that one can make an impression on the heart of the listener."[11]

Whereas Lefin had argued in favor of resisting the temptation to lie, with its (ultimately false) promise of good consequences, Rabinovich contends that good consequences may outweigh ordinary duties to be honest. Whereas Lefin warned against leaders who deceive their followers, Rabinovich embraces an ethic whereby leaders may deceive their followers for the sake of a greater good. Whereas Lefin described "awakening" as taking place when one's "eyes are opened" to the beauty of truth that demands honesty in all ways and circumstances, Rabinovich explains how words of deceit may be necessary for opening hearts and awakening a person to the beauty of higher truths.

Shlomo Rabinovich, *Sefer Nifla'ot ha-Tiferet Shlomo* (mid-nineteenth century)

This is, surely, always good advice for anyone who preaches in public: if he wants to offer a fable to explain words of Torah, he should not call it a "fable," but rather "something that happened," because by doing so, the matter will make an impression in the hearts of the listeners, arousing their imaginations and creating an opening to their hearts. . . .

If you were to ask how it is permitted to speak this lie — "that it was something that happened," when in truth it never was and never existed — you should see this explicit source in the Babylonian Talmud (*Bava Batra* 15a): "Job never was and never existed, but [his story] was only a fable." . . . Nonetheless, it is permitted to speak of it as something that actually happened, and the reason is explained above: in order to make an impression for the one who listens, opening the heart and arousing him from his sleep.

And see the Jerusalem Talmud (Tractate *Berachot* 14d): Rabbi Yonah said in the name of Rabbi Yosi ben Gezerah, "All discussions are bad, except discussions of Torah are good. All lies are bad, but lies concerning Torah are good" — he is speaking of lying, for with Torah one can lie. And see the *Penei Moshe* [commentary on the Jerusalem Talmud] there, as he explains that one is permitted to say, "I have not studied that tractate," referring to the Talmudic teaching [that one may deviate from the truth] regarding three things [one's studies and sexual behavior, and someone else's hospitality] (Babylonian Talmud, *Bava Metzi'a* 23b–24a). And the language of "lies concerning Torah" . . . has the intent that with Torah matters, it is permitted to say that what never existed did exist and was something that happened, in order to make an impression on the heart of the listener.[12]

1.3. HONESTY ABOUT RABBINIC JUDAISM

One of the nineteenth-century figures who shared Lefin's devotion to sincerity and honesty was Rabbi Samuel Holdheim (1806–60), the influential leader of the Reform movement in Germany. But whereas Lefin was fully devoted to Rabbinic Judaism and saw the classical Rabbis as honest and authoritative teachers, Holdheim viewed the Rabbis as having distorted and falsified the nature of Jewish tradition.[13]

So too he condemned modern scholars who dishonestly misrepresented the ancient Rabbis. These scholars sought to further the cause of Jewish emancipation — encouraging Christians to trust that Jews would be good citizens of their modern nation-states — by arguing that Jewish traditions were rational, ethical, and based on the same biblical texts revered by Christians. From this perspective, the Talmud and other Rabbinic sources were to be admired for their biblically based rationality and ethical propriety. Holdheim, however, pointed to irrational, unethical, non–biblically based teachings by the Rabbis that such scholars ignored. Holdheim asserted that he was an intellectually honest scholar who would never cover up the weaknesses of tradition. He was committed to exposing the faults of Rabbinic Judaism (and some of its modern interpreters), in public at that.

It is not certain that Holdheim was the best spokesman on behalf of disinterested honesty. Indeed, his adversary Rabbi Zacharias Frankel (leader of the more traditional faction of Reformers and a major inspiration for the emergence of Conservative Judaism) accused Holdheim himself of sometimes falsifying Jewish tradition for the sake of Jewish emancipation.[14] We might also note that while Holdheim showed a willingness to honestly confront some of the less politically appealing aspects of Rabbinic tradition, he often misrepresented the Bible insofar as he described it as embodying rational, ethical, and immutable divine truth while downplaying its less politically appealing elements and human authorship.[15]

Still, Holdheim offered an ethical vision notable for its insistence on steering clear of political considerations and focusing on the honest investigation of historical truth. In his 1844 response to Frankel's critique, excerpted below, he indicates that he sees such honesty as essential to the development of Judaism.

Holdheim's insistence on honesty helped earn him the admiration of his colleagues within the Reform movement and beyond, even as it provoked historians to improve on his scholarship and develop more accurate understandings of Rabbinic Judaism.[16]

Samuel Holdheim, *The Religious and the Political in Judaism* (1844)

We cannot ignore the fact that the enemies of emancipation can and will misuse many of our statements and arguments to further their own hostile causes. However, this consideration must not lead us to engage in the smallest disguise or minutest ambiguity in our comments on the spirit, essence and contents of the Talmud or of rabbinic Judaism. For this reason, we have never hesitated to call things by their real names, nor have we ever tried to cover up any weaknesses, no matter how embarrassing they might have seemed. . . .

In order to purify our religious convictions, we must succeed in a difficult and sacred fight against antiquated prejudices. Hence, from our point of view, we would be committing a sin if we were to ignore the strict requirements of truth and religion for the sake of emancipation, or if we were to permit any postponement of our search for religious truth for fear that ruthless criticism of any false propositions in our earlier religious ideas and feelings might harm our efforts to achieve emancipation. . . .

We have a firm eye solely on the internal religious conditions and circumstances, which call upon any individual, honest in professing his religious faith and sincere in dealing with coreligionists, to engage in purifying critique and investigation of the truth. . . .

Here, whoever has the courage to recognize the truth and trust therein, must struggle proactively on its behalf. . . . But we have faith in the good sense of the people and the power of the truth, both of which shall soon dispel, at least among the Jews of Germany, that spirit of falsehood and hypocrisy.[17]

1.4. FALSEHOOD FOR THE SAKE OF TRUTH

Rabbi Eliyahu Eliezer Dessler (1892–1953) was a product of the Musar movement, a non-Hasidic Lithuanian Orthodox movement that stressed the cultivation of virtues, especially through the contemplative study of traditional musar literature. He became one of the leading figures of *haredi* (ultra-Orthodox) Judaism in England (where he served at the Gateshead Yeshiva) and then in Israel (where he served at the Ponevezh Yeshiva).

Dessler's work built not only on the legacy of the Musar movement but also on a range of other traditionalist thinkers, including Hasidic rabbis.[18] Some of his teachings closely resemble those of earlier Hasidic thinkers, such as his tenet that Jews must unquestioningly submit to the "Torah understanding" (*da'at Torah*) promulgated by the greatest of rabbis.[19]

The excerpt from Dessler's writings below resembles the teaching on "truth" offered by the Hasidic rabbi Shlomo Rabinovich (section 1.2). Like Rabinovich, Dessler approached questions of honesty from a consequentialist point of view, pointing to the value of deceit if it promoted what God would clearly regard as good consequences. Dessler, though, developed a broad theory of truth and falsehood that goes well beyond the rabbinical preaching of Rabinovich.

As Dessler argues, that which produces good effects is necessarily true and that which produces evil effects is necessarily false. If what seems to be an untrue statement has good effects, it cannot be called untrue, since it ultimately promotes truth—i.e., that which is "in accordance with the will of God." As the scholar Jacob Schacter has put it, for Dessler "truth has nothing to do with the reality of what was or is. Truth, rather, is what is in keeping with God's will." Thus, Schacter writes, in certain cases "disregarding historical accuracy . . . is precisely what the real truth requires, assuming, of course, that one knows the truth about what the real truth requires."[20] Dessler believed, of course, that the greatest of rabbinical authorities had deep insight into "what the real truth requires" and thus should be followed in this regard. His teaching that Jews must accept the truth of such rabbis' rulings, even when they may seem to defy empirical evidence, has remained influential in *haredi* communities to this day.

Dessler illustrates his theory with reference to the biblical story in which Jacob deceives his father, Isaac (Gen. 27). As Dessler points out, Rabbinic tradition justifies Jacob's deceit, teaching that even though Jacob wept at the prospect of lying to his father, God sent an angel to detain Esau and ensure that the deceit would be effective. God, Dessler concludes, values doing what it takes to ensure the victory of "truth," rather than always demanding that the righteous are straightforwardly "honest."

Eliyahu Eliezer Dessler, *Mikhtav me-Eliyahu* (mid-twentieth century)

What is truth and what is falsehood? When we went to school we were taught that truth is to tell the facts as they occurred and falsehood is to deviate from this.

This is true in simple cases, but in life many occasions arise when this simple definition no longer holds good. Sometimes it may be wrong to "tell the truth" about our neighbor, unless overriding purpose and necessity require this. And sometimes it may be necessary to change details, when the plain truth would bring not benefit but injury. In such cases, what appears to be true is false, since it produces evil effects; and what appears to be false may help to achieve the truth.

We had better define truth as that which is conducive to good and in conformity with the will of the Creator, and falsehood as that which furthers the scheme of the Prince of Falsehood, the power of evil in the world.

It follows that no one can succeed in bringing his behavior into line with the veritable truth as long as materialistic, selfish, and evil wills dominate his mind. His eyes will be blinded and he will inevitably pervert everything to accord with his desires.

The verse says: "The remnant of Israel do no injustice and speak no falsehood" (Zephaniah 3:13). Who are they? Presumably the same of whom it is said, "He forgives the sins of the remnant of his inheritance" (Micah 7:18) and whom the rabbis describe as "those who make themselves a remnant" (Yalkut Shimoni 449 on Micah 7:18). That is to say, they make "themselves"—their selfish interests and material desires—a remnant; they give them a very low priority; their main drive is for spiritual achievement. This is what ensures their truthfulness, honesty, and integrity in all their dealings.

One whose driving force is selfish ambition and material desire can never be completely honest or reliable. His urge for gratification will always be stronger than his desire for truth. Even though it happens that his statements or actions may sometimes accord with the truth, they nevertheless count as false. In life everything is subordinate to the main aim. If one's aim is false all is false. . . .

[In the biblical story where Jacob lies to his father in order to take Esau's blessing] it might seem that in this context Esau was the innocent party; he was only doing what his father had commanded him; it was Jacob seemingly who was practicing deceit; why then was an angel sent to prevent Esau from carrying out his commandment?

The point is that the Torah wishes to show us the heavenly judgment regarding truth and falsehood. Jacob did an act which was outwardly deceitful, but in truth he did it unwillingly, weeping, and under higher compulsion. He had no thought for himself; his purpose was solely to bring about that result which would be in accordance with the will of God. "Falsehood for the sake of truth"—such as this—*is* truth.[21]

1.5. HONESTY ABOUT JEWS AND GENTILES

The American-born Orthodox rabbi Meir Kahane (1932–90) immigrated to Israel in 1971 and represented his ultranationalist Kach Party in the Israeli parliament (Knesset) from 1984 to 1988, until the party was banned on account of its racism. An outspoken advocate of Jewish militancy, terrorism, and supremacism, Kahane professed that Jews were superior to non-Jews and empowered to cleanse the Land of Israel of non-Jewish influences. Even though his views were widely seen as anathema to mainstream Judaism, he attained significant influence in his lifetime both in Israel and the United States, and his ideas continue to play an important role in contemporary Jewish public discourse.[22]

Like Dessler, the other Israeli Orthodox rabbi profiled in this chapter, Kahane forcefully advocated for the truths of Torah. But, unlike Dessler, Kahane did not advance any theories about "falsehood for the sake of truth." He consistently extolled the value of intellectual honesty, especially when it came to presenting controversial sources from Rabbinic literature. In particular, Kahane championed the importance of accurately quoting and interpreting Rabbinic sources that Jews seeking integration with non-Jews preferred to remove from the historical record.

In this very specific way, Kahane was an ally of Samuel Holdheim. Considerably unlike Holdheim, though, Kahane hoped that the world would reject the ideal of "integrating" Jews into non-Jewish societies. He maintained that an honest confrontation with Rabbinic traditions would ultimately help non-Jews and Jews alike to recognize that Jews were superior to non-Jews and that—to use the language of the text below—they must live in Israel, "a single, distinctive land of their own, isolated from gentile and foreign influences which can and must influence and corrupt the pure totality and distinctiveness of G-d's society." Kahane relentlessly directed his readers to Rabbinic texts that emphasized the Jews' chosen status, superiority, purity, and need to be isolated from non-Jews. Jews were meant to be living in the Land of Israel under the authority of Torah, not governed by foreign concepts in foreign lands.

Despite Kahane's avowed commitment to honesty, however, he ignored texts at odds with his political vision. Like Holdheim, who described the Bible as a source of immutable divine truth that supported his outlook, Kahane described not only the Bible but also the Talmuds and other Rabbinic texts as sources of immutable divine truth that confirmed his views, and he did not acknowledge traditions that challenged them.

Fundamentally, however, Kahane and Holdheim's views could not have been more different, and Kahane accused Holdheim of ultimately misrepresenting Jewish tradition. In Kahane's eyes, the Reform movement was "conceived in guile," advancing the lie that the Torah was compatible with integration into non-Jewish societies. Kahane singled out Holdheim for covering up traditions that emphasized the value of the Land of Israel and Jewish peoplehood—essentially for misrepresenting Judaism in order to promote the goal of political emancipation.[23]

Further, from Kahane's point of view, it was not just Reform Jews who were engaging in serious forms of deceit. Elsewhere in his article "Jew, Gentile, Judaism and Honesty," excerpted below, Kahane also lambasted Modern Orthodox Jews, Conservative Jews, and secular Jews who joined Reform Jews in their "obsessive, desperate need to pronounce that Judaism decrees" the equality of Jews and gentiles. Kahane especially reproved liberal American Jews of these diverse stripes as pathetically eager to promulgate the falsehood that the Torah affirms Jeffersonian values regarding equality and democracy.[24] He accused American Jews of acting dishonestly so as to maintain their pleasure-filled lives in the "gentile Eden" of America, rather than living the harsher lives they were meant to have in their homeland, Israel.

Like Lefin, Kahane depicted his adversaries in polemical, stereotypical terms. Though he claimed to be speaking honestly, he often misrepresented the motivations of American Jews, which could hardly be reduced to desires for acceptance and pleasure. Like so many other polemicists on behalf of honesty, Kahane was hardly honest when it came to acknowledging the perspectives of his opponents.

Meir Kahane, "Jew, Gentile, Judaism and Honesty" (1985)

The Rabbis say that the seal of the All Mighty is truth [BT *Shabbat* 55a], for it is truth and only truth that is light unto our feet, that gives life meaning and direction. Truth leads us by the hand down the proper path so that we know where we are meant to go, what we are meant to be. And if truth is the lamp that guides us, then falsehood is the darkness and confusion that surrounds the helpless traveler, lost and undecided, wandering as an eternal Cain, forever without compass, direction and knowledge.

And truth is the eternal victim of the man it seeks to guide! For while truth is light, it is often a *painful* light, one that we douse and extinguish, preferring the confusion of falsehood with its comfortable, dark delusions, not knowing that they precede destruction, and this applies to all that we do, even *or especially* to the great Torah concepts which, alone, are the reason for the creation of a world and us.

The truths of Torah are daily victims of both vile and wicked men, as well as those who are simply ignorant or terribly frightened. But the reality is that the ultimate victims are precisely those who kill the truth. For they douse the light that would lead them to that goal of creation which G-d decrees and demands. Those who victimize Torah concepts by perverting and twisting and deforming them, those who dig a pit in which to bury Torah truths — in reality dig the pit in which they must eventually fall.

There is no greater sin than that of the counterfeiting of truth. For such a man passes on falsehood to others, to generations, becoming the false prophet who deceives the Jew while desecrating G-d's creation, and this is the disease and crime of our age, this is the spiritual AIDS of our times.

They band together, an unlikely rag-tag army bearing high the banner of falsehood. . . . They all live in a world of gentiles, loving every material moment of it even as they tremble at the thought of being driven East of this gentile Eden.

And so, theirs becomes an obsessive, desperate need to pronounce that Judaism decrees that gentile and Jew are the same. But despite their most tenacious efforts to persuade themselves that G-d did appear in the form of Thomas Jefferson at Sinai to give the Jews a Torah made up of equality of Jew and gentile, a serpent has slithered into their Garden to shout: Fraud! Nonsense! Judaism differentiates, separates and declares the two to be of different and *unequal* status. . . . The All Mighty wishes the Jews to live as a collective and create a special, holy people . . . [which] can only be done if they live in a single, distinctive land of their own, isolated from gentile and foreign influences which can and must influence and corrupt the pure totality and distinctiveness of G-d's society.[25]

1.6. "PREACHING AGAINST THE TEXT"

One of the most influential figures in shaping Jewish feminism, the American theologian Judith Plaskow (b. 1947), has focused much of her writing on exposing the patriarchal nature of traditional Jewish theology and on developing alternative Jewish feminist theologies. Her major work, *Standing Again at Sinai*, has been described as having "transformed contemporary Judaism" by demanding a revolt against patriarchy and reshaping Judaism based on the experiences of women.[26] In that book and elsewhere in her work, Plaskow also developed an honest understanding of historiography, describing women's presence in Jewish history and explaining how the past has been recorded by men who made tenuous claims to authority as they operated from their own patriarchal assumptions.[27]

The selection below originated as an address to Reform rabbis during a 1997 ordination ceremony at the Hebrew Union College–Jewish Institute of Religion in Cincinnati. Plaskow accused liberal Jews of intellectual dishonesty in ignoring traditional Jewish texts that did not accord with their sensibilities. She asserted the importance of honestly confronting texts that promote injustice—such as the biblical book of Hosea, which suggests that it is appropriate to respond to a promiscuous wife with abuse.

Plaskow thus agreed with Kahane that liberal Jews were misrepresenting Jewish traditions by failing to confront painful texts. But whereas Kahane wanted Jews to read—and then embrace—these teachings, certain as he was that they were divine and true, Plaskow called for Jews to read—and then forcibly reject—these teachings, certain as she was that they were problematic, humanly created texts. For example, she taught that studying the opening chapters of the book of Hosea is valuable not because its misogyny should be affirmed but because its misogyny must be rejected. Studying texts that justify abuse, she argued, can encourage discussion "about the reality of abuse, its origins and emotional dynamics—*and* how one can learn to refuse it."

A century-and-a-half earlier, Holdheim had also called on Reform Jews to honestly acknowledge and reject troubling texts. But whereas Holdheim asked his audience to reject (certain) Rabbinic texts, while affirming the truth of the Bible, Plaskow asked for the rejection of (certain) biblical texts. Ultimately, she encouraged a new generation of Reform rabbis to face up to troubling traditions and "preach against the text."

Judith Plaskow, "Preaching against the Text" (1997)

A rabbi friend once told me that when he was a student at Hebrew Union College, he was taught never to preach against the weekly Torah portion. Instead, he should always seek out something positive in the text that he could lift up as a moral or spiritual lesson that would instruct and inspire. This advice captures a central strategy of many liberal Jews who grapple with issues of continuity and change in relation to Jewish tradition. One way of maintaining a connection with tradition is to affirm its values when they accord with contemporary sensibilities—and ignore them when they do not. . . .

[But] it is intellectually dishonest to focus simply on the positive aspects of tradition. Individual religious ideas and values have contexts; they are connected to other ideas. They are parts of systems that seek to express and establish particular worldviews. Why engage with tradition if we're not prepared to look at the ways it shapes us for good *and* for evil? . . . To wrench what we like out of context and ignore the rest is to engage in a kind of pretense, to act as if we were deriving our values from tradition when what we are actually doing is seeking support for our own convictions.

Such intellectual dishonesty might be excused were it to serve a spiritual purpose. But . . . failure to grapple with the hard parts of tradition is spiritually and socially corrosive, because it leaves destructive ideas intact to shape our consciousness and affect our hearts and minds. . . .

Remaining silent about the negative aspects of tradition not only leaves them to do their work in the world; it also deprives us of an important spiritual resource. In congregations, in Hillels, and in other places rabbis serve, many Jews are in pain. Sometimes they . . . feel they have been wounded directly by some aspect of Jewish tradition.

More often, they have been hurt by injustices or abuse described and sometimes reinscribed by tradition, but not immediately attributable to its influence. . . . What they frequently need and seek are not simply spiritual ideals they can counterpose to the bitterness of their experiences, but places to name and explore the contours and causes of their pain. Passages like the Haftorah [the first chapters of the book of Hosea, which describe a wife as deserving abuse] provide wonderful starting points to talk about the reality of abuse, its origins and emotional dynamics—*and* how one can learn to refuse it. . . .

I do not believe that we have any choice other than to make choices about what we accept and repudiate in tradition. But we do have a choice as to whether we leave the negative to do its silent, poisonous work like an old family secret, or whether we turn and grapple with ambiguity and ugliness, and force them to yield up meaning. Confronting the hard places in tradition and in our lives is neither comfortable nor easy. But it is a necessary step in shaping a Judaism that is inclusive and life-giving, in continuity with tradition and yet responsive to the contemporary world.[28]

1.7. PRIDE AND PATRIOTISM COME FIRST

Daniel Lapin (b. 1947) is a South African–born American Orthodox rabbi, conservative political activist, and business consultant. Though he did not grow up immersed in the Musar movement to nearly the extent that Dessler did, Lapin also had strong ties to the movement, receiving much of his Torah education at the Gateshead Yeshiva where Dessler had served. He has dedicated his career to promoting the study of virtue and teaching "ancient Jewish wisdom" in the United States, especially to conservative Christian audiences.[29] His work has especially championed the idea that Jews and Christians should unite in defense of conservative values found within both Jewish and Christian traditions.[30]

In his 1999 book *America's Real War*, which defends traditional "Judeo-Christian" values as foundational to America, Lapin calls for Jews to be more honest in acknowledging the similar conservative values of Judaism and Christianity; the gifts that Christianity has given the United States and the world; and the ways that liberal secularism threatens Judaism, Christianity, and the United States as a whole.[31] Lapin also asks his readers to be honest in acknowledging the greatness of America—"the greatest country of our time," with a "civilization superior to most others."[32] Though he cautions against ignoring America's faults and problems, Lapin is appalled by the liberal idea that honesty particularly requires focusing on the failings of one's country and its founders. Especially in teaching children, he avows, educators should first focus on honesty about that which is most honorable in America's past before moving on to honesty about America's faults. He suggests in the excerpt below, for example, that students should acknowledge the greatness of America's founding ideals of equality before confronting its history of racial injustices.

In some ways Lapin is like Meir Kahane: an Orthodox rabbi support-ive of certain forms of "religious Zionism," a defender of culturally conservative values, and an outspoken opponent of Jewish liberals who he believes misrepresent Judaism as being aligned with liberal values.[33] But while Kahane denigrated all non-Jewish cultures, Lapin praises Christianity, seeing its values as aligned with Judaism. While Kahane critiqued Jews who attempted to integrate into non-Jewish countries, Lapin defends the Jewish presence in America and relates to his country with great pride. And while Kahane rejected Jewish discourse about human equality, Lapin sees greatness in this idea and urges that it be taught to children in America.

Daniel Lapin, *America's Real War* (1999)

If a nation preserves its national identity by recalling its origins, then it follows that a nation should recall and honor its founding fathers. Three times a day Jews say a prayer that commences with the words, "God of our fathers, God of Abraham, God of Isaac and God of Jacob." . . . It would be hard to find a more important characteristic of durable nations than an ever-present awareness of fathers. . . .

A number of years ago, one of our summer sailing trips took my family to British Columbia at the time of Expo 86. We docked our boat . . . and eagerly disembarked to enjoy the many exhibits from foreign countries. . . . We eagerly anticipated America's pavilion and looked forward to instilling our children with pride in their homeland. To our dismay, this was not to be. . . . One left the pavilion feeling that America was a failure, embarrassed to belong to such a bumbling country. I am not suggesting that . . . we totally ignore our problems and failings. But surely there is a middle course, where we can be honest about both our problems and triumphs, rather than focus only on the latter in a misguided attempt at revisionistic humility.

My wife was once asked to review the reading list for a third grade class in a private school. She disapproved of many of the books. Let me give you one example why. There wasn't an inherent problem with the choice of an excellent book, *Roll of Thunder, Hear My Cry*, by Mildred Taylor. The book is a well-written depiction of the injustices suffered by Southern blacks. My wife's concern was that this book was going to be read by students who . . . knew nothing of those who had made incredible sacrifices for racial equality. These students did not yet even know the phrase, "All men are created equal." There was nothing to place the book, with its valid criticisms of societal injustice, in context. Surely, children should be exposed to pride and patriotism in their country first, for only after that base has been established are they able to put in perspective any wrongs the country has committed. Honoring our country and its history is a traditional Judeo-Christian principle.[34]

1.8. WE ALL STRUGGLE WITH HONESTY

Abigail Treu, a Conservative rabbi, wrote the Torah commentary below while serving as a Rabbinic Fellow at the Jewish Theological Seminary of America in New York City. In this role, as in her more recent position as director of the Center for Jewish Living at one of the largest Jewish Community Centers in the world (the Marlene Meyerson JCC in New York), Treu's work has often focused on making Jewish experiences and traditions more accessible and meaningful to American Jewish adults.[35]

Her commentary on the lies that Jacob tells his father Isaac, excerpted below, depicts Jacob as a figure who, like all human beings, struggles to be appropriately honest. Treu's perspective on Jacob's deception stands in stark contrast to Dessler's view. Rather than accept midrashic interpretations that seek to justify Jacob's lying, she asks readers to acknowledge the Torah's depiction of Jacob as flawed. Rather than idealizing founding fathers and defending their honor and greatness, as Lapin might prefer, she urges readers to recognize a Patriarch like Jacob as a complex, challenged, and struggling human being, like the rest of us.

Ultimately, Treu views Jacob as a source of inspiration, a "worthy . . . patriarch," especially because he matures, eventually turning away from lying and cheating. As far as we are concerned, then, we are to emulate Jacob by *struggling* as he did to become more honest.

Like Lefin, Treu refers to the *yetzer ha-ra*, the evil inclination, which can tempt human beings to speak wrongly. Yet while Lefin views lying as entirely disgraceful, Treu is far more forgiving, intimating that it need not be a source of shame. In Treu's view, lying is part of being human. Since we all partake in this behavior, we should accept it, refrain from harsh self-recriminations when we err, and continue to struggle to overcome it.

Notably, in the full commentary from which this excerpt comes, Treu discusses her own childhood memory of concealing a truth from her mother. Unlike some figures in this chapter who seem fully confident about their own honesty, Treu would appear to take a more honest approach in acknowledging the struggles we all face.

Abigail Treu, "Our Lying Patriarch" (2009)

The most egregious instance of Jacob's less-than-honorable behavior comes in Parashat Tol'dot [Gen. 27] when, at his mother's suggestion, he dons a costume; appears before his old, blind father; and uses a lie to steal the blessing intended for his twin brother Esau. . . .

Of course, interpreters throughout the ages have sought to "correct" the story so as to bolster Jacob's ethical position. . . . [But] what do we gain if we accept the story at face value?

What we gain is a mirror. I wonder if our discomfort in reading Jacob's moral failure here (and elsewhere) is a reflection of the discomfort we feel internally as we struggle with our own morality. We all learned, at some point in life, that we could lie. We all got away with it at some point (in our childhood at least), and had to teach ourselves to refrain from such behavior. Reading the story literally and accepting Jacob's lie means that we don't have to pretend that we are all as innocent as George Washington, who "could not tell a lie," and frees us up to focus inward. Rather than project a holier-than-thou expectation onto Jacob, we can use Parashat Tol'dot as an invitation to scrutinize our own lies and sibling rivalries.

We descend from a patriarch who struggled with his *yetzer ha-ra*, his own temptations to do wrong. So too, each of us struggles. Reading this story without rushing to defend Jacob reminds us that each of us has the capacity to be a liar and a cheat, or a person of integrity and honor. When we hear of the latest scandal involving a bribe, a swindle, marital infidelity, whichever vice *du jour* lands on the front pages, we are incensed, indignant. But when we read Tol'dot, we remember—if we choose *not* to exonerate Jacob—the adjuration of Rabbi Yohanan ben Zakai (BT Berakhot 28b): "May you fear heaven more than you fear one another." Each of us is tempted every day in so many ways, and the integrity that comes from a life of honesty is sacred because it is so difficult to achieve.

The important thing is that Jacob outgrows the behavior we see and dislike. By the time he matures into the father of twelve tribes, he has struggled with God and come to the realization that God dwells in "this place" in ways he did not know in his youth. We don't need to pretend that Jacob never lied; we need to realize that Jacob did lie and cheat, and that he successfully struggled to abandon those behaviors. That is what makes him worthy of being our patriarch.[36]

1.9. AN ORTHODOX TRAVESTY OF INTELLECTUAL DECEPTION

Earlier in this chapter, we saw Kahane and Plaskow critique particular kinds of dishonesty they found in liberal Jewish communities. In the selection below, Shmuly Yanklowitz (b. 1981), an American rabbi affiliated with Orthodoxy's most liberal wing (Open Orthodoxy), critiques Orthodox Jews for the particular kinds of dishonesty he finds in Orthodox communities.

Here, Yanklowitz is responding to his teacher Marc Shapiro's book *Changing the Immutable: How Orthodox Judaism Rewrites Its History* (2015), which documents how ideas such as Rabinovich's and Dessler's have encouraged Orthodox Jews, especially *haredi* Jews, to misrepresent Jewish history by covering up or lying about aspects of that history that do not fit with Orthodox sensibilities. Shapiro demonstrates, for example, that *haredi* Jews have excised views from traditional texts that might appear too sympathetic to the Haskalah, Zionism, feminism, or other approaches rejected by present-day *haredi* authorities. Some *haredi* publications have also doctored photographs to remove men with problematic viewpoints and, moreover, cropped out women altogether, following decrees that publishing images of women is immodest.

In response to this phenomenon, Yanklowitz seeks to develop a new Orthodox ethic. He admits that, on the one hand, classical Rabbinic texts offer some good reasons to be less than fully forthcoming about the truth; and he rejects the sort of approach associated with the philosopher Immanuel Kant that requires honesty in all instances without regard for consequences. Nonetheless, he critiques *haredi* models of rabbinical authority, developed by figures such as Dessler, that allow rabbis to withhold access to texts and certain forms of truth. Yanklowitz describes contemporary *haredi* censors as engaged in a "travesty of intellectual deception" and urges that their publications be regarded with skepticism, as they may have undergone censorship. All in all, he proposes that his fellow Orthodox Jews respond by embracing intellectual honesty: "promot[ing] rigorous study with honest and critical analysis, making it accessible to all, and moving away from unchecked centralized rabbinic authority." Moreover, pushing back against those who would define religious truth in simple terms (such as Kahane, who was certain about the "truths of Torah"), Yanklowitz calls for "embracing the complexity of Jewish history and tradition." While some traditionalist Orthodox rabbis have argued that Yanklowitz misrepresents what can count as authentic "Orthodoxy," Yanklowitz has played an important role in shaping an "open Orthodox" approach that supports controversial perspectives, including those discussed in the excerpt below.[37]

Shmuly Yanklowitz, "Holy Lies?" (2015)

There is some Talmudic basis for censorship and distortion. . . . The rabbis teach *halakhah ve'ein morin ken* (this is the *halakhah*, but we do not teach it). The Rabbis (BT Shabbat 153b) view this as a Divine mandate based upon the teaching that "it is the glory of God to conceal a thing" (Proverbs 25:2). Further, at times *halakhah* allows one to alter the truth *mipnei darkhei shalom* (for the sake of peace), and some have even taught that we should alter religious truths and *halakhah* to establish peace "between us and our Father in Heaven." Although there were many religious exceptions to the pursuit of truth, we can only presume that outside of these few selected areas, the sages were committed to the highest order to the Torah value of truth. The intentions in censorship were likely good: protect sages' honor, promote modesty, enhance peace, foster understanding, etc. These positive intentions are mitigating factors in this intentional deviation from the honest transmission of Torah and history.

To be sure, Kant's categorical imperative is not compatible with the Jewish tradition: telling the truth is not absolute for the Torah. For example, saving a life trumps telling the truth. In the classical critique of Kant, if a Nazi came to one's door, should not a person not tell the truth that Jews are in the basement?

But here [in cases of *haredi* censorship] the stakes were much lower and lines were crossed that should never have been. . . . Earlier rabbinic texts that demonstrate a value higher than truth do not necessarily validate Haredi distortions of truth; Jewish tradition often treats these texts as problems themselves. So how do we in turn respond to the travesty of intellectual deception fully infiltrating not only our religious academies and systems of outreach, but also Jewish history itself?

Here are a few different proposals to grapple with:

1. We must promote rigorous study with honest and critical analysis, making it accessible to all and moving away from unchecked centralized rabbinic authority. This move would necessarily subvert communal hierarchical structures that leave others, especially women, powerless and alienated. Everyone, who so desires, must be granted authentic access to the true law and true narrative. There is indeed a sacred responsibility for scholars to transmit a powerful transformative Torah that helps others grow, but in our day it must be with higher transparency.

2. Ultra-Orthodox works published in the twenty-first century must be read with greater skepticism, and one must be prepared to verify all facts and translations in order to properly understand an issue. There are those who want their Torah to be censored by others they trust and that is fine. But for those of us trying to access the authentic Torah tradition, we must work harder in our critical scholarship.

3. We should begin to embrace pluralism more deeply as a reaction against the current trends toward unswerving absolutism. Embracing the complexity of Jewish history and tradition with full honesty and transparency leads us to understand the diversity of views that existed in the past and that exist today and lessens the need to carve out a false monolithic image of *halakhah* or Torah values. This moves us toward greater tolerance and epistemic humility.

4. We must raise the standards for intellectual integrity within our own communities by never altering facts to serve our arguments. We can learn to cherish our own values while never allowing them to blind us to the values of truth, transparency and intellectual diversity.

We need to work harder to cultivate trust in our fellow Jewish traveler. We can share the complexity of our tradition while trusting and empowering other Jews to create their own meaning and decisions.[38]

1.10. HONESTY WITHOUT MEANING-MAKING

The work of Emily Filler (b. 1980), a scholar of modern Jewish philosophy and professor of Jewish Studies at Washington and Lee University, has focused on the uneasy relationship that modern Jews have had with violent and ethically troubling Jewish texts.[39] In the short essay below, she shifts from considering confrontations with difficult texts to confrontations with difficult and violent histories. Filler asks her readers to look directly at the violence of the twentieth century, including violence committed against Jews and violence committed by Jews.

Filler responds directly to Judith Plaskow's appeal for intellectual honesty concerning Jewish texts (section 1.6). While she supports Plaskow's call for honesty, she raises questions regarding her call for Jews to engage with difficult traditions and thereby force them to "yield up meaning." In confronting catastrophes such as the Holocaust, and then the Nakba (the dispossession of Palestinians carried out for the sake of the State of Israel), Filler points to the value of a kind of honesty that acknowledges irrevocable loss and "refuses . . . to do the work of meaning-making." In her view, honestly confronting disaster requires confronting meaninglessness and destruction that can never be fully restored.

Filler's call to confront not only crimes carried out by Nazis but also crimes carried out by the founders of Israel also clearly contrasts with Daniel Lapin's charge to honor the founding fathers of nations and place their wrongdoings in a context that allows the nation to be viewed more positively (see section 1.7). Filler does not want readers to honor the founders of Israel who perpetrated destructive acts; nor does she seek to qualify and contextualize the crimes in order to ameliorate them. Filler asks us to see catastrophe clearly and honestly, and to refuse to find meaning or hope within it.

Emily Filler, "The Honesty of Radical Pessimism" (2022)

In her very important reflection on the necessity of intellectual honesty, Judith Plaskow argues that Jewish readers and communities must commit to grappling with the many difficult and troubling parts of Jewish text and tradition, instead of ignoring them while they do their "silent, poisonous work" in our lives and the lives of others. We must, rather, confront such texts, forcing them to "yield up meaning," as difficult and painful as such textual and communal confrontation may be.

I certainly agree. But perhaps I would like to call for a kind of honesty — not only toward our texts, but our recent history — that refuses for the moment even to do the work of meaning-making. Perhaps to even begin a process of textual or historical transformation first requires an acknowledgement of the depth and irrevocability of loss. Can we insist on a kind of truthfulness that grapples with the depths of disaster?

We need not look far. The twentieth century presents us with two extended disasters that cry out for this sort of radical and pessimistic honesty. Between 1933 and 1945, most of Europe's Jews were murdered, their bodies flung into trenches or turned to ash, their villages and shuls and Torahs destroyed. Of course, there is no shortage of theorization about the meaning, historical and philosophical, of this particular monstrosity. But perhaps honestly acknowledging the depth of the Holocaust requires a momentary refusal to make any meaning of it at all, but rather to simply insist on the bleak reality and ludicrous meaninglessness of such destruction.

I will go further. It is not uncommon to hear the creation of the state of Israel invoked as a point of Jewish hope after the unthinkable devastation of European Jewry. But what would it take for us to confront the consequences of the state, just as Plaskow calls us to confront the consequences of our destructive and oft-ignored troubling texts? To be intellectually honest in this moment might require us to acknowledge, without qualification or excuse, the catastrophe that the state of Israel was — is — for Palestinians. What depth of honesty is necessary to look squarely at the dispossession of Palestinian homes, land, and olive groves required for the state to come into being, and to know that those things can never be restored? That even in the event of meaningful political compromise or financial reparation, things have been broken that can never again be made whole?

There seems to me to be a radical honesty in our willingness to look at the brutal depths of a disaster and then decline to look beyond it — even for the entirely understandable and important work of locating larger meaning or seeking to repair. Perhaps the beginning of intellectual honesty is the willingness to speak the truth of a disaster aloud, to acknowledge its irrevocability, and to nevertheless refuse to look away.[40]

CONCLUSION

As the array of perspectives in this chapter demonstrates, modern Jewish thinkers have taken diverse positions on how one should best understand, love, and commit oneself to truth and honesty.

Some Jewish thinkers have emphasized the duty to be honest without respect to consequences; others have stressed that good consequences outweigh one's duty to be honest.

Some Jewish thinkers have defined truth as that which corresponds to empirical facts; others have defined truth in terms of its coherence with other ideas they are certain are true.

Some Jewish thinkers have supported creating fictions in service of larger truths; others have derided such fictions as misrepresenting the past.

Some Jewish thinkers have sought to depict widely accepted Jewish traditions as representing "truth"; others have invoked honesty in challenging the authority of such traditions.

Some Jewish thinkers have believed that authoritative leaders may lie in service of a greater "truth"; other Jewish thinkers have found truth in challenging traditional authority structures.

Some Jewish thinkers have admired the deceitful words and actions of biblical Patriarchs, such as Jacob; others have rejected the idea that such deceit can be admirable.

Some Jewish thinkers have expressed concern about truth-telling that challenges patriotism; other Jewish thinkers have emphasized that truth requires exposing the faults of nations and their founders.

Some Jewish thinkers have viewed honesty as a source of meaning; others have emphasized that honesty may require confronting meaninglessness.

And these are only *some* of the disagreements that modern Jewish thinkers have had surrounding the value, function, and cultivation of honesty and a love of truth.

Still, the diverse figures profiled in this chapter would all agree that developing appropriate honesty and love of truth requires more than rules and laws. All would agree on the importance of moral character, and on the need for a kind of musar—the cultivation of a virtuous disposition toward the truth—even as they fiercely disagree on the nature and function of that disposition.

2

Curiosity and Inquisitiveness
(*Sakranut/Ḥakranut*)

The disposition to be interested in and to want to learn new things, a quality generally described in English with the word *curiosity* (in Hebrew, *sakranut*) or, sometimes, with the word *inquisitiveness* (in Hebrew, *ḥakranut*), is seldom singled out as a virtue in premodern musar literature. While that literature often encourages the disposition to want to study Torah, and sometimes encourages wonder about the nature of the created world, curiosity and inquisitiveness became popular and central virtues only among modern Jewish thinkers, especially as they explored new fields beyond the bounds of traditional Jewish learning. This shift was spurred along by the leaders of the late eighteenth-century Haskalah (Jewish Enlightenment) movement, whose adherents—such as Baruch Lindau, discussed in section 2.1—sought to promote modern scientific inquiry as something desired by God.

Compared with figures from the Haskalah, many later Jewish intellectuals who praised scientific inquiry such as Benjamin Gruenberg (section 2.3) were less tied to God-language or Jewish traditions and sometimes viewed Jewish traditions as impediments to proper inquiry. On the other hand, contemporary Jewish thinkers who see curiosity as a virtue are often deeply engaged with Jewish traditions. This is certainly true among rabbis such as Danya Ruttenberg (section 2.7), who encourages curiosity about traditional Jewish texts and practices; Jamie Arnold (section 2.8), who sees the Garden of Eden story as offering a model for curiosity; and Amy Eilberg (section 2.9), who encourages curiosity about those with whom one is in conflict, building on Jewish traditions about relating to enemies.

But while many modern Jewish thinkers have written about curiosity and inquisitiveness in positive terms, others have pointed out that inquisitiveness may be a vice if it seeks knowledge improperly, seeks worthless or incorrect knowledge, or is overly attached to knowledge of certain kinds. Gruenberg, for example, asserts that inquisitiveness is a virtue only when it is guided by the scientific method. Coming from a very different perspective in section 2.2, Naḥman of Bratslav rejects inquisitiveness that challenges what he sees as the proper boundaries of authority. In section 2.4, Eliyahu Eliezer Dessler values curiosity directed toward "Torah" in a narrow sense but views most other forms of curiosity as sinful. In section 2.5, Joseph Soloveitchik stresses that inquisitiveness should be guided by a focus on Jewish law. In section 2.6, Abraham Joshua Heschel insists that one recognize the limits of curiosity and focus one's attention on qualities of wonder and radical amazement. And in section 2.10, Sandra Lawson points out that curiosity about other people may cause deep harm, especially when that curiosity comes from a place of privilege. In short, modern Jewish thinkers have often valued curiosity and inquisitiveness but in different ways, while pointing to diverse problems that may result from these qualities.

2.1. THE INQUISITIVE MASKIL

In the late eighteenth century, a group of Prussian Jewish intellectuals laid the groundwork for the Haskalah, a cultural-renewal movement (sometimes described as "the Jewish Enlightenment") that promoted a broad general education for Jews encompassing non-Jewish literature, science, and philosophy. These *maskilim* (advocates of Haskalah, "intellectuals"), often calling themselves *ḥokrim* (inquirers), enthusiastically promoted inquisitiveness. As the historian Shmuel Feiner has put it, "Intense curiosity and a strong drive to acquire knowledge not easily accessible within the culture of the traditional Jewish society were the hallmarks of the early maskilim."[1]

Baruch Lindau (1759–1849) was among the intellectuals who urged fellow Jews to seek out new scientific knowledge. He himself sought to transmit such knowledge in his own works, which often translated the writings of non-Jewish authors. His Hebrew-language science textbook, *Reishit Limmudim* (The beginning of studies) — largely an abridgment, adaptation, and translation of a German textbook — was widely used by Jews seeking scientific knowledge in the late eighteenth and early nineteenth centuries.[2] Notably, Lindau's curiosity about human diversity was linked with a desire to hierarchically categorize human beings. He divided them into black- and white-skinned groups and promulgated the racist view that white skin is linked with greater beauty, morality, and intelligence. His belief that Jews were "white" would come to take hold among many later Jews (see section 2.10).[3]

In the selection below, from an article in which Lindau discusses the process of collecting pearls at sea, he shares his appreciation of inquisitiveness as a gift from God, a spur to human inventiveness, and an aid to prosperity and human rule over the rest of creation. He ends by encouraging his readers to learn more by reading recent, non-Jewish scientific literature. He does not want his readers to bow to traditional Jewish authorities but rather to give in to the "temptation" (or "inducement") to seek out new knowledge and to learn from new kinds of "sages": natural philosophers, who would soon come to be known as "scientists."

Baruch Lindau, "The History of Natural Species" (1788)

Ever since God first created the human being, a passion has been instilled within his heart and a capacity for inventiveness has been born within him that tempts him to search and seek to know everything that occurs beneath the sun, and to reveal the wonders and secrets of nature, how one may gain some benefit from it that will add to science or wealth . . . and through the effort and diligence of that capacity, which neither slumbers nor sleeps in the heart of all who are wise at heart, the benefits to the existence and glorification of the human race will multiply greatly.... And without this wonder and excitement in the soul, a person would not lift his hand or foot and speak of all this wisdom and science. ...

[In some cases] natural philosophers have gained greater wisdom in our age, disagreeing with earlier authorities.... [God] placed the human being on the earth to rule over all, and endowed him with understanding, knowledge, and intellect to investigate what is hidden in nature and to reveal its mystery. And if these words of mine are [too] brief, here is a gift that will quench the thirst of your soul: do go to a sage, behold and read the books of the natural philosophers....[4]

2.2. THE INQUISITIVE *TZADDIK*

The Hasidic leader Rabbi Naḥman of Bratslav (or "Breslov," Ukraine) (1772–1810), like other leaders of Hasidism, had a very different attitude toward the science and literature produced by non-Jews. With characteristic xenophobia, Naḥman viewed all such "wisdom" (and non-Jews in general) as linked with the "Other Side": the realm of cosmic impurity.

In the selections below, Naḥman describes foreign "wisdom" as a form of prohibited leavening (*ḥametz*) that "soured" and added impurity to Jewish minds. He counsels Jews to seek wisdom only from the *tzaddik*, the true rabbinical leader of one's generation, who links God and Israel (the Jewish people). The true *tzaddik*—which Naḥman seems to believe himself to be—should always be trusted and should never be questioned. Naḥman's Hasidic ideology, granting total authority to the charismatic rabbi, demands that the inquisitiveness of ordinary Jews be limited.

By contrast, Naḥman asserts, the *tzaddik* himself is distinguished by his inquisitiveness. A *tzaddik* is interested in every part of creation, asking about why God endowed each aspect of creation with its particular characteristics. Unlike the inquirers praised by Baruch Lindau, the *tzaddik* is not focused on satisfying his curiosity through empirical observation but instead seeks to understand how God's intent for the People of Israel can be discovered in every animal, vegetable, and mineral.

Whereas Lindau's writing is highly anthropocentric, placing the human being at the center of the universe, Naḥman's writing is highly ethnocentric, placing the People of Israel at its center. Because Naḥman believes that everything in the universe pertains to the People of Israel, he also holds that the *tzaddik*'s inquisitiveness can ultimately be satisfied only when he studies his fellow Jews ("the glory that is in Israel"); thereby the *tzaddik* comes to understand the secrets of the entire created world.

Though Naḥman was not popular during his lifetime, his teachings gained popularity in Israel in the 1970s. The Bratslav Hasidic sect Naḥman founded is now sizable, and Naḥman himself has become a figure of interest to a vast array of Israeli Jews—Hasidic and non-Hasidic, Sephardi and Ashkenazi, even secularists who would not accept many of his stricter teachings. As the scholar Zvi Mark has noted, Naḥman has become "a cultural icon in contemporary Israeli society," where "his image is ubiquitous and his influence widespread."[5]

Naḥman of Bratslav, *Likkutei Moharan* (1808)

I. It is necessary to clear the mind of leavening—external [non-Jewish] wisdom and foreign thoughts—so that one does not sour one's wisdom with external wisdom and appetites. . . . When the sphere of the mind is blocked by impurity (as it is written, "you shall not become unclean through them" [Lev. 11:43]), then one's voice [of true prayer] will not be heard. One must also guard one's fear [*yirah*] of God . . . so that it will not be externally imposed fear: "If there is no wisdom, there is no fear; if there is no fear, there is no wisdom" (*Mishnah Avot* 3:17).[6]

II. Fear and love [of God] can only be achieved through the *tzaddik* of [one's] generation, for the *tzaddik* of the generation reveals fear and love. For the *tzaddik* continually seeks and searches for God's will, as God's will is within everything. . . . To understand and know God's will for everything, the *tzaddik* continually seeks and searches: for example, why it is the will of God that the lion has such strength and might, and such a form, and the lion's nature and behavior; and on the other hand why a tiny flea is so very weak and has another nature and form and behavior. . . . So too for other creations in the world, whether mineral, vegetable, animal, or human. . . . All this is due to God's will, that He wanted that this should be thus and this should be thus. The *tzaddik* continually searches for this will, and he understands and finds it through the glory that he finds in [the People of] Israel . . . because the whole world was created only for the sake of Israel. . . . By continually seeking and searching and finding the glory that is in Israel (generally, particularly, and in the smallest details) . . . the *tzaddik* knows and understands God's will for all of creation (generally, particularly, and in the smallest details).[7]

III. The main principle and basis upon which everything depends is to connect oneself to the *tzaddik* of the generation, and to accept his words, whatever he says, whether important or unimportant, and not deviating (God forbid) from his words to the right or left. . . . Cast aside all [external] wisdom and purge your mind so that it is as if one had no intellect other than what one receives from the *tzaddik*, the rabbi of one's generation. As long as any of one's own intellect remains, one is not completed and connected to the *tzaddik*.[8]

2.3. SECULAR SCIENTIFIC CURIOSITY

The Russian-born American Jewish scholar and educator Benjamin Gruenberg (1875–1965) authored and edited many popular books on science, including *Science and the Public Mind*, the source of the selection below. A member of the secularist New York Society for Ethical Culture as well as a number of secular Jewish organizations, Gruenberg encouraged his fellow Jewish immigrants to study science, which he believed would lead to their intellectual and moral improvement. The widespread cultivation of scientific inquisitiveness through training in the scientific method, Gruenberg believed, would not only reveal new knowledge but also help Jews and others realize the limits of their own knowledge and question "orthodoxies of all sorts."

Among the orthodoxies he believed should be eviscerated by the spirit of inquiry were ideas about one's own people being "God's chosen people" (the sort of belief exemplified in the writings of Naḥman of Bratslav above). Gruenberg hoped that all people would come to cast off their various ethnocentrisms and be linked instead by a common commitment to scientific inquiry transcending cultural boundaries.[9]

Benjamin Gruenberg, *Science and the Public Mind* (1935)

However far our technicians may go in making our machinery automatic and fool-proof, there will still remain, for some people at least, a curiosity as to how things work, as to the nature of the world; and some of these are willing to make serious efforts for the mental satisfactions which they get as a result.... People want to know, not only for the power which knowledge may yield, but for the satisfaction that knowing yields, or the attaining of knowledge as an experience.... It thus becomes urgent for people in general to get a clearer understanding than now obtains as to just what this "science" is, as to just how it produces its results, as to just how it affects our ways of living, as to just what we can do with it, or about it....

Science makes us perceive that there are certain matters which nobody knows, however much assurance any group may have as to the soundness of its own doctrines. Science proceeds, in fact, on the assumption that in specific areas the best we can do is to find out by trying. Hence the significance of assimilating the experimental method as a common way of life. Science may be urged "for everybody" not in the confidence that it will give us common beliefs to guide us harmoniously always and everywhere, like the guiding principles of an established and accepted religious system, but rather in the hope that we can arrive at a common reliance upon the experimental attitude....

The chief obstacles to science have always been fixed ideas and vested interests. Reliance upon a body of doctrines that rationalizes an institution makes investigation a source of danger—to the institution. Orthodoxies of all sorts, whether religious or political, whether moralistic or intellectualistic, are inimical to the spirit of inquiry. The assurance that "the truth" is already at hand makes further search seem futile. Such obstructive confidence in the truth is well illustrated by the religious fervor with which many people hold and urge their theological doctrines. It is not, however, confined to this area but is characteristic of self-complacent ignorance in every realm of human thought. It is exemplified by the intellectual provincialism which assumes that those whose views differ from ours must be either foolish or dishonest, if not both; or which naively identifies its own sect or class or tribe or race or nation with God's chosen people, interpreting that mystic symbol of approbation, "O.K.," as meaning "Our Kind." Science cannot proceed without the open mind, and the human mind, if not constitutionally disposed to close automatically, is at least easily induced to shut up tight early in life. A major task of adult education is to reverse that process.[10]

2.4. CURIOSITY AS THE GATEWAY TO SIN AND HERESY

Rabbi Eliyahu Eliezer Dessler (introduced in section 1.4) was a major figure in the development of *haredi* (ultra-Orthodox) thinking, first in England and then in Israel. A product of the Musar movement, Dessler was also inspired by his studies of Hasidism including, as the selection below indicates, the ideas of Naḥman of Bratslav (section 2.2). Dessler joined Naḥman in counseling obedience to rabbinical authority (see section 1.4), and, as indicated below, he also appreciated Naḥman's vision of faith that transcends the intellect.

Dessler shares Naḥman's concern about the dangers of intellectual inquiry. The curious intellect may be motivated by desires to fulfill physical appetites or to engage in idolatrous "foreign worship." Like Naḥman, but here speaking to an audience of yeshiva students more likely to have access to heretical or foreign ideas (through books or universities, for example), Dessler urges avoiding any "books that have heresy mixed within them." And, like Naḥman, he also urges readers to beware of the "Other Side," the dimension of metaphysical evil and impurity. Curiosity about this ontologically distinct realm can have not only natural effects but unexpected metaphysical consequences, as it did for Adam in the Garden of Eden.

Dessler is assured that as God's Chosen People, Jews have access to the truth and need not inquire into anything else other than the Torah. In his view, curiosity can be a positive virtue, but only if it directs a Jew to be curious about God's Torah and to engage in in-depth Torah study.

Eliyahu Eliezer Dessler, *Mikhtav me-Eliyahu* (mid-twentieth century)

I. A person may be separated from sin but, nonetheless, interested to know about the nature of sin and matters related to it—not to engage in it, God forbid, but "just to know." This power is known as "curiosity," and it is the gateway to sin itself.

If one could ascend to the level closest to the truth, one's curiosity would necessarily come to an end, and one would recognize that, outside of the truth, there is nothing to know and nothing to see, for all else is an illusion and has no value. . . .

In a way ever so slightly like this, our sages of blessed memory have revealed to us the process of the temptation of Adam, the first human being. In knowing that there was a reality of "knowledge of good and evil" that was prohibited to him, there entered into his thought the shadow of an idea, the speck of a desire, to know about it, not for the sake of sinning (God forbid) but "just to know." And with this, the gateway widened, and the temptation continued further on. . . .

It is incumbent upon us to learn and to understand the extent to which a person needs to flee from the domain of the evil inclination. If even [Adam's] mere knowledge of [the evil inclination] led to all the evils in the world—filth and impurity and death and suffering—how much it is incumbent upon us to strive, in accordance with our low level, to distance ourselves from evil with all of our strength. It is incumbent upon us to understand and to feel that even coming close to its borders, whether by seeing or hearing or reading something forbidden, is liable to lead to unexpectedly evil consequences. It is incumbent upon us to overcome the tempting of our desire—which is liable to sometimes awaken within us, seemingly without any evil intention, but which will momentarily peek over the border of the [evil] Other Side, "just to look" without any intention to act—for this, on our level, is truly comparable to the sin of Adam, about whom it was said that, in accordance with his level, "he wanted to taste the dish." All we can do is focus all of our strength on Torah and on holiness.[11]

II. The ascent in inner faith, level after level, comes not through abstract intellectual inquiry but through delving into the Torah itself. It is a mistake to think that one can attain complete faith through intellectual or philosophical inquiry, for the intellect is prejudiced by all kinds of biases. . . . The intellect is also limited, for thought is based on limited, material images. But faith that comes from a person's interiority is not ruled by these limits. Our teacher, Rabbi Naḥman of Bratslav of blessed memory, has already written that faith begins at the limit of the intellect. . . .

[And so] "do not follow your heart and eyes [in your lustful urge]" (Num. 15:39). There is a power within the human being known as curiosity that wants to taste and figure out the character of things beyond oneself. This power has been given to us in order to awaken our capacity for in-depth study of words of Torah—that we are drawn to them even before we have tasted [i.e., discerned] their meaning. But the evil inclination tempts the human being and uses the power of curiosity to draw [a person] to taste things of this world. Even before one has tasted evil, a person's evil inclination tempts and says to him to try it, even just one time.

"'[Do not follow] your heart' to heresy, and '[Do not follow] your eyes' to yearning for sin" (Babylonian Talmud, *Berachot* 12b). Even before he has tasted the sin, and still has no connection to it, a person will desire and have an appetite to taste these two things, out of curiosity. And after tasting, the evil inclination already has an entrance into the person, and he comes into "your lustful urge," already dragged after his appetite. "Keep yourself far away from her; do not come near the doorway of her house" (Prov. 5:8)—for just one step separates you from sin.

Appetite and foreign worship[12]—heresy—reinforce each other. First comes appetite, and then foreign worship: for appetite is the reason for foreign worship, as our sages of blessed memory said: "The Israelites knew that foreign worship had no substance, and only engaged in foreign worship so that they could permit themselves to publicly engage in sexual transgressions" (Babylonian Talmud, *Sanhedrin*, 63b). A person pursues heresy in order to permit all of his desires for himself without interruption; the biases [that prejudice the intellect to pursue desires] are the reason for heresy. . . .

The one who has traits of appetite, who is full of biases that draw him to values of this world—what should he do? He will not come to faith by intellectual inquiry, for his desires will ruin this; rather, he should immerse himself in simple faith, without philosophizing, in becoming accustomed to the performance of commandments . . . and in the continual study of Torah. And slowly, slowly, his appetites will weaken and his heart will be purified, and then he will permit pure inner faith. But woe to the one . . . who studies books that have heresy mixed within them, and clings to improper motivation, drawn to values of this world.[13]

2.5. THE CURIOSITY OF HALAKHIC MAN

Rabbi Joseph Soloveitchik (1903–93), the longtime *Rosh Yeshivah* of Yeshiva University in New York City and an influential leader of Modern Orthodox Judaism, was a staunch defender of the Orthodox belief, also held by Eliyahu Dessler and Naḥman of Bratslav, that Orthodox practices are divinely ordained and unchangeable. At the same time, though, Soloveitchik viewed both Naḥman's Hasidic movement and the Musar movement with which Dessler was associated as problematic: Hasidism was overly focused on metaphysical speculation, Musar was too centered on psychological introspection, and both were insufficiently attentive to the proper focus of a Jew's inquiry—halakhah (Jewish law).

Furthermore, unlike his fellow Orthodox Jews, Soloveitchik saw the study of secular subjects such as science and philosophy as necessary for properly engaging with Jewish law.

Soloveitchik described the ideal Jew as "halakhic man," and in the selections below he indicates that this ideal type is both similar to and different from "cognitive man" (or "theoretical and scientific man"), the ideal type praised by many Western philosophers. Much like the ideal types described by Lindau or Gruenberg, "cognitive man" is characterized by intellectual curiosity. Soloveitchik agrees that one should have intellectual curiosity and study the world, but his "halakhic man" is motivated not by "plain curiosity" but by questions of Jewish law. He may be curious about a bubbling spring because of the importance of springs in Jewish law. He may even be curious about heretical books, such as the works of the liberal Jewish philosopher Hermann Cohen (profiled in section 4.2, an influence on Soloveitchik's view of law); but, as Soloveitchik's student Rabbi David Hartman has put it, "Halakhic man is not especially curious about anything outside the halakhic framework. He lacks an aesthetic sense. The beauty of nature does not capture his attention. He is not concerned with existential issues, such as human mortality and the absurdity of human existence. He shows no interest in metaphysical speculation; the sense of radical wonder . . . has no place in his religious life."[14] Soloveitchik thus encourages curiosity only of a very certain, limited kind.

Joseph Soloveitchik, *Halakhic Man* (1944)

When cognitive man observes and scrutinizes the great and exalted cosmos, it is with the intent of understanding and comprehending its features; cognitive man's desire is to uncover the secret of the world and to unravel the problems of existence. When theoretical and scientific man peers into the cosmos, he is filled with one exceedingly powerful yearning, which is to search for clarity and understanding, for solutions and resolutions. Cognitive man aims to solve the problems of cognition vis-à-vis reality and longs to disperse the cloud of mystery which hangs darkly over the order of phenomena and events. . . .

Halakhic man . . . resembles in various ways cognitive man, yet, he differs in many respects from him as well. . . . Halakhic man studies reality not because he is motivated by plain curiosity the way theoretical man is. . . . Halakhic man orients himself to reality through a priori images of the world [organized according to halakhah] which he bears in the deep recesses of his personality. . . . There is no phenomenon, entity, or object in this concrete world which the a priori Halakhah does not approach with its ideal standard. When halakhic man comes across a spring bubbling quietly, he already possesses a fixed, a priori relationship with this real phenomenon: the complex of laws regarding the halakhic construct of a spring. The spring is fit for the immersion of a *zav* (a man with a discharge); it may serve as *mei ḥatat* (waters of expiation); it purifies with flowing water; it does not require a fixed quantity of forty se'ahs; etc. (See Maimonides, *Laws of Immersion Pools*, 9:8.) When halakhic man approaches a real spring, he gazes at it and carefully examines its nature. He possesses, a priori, ideal principles and precepts which establish the character of the spring as a halakhic construct, and he uses the statutes for the purpose of determining normative law: does the real spring correspond to the requirements of the ideal Halakhah or not? Halakhic man is not overly curious, and he is not particularly concerned with cognizing the spring as it is in itself.[15]

2.6. WONDER, NOT INTELLECTUAL CURIOSITY

Rabbi Abraham Joshua Heschel (1907–72), an influential theologian and activist who spent most of his career as a professor at Conservative Judaism's Jewish Theological Seminary in New York City, describes a very different ideal human type than Soloveitchik's paragon. Even as halakhic observance is central to his vision, Heschel encourages his audience to consider the world beyond the framework of halakhah and to respond to it with a sense of radical wonder. Whereas Soloveitchik encourages Jews to approach a spring with questions about halakhah in mind, Heschel wants his audience to be filled with wonder upon seeing the spring—to be amazed by its very existence and aware that words and concepts are inadequate to describe its sublime character. While he recognizes that intellectual inquisitiveness about halakhah (as promoted by Soloveitchik) can be valuable, just as scientific curiosity (as promoted by Lindau and Gruenberg) can be valuable, Heschel urges his readers to cultivate a sense of wonder that goes far beyond philosophy, science, and intellectual curiosity.

Speaking of the importance of analytic inquiry in his book *God in Search of Man*, Heschel argues that "the sense of wonder and transcendence must not become 'a cushion for the lazy intellect' . . . a substitute for analysis where analysis is possible."[16] That said, Heschel depicts his era as overly obsessed with inquiry and analysis, spurred on by popular-science writers—in the mold of Benjamin Gruenberg—who have taught that "all enigmas can be solved." Such an attitude, Heschel writes, leads to the "indifference to the sublime wonder of living" that is the "root of sin"—encouraging a focus on human power and achievement and neglecting God's transcendence.[17]

In his book *Man Is Not Alone*, the source of the selections below, Heschel warns that curiosity is a trait of self-assertion and expediency. He sees the outcomes of curiosity that so excited Baruch Lindau—the attainment of knowledge, material benefits, and power over nature—as leading to a corrupt self-centeredness: a focus on our own human questions and needs when we should be focused on God's questions and God's needs, a tendency to see ourselves ruling the world when we should see God ruling the world. Intellectual inquisitiveness can therefore be a gateway to sin, though for very different reasons than Dessler thought.

And Heschel offers a different remedy for errant inquisitiveness. For Heschel, we must cultivate wonder, the virtue that lies at the heart of what he defines as true "religion." Wonder allows us to turn away from our self-centered curiosity, focus on God's questions rather than our own, see our unity with the rest of creation, and ultimately find greater awareness and knowledge.[18] As Heschel writes, "The greatest hindrance to knowledge is our adjustment to conventional notions, to mental clichés. Wonder or radical amazement, the state of maladjustment to words and notions, is . . . a prerequisite for an authentic awareness of that which is."[19]

Abraham Joshua Heschel, *Man Is Not Alone* (1951)

There is no knowledge that would be an answer to endless wonder, that could stem the tide of its silent challenge. When we are overtaken by endless wonder . . . [we] realize that our concern is not: What may we know? How could we open Him to our minds? Our concern is: To whom do we belong? How could we open our lives to Him? Where self-assertion is no more; when realizing that wonder is not our own achievement; that it is not by our own power alone that we are shuddered with radical amazement, it is not within our power any more to assume the role of an examiner of a subject in search of an object, such as we are in search of a cause when perceiving thunder. Ultimate wonder is not the same as curiosity. Curiosity is the state of a mind in search of knowledge, while ultimate wonder is the state of knowledge in search of a mind; it is the thought of God in search of a soul. . . .

What gives birth to religion is not intellectual curiosity, but the fact and experience of our being asked. As long as we frame and ponder our own questions, we do not even know how to ask. We know too little to be able to inquire. Faith is not the product of search and endeavor, but the answer to a challenge which no one can forever ignore. It is ushered in not by a problem, but by an exclamation. Philosophy begins with man's question; religion begins with God's question and man's answer.[20]

2.7. A NEW FEMINIST CURIOSITY

An influential scholar and activist with particular expertise on issues of gender and sexuality, Rabbi Danya Ruttenberg (b. 1975) takes a feminist approach to curiosity. In the selection below she advocates a new feminist hermeneutics (approach to interpretation) where curiosity is the core hermeneutical virtue, the trait that guides one's study.

Ruttenberg advises approaching Jewish texts and practices with curiosity about their history. She encourages her audience to investigate the ways that many traditions have historically sought to subjugate women. Meanwhile, she also asks readers to be curious about how texts and practices might be reinterpreted in ways that build better connections among human beings and between humans and God.

A Conservative rabbi, Ruttenberg is committed to studying the sometimes disturbing history of Jewish traditions, to maintaining traditional practices, and to finding new meanings in them. Thus, for example, in a portion of the essay not printed below, she comments that while feminists have often rejected the practice of abstinence during menstruation because of its misogynistic history, she can see much goodness in the practice when she is curious about how it can be reframed as "sanctifying intimate relationships."[21]

A very different kind of questioning is at work here than in the writing of Joseph Soloveitchik. When Soloveitchik's halakhic man approaches a spring that might be used for immersion following menstruation, his questions are about whether the spring is fit to be used according to the fixed rules of halakhah. Ruttenberg's curious feminist would approach the same spring with what she calls a "hermeneutics of curiosity": about how it has been used as a tool of patriarchal domination (with the claim that it cleanses women from "filth"), and also about how immersion practices can lead to connection with God and to experiences of renewal within a couple's relationship. Like Dessler, Ruttenberg values how curiosity can lead to in-depth Torah study, but she challenges Dessler's "simple faith" that commits to traditional practices without considering their histories. And while, like Gruenberg, Ruttenberg supports efforts to question orthodoxies, she also supports questioning those who question orthodoxies and who too quickly discard too much of tradition.

Danya Ruttenberg, "The Hermeneutics of Curiosity" (2009)

Earlier feminist work had to correct a long-standing imbalance by jettisoning much of what was downright hostile to women. This reminds me of the old story (that has no basis in truth) of Elizabeth

Cady Stanton sitting on the floor of her church with a Bible and a pair of scissors, snipping away everything in the book that was problematic from a gendered perspective, until she was left with a very slim volume indeed. Now, at this late date, I think that we're able to look around at the scraps on the floor, to think about integrating, on feminist terms, parts of tradition that may have been initially discarded as a necessary part of the feminist process. What treasures are waiting for us to pull them out of the feminist garbage heap? . . .

I wonder if, rather than operating with the famous "hermeneutics of suspicion"[22]—that is to say, the default assumption that a text or practice is misogynistic until proven otherwise—we might want to try a hermeneutics of curiosity. For example, when we come across something that makes us deeply uncomfortable, we might ask ourselves, what is this ritual (or rule, or piece of liturgy) really about? What are some of the ideas underlying it? How did it get to its current incarnation? How have people understood it in different times and places? And, perhaps most important, what potential does it have? . . . As feminists, we aren't obligated to accept everything handed to us by our patriarchal tradition. But as Jews, it behooves us to turn our traditions around a few times. Through a hermeneutics of curiosity, we may not necessarily find everything we need already there from the start, but it's worth the extra spin to see if some notions can help us better learn how to connect to one another and to God. . . .

While we can't blindly accept practices and traditions inside Judaism that destroy or subjugate women, we have the ability to transform many aspects of our tradition into vehicles that can help us to seek the holy, and to serve God by learning how to better relate to others in caring and connection. It is tempting to leave behind anything that suggests patriarchal domination, but sometimes, mixed in with troubling notions about gender are centuries of questions about how best to live in relationship to the Divine. I think that we do ourselves a disservice when we do not try to find those questions, and when we do not engage them on our own terms. Through a hermeneutics of curiosity, we may be able to help repair a broken Judaism, to turn it into something more whole and complete than it's ever been. And who knows? We may even find ourselves repaired in the process.[23]

2.8. EVE'S CURIOSITY WAS NOT A SIN

When Eliyahu Dessler condemns the curiosity that leads to sin in the Garden of Eden, he focuses on the curiosity of Adam, not that of Eve. But, as Rabbi Jamie Arnold (b. 1969) observes in his Rosh Hashanah sermon at Congregation Beth Evergreen (a Reconstructionist congregation in Evergreen, Colorado), Eve's curiosity has often been singled out for particular blame. In the selection from that sermon below, Arnold inverts this message, urging his audience to be more like Eve—always reaching "for the new fruits of new knowledge." As he views eating the fruit in the Garden of Eden as a positive step, he describes the snake that provokes Eve's curiosity in positive terms as well. Traditional kabbalistic teachings describe the snake as an agent of the evil "Other Side," bringing (to use Dessler's language quoted above) "filth and impurity and death and suffering" into the world; one tradition suggests that a messianic "holy snake" will ultimately destroy the evil snake that had successfully tempted Eve. Yet here too Arnold inverts this tradition, regarding the snake in the garden as holy and messianic, "the savior of our story."

Like Heschel, Arnold is also intrigued by God's questioning of human beings. But Heschel teaches that the primary lesson to learn from this questioning is that we need not curiosity but greater responsiveness, wonder, and awe; for Arnold, by contrast, the primary lesson is to be as inquisitive as God. Heschel sees his generation as too self-assertive and in need of paying greater attention to God's questions rather than their own; Arnold, by contrast, encourages his audience to be more self-assertive with their curious questioning.

Jamie Arnold, "The Snake, the Skylight, and the Seeker" (2013)

There are those who've claimed that Eve's curiosity was a sin. Had she not been curious, she wouldn't have transgressed, and we would still be in the Garden of Eden. They claim that her curiosity caused the curses of pain in childbirth and exile from Eden. Curiosity killed the cat. Pain in childbirth, maybe? Curiosity, anthropologists tell us, was and is integral to stimulating new learning and the enlargement of our brains. Those big heads, I'm told, are a bear to get through the birth canal. *But there is a difference between a punishment and a price.* Curiosity is no sin, and without it we'd still be stuck in a world in which there is nothing new under the sun....

So if not curiosity, what was the sin of the Garden of Eden? The sin was that they stopped being curious. After Eve eats and shares the fruit of the new knowledge, "the voice of God walks in the breeze of the garden" and asks, "Where are you?" (Gen. 3:8–9). The sages point out that with compassion, patience and trust, God wants to give them an opportunity to admit what they did. "Where are you?" With this inquiry God is also modeling curiosity for them—*asking instead of accusing.* They have a difficult choice to make. Will they own up to what they have done or try to hide? Will they share responsibility and reconcile, or will they try to save their own skins? They, like the snake, are now naked, their curiosity exposed. God asks rather than accuses, not because God does not know, but because *God wants them to stay curious....* Curiosity is not the sin, it is the salvation.... The snake is the savior of our story....[24]

It is time. Like Eve, let's get curious about the possibilities, ask "What if ...," embrace the temptation to reach for the new fruits of new knowledge.[25]

2.9. CURIOSITY AND THE PURSUIT OF PEACE

Rabbi Amy Eilberg (b. 1954), the first woman ordained as a Conservative rabbi (in 1985), has served in many roles throughout her career including chaplain, pastoral counselor, spiritual director, peace and justice educator, interfaith activist, musar teacher, and conflict-resolution teacher. The selection below is excerpted from her book *From Enemy to Friend: Jewish Wisdom and the Pursuit of Peace,* which explores how Jewish sources may support reconciliation and peace-building work. Its last chapter, focused on musar, considers a number of virtues, including curiosity.

One of the distinguishing characteristics of the previous texts by Naḥman and Dessler is their certainty that Jews should not be curious about texts written by non-Jewish authors or promoting "foreign worship." The authors view themselves as clearly superior to non-Jews and write off non-Jewish wisdom as foolish and downright evil. Eilberg takes a very different attitude toward the "other," refusing to write others off. Focusing on those who may seem to be "enemies," she asks her audience to show appreciative curiosity toward all others, even "enemies."

The idea that one should not dismiss others echoes a theme in Gruenberg, and, like Gruenberg, Eilberg encourages her audience to learn from contemporary science.[26] But she does not share Gruenberg's optimism that a common commitment to secular scientific inquiry will lead to peace. More important, in her view, is appreciative curiosity for people of all genders, races, religions, nationalities, political parties, and all other identities. And whereas Gruenberg has little interest in early Jewish texts, Eilberg's discussion is grounded in ancient traditions. Underlying her vision is the age-old Rabbinic statement that gives her book its title: "Who is the hero of heroes? . . . One who makes an enemy into a friend."[27]

Amy Eilberg, *From Enemy to Friend* (2014)

In the midst of polarized conflict, locked in an intellectual version of combat, with the limbic brain on high alert, we can only repeat our own version of things as loudly and powerfully as possible. The opposing view is regarded as incomprehensible, foolish, ignorant, or unconscionable. It is a straw person to be demolished if possible or at least strenuously defended against. Just as we cannot show physical weakness when a wild animal is attacking us, in rhetorical battle we instinctively present the most powerful, aggressive form of our own belief and see only the flaws in the other's view. I certainly know the feeling.

I have long seen listening as the single most important skill for dialogue across conflict, whether interpersonal, intergroup, or international. I have come to recognize that the restoration of curiosity about one's opponent is an equally important capacity. . . . To the extent that we consider ourselves superior to or unconnected to others, our natural desire for knowledge about them will be shut down. The result is that we live in worlds of our own construction, listening only to the people we deem worthy, reading only the commentators whose views match our own. The irony is that this attitude of self-satisfied superiority makes us ignorant, without access to sources of possible wisdom beyond our chosen circle of acceptable people and opinions. In the process, we impoverish ourselves, denying ourselves the possibility of learning new ways of seeing the world.

By contrast, an attitude of curiosity means that opportunities for learning and expansion of our horizons are everywhere. Every moment of our lives can be a laboratory, an occasion for growth both interpersonally and intellectually. . . .

The deceptively simple act of stopping to observe that our natural capacity for curiosity is locked down can be a moment of awakening in the midst of conflict. In such a precious moment, when we notice that we actually don't have any interest in what a Democratic or Republican voter in the United States or a Likud or Meretz voter in Israel thinks, we might feel a pang of regret for the lost opportunity to learn something more about God's world. This might lead to a brief moment of humility and honesty, in which we admit to ourselves that we actually do not know everything about the other side or even about the issue we are discussing.

Can you think of a moment when someone unexpectedly inquired about an important aspect of your life? Generally this is an experience of respect, an affirmation that you are important enough for the other to want to know more about you. It is an experience that fosters connection, as you share something you value and see that the other person wants to hear and understand your perspective.

When one side in a dispute interrupts the continuous flow of aggressive communication to ask a question of genuine curiosity, a crack may appear in the previously impenetrable wall of animosity. The very expression of interest and inquiry creates a thaw in frozen rhetorical combat, inviting the two parties to step beyond their well-worn embattled positions and experience one another as whole human beings, not only straw figures representing an objectionable point of view.[28]

2.10. CURIOSITY AND WHITE PRIVILEGE

Rabbi Sandra Lawson (b. 1969), the world's first Black openly lesbian rabbi, was ordained by the Reconstructionist Rabbinical College in 2018. An influential voice on questions of race and racism in Jewish communities, she serves as director of racial diversity, equity, and inclusion at Reconstructing Judaism. In one 2018 article, Lawson and coauthor Rabbi Donna Cephas argued that "holding a Jewish American, or American Jewish, identity does not always lead to an appreciation of difference" and discussed how "we often treat Jews of color as other, as objects of curiosity, and sometimes as objects of distrust," especially given the ubiquitous assumption that Jews are white (see section 2.1). Lawson describes how Jews who meet her often question her as to whether she is Jewish, how she became Jewish, or when she converted. "These questions," Lawson writes, "never seem to happen in a context of wanting to know me as a person. They are about the questioner's own curiosity as they attempt to see how I fit into Judaism. When people start to ask me questions about my Jewish identity, I feel as if they are trying to assuage some type of uncomfortable feeling they have regarding my Jewishness."[29]

Lawson agrees with Eilberg that curiosity is, for the most part, a good thing, but whereas Eilberg's writing describes how curiosity about another person may reflect humility, respect, positive connection, and seeing another as a whole human being, Lawson points out how curiosity may reflect selfishness, disrespect, and negativity. In the brief meditation below, she discusses how questions directed at her and other Black Jews by white Jews operating from a position of privilege can be harmful, invasive, hurtful, selfish, and othering.

Sandra Lawson, "Curiosity Can Be Invasive and Hurtful" (2022)

Human beings are naturally curious about the world around them. For the most part, this type of curiosity is good and usually causes no harm. But when we are curious about people, even though our intentions may seem innocent, we can cause harm.

The Torah has countless examples about how we as Jews are to treat the stranger, the foreigner, and the other. Sadly sometimes, when it comes to members of our own community, we often miss the mark. As a Jew of color, I know that I do not look like what many people expect a Jew to look like; and I am reminded of this every time I out myself as a Jew to Jews who are White. Jews who are white often treat Jews of color as the other, as objects of curiosity and sometimes as objects of distrust. They are often so curious, with their line of questioning about, *"How are you Jewish?"* that their questions become invasive and hurtful. And the questioner comes off as having a sense of entitlement about knowing personal information about the person they are asking. This type of curiosity is selfish and othering, and it tells people like me that we don't belong.[30]

CONCLUSION

Jewish thinkers have clearly disagreed over questions of how curiosity might be a virtue. Is it a virtue that all people may cultivate or is it only for a select few? May one direct one's curiosity only to Jewish wisdom sanctioned by rabbinical authorities or may one be curious about all forms of wisdom? Is scientific curiosity compatible with theological orthodoxies? Do we need more intellectual curiosity, or, rather, more wonder? Is curiosity more likely to be a dangerous quality or a source of peace? How might curiosity be connected with sin, if at all? How should we understand the curiosity of Adam and Eve? How should one respond to curiosity about Jewish traditions or other traditions? What about when those traditions appear dangerous or hostile?

Debates about who has the authority to guide inquiry are foundational to these disagreements. At one extreme, Naḥman of Bratslav shows one model of rabbinical authority as he demands that his followers submit entirely to his word ("as if you had no mind of your own"). On the other hand, Danya Ruttenberg encourages curiosity about Jewish traditions without dictating what particular traditions Jews should take up. Other thinkers, such as Baruch Lindau and Benjamin Gruenberg, point to scientists as authoritative guides, while Abraham Joshua Heschel urges his audience to focus on God's authority and give less authority to scientific models. While many other authors in this chapter might also describe God as possessing ultimate authority, they have very different ideas of what God wants and of how the divine ideal or divine will might be known.

Debates about humility are also foundational to these debates. Does facing the divine ideal or divine will require humbling oneself before God, and, if so, what does it mean to humble oneself? Does humility require submitting to certain authority figures? Does humility require certain limits to one's inquiry? How much should we assert ourselves, and how do we avoid too much or too little self-assertion? Can the cultivation of humility help us to avoid causing harm to others? These and other questions will be the subject of the following chapter.

3

Humility (*Anavah*)

Unlike curiosity, the virtue of humility (in Hebrew, *anavah*) is often singled out for particular praise in premodern Jewish literature. In the written Torah, Moses is described as "a very humble [*anav*] man, more so than any other man on earth" (Num. 12:3). Using different Hebrew terminology, a biblical verse in the book of Micah sums up God's requirements "only to do justice, and to love goodness, and to walk humbly [or "modestly," *hatznea lekhet*] with your God" (Mic. 6:8). Elsewhere in the Bible, God is said to "adorn the humble with salvation" (Ps. 149:4), while "the fear of the Lord is to hate evil: pride and arrogance and the evil way" (Prov. 8:13). As we will see, modern Jews constructing their own approaches to humility have sometimes engaged with verses such as these.

Many statements in the foundational ethical tractate of the Mishnah, *Avot*, also urge humility and caution against pride and arrogance. Rabbi Levitas of Yavneh teaches, "Be very, very humble, for the end of the human being is the worm" (*Avot* 4:4). Hillel warns, "Do not judge your fellow until you have stood in his place" (*Avot* 2:5). Yohanan ben Zakkai advises, "If you have studied much Torah, do not ascribe merit to yourself, for you were created for this" (*Avot* 2:8). Elazar ben Shamua warns teachers against arrogance toward students: "The dignity of your student should be as precious to you as your own" (*Avot* 4:15); Ben Zoma sees wisdom in "one who learns from every person" (*Avot* 4:1); and the Mishnah cautions that one should respect the colleague from whom one has learned anything, "even one letter" (*Avot* 6:3). Talmudic literature adds many other warnings against arrogance—for example, a warning from Rabbi Yehudah in the name of Rav that if a Rabbinic sage is arrogant, "his wisdom will disappear" (BT *Pesachim* 66b).

Other rabbis quoted in the Talmud, however, suggest that rabbis themselves need a bit of arrogance, at least so that others will accept their authority.[1] Many are concerned about those who "dishonor the Torah" (*Avot* 4:6) by disrespecting those who teach it, and they are especially concerned about the "ignorant masses" (*ammei ha-aretz*) among the Jewish people who fail to respect Torah scholars. Various Rabbinic texts ask rabbis to recognize their own superiority vis-à-vis ignoramuses, view them as mere animals, and separate themselves from them. One talmudic text, for example, warns scholarly men against marrying the daughter of an ignoramus, equating the end result with "lying with a beast" (BT *Pesachim* 49a–b). Other Rabbinic texts assert the superiority of law-abiding Rabbinic Jews over those whom they see as sinning. They often describe sinners as arrogant and sometimes associate particular transgressions—such as same-sex male intercourse—with arrogance.[2] Although some rabbis caution against being overly judgmental of others, they seldom see themselves as arrogant when they are enforcing what they see as God's clear judgments and God's law.

Other Rabbinic texts encourage other sorts of hierarchies. Many encourage males to see their own superiority vis-à-vis women—for example, when they speak of men "acquiring" or "possessing" women in marriage. Many Rabbinic texts also ask Jews to recognize themselves as "the Chosen People," superior to non-Jews; and various traditions assert the superiority of human beings over animals. At the same time, other Rabbinic traditions affirm the dignity of all Israelites regardless of gender or education, all human beings regardless of nationality, and all animals.

As we will see in this chapter, those traditions that stress inequality are sources of deep tensions when it comes to humility. Tensions around how humility may or may not be compatible with social hierarchies among Jews become apparent when we contrast perspectives from Pinhas of Polotsk (section 3.1) and Nahman of Bratslav (section 3.2) with more egalitarian perspectives from Mordecai Kaplan (section 3.4), Rebecca Alpert (section 3.7), and Ira Stone (section 3.9). Perspectives from Naḥman, Alpert, Shalom Noah Berezovsky (section 3.5), and Ruth Abusch-Magder (section 3.10) reveal tensions around how humility may or may not be compatible with male chauvinism and heterosexism. Perspectives from Kaplan, Berezovsky, Aharon Shmuel Tamaret (section 3.3), and Meir Kahane (section 3.6) evince tensions over how humility may or may not be compatible with assertions of national pride and "chosenness." Jeremy Benstein (section 3.8) addresses the tensions over how humility may or may not be compatible with anthropocentric (human-centered) approaches to morality. The debates about humility in this chapter are also intertwined with very different perspectives on anger, war, the evil inclination, selfhood, idolatry, and God.

3.1. BEWARE THE FALSE CROWN OF HUMILITY

Rabbi Pinḥas of Polotsk (d. 1822), the author of the text below, was a student of the Vilna Gaon, the leader of traditionalist scholars in Lithuania who were fierce opponents (*mitnagdim*) of the emerging Hasidic movement. A scholar and traveling preacher who, like his teacher, bitterly criticized the Hasidic movement, Pinḥas disparaged the Hasidic model of leadership, which granted tremendous authority to a single rabbinical leader—a *tzaddik*, an intermediary between God and human beings distinguished not by his learning but by his charisma. To Pinḥas, the *tzaddik* denigrated the honor of Torah study and often associated with ignorant and sinful Jews.[3]

In opposition to this model, Pinḥas contended that proper rabbinical leadership was found among elite scholars (*talmidei hakhamim*) who maintained social distance from the "ignorant masses" (*ammei ha-aretz*). In the text below he warns aspiring scholars that the evil inclination (*yetzer ha-ra*) might seek to persuade them that, in order to be properly humble, they should not only associate with the ignorant masses but should defer to them. Pinḥas objects that this is a false notion of humility, one that dishonors God's Torah by dishonoring its learned scholars. While a scholar should have the humility to refuse honors that confer personal benefits, he should never refuse honor for the Torah. Furthermore, properly honoring the Torah requires acknowledging the superiority of Torah scholars like himself—and the inferiority of the ignorant masses.[4]

Pinḥas's perspective on humility builds on ancient Rabbinic texts that castigate the unscholarly masses for their ignorance and urge scholars to keep their distance from them. Rabbis quoted in the Babylonian Talmud, for example, demand that scholarly men never marry the daughter of an ignoramus; they depict her as less than human, such that sex with her would be like sex with an animal—and as the book of Deuteronomy teaches, "Cursed be he who lies with any beast" (Deut. 27:21). Pinḥas laments that, in his era, the tables have been turned: scholars are poor and degraded, and the ignorant masses refuse to marry the daughters of scholars, whom *they* regard as beasts.

The model of humility unveiled here helps bolster the authority of elite male scholars. Unscholarly men are condemned for their arrogant attempts to degrade those scholars; women, referred to solely as marriage prospects, are not empowered to be potential scholars nor given a voice in the debate about proper humility. These views are well within the mainstream of traditionalist rabbinic thought and have continued to be influential in some Orthodox circles to the present day.[5]

Pinḥas of Polotsk, "The Crown of Torah" (1788)

[The evil inclination] will tell you: "Because you have merited divine wisdom and the crown of Torah, it is fitting that you should also be crowned with humility, such that you should regard every man in Israel as more important than yourself and you should renounce your honor before every man, in line with the statement of our sages: 'If you have studied much Torah, do not ascribe merit to yourself, for you were created for this' (*Mishnah Avot* 2:8). You should show no sign that would mark you as a scholar [*talmid hakham*], and you may speak with anyone, join gatherings with anyone, and eat with anyone. . . . Thus you will demonstrate your humility and derive no benefit from the honor of your Torah."

Woe, my brother! Beware and be on guard against this cursed serpent that tempts and seduces, for its intention is only to dishonor the Torah in the eyes of the masses and the students. . . . It prefers to equate everyone—the layman and the priest, the unworthy and the great, the ignoble and the honored—such that "every man does as he pleases" (Judg. 17:6, 21:25) without reproof. . . .

It is true that a man needs to distance himself from arrogance as far as possible, so that he does not pursue honor or (God forbid) seek it for himself or act haughtily. As the sages said, "If a scholar acts haughtily, his wisdom departs from him" (BT *Pesachim* 66b). . . . But in forgoing his own honor, he must not forgo the honor of the Torah, God forbid. . . .

The sages said, "Whoever dishonors the Torah is himself dishonored by the people" (*Mishnah Avot* 4:6). Woe to us, that this has happened in our era! Under the leadership of those seduced by the evil inclination and crowned with the "crown of humility," the Torah and its scholars have been utterly degraded in the eyes of the masses. To the ignorant masses, it seems that this is the way of Torah: anyone who touches it must be degraded and ridiculed in the sight of all people, and must go out in filthy, soiled, muddied clothes, and must rise in the presence of every ignoramus . . . and revere each and every one . . . and eat at his table. . . . [Meanwhile, the ignorant masses] fear [the scholars'] touch lest they defile their vessels and their palatial residences. They will not join their gatherings or, God forbid, eat with them, and with regard to their daughters they say, "Cursed is the one who lies with any beast" (Deut. 27:21). . . . The way that the scholar should be treating the ignorant masses, with all of this distancing, is the way that they treat him. . . .

Now this cursed serpent wants to crown you with the "crown of humility." . . . And is it not because of this crown of humility that those who come before judges come with no reverence, embarrassment, or shame? . . . They insult and curse each other before the judges, and the judge stays silent out of humility, deferring to heretics. (So said the sages: "One who denigrates another in the presence of a scholar is a heretic" [BT *Sanhedrin* 99b], and how much the more one who denigrates a scholar himself.) Is humility like this commanded by the Torah? It is not humble—rather, this totally destroys the law of Israel, darkening and degrading and extinguishing the light of the Torah, such that one's words will not be heard. . . .

[Scholars] must adhere to these measures: minimize conversation with the ignorant masses, and flee from their company and gatherings as one would flee from a serpent . . . and respect the holy crown, and do not defile it by honoring one who is not fit for honor before God.[6]

3.2. NAḤMAN OF BRATSLAV ON ARROGANCE

In his *Sefer ha-Middot* (The book of character traits), the Hasidic teacher Rabbi Naḥman of Bratslav listed significant teachings regarding a series of virtues and vices. His entry regarding arrogance, the beginning of which is printed below, offers ideas about arrogance and humility that are in tension with most of the other entries in this chapter.

In the previous chapter (section 2.2), we saw Naḥman's belief that total authority should be granted to a true *tzaddik* such as himself. His belief in the power of the *tzaddik* is also manifest in the selection below. Scholars who think they are superior because of their scholarly insights— like Pinḥas of Polotsk—should realize that their insights are not due to their own efforts but to "the *tzaddik* of the generation," who uses them just as a scribe uses a pen. A key way to remove arrogance is to cleave to the *tzaddik*—something that any common person can do, for even wearing the sort of hat that a *tzaddik* wears will have the effect of removing arrogance. Other auspicious behaviors with the same effect include gazing at the sky; refraining from food, alcohol, and illicit sexuality (the latter of which is a central theme for Naḥman); and taking part in the suffering of one's fellow Jews (there is no mention of the suffering of others). Common Jews engaging in such behaviors are in fact more likely to be humble than rabbis.

Naḥman warns against "one who arrogantly imposes rabbinical authority" but believes that a true *tzaddik* could not be guilty of such arrogance.

The *tzaddik* is defined as a rabbi who is free from sin and arrogance (no. 29 on the list below), and his authority is assumed to come from a place of humility, though "it may be permissible" for him "to act in a way that appears arrogant" (no. 24). Similarly, Pinḥas believes that Torah scholars should take on what might appear to be pride in order to uphold their social status. For Naḥman, as for Pinḥas, discourse about arrogance and humility functions to justify certain social hierarchies.

The selection below also reveals what Naḥman saw as possible consequences of arrogance: famine, adultery, male homosexuality, female infertility, and slipping and falling in public marketplaces. A discerning individual, seeing such things, will recognize the arrogance causing them. The references to sexuality hint at the idea, more fully developed elsewhere in Naḥman's writing, that the "evil inclination" is particularly linked with illicit sexual desires.[7] (Naḥman writes elsewhere, for instance, that the arrogance of unworthy Jewish leaders "increases desire for illicit sexual behavior in the world"[8] and that "through excessive arrogance, [a man] will be sodomized like a woman."[9])

Naḥman of Bratslav, "Arrogance" (early nineteenth century)

1. The Messiah will not come until all arrogance is gone from the world.
2. Through arrogance, one comes to desire male homosexual intercourse; one also comes to anger; also, sometimes, a woman cannot conceive because she adorns herself, possessing arrogance.
3. Through arrogance, famine comes to the world.
4. Through arrogance, one comes to drunkenness, and vice-versa.
5. Through arrogance, one comes to fear.
6. Giving charity is an auspicious practice for annulling arrogance.
7. One who arrogantly imposes rabbinical authority, God arouses enemies against him.
8. One who experiences an uplifted heart should know that the time will be successful for him.
9. One who saves the poor has power in his gaze to humble the arrogant.

10. One who walks in a marketplace and falls: it is known that he has a large ego.

11. An auspicious practice for overcoming arrogance is to join in the suffering of Israel.

12. A poor man who is pursued by a wicked man: know that the poor man possesses arrogance.

13. Through arrogance, one loses one's faith.

14. Through arrogance, one's heart and eyes are blocked from seeing the wonders of the Blessed One and from being in awe of Him.

15. One should not make oneself arrogant on account of great insights or good deeds, for it all comes through the Tzaddik of the generation, and one is related to the Tzaddik like a pen is related to a writer.

16. Eating and drinking lead to arrogance.

17. A rectification for arrogance is that one should fast.

18. An auspicious practice for overcoming arrogance is to look at the sky.

19. A person is frightened by one's dreams in order to remove embedded arrogance, which is concealed from him, which he does not recognize.

20. Anyone who is haughty: his wisdom and prophecy depart.

21. The intellect does not tolerate an arrogant pauper. In time, he too has regret and is despised in his own eyes.

22. The arrogant one is unable to humble his intellect and will come to forgetfulness.

23. A haughty person is blemished.

24. It may be permissible to act in a way that appears arrogant, depending upon the necessity of the matter.

25. An impertinent person will in the end commit adultery, and is like an idolater, like a complete heretic, like one who commits all forms of sexual transgression, and like one who built an idolatrous altar. His importance diminishes to nothing; it is appropriate to cut him down like the [idolatrous] Asherah tree; nor will his remains be resurrected; the divine presence wails over him.

26. An auspicious practice for removing arrogance: [wearing] the hat of a Tzaddik.

27. Through faith, you will have the strength to break yourself of arrogance, and rule over the vice of arrogance.

28. An arrogant person: his plans do not succeed.

29. When you happen to transgress, unaware, it is certain that you possess arrogance, and this shows you that you are not yet a Tzaddik. . . .[10]

3.3. THE IDOLATROUS ARROGANCE OF NATIONALISM AND WAR

Like the two previous authors, Aharon Shmuel Tamaret (Tamares, 1869–1931) was an Eastern European Orthodox rabbi who preached on themes of humility and against the temptations posed by the evil inclination. While he was trained in the world of non-Hasidic traditionalism shaped by figures like Pinḥas of Polotsk, the concerns that animated him were very different than those that stirred Pinḥas or Naḥman of Bratslav. Rather than portraying the evil inclination as disparaging scholarship or encouraging illicit sexuality, Tamaret characterized it as an egotistical impulse that sought political power and found its ultimate expressions in nationalism and war.

The selections below were written amid World War I. Tamaret describes the world as engulfed by idolatry: worshipping the ego and the nationalism that satisfies the egotistical desire for superiority, and approving of the slaughter of millions in order to satisfy that desire. Here, the evil inclination takes the form of a demonic "angel of destruction and devastation."

A committed pacifist whose writings have continued to inspire Jewish pacifists to this day, Tamaret was opposed to nationalists of all sorts, including Jewish nationalists—Zionists—who sought to restore "national honor" through the use of force. In the selections below, he insists that the ancient rabbis favored a society that would be built "in the spirit of humility" rather than out of a desire for honor, aggrandizement, and earthly power. But, for Tamaret, Jews could be properly humble and still feel proud—proud to be chosen by God to be an ethical nation committed to peace and opposed to gross egotism, arrogant nationalism, and war.

Aharon Shmuel Tameret, *The Assembly of Israel and the Wars of the Nations* (1918)

I. War is modern idolatry; out of all of the foolish forms of idolatry, it is the one preserved by [today's] "enlightened" generation. . . . It is in accordance with the well-known proverb: God created the human being in [God's] image, and people go forth and construct idols in their image and spirit. Thus we can understand that the idol of the "homeland" that the modern human being worships has been constructed by nations to fill the great emptiness created in their souls by their continual preoccupation with matters of nationalism and by their nationalist, egotistical spirits. . . . With great tumult, contemporary nations busy themselves with civilizing the world—sowing, planting, building bridges, paving highways, holding fairs, and so on—but the spirit animating all their activities is the basest form of egotism. All of this business and all these activities stem from the passionate pursuit of wealth, possessions, and power. An [evil] Angel of Destruction and Devastation stands behind, mocking, supervising these activities and the building of buildings out of gross egotism . . . and, without stopping, they sink further into egotistical matters. . . .

But the eyes of the Destroyer-Angel, who was created from the building of an egotistical world, are now looking at a greater opportunity for destruction: overthrowing people and their creations, as Sodom was overthrown, returning the world to being formless and void.

Our rabbis of blessed memory stated: "Every house in which words of Torah are not heard"—that is, not established and intended for a spirit of humility and the nobility of Torah, but rather for a spirit of gross materialism—"will in the end be destroyed." They said this not only regarding a person's private home but also regarding that which is built by peoples and whole states. The Destroyer-Angel is not satisfied with the idols of small taverns and limited destruction, when there is the opportunity to use the character of peoples to pour out a giant idol that can be shared by all people of a state, of such a size that its influence can be blinding and overpowering, and the power of its arm will be great enough to enslave all others, and to destroy and annihilate so that none remain. The name of this great idol is "the honor of the homeland," and it is formed by joining together the private egotisms found in the hearts of each inhabitant of the state. It is worshipped by slaughtering millions of people in war for the homeland. . . . And [this] wolfish way of relating to the spilling of blood will not be extinguished until our hearts are properly trained, and the filth of egotism ceases to be the spirit animating all human actions. . . .[11]

II. We [Jews] are permitted—and it is our sacred obligation—to awaken within our hearts a feeling of pride in our antiquity. For preserving our uniqueness, for saving us from being assimilated among the nations, this pride is a virtue and is not a defect, given the ethical mission of repairing the world that we carry as our obligation. This pride is a virtue as a means to an end, for the sake of our ethical mission—because our mission to repair the world depends on our having been separated from the world, and our courage to stand in isolation depends on recognizing our essence. Furthermore, our pride . . . is a virtue for our ethical mission, not only as a means to an end—rather, because this pride is in opposition to the pride of the sword, and it sends forth good fragrances into the world, ever-so-slightly purifying the air of the terrible odors of nationalist pride.[12]

3.4. THE ARROGANT CONCEPT OF "CHOSENNESS"

All of the thinkers quoted above believed that humility was compatible with the doctrine that Jews are God's Chosen People; Pinḥas and Naḥman also emphasized that certain individuals within that Chosen People (whether scholars or *tzaddikim*) were further chosen by God as indispensable leaders. In the selection below, Rabbi Mordecai Kaplan (1881–1983), the founder of Reconstructionist Judaism, argues that any of these sorts of claims to chosenness and indispensability are a sign of arrogance.

Kaplan is responding directly to an article by a Reform rabbi, Bernard Bamberger, who had also argued that the Jews are a Chosen People. Bamberger stressed that the Jews must recognize their obligations as "teachers of mankind and exemplars of religious living" who have been elected to play a unique role in history; he proudly made such claims even though "it may be immodest (according to the conventions of Anglo-Saxon taste)" to do so.[13] Kaplan responds in his book *The Future of the American Jew* that such claims are not merely immodest according to Anglo-Saxon conventions but according to Jewish tradition. The idea that one should not view oneself as chosen by God was first advanced by Moses, he argues; after all, following the sin of the Golden Calf, Moses was willing to sacrifice himself for the sake of his people, and, as the most humble of all people, he hoped that his fellow Jews would join him as prophets. Just as it would be incompatible with his humility for Moses to see himself as uniquely chosen, for the Jewish people to see themselves as chosen is incompatible with their ideal of humility. It is worth noting that Kaplan sees the idea of a God who has chosen favorites as an idea created by ancient peoples who were (understandably) inclined to see themselves at the center of the world. Kaplan does not believe that such a God exists; he himself favors God-language only when used to describe natural forces that make for goodness and salvation.

It is also worth noting that Kaplan shared many of Aharon Shmuel Tamaret's concerns about aggressive nationalism and war; but he supported forms of nationalism (including Zionism) that did not claim the superiority of one's nation, and he supported what he saw as just wars, including efforts by America and its allies in World War I and World War II. Elsewhere in *The Future of the American Jew*, published in the wake of World War II and amid the 1948 Palestine War, he argued that pacifism was inadequate for resisting certain evils.[14] In contrast to Tamaret, Kaplan did not see war as incompatible with humility, but he saw humility as incompatible with any conception of one's nation as superior to another.

Mordecai Kaplan, *The Future of the American Jew* (1948)

Just as, in ancient times, men thought that the earth was the center of the universe, and that their own homes, being equi-distant on all sides from the horizon, were the center of the earth, so our fathers, in pre-modern times, regarded the drama of human life as exhausting the whole meaning of creation, and the Jewish people as the hero in that drama, with all other nations merely the supporting cast. . . . [But] nowadays for any people to call itself "chosen" is to be guilty of self-infatuation. . . .

It is said that to express at this late date dislike of what sounds like pretension is merely to yield to "the conventions of Anglo-Saxon taste." Since when is humility a virtue prized by the Anglo-Saxon rather than the Jewish tradition? Our Torah praises Moses for his meekness. It records the prayer of Moses that he be blotted out of God's book, if only his people might enjoy God's grace (Exod. 32:32). It tells of his refusing to be disturbed by the news that Eldad and Medad were prophesying in the camp and his exclaiming in response, "Would that all the Lord's people were prophets!" (Num. 11:29) Can we imagine Moses thanking God that He had not made him like the rest of Israel, but had made him the chosen vehicle for conveying God's message to his spiritually inferior brethren? . . .

The assumption by an individual or group that it is the chosen and indispensable vehicle of God's grace to others is arrogance, no matter how euphemistically one phrases the claim to being chosen.[15]

3.5. HASIDIC SELF-NULLIFICATION

Rabbi Shalom Noah Berezovsky (1911–2000) was the leader of the Jerusalem-based faction of the Slonim Hasidic sect and author of the popular musar book *Netivot Shalom* (Paths of peace), from which the selections below are taken. Here, he describes the concept of "self-nullification"—a notion also present in the writings of many earlier Hasidic masters, including Naḥman of Bratslav—as an ethical ideal.

To Berezovsky, proper humility requires the total annihilation of the ego, the complete elimination of any sense of one's existence separate from God, and the acceptance that one is "nothing." Like Tamaret, he describes egotism with the language of idolatry—but whereas Tamaret emphasizes idolatry as expressed in nationalism and war, Berezovsky sees idolatry in the very expression of selfhood independent from God.

Berezovsky also has a strong sense of how the Jewish people have been chosen by God, and this feeds into his vision of self-nullification. Being chosen by God, in his view, means being singled out as God's treasured "possession"—entirely possessed by God, with no independent sense of self. With characteristic sexism, Berezovsky expresses this with a gendered metaphor: just as a woman should be totally possessed by her husband and nullify her own will before him, so too Israel must be totally possessed by God and nullify her will. Berezovsky further explains that Israel must admit to being like a "country girl" who must recognize her own ignorance when she is brought to a royal palace to marry a king. Both submitting to God and seeing one's own ignorance are gendered as female. These ideas have helped shape a social reality in which men are viewed as superior to women just as God is viewed as superior to human beings.

Shalom Noah Berezovsky, *Netivot Shalom* (1981)

I. In taking them to be his treasured [chosen] people, the Holy Blessed One said to [the People of Israel] that the essence of Judaism is that "you shall be My treasured possession among all the peoples" [Exod. 19:5]. [Midrash] *Mekhilta* explains that this means: "You will be possessed by me."[16]

Though "the earth is full of your possessions" [Ps. 104:24], this may be explained through a parable of a king who desired to marry a country girl. In addition to all that he must stipulate so that her behavior will be appropriate for a king's palace, he will also place her in the high status of being queen of the realm, such that she must replace her whole prior worldview with the worldview of royalty and nobility fit for her status. In this way, the Lord spoke to his people: "You must know that you are possessed by me." The essence of Judaism is that one is married, as it were, to the One Above, as it is written: "I betroth you to me forever" (Hosea 2:21). And in order to reach this lofty status . . . "she must agree to the betrothal of the man, and she must nullify her mind and her will, making her soul like something freely available for her husband's acquisition."[17] . . . The inner purpose of Judaism is that the Jew nullifies one's self, one's mind and will, for the Holy Blessed One, and that one completely give oneself to the Blessed One, like one who says, "I and all I have are yours" [1 Kings 20:4].[18]

II. It is written: "walk humbly with your God" (Micah 6:8) . . . that your walking in the service of the Lord should be in humility, that no outsider should know of it, so that you will not blemish your holiness through additional motives and the like. . . .[19]

III. What is the "stock sprouting poison weed and wormwood" [Deut. 29:17] upon which a person's negative character traits grow? . . . It is the egotism . . . within human beings—when a person sees only his own good, and always worries only about himself. . . . The Baal Shem Tov . . . explained the verse "I stood between the Lord and you" (Deut. 5:5): the "I," a person's egotism, stands like a barrier that separates the Lord from you. The one who loves himself does not love the Blessed Creator, and so he does not love the People of Israel, because his character trait of love is occupied with self-love, and there is no further room for the love of God and Israel. . . .

[The sages] compared pride to idolatry, because a sense of independent existence is a kind of idolatry, as idolatry includes the idea of a distinct and separate reality that is not nullified before the Blessed Creator. . . .

The essence of a Jew's work is to be "nothing"—totally nullified before the Blessed One. Thus our father Abraham said, "I am but dust and ashes" (Gen. 18:27), and Moses our teacher (peace be upon him) said, "What are we?" (Exod. 16:8). One who is nothing takes up no space, and does not seek anything, and does not need anything. And so he does not have jealousy or hatred, for no one stands in his way, and he does not become angry, and he does not become proud, and he does not have the craving to fulfill his appetites and his desires for pleasures.[20]

IV. As long as the human being is ruled by materiality and his animal soul, he cannot achieve nullification. One can nullify one's sense of independent existence only through the trait of holiness — when one's materiality and willfulness humbly submit before the Blessed One.[21]

3.6. HUMILITY, REVENGE, AND SELF-SACRIFICE

An Orthodox rabbi, Israeli politician, and advocate of Jewish militancy and terrorism, Meir Kahane (see section 1.5) championed a very different sort of Israeli Orthodoxy than Berezovsky. Though Kahane joined Berezovsky in advancing the idea that Jews are God's Chosen People and in seeing this idea as fully compatible with humility, Kahane stressed the pride Jews should have in their status and the need to be vengeful in defending the honor of the God who had chosen them. Whereas Berezovsky viewed anger as a sign of arrogance, Kahane viewed anger as an appropriate motivation for defending against those who are truly arrogant. Whereas Berezovsky saw little spiritual benefit to Jewish political sovereignty in present-day Israel,[22] Kahane emphasized Jewish political power and the violence that sovereignty requires. Whereas Berezovsky contended that a Jew should "take up no space," Kahane called on Jews to collectively take up significant space as they asserted their presence in the Land of Israel.

Kahane, too, wanted individual Jews to think little of their personal interests; yet he trusted that God had granted power to His Chosen People who follow His Torah, and therefore viewed any efforts to promote the power of such people as signs of humble submission to God's will rather than assertions of personal self-interest. While the arrogant quest for human power in violation of God's will would obscure God's omnipotence, the quest for power by those who humbly submit to God's will would help "restore" God's power—"resurrecting" God, as it were. To Kahane, God's power is affirmed as the humble among the People of Israel vanquish their enemies, who are also God's enemies. This is true whether those enemies are foreign idolaters, who are clearly not created in the image of God, or idol-worshipping Israelites who arrogantly disobey God.[23]

The selections below are taken from Kahane's posthumously published magnum opus *The Jewish Idea* (*Or ha-Ra'ayon*), which devotes chapters to a series of character traits central to Kahane's understanding of Jewish tradition including kindness, vengefulness, trust, and humility.

In section 3.4, Kaplan offered his assurance that Moses could not have possibly imagined himself as "the chosen vehicle" held above his "spiritually inferior brethren." Kaplan cited Moses' willingness to sacrifice himself so that his people might survive (Exod. 32:32). Here, Kahane points us to Moses' words five verses earlier, instructing the Levites to kill even their friends and family members who had participated in the idolatrous worship of the Golden Calf (32:27). In Kahane's view, Moses is quite wise in holding himself and his fellow righteous Jews above his spiritually inferior brethren, and (as stressed elsewhere in his writings) right to seek revenge against the non-Jewish nations that humiliated God and God's Chosen People.[24] Whereas Kaplan viewed assertions of Israel's chosenness as a sign of arrogance, Kahane saw Jews exercising great humility when, acting not for the sake of personal gain but to glorify God, they accepted their chosen status and humbled their arrogant enemies.

Meir Kahane, *The Jewish Idea* (late twentieth century)

I. Words do not suffice to explain the great purpose served by recognizing God's greatness and sovereignty, and man's lowliness before Him. No traits are more disgraceful than haughtiness and egotism. They are the root of evil and ugliness. God hates haughtiness, as it says, "The Lord hates . . . haughty eyes . . ." (Prov. 6:16–17). . . . If God hates arrogance, we, too are clearly commanded to hate it, as it says, "The fear of the Lord is to hate evil: pride and arrogance and the evil way" (Prov. 8:13). . . . Haughtiness takes a humble person and fills him with self-importance and a craving for the honor, power and majesty enjoyed by kings. Such a person ultimately usurps God's throne, so to speak, rebelling against God, denying His omnipotence. . . .

"The Lord upholds the humble. He brings the wicked down to the ground" (Psalms 147:6). He who thought to ascend to the heavens in his conceit, like the King of Babylonia who said (Isaiah 14:14), "I will ascend above the heights of the clouds, I will be like the Most High," God brings down low. Conversely, He upholds and adorns the humble in victory in their war against the arrogant: "He adorns the humble with salvation" (Psalms 149:4).

The Jew is commanded to ascend via humility and lowliness and to break down his own egotism. He is obligated to liberate himself from his enslavement to himself and to be a free man vis-à-vis everyone but God. . . . [But] certainly, the Jewish people, as a people and nation, the nation of God, are a chosen people. In their role as the nation chosen by Him Whose word created the world, pride is befitting and proper for them. . . . Pride is becoming to Israel as God's holy, erect nation, but not to the individual Jew.[25]

II. [For the nation] it is a great mitzvah to take the revenge of the righteous and humble from the evildoer. . . . The evildoer's victory is the very worst profanation of God's name, because it implies the defeat or impotence of God. . . . Only via revenge does God "recover" and "awaken," bringing Himself back to life, so to speak. . . . Great is revenge for it resurrects God . . . and humbles the arrogant sinner.[26]

III. Self-sacrifice is the ultimate proof of trust in God. . . . When Moses saw the terrible *Chilul Hashem* [desecration of God's name] of the Golden Calf episode . . . he immediately understood that only self-sacrifice and *Kiddush Hashem* [sanctification of God's name] would save Israel from God's ire. It therefore says (Ex. 32:26–27, 29): "Moses announced, 'Whoever is for the Lord, join me!" All the Levites gathered around him. He said to them, "This is what the Lord God of Israel says: Let each man put on his sword. . . . Let each one kill [all those involved in the idolatry], even his own brother, close friend, or relative." . . . This *Kiddush Hashem* was intended so that Israel would achieve spiritual perfection rather than remain incomplete like those who avoid self-sacrifice for *Kiddush Hashem*. . . . We must understand that it is man's arrogance and selfishness . . . which tarnish him and lead him to sin. Even in the most saintly, selfishness blocks the path to spiritual perfection.[27]

3.7. LESBIAN SELF-ACCEPTANCE AND WALKING HUMBLY WITH GOD

Rebecca Alpert (b. 1950) is a Reconstructionist rabbi and scholar with particular expertise on issues of sexuality, gender, and race. Her book *Like Bread on the Seder Plate: Jewish Lesbians and the Transformation of Tradition* has been described as "the first and only full-length Jewish theological work that takes lesbian Jewish experience as its orienting lens."[28] Portions of the book focus on interpreting the injunction (in Mic. 6:8) "only to do justice, and to love goodness, and to walk humbly with your God"; the third of those commands is discussed in the selection below.

Heir to the Reconstructionist legacy of Mordecai Kaplan, Alpert shares many of Kaplan's concerns about ideas of "chosenness" and supernatural conceptions of God. God, she writes, may be defined as "anything that helps one perceive holiness in the world." Humbling oneself in relation to God, for Alpert, does not require submission to the authoritative commandments of an omnipotent being, as it did for Kahane; rather, it requires accepting oneself and one's desires, accepting the holiness of all humans, and loving oneself and all others.

Alpert does agree with many of the aforementioned figures that humility must make space for legitimate pride. But in clear opposition to Pinḥas, Naḥman, Berezovsky, and Kahane, she emphasizes that all human beings are equal and that all may be legitimately proud of who they are — including Jewish lesbians, whom Pinḥas and the others would judge as flagrantly violating Jewish law. She responds to such judgments with the teaching in *Mishnah Avot* not to judge others "until we have stood in their place." Pinḥas had warned that the evil inclination would quote *Avot* in order to subvert traditional hierarchies; no doubt he would see Alpert as engaged in the "evil" work of overturning eternal values. From Alpert's perspective, Pinḥas (and Naḥman, Berezovsky, and Kahane) are overturning the clear meaning of humility: they would seem to embody the arrogance of those who, in Alpert's words, "assume that [they] can determine the right way for everyone."

Alpert's vision of humility stands in particular opposition to that of Naḥman of Bratslav, for while Naḥman had seen sexuality as linked with arrogance, Alpert sees "our sexual attractions as a holy pursuit," and while Naḥman particularly denounces homosexuality, Alpert seeks to create a world where sexual orientation is not stigmatized. Nor, more generally, does Alpert believe that desires for personal pleasure are the sign of arrogance that Pinḥas, Naḥman, or Berezovsky believe them to be. Berezovsky, for instance, idealizes the truly humble person who "does not have the craving to fulfill his appetites and his desires for pleasures." Alpert's ethic of modesty, on the other hand, requires an acceptance of one's whole self, including "our sexual joys and pleasures." And while Berezovsky sees the injunction to "walk humbly [*haẓnea lekhet*] with your God" as pointing to private acts about which "no outsider should know," Alpert quotes the same verse as she encourages lesbian Jews to be public about their sexuality. Though she teaches that one should not pressure people to be public about their identities—as that would be a sign of arrogance—Alpert encourages her readers to see self-acceptance as at the core of walking with God, and she reasons that self-acceptance should ideally lead to openness about one's identity.

Rebecca Alpert, *Like Bread on the Seder Plate* (1997)

"Haẓnea lekhet im elohekha" [Mic. 6:8]. Traditionally, this has been translated "walk humbly with your God," but more recent translations have suggested it to mean to walk modestly or with decency. I interpret this statement to be about the way an individual understands her own place in the world. I assume that the way in which a person approaches her own life will determine her ability to behave ethically toward others. A central Jewish precept demands that we love our neighbors as ourselves. Commentators have understood this to mean that we can only learn to love our neighbors if we learn to love ourselves.

Walking with God is a metaphor for the way each person approaches her own life. It is a way to conceptualize one's innermost feelings and thoughts. It is not necessary to hold a traditional concept of God, or to imagine God in human form, to appreciate this metaphor. To see oneself walking with God requires a vision of God as the most important value in life, that which is with the individual always and everywhere. God may be in the image of a human being, but God could also be a power, force, feeling, idea, or anything that helps one perceive holiness in the world.

As Jewish lesbians, we begin with the assumption that we can only walk with God if we know and accept ourselves for who we are. Walking with God begins with self-acceptance and requires that we tell ourselves the truth about ourselves. This stance describes coming out, declaring oneself to be lesbian, as a necessary prerequisite to walking with God. Walking with God requires self-knowledge. Those who walk with God know their way and consciously claim a path in the world. They are guided by the understanding that all human beings are holy, having been created in God's image. . . .

Accepting and acting on this erotic attraction is an example of haẓnea lekhet because it indicates self-acceptance. Jewish lesbians claim our sexual attractions as a holy pursuit. What makes our sexuality holy is not intrinsic to it. It is the acceptance in ourselves of our sexual joys and pleasures, of not seeing our erotic lives as cut off from the rest of ourselves, but integral to making our lives rich and meaningful. Too often lesbians, especially when our homosexuality is first awakened, feel shame about our feelings and desires. Haẓnea lekhet means accepting desire and finding creative ways of expressing it. Of course, those expressions must conform to other ethical standards of behavior toward ourselves and others. But those desires and behaviors will also unleash our creative powers and enable us to be in the world in a holy and positive way. When the connection between the sexual self and the rest of the self is cut off, we cannot walk with God. . . .

Walking with God is not limited to self-acceptance as a lesbian in the privacy of one's own inner world. The next stages of self-acceptance suggest being out with family and friends and in the lesbian and gay or Jewish lesbian worlds. But I want to suggest that truly walking with God moves beyond this stage. The ultimate way to walk with God with self-acceptance also requires coming out publicly. . . .

To walk with God . . . also requires that we persuade the closeted to come out. But the quotation from Micah suggests not only that we find a way to walk with God but that that way be modest, decent, and humble. Haẓnea lekhet does not carry with it the assumption that we are not proud to be lesbians. The fact that being open and comfortable with being a lesbian is understood as a way to walk with God should illustrate this clearly.

It does imply, however, that we are not so arrogant as to assume that we can determine the right way for everyone. Walking humbly with God means self-acceptance, not requiring that others follow your example. This is not a mandate for outing others. Our humility must keep us from arrogant assumptions about who must declare their lesbian identity. This humility outweighs the burden placed on us by closeted lesbians to keep their secrets. We must be mindful of the idea that we cannot judge others until we have stood in their place (Mishnah, Avot 2:5). . . .

To walk with God in humility, modesty, and decency is a daunting task. It is not easy to eschew arrogance; it is not easy to be modest about our accomplishment of self-acceptance in the Jewish world that tells us daily that we do not fit, do not belong. Haẓnea lekhet im elohekha requires a delicate balancing act between feeling pride and joy at being able to be at peace with ourselves but not expecting others to travel the same path. Our goal is to create a world where coming out is not an issue because sexual orientation is not stigmatized.[29]

3.8. A NONANTHROPOCENTRIC PERSPECTIVE

Jeremy Benstein (b. 1961) is an Israeli anthropologist and environmentalist whose approach to humility may, like Alpert's, be connected with the approach of Mordecai Kaplan. In section 3.4, Kaplan mentioned the premodern error of regarding "the drama of human life as exhausting the whole meaning of creation." In the source below, Benstein further critiques those who make this error, asking his audience to be not only less ethnocentric but also less anthropocentric. His critique takes to task many of the authors quoted above in this chapter. In response to Naḥman of Bratslav teaching that "to take part in the suffering of the Jews" is "conducive to overcoming arrogance," Benstein might add that overcoming arrogance also requires sensitivity to the suffering of people from other cultures, and, moreover, sensitivity to the needs of animals. As he notes elsewhere in his book *The Way into Judaism and the Environment*, from which the selections below are taken, the Jewish legal principle that prohibits cruelty to animals (*tza'ar ba'alei ḥayyim*) is especially important in an era when much cruelty to animals is for the sake of luxury or convenience (e.g., so that people can eat certain kinds of meat) and is shielded from view (in labs or factory farms).[30] Humility requires recognizing our kinship with nonhuman animals and considering their suffering.

Benstein's concern for animals is also in tension with the authors in this chapter who have referred to animality with derision and disdain. Pinḥas of Polotsk, for example, indicated that his scholarly audience should keep themselves separate from the ignorant masses, referring to the talmudic teaching that their daughters were like mere animals. Shalom Noah Berezovsky discussed the need to overcome the appetitive "animal soul" within the human being, a label that reflects the idea that nonhuman animals have little to commend them other than their gross appetites. Benstein, by contrast, advises us to consider ourselves in relationship with nonhuman animals, and he does not define animals merely in terms of their appetites. As he notes in his book, there are long-standing Jewish traditions that see nonhuman animals as capable of moral choice.[31]

A founder and deputy director of the Heschel Center for Environmental Learning and Leadership in Tel Aviv, Benstein's injunction to take a less anthropocentric view echoes the teaching of his organization's namesake, Rabbi Abraham Joshua Heschel, that we saw in section 2.6. But, as we saw there, Heschel taught that anthropocentrism should be replaced by *theocentrism*, the perspective of "religion" that places God at the center of the universe. Benstein's comments below build directly on his appreciation of Heschel's conception of religion;[32] but he seeks to go well beyond Heschel by arguing that a secular environmentalist approach may do just as well as "religion" in helping human beings to be less anthropocentric — with no reference to God, but rather through a "biocentrism" that is centered on life in general rather than human life in particular. Secular biocentrism, like theocentrism, can instill proper humility in human beings by helping them not to see themselves at the center of the universe.

Jeremy Benstein, *The Way into Judaism and the Environment* (2006)

I. Both ecological thought (with its recognition of interdependence and the trans-human complexity of ecosystems) and religion (with an all-embracing God at the center) share a crucially important perspective, which I shall call "something-else-centrism." Whether in the theocentric approach of religion or the biocentric approaches of many types of environmentalism, something other than human needs and perspectives is paramount — the upshot being some version of human humility in the face of an existence greater than ourselves. Whether the earth belongs to God or simply to itself, it surely isn't ours. [These] shared views on human humility and hubris are relevant to the environmental claim that our behavior has reached and breached limits of ecological life support, putting us in peril. We need to disavow the ingrained belief that we can "invent" ourselves out of the current crisis with technology. We must work within the limitations the world places on us, not pretend they don't exist or that we can ignore them. This requires changing our notions of progress, from mere economic growth to holistic conceptions of fundamental human welfare for current and future generations.[33]

II. True concern for animal welfare is [also] a lesson in humility, both in learning the deep connections we have with the nonhuman, animate world and in confronting its ultimate otherness. We expand our moral universe when we break out of the shell of the self to include others in relationship, when we develop a multicultural sensibility to appreciate the contributions of other peoples. Insensitive "species-centrism" is a similar blinder, and we need animals to help put ourselves in perspective.... Not inflicting suffering [*tza'ar ba'alei ḥayyim*] on creatures that feel is a moral and ethical imperative, and it should certainly trump considerations of convenience or luxury.... It's time we reevaluate whom we include among those worthy of moral consideration, our circle of friends.[34]

3.9. THE OTHER IS OUR TEACHER

The American Conservative rabbi and theologian Ira F. Stone (b. 1949) has sought to revive many of the nineteenth-century Lithuanian Musar movement's models for focusing on character traits and, especially, concern for the other. In the selection below, Stone discusses humility as the virtue that allows for embracing strangers and viewing them as teachers rather than threats. Like Rebecca Alpert, Stone turns to *Mishnah Avot* in order to explain his perspective, pointing out that *Avot* demands respect and reverence toward the colleagues from whom one learns— and that anyone can be a colleague from whom one learns.

Pinḥas of Polotsk had warned that the *yetzer ha-ra* (evil inclination) would seek to upset traditional distinctions between true scholars and the "ignorant masses" by quoting *Avot*, and Stone would seem to be doing precisely this. Even more directly than Alpert, Stone speaks the very language that Pinḥas saw as incited by the *yetzer ha-ra*—equating all human beings, advocating for learning from everyone, seemingly urging even scholars to forgo their own pride and defensiveness when confronted with strangers. From Pinḥas's perspective, *Mishnah Avot* should properly be understood as teaching a very different message: scholars are to respect other scholars.

But Stone, like Pinḥas, also sees the *yetzer ha-ra* as pervading human consciousness; and just as Pinḥas would see Stone as promoting the cause of the *yetzer ha-ra*, Stone would likely see Pinḥas as doing the same. Stone describes the *yetzer ha-ra* as the inclination to serve oneself, to proudly defend oneself against the threat of the other, to magnify one's own virtues, and to leave little space for the other. From Stone's perspective, when Pinḥas describes the masses as threats against whom scholars must proudly defend themselves, it is Pinḥas who is giving too much space to the *yetzer ha-ra*. All the more so, this critique would apply to Meir Kahane when he depicts idolaters and foreigners as terrible threats to the Chosen People.

Stone, however, does not define the *yetzer ha-ra* as do most other thinkers. To him it should not be understood as "the *evil* inclination" but as "the inclination to serve oneself." Building on a Rabbinic tradition that sees the *yetzer ha-ra* as necessary for human life, Stone stresses that this selfishness cannot be fully "nullified," to use Berezovsky's language.[35] Still, it can be constrained or transformed. A person must strive to continually choose humility and the *yetzer ha-tov* ("the good inclination," as it is conventionally translated—in Stone's terms, "the inclination to serve the other") over pride and the *yetzer ha-ra*.

As Stone makes clear elsewhere in his writings, moments of choosing to be responsible for the other are appropriately described as moments of being "chosen." When we encounter another human being, we are elected and obligated to act with responsibility.[36] The other, as the source of chosenness, stands in the place of God, "in a commanding position above us."[37] This theology shapes Stone's conclusion in the selection below that the other is "a stand-in for God." Indeed, for Stone, submitting to God occurs only through submitting to our responsibilities to the other. Like Kaplan, Stone does not see God as an independent, supernatural being who has elected the People of Israel; rather, all human beings are elected for our particular responsibilities, and we encounter God through the face of the other. Indeed, thinking that any of us are uniquely loved by God tends to cause us to avoid our own responsibilities to others.[38]

Although, unlike Kaplan, Stone is comfortable with using the language of chosenness, he would seem to share much of Kaplan's critique of the concept, and he uses it only to show how human beings in general may be called to responsibility. Note that whereas Berezovsky makes mention of Psalm 104's proclamation that the whole earth is possessed by God but then immediately pivots to stress that Israel is uniquely chosen by God, Stone cites Psalm 104 only to stress that all human beings can renew their souls by "making room for the face of the other" and that anyone can be the "other" who makes that renewal possible. Not only Jews, and certainly not only *tzaddikim*, are to stand in the place of God and instruct us in humility.

Ira Stone, "Anavah (Humility)" (2013)

The moment that another person enters our field of vision our *yetzer ha-ra* (the inclination to serve oneself) prepares to defend us. The *yetzer ha-ra* enlarges itself and fills all the "space" that would ideally be available for the other. The cost of this is the potential of our soul. This enlargement of the *yetzer ha-ra* can be expressed in a number of ways . . . all of which are manifestations of *ga'avah*, pride.[39] The *middah* [character trait] that addresses the insidious nature of pride is *anavah*, humility.

The *yetzer ha-ra* deflects the approach of the other by multiplying our consciousness of our real virtues, [in] which we are already predisposed to take appropriate pride. In fact, not taking appropriate pride in our own achievements, feigning humility rather than acknowledging our accomplishments, turns out to be one of the types of pride that we use to deflect the approach of others.

However, despite the legitimacy of these virtues, thinking about them in such a way as to fill ourselves up with them diminishes the possibility of our maintaining our soul in that moment. Maintaining and expanding the soul is the moment-to-moment challenge, which is the focus of our *middah* work. The choice between the *yetzer ha-ra* and the *yetzer ha-tov* (the inclination to serve the other) is the moment-to-moment mechanism by which the soul is either renewed or abandoned.

This is what our tradition expresses when it teaches "every day God renews the face of creation" (Psalm 104:30). This metaphor of God's daily renewal of creation expresses the fact that we are responsible every day to renew our soul by appropriately constraining or transforming our *yetzer ha-ra* and making room for the face of the other. The ability to embrace the other in this space, we call our *yetzer ha-tov*.

The instinct to deflect the other is not easily overcome. The moment another person enters our field of vision, our *yetzer ha-ra* rises in our defense against the perceived threat of the stranger. Pride swells within us almost unconsciously when another approaches. Containing pride requires an enormous act of will; an act of will, in fact, almost beyond our ability. In order to aid and ease this act of will—in truth to mask it—it is actually more helpful not to attempt to change our inner consciousness, but rather to change our perception of the other person so that from the beginning he or she does not elicit the kind of defensive response that engenders pride.

How, the tradition asks, can we turn around the natural threat of another, his or her very otherness, in such a way as to short-circuit pride? If we conceive of another in his or her role of parent, sibling, friend, or lover, we make that person into the stranger. Instead, our tradition asserts, precisely because he or she is another, we can learn something from them. In fact, we should attempt to learn something from every person we encounter.

Anything we do learn from them makes them our teacher, and as we learn in Mishnah tractate Avot, our relationship with them is transformed. Rather than crowding out the space for the other within us with our own virtues, we can allow the embrace of the other by the *yetzer ha-tov* in the same way that we embrace our teacher, which in turn is a sacred relationship extended infinitely toward God.

In Mishnah tractate Avot, chapter 6 mishnah 3 we read: One who learns from a colleague one chapter, or one halachah, or one verse, or one expression, or even one letter, is obliged to show respect. This we learn from David, King of Israel, who learned but two things from Ahitofel, yet called him his master. . . .

In Mishnah tractate Avot, chapter 4 mishnah 15 we read: Rabbi Elazar ben Shamua taught: The dignity of your student should be as precious to you as your own; the dignity of your colleague should be as precious to you as your reverence for your teacher; your reverence for your teacher should be as great as your reverence for God.

The middah of *anavah* can be defined truly as the embrace of the other in a sacred and satisfying relationship. . . . It is precisely our perception of another as a teacher that transforms that person from being a potential threat into being a stand-in for God.[40]

3.10. "SHOULD A WOMAN BE HUMBLE?"

The American Reform rabbi Ruth Abusch-Magder is rabbi-in-residence at Be'chol Lashon, an organization that focuses on ethnic, cultural, and racial inclusiveness in Jewish communities. Her concerns about gender and humility raised in the essay below build on Alpert's contention that the prophet Micah's injunction to "walk with God" should be understood to require decency and modesty but also considerable pride. Abusch-Magder stresses that such pride is essential for women, who are often ignored and unsupported unless they demonstrate "a healthy ego and sense of reasonable entitlement." Therefore, she notes, it is helpful for women to think about humility in terms suggested by the contemporary musar teacher Alan Morinis (see section 6.7): as was known to the prophet Moses, humility requires taking up a proper amount of space—no more than the space to which one is entitled, but also no less than the space to which one is entitled.[41] Such a framing of humility stands in particularly clear contrast to that of Shalom Noah Berezovsky, for whom a truly humble person—like Moses—is "nothing" and "takes up no space."

Berezovsky clearly thinks about men "taking up space" in very different terms than how he thinks about women "taking up space." We saw him characterize "taking up no space" as a feminine quality—the sort of quality a married woman must possess in relationship to her husband. For Berezovsky, though, men like Moses are particularly suited for public-leadership roles when they "take up no space," whereas women's public leadership is not advisable. The voices of women who "take up no space" are easily ignored; by contrast, the men who "take up no space" have their voices amplified and may be honored as the greatest prophets and rabbis.

While the American gender norms Abusch-Magder confronts are not as severely differentiated as they are in Berezovsky's ultra-Orthodox social reality, they are influenced by similar patterns of patriarchal thinking, leading to a reality where women who accept societal expectations for female modesty "are unlikely to get noticed."

As Abusch-Magder explains, Morinis's model of taking up sufficient space serves as an important correction to these expectations. Yet women who seek to take up the same amount of space as men are readily criticized for their arrogance. So it is that pioneering female rabbis who are proud of their identities are commonly viewed as overly aggressive, whereas male rabbis showing similar traits are viewed as legitimately proud. As Abusch-Magder makes clear, patriarchy has left a significant imprint on how Jews, like so many other groups, understand humility.

Ruth Abusch-Magder, "Should a Woman Be Humble?" (2017)

"He has told you, O man, what is good, And what the LORD requires of you: Only to do justice, And to love goodness, And to walk humbly with your God" (Micah 6:8). . . .

As we read in the Bible, humility is a positive when it comes to walking with God. And walking with God is at the core of my understanding of the role of the rabbi. Humility is essential to keep rabbis from confusing the work we do in the service of God with being as great as God.

But at the same time, I'm not just a rabbi, I'm a woman rabbi.

And when it comes to women, humility gets complicated.

Humility is freedom from pride or arrogance. It comes from the Latin word *humilis*, which literally means low, and also suggests modesty or a lower sense of self-importance. But what passes as pride or arrogance is often judged more harshly in women than men. And when women do not push through the modesty thrust upon them by societal expectations of womanhood, they are unlikely to get noticed. In other words, for women being humble can get in the way of doing God's work, or any work for that matter.

Take for example Dorothy Vaughn . . . one of a group of female African-American mathematicians who worked as human calculators at NASA in the 1960s. . . . Left without a supervisor, Vaughn took on organizing the group and distributing assignments. Given the double burden of racism and sexism, humility would have been the end of the line. Instead, knowing her worth, she approached a white female supervisor and clearly stated her capacity to become a supervisor. When that failed, she persisted, daringly pioneering and training other black women in computer programming. Under her leadership and innovative visioning, new realities became possible. Humility would have been a hindrance; only a healthy ego and sense of reasonable entitlement by Vaughn made any of this possible.

Humility seems to be one of the barriers to having more women in public office. Unlike men who are often glad to put themselves forward to run, women usually have to be asked more than once, in no small part because they don't feel qualified, even when they are.

Once women are in office . . . they still have to battle with gendered visions of humility and the "proper" place of women. Unless women speak up they are unlikely to be heard, and if they speak up too loudly they may be seen as too forward, even if the ideas they present are smart and mission critical. In the Obama White House, which had a large number of professional women, the women actively countered these tendencies by reinforcing the ideas that individual women suggested so they could not go unnoticed or unattributed. Collectively fighting against expectations of modesty was the only way these women could possibly give the best they had to offer to their country.

The first women rabbis were similarly filled with a healthy sense of self and their right to step into a role that had historically been denied to them. Even today, women rabbis cannot truly afford to be humble lest their other God-given talents, so essential for their success, be overlooked.

Alan Morinis, one of the leading teachers of the Jewish study of character traits, offers a more textured vision of humility. One that encourages each of us to take up the space that we are expected to. "Being humble doesn't mean being 'nobody,' it just means being no more of a 'somebody' than you ought to be. After all, Moses, the greatest of the prophets, is described in the Torah as 'very anav [humble], more than any other men who were upon the face of the earth' (Numbers 12:3)."

Unfortunately, I know from my own experience, from countless conversations with other women professionals, and from watching women, from Hillary Clinton to Kellyanne Conway, that when women fulfill Morinis' vision of humility and boldly step forward to share what they have to give, they are derided instead of celebrated.

For women, women rabbis included, humility cannot be a fixed trait. Until women are able to be as strong and decisive as Moses without being labeled nasty or aggressive, they will never be able to reach . . . their full potential. Until women's voices and contributions are valued without undue censure or disregard, they will never be able to be humble without sacrificing capacity or self-regard. And then, and only then, will we really be able to both walk with God and be humble.[42]

CONCLUSION

Those who confidently instruct others in humility may seem anything but humble, and some of the figures instructing us in this chapter may seem particularly guilty of arrogance while they teach about humility.

We have even seen rabbis invoke humility as they ask their followers to view them as the source of all knowledge (Naḥman of Bratslav), denigrate nonscholars (Pinḥas of Polotsk), or call for violence against non-Jews (Meir Kahane).

We might also consider how other thinkers have been or might be judged as speaking with arrogance. Mordecai Kaplan, for example, has been accused of arrogantly seeking to abrogate traditional concepts that his critics claim should be approached with greater humility. As Ruth Abusch-Magder suggests, women like her or Rebecca Alpert are especially likely to be labeled as insufficiently humble, given societal expectations that women should take up less space than men.

The thinkers in this chapter all agree that there are some forms of legitimate pride as well as times when pride must yield before some higher value. But many of them disagree deeply about what pride is legitimate and what values are ultimately sovereign. Both Alpert and Kahane, for example, ask their readers to have pride, but for Kahane legitimate pride is limited to pride in being chosen by God, and human beings must submit to an ideal of God characterized by particular love for Israel. Alpert, by contrast, holds that legitimate pride must respect the holiness of all human beings and advocates self-acceptance as at the core of walking with God. Both of these thinkers invoke the need for humility in relationship to God, but they offer very different portraits of the God with whom one must walk humbly.

Other thinkers in this chapter hold up other constructions of authority, ethics, and God before which they believe human beings must submit. Aharon Shmuel Tamaret counsels submission to a vision of ethics grounded in an ideal of nonviolence among humans, while Jeremy Benstein counsels widening one's perspective and considering the broader ecosystem. Pinḥas of Polotsk seeks submission before only certain kinds of scholarly authorities; Ira Stone seeks submission to the needs of any stranger before whom one stands.

These sorts of disagreements often reflect diverse positions on the status of various individuals or groups. As we have seen, Jewish thinkers pushing for certain models of humility have often done so while making claims about God's chosen rabbis, treasured people, preferred gender, or favored species and concurrently explaining that God has revealed these preferences, to which they are merely submitting. Other Jewish thinkers have argued that such claims are mere human constructions, often reflecting the self-centered preferences of particular individuals and groups. With humility, differing conceptions of virtue often correlate with different claims about God and the very nature of the world.

We will see similar correlations in the next chapter, as we explore the virtue of courage.

4

Courage and Valor
(*Ometz Lev/Gevurah*)

Courage, valor, and bravery are dispositions "to do what needs to be done despite fear."[1] Hebrew words such as *ometz* (courage, bravery), *ometz lev* (courage of the heart), and *gevurah* (bravery, strength, valor, heroism) point to the same concept.

In our discussion of humility (chapter 3), we saw diverse Jewish thinkers pronounce that human beings should proudly assert themselves, while fiercely disagreeing over when and how as well as what constitutes inappropriate arrogance. Similar tensions arise in this chapter: the thinkers here agree that some contexts require the assertion of courage but disagree over when and how as well as what constitutes inappropriate brazenness or impudence. And just as we saw disagreements over what constitutes too much meekness, here we will see disagreements about what constitutes too much cowardice, faintheartedness, or timidity.

Many thinkers in this chapter point to biblical models of courage: for example, Abraham's courage to argue with God over the destruction of Sodom and Gomorrah and to submit to God's command to sacrifice his son; or Moses' courage to stand up both against Pharaoh and the "mixed multitude" escaping Egypt along with the Israelites. Some thinkers herald biblical figures who courageously engage in violence: for example, the Levites, who killed those who worshiped the Golden Calf (Exod. 32:26–29); or Samson, who pulled down a building that was home to his Philistine captors, killing himself as well (Judg. 16:21–30). On the other hand, some point to biblical associations of valor with nonviolent ideals—for example, the "woman of valor" described in the book of Proverbs—or God's teaching that triumph will come "not by valor, nor by power, but by My Spirit" (Zech. 4:6).

Some thinkers pay homage to the courage of postbiblical Jewish warriors: the Maccabees, who revolted against the Seleucid Empire in the second century BCE; the Zealots, who fought against the Roman Empire in the first century CE (including those who killed themselves at Masada); or Simon bar Kochba, who rebelled against Rome in the second century CE. Other thinkers, however, offer paeans to the courage of those who did not fight against Rome, such as Rabbi Yoḥanan ben Zakkai, the ancient Rabbinic hero who escaped the besieged city of Jerusalem in a coffin and asked the Romans to preserve the Rabbinic academy at Yavneh (*Avot de-Rabbi Natan* 4 / BT *Gittin* 56a–b).

While ancient Rabbinic texts sometimes valorize violence, they often valorize courage in Torah study rather than bravery in armed battles; and rather than always condemn those who shy away from fighting, Rabbinic sources see timidity as a legitimate reason for exemption from military service (BT *Sotah* 44a–b, based on Deut. 20:8). Some texts explicitly reject the idea that the *gibbor*—"the hero," "the mighty one," "the person of courage"—should be primarily associated with the warrior. Thus, in *Mishnah Avot* (4:1), Ben Zoma asks, "Who is the person of courage?" and answers, "He who conquers his impulse [or "evil inclination"], as it says, 'Better to be forbearing than to be a hero, to rule one's soul than to conquer a city'" (Prov. 16:32). A version of this teaching in the *Avot de-Rabbi Natan* collection adds another, alternative answer: "He who makes an enemy into a friend" (*Avot de-Rabbi Natan* 23). Elsewhere in *Avot* (5:20), Judah ben Tema teaches the ideal of being "as courageous as a lion to do the will of your Father who is in heaven."

Rabbinic literature associates a very different kind of fearlessness with the word *chutzpah*: impudence, insolence, and the arrogant refusal to perform God's will. The talmudic rabbi Rav Naḥman describes the prophet Balaam, who is hired to curse the Israelites, as possessing "chutzpah, even in the face of heaven" (BT *Sanhedrin* 105a), and while Rav Naḥman seems to view this impudence as effective in convincing God to let him go on his mission, it is clearly far from the ideal, humble courage to do God's will. The Mishnah (*Sotah* 9:15) lists chutzpah as among the tribulations to come before the arrival of the Messiah: "In the time of the footsteps of the Messiah, impudence [chutzpah] will swell."

For some Rabbinic Jews, one sign of particular impudence is breaking the oaths sworn by the People of Israel (according to many understandings of BT *Ketubot* 110b–111a) that they would not attempt to retake the Land of Israel by force or rebel against the nations.[2] In their understanding, Jews are forbidden to rise up against other nations; they should sanctify God's name as martyrs rather than dishonoring God's name by breaking their oath; and they should accept their destiny to live in exile surrounded by hostile nations—as some midrashic traditions put it, like a solitary ewe surrounded by seventy wolves. They should not trust in their own power but in God's power, which will preserve them and eventually restore them to power in their land in the days of the Messiah. In the words of one midrash: "Hadrian said to R. Joshua: 'Mighty is the ewe that can survive among seventy wolves.' And [R. Joshua] replied: 'Mighty is the shepherd who can save and protect the ewe, and destroy the wolves surrounding her.'"[3] God, the shepherd here, is the true hero who does what is necessary to preserve the People of Israel in their exile and promises to eventually destroy the seventy nations of the world. The People of Israel are not to defend themselves; Israel's courage is required not for war but for cultivating self-restraint and love, engaging in prayer and Torah study, and performing the will of their Father in heaven.

Some modern Jews have forcefully rejected these sorts of Rabbinic traditions. In the late nineteenth and throughout the twentieth century, many of these traditions drew the ire of Zionists who argued that Jews should instead recover the courage of warriors—the courage to rise up and regain power in the Land of Israel. Various Zionist, non-Zionist, and anti-Zionist Jews, in turn, countered with their own claims about how Jews should think about the virtue of courage.

As different attitudes about Zionism have shaped many modern Jewish debates about courage, this chapter gives particular focus to these debates.

The Zionist leader Heinrich Loewe seeks to recover the warrior ethos of the Maccabees and Bar Kochba, while also arguing that German-Jewish warriors will be loyal and valiant in defense of their adopted country, Germany (section 4.1). The anti-Zionist liberal philosopher Hermann Cohen stresses the value of martyrdom in defense of monotheism and morality (section 4.2). The secular Zionist thinker Mikhah Yosef Berdichevsky condemns many of the aforementioned ancient Rabbinic traditions and seeks to advance older conceptions of warrior courage (section 4.3). The Religious Zionist leader Abraham Isaac Kook upholds Rabbinic traditions while also admiring the courage of secular Zionists (section 4.4). The anti-Zionist leader Yeshaya Asher Zelig Margaliot writes of the courage needed to fight and humiliate Zionists of all kinds (section 4.5). The Religious Zionist leader Tzevi Yehudah Kook speaks of courage in connection with the modern conquest of the Land of Israel (section 4.6). The *haredi* authors Yoel Schwartz and Yitzchak Goldstein (section 4.7) forcefully reject dominant Zionist discourses about courage, especially with regard to the Holocaust.

In closing, four American Jewish leaders articulate their own distinctive approaches to courage. Sherwin Wine's understanding stresses reason and the value of Secular Humanism (section 4.8). Edward Feinstein emphasizes how "chutzpah" may be understood in very positive terms and as the essence of Judaism (section 4.9). Pushing back against violent and sexist conceptions of courage, Amy Eilberg underscores the strength required to "make an enemy into a friend" (section 4.10). Finally, Stosh Cotler (section 4.11) advocates risking one's power, one's privilege, and even one's life in order to stand up for vulnerable immigrants.

These various perspectives also reveal deep tensions in other areas: trust, gender, God, the meaning of the Exodus, and relations between Jews and non-Jews.

4.1. COURAGE TO DEFEND THE GERMAN FLAG

Heinrich Loewe (1869–1951) was a German-Jewish journalist, editor, University of Berlin librarian, scholar of Jewish folklore, and Zionist leader. During the late nineteenth and early twentieth centuries, like many other German Zionists, he combined his devotions to Jewish nationalism and German nationalism. In his view, Germany was the protector of the Jewish people that would ultimately ensure Jews had a state of their own in Palestine.[4]

Loewe's German nationalism is clearly visible in the selections below, which were written amid the outbreak of World War I and titled with the then-popular German phrase "Enemies on all sides of us!" ("Feinde Ringsum!"), a propagandistic slogan justifying Germany's use of force to protect itself from enemy nations. Asserting the need to defend "progress, freedom, and culture" in the face of the "terrible tyranny, bloody cruelty, and dark regression" enveloping Europe,[5] Loewe went on to describe how Jews would defend Germany with particular bravery. They possessed "manly courage" and would carry on the ancient legacy of Jewish warriors.

As the scholar Todd Presner points out in his book *Muscular Judaism*, Loewe was among many European Jews who advanced images of courageous, muscular Jewish men fit for combat to fight against the widespread stereotype that Jewish men were cowardly and weak.[6] Loewe drew particular inspiration from the examples of the Maccabees (who rebelled against the Seleucid Empire in the second century BCE) and Bar Kochba (who rebelled against the Roman Empire in the second century CE). The Maccabees were especially compelling, Loewe noted in a 1908 article, since they possessed "the greatest courage and heroic martyrdom for people and freedom" and demonstrated that "heroes [could be] created from a cowardly tribe."[7] Twentieth-century German Jews, Loewe contended, should devote themselves to training their bodies and hearts so that, as "new Maccabees," they could bravely defend the German fatherland and further the Zionist cause.

Heinrich Loewe, "Enemies on All Sides of Us!" (1914)

In these hours, it must be shown anew that we—as tribally proud Jews—belong among the best sons of the fatherland. The nobility of our millennia of history obliges us. We expect that our youth will voluntarily and cheerfully defend the flag. . . . We trust that our youth—strengthened by the cultivation of their Jewish consciousness and their physical education in ideal conviction and manly courage—will distinguish themselves in all war-like virtues. . . .

When we fight as citizens of our fatherland, the bravery of our ancestors, the courage unto death of the Maccabees, the tremendous fight of Bar Kochba, and the heroic death of hundreds of thousands of our people throughout the ages comes shining through as a glorious example. We will be victorious. We have the confidence in the German Emperor that he is leading us right. We have confidence in the German people that they will fight to their last breath, and we have the unshakable confidence in the divine justice that will bring victory to our honest brothers in arms.[8]

4.2. HUMANITARIAN, THEOLOGICAL, MESSIANIC COURAGE

The German-Jewish philosopher Hermann Cohen (1842–1918) had much in common with Heinrich Loewe. He was also a Jewish scholar who spent much of his life affiliated with a German university (he was the first Jew to hold a full professorship at one, the University of Marburg). A passionate German patriot who also defended his country's entry into World War I, he similarly saw loyalty to German patriotism as fully compatible with his loyalty to Judaism.

But, unlike Loewe, Cohen was associated with Reform Judaism, and his philosophy was centered on God and liberal Jewish religion. Moreover, unlike Loewe, he was an outspoken opponent of Zionism, and his writing after the war emphasized pacifism and nonviolent martyrdom.[9] These emphases manifest in Cohen's chapter on the virtue of courage in his posthumously published *Religion of Reason out of the Sources of Judaism* (1919), from which the selections below are taken.

Cohen points to ways in which the meanings of the words *gevurah* (heroism, courage, valor), *gibbor* (hero, person of courage), and *ḥayil* (army, valor) have changed over time. While the language of heroism once described only male warriors, the same language came to depict those who were dutiful and restrained, whether male or female. Cohen sees courage exemplified not in the "manly courage" of the Maccabees but in the "upright housewife" (*eshet ḥayil*, a woman of valor) described in the book of Proverbs and in the Rabbinic hero who "conquers his desire."

Cohen also considers whether that Rabbinic hero might embrace asceticism (abstinence from sensual pleasures). But, he reasons, asceticism is in fact a form of slavery to one's desires, whereas a true hero accepts desires, tames them, and makes use of them. Ideal courage requires not fleeing from one's sensual desires (a response Cohen associates with Platonism) but mastering them. As Cohen puts it elsewhere in his book, "self-restraint, the taming of the passions, is true courage. Courage is equivalent to the rational knowledge of God."[10]

How is courage equivalent to the rational knowledge of God? God, for Cohen, is not a being but is, rather, the ethical ideal, "the archetype of all human morality."[11] The rational knowledge of God is ethics; when one acts ethically, one testifies to one's knowledge of God. Recognizing the ultimate ethical ideal is a recognition of God—it is "pure monotheism," in Cohen's language—whereas a failure to recognize ethics is "idolatry." And, as Cohen indicates, the Talmud teaches that a Jew should die rather than engage in idolatry (or murder or incest). Jews are thereby required to muster the courage to risk their lives for the sake of ethics—above all, for the sake of love and justice toward other human beings. One must summon the courage to tame one's passions for the sake of acting ethically toward others—and that ethical commitment requires the courage to risk one's life. This ethical courage is emblematic of Jewish life, at least insofar as Jews have chosen martyrdom rather than forsake Jewish ethical monotheism.

Cohen does not trust in the kind of providential "divine justice" envisioned by Heinrich Loewe that guarantees military victory for righteous nationalisms (for Loewe, German and Jewish nationalisms). In Cohen's words, rather, "Messianism breaks the backbone of nationalism." Whereas before World War I Cohen had imagined that the German military would spread the (Jewish) idea of ethical monotheism throughout the world, the postwar text below imagines that the spread of ethical monotheism will happen only "by means of the Jew bearing witness as the suffering servant," as the scholar Robert Erlewine has put it. For Cohen, it is not courageous military triumph but the courage to be martyrs for the sake of the ethical ideal that can best educate others and guide the world toward a messianic age.[12]

True martyrdom, Cohen goes on to teach, is ultimately "in the service of history." Courageous Jewish martyrdom for the sake of ethics (exemplified by martyrs including Jesus of Nazareth) will help teach the ideal of ethical monotheism to the world and will hopefully ultimately usher in a messianic age in which all human beings recognize God and ethics—though it is doubtful whether human beings can ever reach the level of total goodness that such an age would require.[13]

Hermann Cohen, *Religion of Reason out of the Sources of Judaism* (1919)

In the Hebrew language the word "hero" originates out of the same idea of virtue as in the Greek (*arete*) and in the Latin (*virtus*), which both originate from "man" and originally mean manliness. In the same way the Hebrew "hero" (*gibbor*) and "heroism" (*gevurah*) originate from "man" (*gever*). However, man does not remain the sole possessor of heroic virtue. Just as the hero did not remain preeminently the hunter hero (*gibbor tzayid*) but became the war hero (*gibbor milḥamah*), so also did the woman become the woman of the army (*eshet ḥayil*), as the war hero became the hero of the army (*gibbor ḥayil*). However, this appellation of woman, which is found in the significant hymn at the conclusion of the Proverbs of Solomon, does not designate her ability as a warrior; the army also is rather thought of as the administrative area of courage and faithfulness to duty in general. This change in the meaning of the concept of heroism affected the transference of the heroic title from the woman of the army to the upright housewife. How was this lowering in meaning accomplished?

In the Sayings of the Fathers [*Avot* 4:1] it says, "Who is a hero?" And the answer is: "He who conquers his desire" (*ha-kovesh et yitzro*). Now the hero has even become an ascetic. However, he who subdues his passion is not thereby an ascetic but a true hero, who does not permit the senses to rule him, does not become their slave, but their master. He therefore uses their powers, whereas the ascetic, by not using the power of the senses, makes himself negatively the slave of passion. He who conquers sensual desires rules them and accepts their slave services. . . .

If . . . idol worship, or murder, or incest is demanded under threat of death, the Talmud [BT *Sanhedrin* 74a] orders martyrdom. Thus, courage becomes a virtue which accompanies the life of the Jew. For the sword of Damocles has hung over the Jew throughout his history, in order to seduce him to idol worship or to the denial of his pure monotheism. Therefore, one may in all sobriety call the historical life of the Jew the life of courage. . . .

The Jewish martyr . . . is a hero of the unique God of Israel, who is not only his God, the God of his theory and, it may be, even of his faith, but he is at the same time the God of his fathers, the God of his history, who therefore can also be thought of as the God of mankind. . . . Furthermore, Messianism breaks the backbone of nationalism, so that the courage of the Jew cannot be degraded to a merely national virtue. The human courage of the Jew is, as an historical virtue, humanitarian courage, the courage for the truth of the religious ideal of mankind. . . . Martyrdom is an historical act, which the individual does not take upon himself for his own sake, or for the sake of his soul, but in the service of history. . . .

For thousands of years, as also at present, each Jew has been . . . taking the virtue of courage upon himself as his historical lot. Surmounting the worldly life of actual history, the Jew took upon himself the courage to live and, if necessary, to die in joyous resolution for the deepest and most holy idea of the human spirit, the idea of the unique God. Vicarious justice is the Jewish virtue of courage.[14]

4.3. REVIVING ISRAEL'S NATURAL COURAGE

Mikhah Yosef Berdichevsky (Berdyczewski, 1865–1921) was a Ukranian-born Hebrew writer, journalist, and influential secular Zionist. Angered by claims like Cohen's about the virtues of Jewish martyrdom, the nonnationalistic character of Judaism, and the spiritual, ethical, and religious character of the Jewish people, Berdichevsky sought power for the People of Israel in the Land of Israel and praised Jewish heroes who died fighting their enemies. Whereas Cohen saw courage at work in Jews who subdued their passions and dedicated themselves to biblical and Rabbinic ethical ideals, Berdichevsky asked Jews to reject those ideals and instead unleash their natural passions. Applying a similar critique to Judaism that the philosopher Friedrich Nietzsche applied to Christianity, Berdichevsky called for the "transvaluation of values," promoting strength, love of natural beauty, and the culture of the "sword" rather than values that he associated with bookishness, weakness, otherworldliness, and restraint.[15]

In part I of the selections below, Berdichevsky invokes a midrash that God threatened the People of Israel to accept the Torah by holding Mount Sinai overturned above their heads. For him, this overturning alludes to the way in which the laws of the Torah forced the people to overturn their natures—to conquer their desires, subdue their natural passions, and submit to unnatural standards of "good and evil." For Berdichevsky, there is nothing heroic about such submission. Rather, true heroism was best found among the people of Israel before the giving of the Torah, when the Israelites were "healthy," unshackled by conventional morality, and naturally courageous. True heroism is found not in the study of desiccated scriptures but in the unscripted embrace of strength and passion. Berdichevsky calls for the recovery of a form of ancient Jewish living rejected in Jewish literature for many centuries.

In part II, Berdichevsky attacks the Rabbinic midrash that describes Israel as a solitary (female) sheep surrounded by seventy (male) wolves—the seventy nations of the world. According to the midrash, this arrangement reveals not the might of the ewe but that of the shepherd, who miraculously ensures her survival and promises to destroy her tormenters.[16] For Berdichevsky, this midrash inexcusably justifies

Jewish weakness: teaching the fiction that God will intervene in history, it encourages Jews to accept suffering and martyrdom at the hands of their enemies. Jews should, instead, act like wolves themselves, recovering their national will to power (and, it is implied, their masculinity). Whereas rabbis have taught that God punished the Jews with exile because they *failed* to uphold ethical and religious responsibilities, Berdichevsky thinks that the exile happened for the opposite reason: because they *chose* a path of ethics and religion rather than courageously fighting for political power in their homeland.[17] Rabbi Yoḥanan ben Zakkai, for example, made the cowardly choice to be carried out of Jerusalem in a coffin so he could save the Torah academy in Yavneh, instead of joining the Zealots who defended the walls of Jerusalem against Rome; his error led to weakness and exile.[18]

While Berdichevsky's heroes, like Loewe's, include the Maccabees and Bar Kochba, they also include figures who took particularly brazen risks or willingly took their own lives: the Zealots who burned their own food while Jerusalem was under Roman siege; those at Masada who courageously killed themselves rather than submitting to Rome (a story that Berdichevsky was instrumental in reviving); and Samson, who refused to submit to or flee his Philistine captors but instead took vengeance upon them while killing himself in the process.[19]

To Berdichevsky, the fight for the future of the Jewish people can be characterized as a battle between those who are dedicated to the cautious upholding of the commandments and those truly courageous warriors whom "Judaism" might characterize as doing "evil in the eyes of the Lord" (see part III below). Jews today must act like these warriors who fought for their land.

Berdichevsky sees no place for the Jews in the Diaspora—not to defend European fatherlands as Loewe would have it and certainly not to die as martyrs as Cohen would have it. Rather, like the ancient Israelites who rejected conventional morality and fought for their land, Berdichevsky urges his fellow Jews to reject such morality and courageously fight for their land again.

Mikhah Yosef Berdichevsky, *On the Road*
(late nineteenth / early twentieth century)

I. "It teaches that [the Holy Blessed One] overturned the mountain above them like a basin" (BT *Shabbat* 88a). Our origin, our book, our life—these all teach us that they have overturned the mountain above us—that is to say, they have forced us to overturn our nature. . . .

We know of Israel's origins and original character only from the books of teachings and ideas that defeated it, that fought it and its path, and that taught us to say that the deeds of those [original Israelites] were evil. But it is our duty to describe, for ourselves, the life of those "rebel" Israelites with their purity, their courage, and the natural feeling that they possessed. Before the giving of Scripture, this life was so beautiful, so proud, so attractive, so courageous; "so fair [were] your tents, O Jacob . . ." [Num. 24:5]. The innocence and purity before the giving of "good and evil," before the giving of ideas and laws for life, before the strengthening of moral loathing for the healthy feelings of life—all these gave the Israelites, then, a life of natural beauty that was not set out for them.[20]

II. I remember that the writers of the Talmud compared the Assembly of Israel among the nations of the world to a ewe among wolves; it was a great miracle that the ewe was not prey for the wolves' teeth. I do not comprehend how a whole nation can turn itself into a ewe and be content with that . . . I will not comprehend how we can turn ourselves into a people that is beaten and tortured all our days. . . .

It is easy to say that the Holy Blessed One exiled us from our land and scattered us among the peoples. But we also hurried to go into exile, and chose to be wanderers among the peoples sitting under their vines rather than choosing to dwell in our empty land. . . . We know all the historical reasons for our scattering among the peoples, but these reasons are no longer absolutely necessary, and we could change them through a strong national will—if, truly, there is one spark of life remaining in our midst.

The best of the people knew the quality of the land for the people, and they fought for it with courage. For them, there was a living and feeling spirit. But, through their counterfeit spirituality, the leaders of the people deflected the people's natural inclinations and taught them to favor Yavneh over the fortress of Jerusalem—that is, over the fortress of the people and its survival. . . . Those who fell on their swords were superior to those who fled from the walls [of the city] and hid themselves in coffins. . . . Samson who said "Let me die with the Philistines!" [Judg. 16:30] would be superior to a Samson who, blinded, fled. . . .[21]

III. Even those who believe in the absolute value of Judaism do not deny that the era of Israel's courage, and the foundation of the people of Israel as a nation, was mostly during the very time that it did what was apparently "evil in the eyes of the Lord."[22] True, the spirit of Judaism won out at Yavneh, and then the remnant of Israel was a nation for guarding faith; but how can those who are "as cautious with a minor commandment as with a major one" [*Avot* 2:1] compare to those courageous Israelites who conquered the land and fought for it?[23]

4.4. COURAGE DRAWN FROM PURE SOURCES

Abraham Isaac (Avraham Yitzḥak) Kook (1865–1935), originally from the Lithuanian/Latvian regions of the Russian Empire, was an Orthodox rabbi shaped by a range of intellectual currents, including Chabad Hasidism, non-Hasidic kabbalistic pietism, Lithuanian Talmudism, the Musar movement, and Zionism. He eventually became Ashkenazi chief rabbi of Palestine and the major theologian and musar writer of messianic Religious Zionism—the Orthodox movement that attributes messianic significance to the Zionist enterprise.

Kook believed that the influx of Jews to the Land of Israel in the late nineteenth and early twentieth centuries marked the beginning of the process of the redemption of the world. Even secular Jews who returned to the land (and those who advocated secular Zionism, such as Heinrich Loewe or Mikhah Berdichevsky) thus contributed to redemption, and they showed yearnings and qualities of courage that reflected deep holiness.

In part I of the selection below, we see Kook's understanding of such apparently "secular" desires and qualities. Kook concludes that even "the empty ones" and the "sinners" among the Jewish people are (unbeknownst to them) seeking a connection to God (who is more fully known in the Land of Israel) and God's commandments (which can only be fully practiced in the Land of Israel). In his view, all the People of Israel are uniquely attached to God and possess a holy, divine flame within their souls that allows for singular qualities of courage. Kook thus finds courage not only in expressions of morality and monotheism (where Cohen saw courage exemplified) but also very much in the longing of a figure like Berdichevsky to renew Jewish identity and return Jews to their land.

Berdichevsky had been Kook's classmate at the Volozhin Yeshiva, and Kook agrees with Berdichevsky that Jews must throw off "exilic" passivity and recover the valor and vitality of ancient Jewish leaders who fought to defend the Land of Israel. But whereas Berdichevsky admired ancient warriors precisely because they were not concerned with God, Torah, and "good and evil," Kook points to biblical figures such as Abraham, Moses, Joshua, and David who in his view combine courage in battle with prophecy and dedication to the laws of Torah. In part II of the selection below, Kook urges his fellow Jews to recover the courage of these biblical heroes, which was bolstered by their confidence that God was with them and expressed in both spiritual and physical bravery.

Kook emphasizes that models of courage should be drawn from the divine spirit uniquely found within Jewish souls and not from "foreign wells" (such as some of those heralded by Loewe, Cohen, and Berdichevsky). Though Kook himself was inspired by non-Jewish, European models of culture and philosophy in various ways, he claims that Jews must rely only on their unique Torah and relationship to God in "the spiritual realm of faith and morality."[24]

Kook has particular contempt for liberal, anti-Zionist views associated with the Reform movement (e.g., the views of Hermann Cohen) that may seem focused on God and Torah but that he regards as utterly corrupted by foreign wisdom.[25] He sees much more value—indeed, more "holiness"—in the secular Zionism of Berdichevsky that rejects God and Torah but does so while celebrating Jewish vitality, distinctiveness, and courage. In his view, secular Zionists like Berdichevsky are in fact playing a pivotal role in the drama of history because of their Zionism *and* their audacity, arrogance, and impudence (chutzpah).

The Mishnah (*Sotah* 9:15) offers the cryptic teaching that "in the time of the footsteps of the Messiah, chutzpah will swell," and Kook understands this to indicate that chutzpah-filled secular Zionists are directly ushering in the Days of the Messiah. As Kook indicates in part III below, their brazen willfulness contains some holy courage and will have positive effects. For one thing, it will inspire deeper courage among others, especially by challenging the "moderate," "weak," and cowardly Jews (e.g., liberal Jews like Hermann Cohen or Orthodox Jews like Yeshaya Margaliot, section 4.5) whom Kook sees as resisting Zionism's redemptive power. Moreover, the strength that wicked secularists bring into the world will ultimately be passed along to the righteous—to Jews (like Kook himself) who will combine the strength of Zionism with the righteousness and faith of Torah, thus replacing the impudence of chutzpah with a pure, holy, and lucid courage. Secular chutzpah, like everything secular, is ultimately transient and must give way to the Torah-based courage that will represent the true strength and stability of the messianic era.[26]

Kook trusts that all forms of evil will ultimately lead to good, as divine providence is guiding the world toward a glorious messianic age. Unlike Hermann Cohen, whose doubts that the messianic ideal can ever be fully reached correlate with his view of God as an ideal who cannot be fully brought into the world, Kook is certain that God is very much immanent within the People of Israel and within the Land of Israel, where God's plan for history is unfolding. As Kook puts it in part IV below, all that is frightening in the world is part of a "great vision" that one need not fear. Jews may find courage through trust in God's presence and providence.

But as much as Kook embraced boldness, he unsurprisingly saw public boldness as more valuable for men than for women. Part V contains selections from Kook's writing (in 1919–20) in opposition to women's suffrage in Palestine, and there we can see Kook asking for those seeking an expanded public role for women to be more patient in waiting for entry into the messianic age, which may eventually offer the Jewish woman new opportunities to act as a "woman of valor" and as a "crown for her husband" (Prov. 12:4). In the present era, from Kook's perspective, Jews must have the courage to maintain their uniquely patriarchal society, which clearly does not permit women to participate in political elections. Kook saw women's political empowerment as threatening, especially to domestic tranquility; for the time being, at least, women's valor surely required restraining their desires for a more public voice. Kook recognized courage in precisely this sort of restraint, which required resisting the lure of non-Jewish European concepts of gender egalitarianism. In his view, Jews needed to cultivate the courage and strength to draw political guidance from pure, Jewish sources — and from the presence of God within their holy souls — and to reject foreign political ideas that allowed for women's suffrage.[27]

Abraham Isaac Kook, *Lights*, "The Moral Principles" and "On Women's Voting" (early twentieth century)

I. Within the inner heart, in the chambers of its purity and holiness, the flame of Israel grows stronger, forcefully demanding a courageous and constant connection of life to all of God's commandments. . . . The fire burns and blazes deep within, [even] in the hearts of all the empty ones among the people of Israel, and in the hearts of the sinners of Israel. In the entirety of the nation is all of the desire for freedom and all of the longing for life . . . and this longing is the longing for the Land of Israel, the land of holiness, the land of God, within which all of the commandments are embodied and expressed in their finished form. . . . The courage in the heart, demonstrating to the whole world the courage of the nation that maintains its character, name, values, faith, and desires, is included within this longing for a life of truth and a life of all the commandments, which the light of Torah in all of its fullness and goodness will illuminate.

One who stands at a distance may wonder: How is it possible that all these souls, apparently distant from faith, have the spirit of life beating within them, with inner force, not only to come close to God in general but also to the true life of Israel, to the commandments in their finished form, in image and idea, song and action? But it is no wonder to anyone who is connected in the depth of his spirit to the depths of the Assembly of Israel and knows its wondrous divine powers. This is the secret of courage, the exaltedness of life that will never cease. These are the commandments "that a person should perform, and live by them" [Lev. 18:5]; to "walk before God in the land of life" [Ps. 116:9]—this is the Land of Israel.[28]

II. We look upon the first generations—the generations engaged in wars recounted in the Torah, Prophets, and Writings—as the truly great, whom we cherish and whom we see as greatly holy. We understand that the spark of their souls was the foundation. The state of the world had evolved to require war, and this caused the appearance of these souls, with their perfected inner feelings. They had the inner recognition that the war of the nation, the war for their existence, was God's war. They were bold in their spirits, and in the depths of the darkness they knew how to choose good and reject evil—"though I walk through the valley of the shadow of death, I will fear no evil" [Ps. 23:4]. When we contemplate them with all the spirituality for which we yearn, we yearn for their courage, for the life force embodied within them in its finished form, firm and strong within them; and out of this longing, our spiritual strength is encouraged and the force of our [physical] courage is refined, and those strong souls return to live within us, forever. . . .

When she recognizes God within her, [the Assembly of Israel] will recognize how to reveal the source of her life. . . . She is not called to draw from foreign wells but to draw from her own depths. She will draw will from the depth of her prayer, life from the well of her Torah, courage from the root of her faith, order from the uprightness of her mind, valor from the strength of her spirit, and all that arises in the canopy of her heavens is from the spirit of God that hovers over the fullness of the universe from the days of Creation until the end of days—"For I am with you, says the Lord of Hosts . . . My spirit is still in your midst. Fear not!" [Hag. 2:4–5].[29]

III. The brazen ones of this generation, who are wicked as a matter of principle . . . they soil the world and they are soiled. But the essence of courage that is in their wills is a bit of holiness. . . . They are most revealed at the end of days. . . . In [these] times of redemption, chutzpah increases. A storm gathers and rages, breach after breach emerges, chutzpah breeds chutzpah. These fiery souls display their strength, which no fence or boundary can restrict, and those in this ordered world who are weak, moderate, and polite are frightened by their forcefulness. . . . But those with [true] strength of courage know that what is being revealed is one of the revelations that are necessary for the improvement of the world, for bringing courage to the nation, to humanity, and the world. Though at first this revelation of force is in the form of chaos, in the end it will be taken from these wicked people and given to the righteous who are [truly] "courageous as lions," who will reveal with a mighty spirit of lucid and courageous thinking . . . [that] these storms will bring abundant rain, these dark clouds will be vessels for great lights, and "from pitch darkness, the eyes of the blind will see" [Isa. 29:18].[30]

IV. Fear is complete foolishness. A person must not be afraid, he only needs to be careful. The more he is afraid, the more he falls, and when he is frightened, the fright itself produces the stumbling. It is therefore important for him to strengthen himself in the understanding that there is no reason for him to be afraid. All the frightening images are only the fragmented colors of a great vision that needs to be completed, and when it is completed they all merge to engender confidence [bitaḥon] and great strength that fill the soul with firmness and courage.[31]

V. We are marching on our path of redemption, not in order to be mere followers of European culture (which is bankrupt, at least with regard to morality and purity of character traits, from the perspective of all deep critics who do not fear its appearance and great stature) but in order to proclaim our invigorated, holy, clear message, just as it is drawn from our inner source. In any case, it is fitting at this time of great need . . . that we walk upright, to emphasize the [distinct] national character of our social life in our land. We can be confident that this courage will bring us far more honor in the world than all of the imitation of externals, which usually comes from inner weakness. . . . [It is only in the future] that the world will be purified, and then safe and honorable ways will be found (generally and particularly) for the pure, delicate, and holy activity and influence of the woman—the mother in Israel—for the fullness of her influence appropriate for her special inner worth, fulfilling the vision that every "woman of valor is a crown for her husband" (Prov. 12:4). . . . A bit more moderation, equanimity, and faith are very much required of us at this time . . . [to] give us splendor and glory, increase peace, harmony, and mutuality among us, and grant us the courage to actualize the revival to which we all aspire.[32]

4.5. THE COURAGE OF THE FEW AND THE WEAK

Rabbi Yeshaya Asher Zelig Margaliot (Margolis, 1894–1969) was a leader of the most radical anti-Zionist Hasidic Jews of Jerusalem. Born within a Belz Hasidic family in Chelm (part of the Austro-Hungarian Empire), he became a follower of Rabbi Ḥayyim Elazar Shapira, the Munkaczer Rebbe (the great-great-grandson of Rabbi Tzevi Elimelekh Shapira, section 7.2).

Margaliot insisted that Jews were absolutely forbidden to establish their own state until the coming of the Messiah; that Zionism was an ideology created by Satan; and that Zionists were not truly a part of the People of Israel but part of the demonic "mixed multitude" of Egyptians that had accompanied the true People of Israel out of Egypt and continually led Israel astray.[33]

He would have been appalled by the other perspectives in this chapter: by Hermann Cohen's liberal Judaism and its rejection of traditional authority; by figures such as Heinrich Loewe who supported the "satanic" movement of Zionism; and all the more so by figures like Berdichevsky who combined Zionism with a fierce rejection of God and Torah. Yet he was particularly disgusted by Abraham Isaac Kook, who had the audacity to describe Zionism as the path demanded by the Torah that would lead to the redemption of Israel. Margaliot seemingly had much in common with Kook—both were pious Orthodox Jews and kabbalists, both stressed that Jews must be informed only by "pure" Jewish sources, and both rejected what they saw as foreign ideas (such as gender egalitarianism). But Margaliot viewed Kook as taking a clearly foreign idea—Zionism—and transforming traditionalist Jews into great sinners by deceitfully arguing that this was in fact a pure Jewish idea. For convincing countless worshipers of God to become worshipers of Satan, Kook could never be forgiven. The selection below comes from Margaliot's book *Ashrei ha-Ish* (Fortunate is the man), a volume addressed to a wide range of anti-Zionist *haredi* Jews that has been viewed as, above all, a work intended to criticize Kook.[34]

Unlike Kook and many other thinkers, Margaliot refused to link courage with physical might. Margaliot describes how throughout history the true People of Israel, though physically weak and few in numbers, courageously relied on God to miraculously defend them against stronger and more numerous enemies: demonic, impure nations like the Egyptians, Canaanites, and Amalekites; or the demonic, impure mixed multitude that infiltrated the People of Israel. Thus, for example, when the People of Israel engaged in idolatrous worship of the Golden Calf, only the tribe of Levi courageously defended God against the threat of idolatry by massacring the idolaters (even their own family members), with God's help (Exod. 32:26–29). So too, God aided the Maccabees ("the Hasmoneans"), who were few and weak (not distinguished by physical strength as Loewe, Berdichevsky, and Kook imagined), when they courageously stood up against impure Hellenizing Jews and their Greek allies. Moses stood up to Pharaoh with his words, knowing that God would intervene (Exod. 5–11). God gave the zealous Phinehas the courage to impale the powerful, sinful prince Zimri and his consort with a spear (Num. 25:7–8). Moses assured the Israelites that God would be with them in the battle to dispossess the numerous and strong Canaanite nations, so they could fight without fear (Deut. 7:17–21). Likewise, God imbued David with the courage to fight Goliath (1 Sam. 17:32), Elijah to slaughter the 450 prophets of Baal (1 Kings 18), and Israel to defeat the Amalekites (Exod. 17:16).

Examples such as these offer templates for Margaliot's own courageous confrontation with the mixed multitude of Zionists in his day. Margaliot saw himself as part of a small, embattled community whose only weapons were prayer, study, performance of commandments, and the use of words to forcefully rebuke their wayward neighbors. But Margaliot was confident that messianic redemption was coming soon. Deeply debased humanity would not actualize that redemption alone, of course—it could only happen through God's miraculous intervention on behalf of the righteous. God had given him the courage to forcefully remind other Jews of this truth and to rebuke those Zionists who considered themselves "redeemers of Israel" when in truth only God would be the "redeemer of Israel."

For Margaliot, using one's words to rebuke sinners in this way is a kind of war, and all Jews should choose to ally themselves with the forces of righteousness and join him in his war. While the Torah recognizes timidity as a legitimate reason for an exemption from battle in certain kinds of wars (Deut. 20:8; BT *Sotah* 44b), Margaliot indicates that the war against the mixed multitude in the present day is a "commanded war" from which no man can be exempt; all are required to cultivate the courage necessary to fight against Zionism.

Yeshaya Asher Zelig Margaliot, *Ashrei ha-Ish* (1921)

All those "who have not taken a false oath by [God's] Life or sworn deceitfully" [Ps. 24:4] should go forth like the tribe of Levi [who massacred idolatrous Israelites, Exod. 32:28]. Moses our teacher . . . praised them for submitting in sacrifice to sanctify God's name at the time of the sin of the Golden Calf. . . . Thus would our forefathers always act when the wicked rose up in the land. . . . Thus let us stand up against them, and be not afraid . . . even though they are many and we are few, and they are mighty and we are weak. It has already been this way, always, and nonetheless Israel triumphed.

At the time of the Hasmoneans [the Maccabees], God assisted and delivered "the mighty into the hands of the weak, the many into the hands of the few, the impure into the hands of the pure, the wicked into the hands of the righteous, and those who do evil into the hands of those who are immersed in the Holy Torah."[35] Even if there is only one righteous person in the city, "let him be strong as a leopard, swift as an eagle, fleet as a gazelle, and courageous as a lion," as the *tannaitic* rabbi [Judah ben Tema] said [*Avot* 5:20]—this is the true courage that every God-fearing person must possess. . . . Especially now in this era, when (God forbid) the wicked want to destroy all that is holy, we must break the jaws of the sinners and humiliate those who engage in crimes and falsehoods, with all of our force and strength, and strengthen God's Torah so that it spreads and is exalted, and strengthen the hands of people of truth. With the force of God who gave us the Holy Torah we will battle against [the wicked], with no fear or fright, and certainly rebuke them with no fear or fright, as Moses our teacher of blessed memory spoke when he prophesied before Pharaoh the King of Egypt, before every plague, and did not fear him, and always said to him, "Thus says the Lord"; . . . and so Phinehas stood up against Zimri [Num. 25:7–8], even though he was a prince of Israel and his tribe protected him.

And so it is written, "Should you say to yourselves, 'These nations are more numerous than we; how can we dispossess them?' You need have no fear of them. . . . Do not stand in dread of them, for the Lord your God is in your midst, a great and awesome God" [Deut. 7:17–21]. . . . And so the heart of King David, peace be upon him, was upright and confident, and he said, "Let no man's courage fail him. Your servant will go and fight" [1 Sam. 17:32]. And so Elijah stood up with courage against Ahab and the 450 prophets of Baal and that whole generation that thronged after them [1 Kings 18]. . . .

It is a holy obligation upon each member of the People of Israel to stand up for this commanded war, as it is written: "The Lord will be at war with Amalek throughout the ages" [Exod. 17:16], and no Israelite man may exempt himself. . . .

We will raise the banner of the Lord our God and the Holy Torah . . . and with God's great strength, for He is the one who girds Israel with courage, we will clothe ourselves with the spirit of courage to humiliate those who engage in falsehoods . . . and we will declare and announce to all of our brothers in the House of Israel wherever they may be, and to the entire world, that all of these [Zionists] are heretics. . . . They and those who assist them are from the "mixed multitude," who have come from Egypt, and they do not belong to the People of Israel, and they have no right to speak anywhere in the name of Israel, and certainly not to call themselves the "guardians and redeemers of Israel."[36]

4.6. ABRAHAM'S COURAGE AND THE CONQUEST OF THE LAND

Rabbi Tzevi Yehudah Kook (1891–1982), the son of Abraham Isaac Kook, passionately endorsed his father's teachings, which he edited, published, and expanded. A prominent leader of Israeli Religious Zionism himself, Kook stressed the need for Jewish control of the entire historic Land of Israel. After the 1967 Six-Day War, he became the leader of the Gush Emunim (Bloc of the Faithful) settlement movement, which sought to establish Jewish control of the areas Israel had conquered in the war.

Kook's discussions of courage echoed his father's in many respects, but they sometimes expanded on them by including his characteristic emphasis on conquest and control of the Land of Israel. Many of his statements reflect his trust that Israel had moved far along in the redemptive process in the years since his father's death, given the military prowess of the State of Israel that his father did not live to see, and his confidence that asserting control over the land was absolutely necessary for the redemptive process to continue.[37]

In one characteristic statement, Kook argued against retreating from even a single kilometer of the Land of Israel. Insisting that "the State of Israel is divine," he avowed that "the Glory of Israel does not deceive or change His mind" (1 Sam. 15:29) — since God had granted so much territory to the Jews, surely God would not revoke that grant, and would in fact want Israel to "conquer and liberate more and more." He concluded, "Heaven protect us from weakness and timidity. . . . In our divine, world-encompassing undertaking, there is no room for retreat."[38]

The text below explores the courage of the biblical character who began that divine undertaking, never retreated, and never showed weakness or timidity: Abraham. Kook, like his father, emphasizes the importance of both physical and spiritual courage, and in Abraham he finds admirable deeds of physical courage (e.g., the war in Gen. 14) as well as deeds of spiritual courage (e.g., supervising conversions, according to midrashic tradition). Then, looking to the deed of ultimate heroism, Kook points to the way in which Abraham submits to God's command to bind his son Isaac as a sacrificial offering (Gen. 22) — a command that requires him to give up not only his son's life but also the very principles that had become core to his spirit.[39]

For Kook, Abraham's courage to sacrifice for the sake of God becomes a model for later generations of Jews, who are called on to make spiritual sacrifices (dedicating themselves to what Kook calls "the war of Torah") as well as physical sacrifices (e.g., in the army). Courage, for Kook, plainly requires not only what *Mishnah Avot* described as "conquering one's desire" but also the physical conquering of the land.

Only a year after Kook offered these words to his students, he was able to see the further fulfillment of the promise to Abraham and the opportunity for new heights of Abrahamic courage. In 1967, once Israel had conquered much of the land on which Abraham had walked, Kook called on his students to courageously settle it, defend it, and support its military occupation, continuing the physical and spiritual wars that had begun with Abraham.[40]

Tzevi Yehudah Kook, *Siḥot* (1966)

The steps of our father Abraham in the Land of Israel are linked to the conquests of his children. His walking has a goal: "that his children might easily conquer the land" (BT *Bava Batra* 100a). The oaths of the fathers and the conquests of his children are one: the conquests of the children—the conquest of Joshua, and then our conquest [as Israelis]—fulfill the oath given to the patriarchs. . . .

Our father Abraham is the seed of the great nation, the foundation, "the rock we were hewn from" (Isa. 51:1). . . . Our father Abraham appears as "a great man among giants" (*Soferim* 21:9), as a giant full of tremendous and awesome courage in all respects, great in deeds in all respects: he went and "invoked God by name" (Gen. 12:8, 13:4, 21:33); he "went on his journeys" (Gen. 12:9, 13:3); he educated, as when "he armed his educated men" (Gen. 14:14) and "the souls whom he converted in Haran" (Gen. 12:5), and he fought wars (Gen. 14). He was full of noble and mighty deeds, culminating in the extreme and final one (Gen. 22): submission through sacrifice with the Binding of Isaac, the sacrifice of body and sacrifice of soul. . . . The mighty abundance of wealth, wisdom, spirituality, and courage was all found in this one noble and mighty personality, our foundation for all generations, the foundation of the "great nation" (Gen. 12:2), the foundation for his children's conquest . . . whose value was for the nation and for the whole world—"all the families of the earth shall bless themselves by you" (Gen. 12:3).

The particular divine creation that emerged with the decision, decree, and formation of "God said to Abram" (Gen. 12:1)—this continues for us, in the courage of Israel through all generations, in this miraculous people's submission through sacrifice: the spiritual courage of the war of Torah and the practical courage of concrete activities, practical war and maintaining a position. This wonderful divine strength that was found in the original patriarch, the seed of the great nation, continues to reveal itself in the community of the People of Israel, in every generation, in the greatness of spiritual and practical activities.[41]

4.7. AGAINST THE "ZIONIST" MYTH OF THE HOLOCAUST

Rabbi Yoel Schwartz (b. 1939) is a prominent Israeli teacher and scholar who identifies with *haredi* Judaism while also supporting Zionism. He serves as a senior lecturer at the Dvar Yerushalayim Yeshiva and as the spiritual authority for the Nahal Haredi battalion in the Israel Defense Forces, a battalion for *haredi* Jewish men established despite opposition from non-Zionist and anti-Zionist *haredi* Jews and concern from many secular Israeli Jews.

Seeking to build on the legacy of the Musar movement, Schwartz has written a number of books on the cultivation of character traits.[42] He also joined with his student and colleague Yitzchak Goldstein in writing *Shoah*, a volume that has come to shape contemporary *haredi* approaches to Zionism and the Holocaust. Schwartz and Goldstein see goodness in the establishment of the State of Israel after the Holocaust but do not view the state as divine or messianic (as Tzevi Yehudah Kook did).[43]

In the selection from *Shoah* below, Schwartz and Goldstein address the myth that Jews failed to show courage during the Holocaust, passively going "like sheep to the slaughter."[44] Secular Zionists developed this myth, they argue, drawing on "foreign," non-Jewish ideas to portray Jews as passively accepting their fate as God's will, and thereby mocking traditional Jewish ideas about divine intervention. As we have seen, secular Zionists had developed similar myths about Jewish weakness well before the Holocaust: Berdichevsky had condemned Jews for accepting the fate of sheep surrounded by wolves and for relying on divine miracles rather than fighting back against their tormentors.

Berdichevsky played a significant role in constructing the secular Zionist ethos to which Schwartz and Goldstein are responding—an ethos that asks Jews to venerate strength, to affirm the courage of heroes such as Samson and the Zealots of Jerusalem and Masada, and to reject the oppressive theological and ethical ideals said to have been revealed by God at Mount Sinai. Schwartz and Goldstein voice precisely those views that Berdichevsky so strongly opposed. They suggest that the secular veneration of physical strength reflects the very same European culture that produced Nazism, and that the authentic Jewish ideal is instead found in the person of courage (the hero) who, in the language of *Avot*, "conquers his impulse." In their view, the experience of standing at Mount Sinai means being subject to moral principles that permit the use of force in self-defense but restrain those who idealize physical strength. Thus when Samson takes vengeance upon the Philistines and kills himself in the process, he represents a foreign, non-Jewish ideal of courage. Jews with real courage should never engage in such cowardly, suicidal behavior but always hope for divine intervention. As such, the Zealots who killed themselves at Masada represent another cowardly, non-Jewish model; the more courageous choice would have been to accept Roman rule, slavery, or even martyrdom at Roman hands.

Accepting the decree of being like sheep among wolves, for Schwartz and Goldstein, should not suggest passivity or cowardice. As they emphasize elsewhere in their book, Jews who were killed by the Nazis for being Jewish were not passive sheep but martyrs whose deaths "sanctified God's name." Sometimes they expressed their courage by physically resisting, but others expressed their courage by accepting sacrifice with the conscious and courageous awareness of Abraham and Isaac in Genesis 22.[45] In any case, Schwartz and Goldstein are clear, no martyr should be derided as a mere sheep who passively went to the slaughter.

From their perspective, Berdichevksy and other so-called "Zionists" who see courage as requiring physical strength, armed resistance, and a concern with honor are defaming martyrs and cannot be viewed as true "Zionists." Schwartz and Goldstein are interested in defining a new type of Zionist identity that reimagines what it means to be courageous, recovering the ancient models that Berdichevsky sought to overcome.

Yoel Schwartz and Yitzchak Goldstein, *Shoah* (1988)

The accusation of "timidity" [against Holocaust victims] and the veneration of "courage" [of those who physically fought the Nazis] is based on an error, and its roots are in foreign cultures. Timidity is . . . recognized in the Torah as a legitimate reason for exemption from military service [Deut. 20:8; BT *Sotah* 44b]. . . . The scorn for "cowards" is rooted in the culture of power that venerates the strong (in body and spirit) and scorns the weak. How dreadful it is when those discussing the Holocaust use ethical standards taken from a culture that itself produced the Nazis! . . . It was from the murderers that we heard the epithets "rag dolls" and "cowards," and they were the ones who idolized physical force alone.

The Jewish hero is the one who "conquers his impulse" [*Avot* 4:1], acting with restraint and patience. This is not external valor but superior internal strength. He does not need physical exploits in war and concrete struggle. He makes use of them when needed, but he does not see them as ideal in and of themselves. Sometimes he even sees them as defective, as stooping to the level of the enemy and as using means that are not appropriate for someone whose fathers stood at Mount Sinai. He does not want to react to terror with terror, to murder with murder, lest he become one who sheds blood. Sometimes he has no choice, and he must make use of the principle that "if someone comes to kill you, kill him first" (BT *Berachot* 58a) — but he does not see any heroism in this.

The demand "to die honorably" is as far distant from the ideas of the Torah as the east is distant from the west. It contains the assumption that death is inevitable, that there is no hope to live, as [when Samson said] "Let me die with the Philistines!" [Judg. 16:30]. Such dark despair is not from a Jewish source. . . .

[The assertion that Jews killed by the Nazis went] "like sheep to the slaughter" follows from the myth created by "Zionist" education (the quotation marks should be emphasized). . . . One of the most important symbols of this myth is the story of Masada, a story that is still taught to tens of thousands of youth. Again and again it is told how the Zealots took their own lives so they would not fall into the hands of the Romans, for "we shall die before becoming slaves to our enemies, and remain free men by leaving the land of the living" (in the words of Elazar ben Yair, commander of the Zealots, according to Josephus). The veneration of the "courage" of the Zealots gave rise to the slogan "Masada will not fall again" — that is to say, "We, with our strength and courage, will not allow another defeat to occur." . . . [But] this concept of "courage" is problematic. If — God forbid — the residents of Jerusalem and the Galilee had acted like their brothers at Masada, and all committed suicide so that they would not have had to surrender to the Romans, we would not exist today. Even the very substance of the "courage" of Masada is doubtful: Is there not greater courage in confronting the difficult life of slavery to the Romans that awaited them, in order to stay alive and to keep the Jewish people alive, rather than dying "as free men"?[46]

4.8. THE COURAGE OF SECULAR HUMANISTS

Rabbi Sherwin Wine (1928–2007) was the founder of the Society for Humanistic Judaism and the intellectual framer of Secular Humanistic Judaism as a worldwide movement. Born in the United States and originally ordained by the Reform movement's Hebrew Union College–Jewish Institute for Religion, Wine declared himself an atheist and broke with Reform Judaism to found his own Jewish denomination, often known simply as Humanistic Judaism.

Wine was deeply concerned with questions of moral character and wrote about virtues including honesty, justice, love, self-respect, self-control, and courage.[47] Courage played a particularly central role in his book *Staying Sane in a Crazy World: A Guide to Rational Thinking*, from which the selections below are taken.[48]

For Wine, courage requires "realistic living" — facing the world as it is, from the perspective of reason, rather than taking refuge in fantasies that God exists or that things are guaranteed to turn out well. Wine rejects the various conceptions of God affirmed in this chapter as well as any expectations of providence, life after death, or "stability" in general.

Though Wine joins Hermann Cohen in passionately affirming the value of reason, Wine's reason leads him to conclude that the abstract ideal that Cohen calls "God" is not real (although Wine does think that reason should affirm the reality of other abstract concepts, including "happiness" and "usefulness"). Like Cohen, Wine also sees courage manifested by nondescript people in ordinary settings, but whereas Cohen focuses on the courage of ordinary Jews who testify to the value of monotheism and morality, Wine sees courage in any manifestation of "realistic living" and what the philosopher Hannah Arendt (see sections

7.3, 8.4, and 9.6) describes as "the willingness to act and speak at all." Furthermore, Wine does not attribute particular courage to Jews who proclaim their monotheism—he sees all theisms as signs of cowardice rather than courage.

Rejecting traditional Jewish beliefs regarding God and Torah as lies and fantasies chosen out of cowardice, Wine has a good deal in common with Berdichevsky. Elsewhere in his writing he mentions Berdichevsky as an important thinker in the history of Jewish secular humanism "who rejected supernatural authority and who sought to persuade the Jews to take their own destiny into their own hands."[49] Wine is supportive of secular liberal Zionism and affirms the secular humanistic Israeli identities Zionism made possible.[50]

But Wine also discusses courage in very different ways. Whereas Berdichevsky idealizes the courageous expression of instinctual and natural passions, Wine stresses the importance of controlling feelings. Wine does not romanticize the courage of ancient Israelites who lived free from the fetters of Jewish morality—rather, he sees certain valuable moral truths in Jewish tradition. As he puts it in one essay, "Character building and ethical training are the aspects of historic religion which are still appealing."[51] Whereas Berdichevsky sees no hope for Jews in the Diaspora, Wine affirms the potential for courageous, secular Jewish living in all places.[52]

Wine does not idealize fighting for one's land or the courage of those who took their own lives rather than submit to enemies; rather, he stresses everyday expressions of sanity and reason, while encouraging his readers not to be embarrassed by their fears. Challenging conventional models of masculinity as well, Wine encourages his audiences to reject traditional conceptions of "masculine virtue" that stress the conquest and elimination of fear.[53]

Sherwin Wine, *Staying Sane in a Crazy World* (1995)

I. Fear . . . [can be] embarrassing. For many people to be afraid is a sign of weakness. They would rather confess to almost anything than to fright. Masculine virtue means not only the conquest of fear but also the elimination of fear. Brave men do not fear. When they are asked, "Are you afraid?" they always protest. "Not me, I'm not afraid."

People who are embarrassed by their fear will resort to strange ways of hiding it. They will often plunge into reckless and foolish action in order to prove that they are brave. Or, if they are unable to be brave, they will pretend that they never really wanted what they are too afraid to achieve. We call this rationalization "sour grapes."

Being realistic about fear is essential to sanity. If we are too indulgent and turn everything and everybody into an insurmountable danger, we will live in an illusory world of terror. If we are too embarrassed and hide from our fear, we will spend too much time covering up our feelings and too little time solving our problems. And if we are too eager to be guided by our feelings and not control them, we will pursue their agenda and not our own. Taming fear is part of training for realism. . . .[54]

II. Choosing the life of courage is not easy. The world we live in is filled with so many risks, so many dangers. The world we have is so different from the world we want. We want a loving and just providence, but it is not there. We want guarantees of happy endings, but they do not exist. We want eternal life, but it is most likely a fantasy. We want stability, but everything is change. We even want to be surrounded by sane and caring people, but they are few and far between.

Choosing cowardice seems so much more attractive. Cowards never have to face the real world. They can invent their own "reality," fill it with whatever they need and want and play make-believe. Yet cowardice exists at its own price. It forces us to lie about our experience. It makes us deny what we see with our own eyes. It humiliates us with our weakness. It exhausts our energy in the battle to resist the truth. It turns us into begging children, grateful for abuse and suffering. It prevents us from assuming responsibility for our own lives. It forces us to negate the one power we do have to cope with reality, our own power. It makes us as crazy as the world we live in.

The life of courage is hard. But it is, ultimately, rewarding. It makes us pay attention to our own experience. It makes it easy for us to admit the truth. It notices our strength. It protects our dignity. It enable[s] us to assume responsibility for our own lives. It celebrates our own power. It makes us sane in the face of the crazy world.

It even makes us pay attention to the opportunities, as well as the dangers, of the real world. Pleasure is real. Happiness is real. Usefulness is real. Loving and supportive relationships are real. But, if they happen, they are not gifts of destiny. They are human achievements—sometimes against overwhelming odds.

The life of courage rests on the foundation of reason—but it is made out of passion and emotional power. It turns every ordinary day into an extraordinary event of personal resistance and every ordinary person into a hero of determination. As Hannah Arendt, the German Jewish refugee philosopher said, "The connotation of courage, which we now feel to be an indispensable quality of the hero, is, in fact, already present in the willingness to act and speak at all, to insert oneself in the world and begin a story of one's own" (*The Human Condition*).

Realistic living has a heroic touch to it—even for the most nondescript men and women—even in the most pedestrian of settings—because the dangers of failure and death are so real.[55]

4.9. JUDAISM'S CHUTZPAH IMPERATIVE

Edward Feinstein (b. 1954) is a Conservative rabbi who serves as senior rabbi of Valley Beth Shalom in Encino, California, and on the faculty of the American Jewish University's Ziegler Rabbinical School. In his book *The Chutzpah Imperative: Empowering Today's Jews for a Life That Matters*, Feinstein stresses the importance of cultivating a sort of moral courage that he describes with the Hebrew word *chutzpah*. As noted above, traditional Rabbinic literature often used the term to describe a negative (though sometimes effective) sort of audacity, arrogance, and impudence, though Abraham Isaac Kook saw some sparks of holiness in the chutzpah of secular Zionists. In part I of the selections below, Feinstein gives chutz-pah a far more positive valence, arguing that it is a holy form of courage and that even the Talmud suggests positive connotations of the term: the Jerusalem Talmud describes the fertility of the Land of Israel using "chutzpah," and in the Babylonian Talmud, Balaam, the prophet hired to curse the Israelites (Num. 22–24), is said to possess "chutzpah even in the face of heaven." The talmudic text suggests that Balaam's insistence and impudence toward God has some effect in convincing God to let him go on his mission, but the Talmud does not suggest that Balaam is morally courageous. Feinstein, however, understands the phrase to point to a concept of moral courage that stands at the heart of Judaism: a courage to insist on justice even when God seems to deny it.

Feinstein sees many ancient cultures as having taught "myths of moral surrender" (see part II below)—teaching that human beings must be passive, resign themselves to powerlessness, and submit to whatever the Divine commands, even when the commandment is immoral.[56] He describes the Bible and Judaism as launching a war against this myth, teaching that human beings must be active and empowered and that God wants to be challenged by courageous human beings who insist on justice. Feinstein locates this idea in biblical texts such as the story of Abraham at Sodom and Gomorrah, where Abraham has the chutzpah to successfully challenge God's sense of justice (Gen. 18:23–32).[57]

What about the story of the Binding of Isaac, where Abraham surrenders to God's command to sacrifice his son Isaac without challenging God's justice (Gen. 22)? Whereas Tzevi Yehudah Kook saw this story as showing Abraham's heroic "submission" (section 4.6) and Yoel Schwartz and Yitzchak Goldstein (section 4.7) note Abraham and Isaac's courageous surrender to God's will, Feinstein points to an ancient midrashic tradition in which Abraham is not silent after submitting to God's command but extracts a commitment from God that God will grant forgiveness to his descendants. Though the ancient midrash does not depict Abraham as directly challenging God's justice, Feinstein sees a note of protest and chutzpah within it that brings him to conclude that here too, Abraham is demonstrating moral courage (see part III below).[58]

Just as Feinstein differs from other sources in his understanding of Abraham, he also differs in his understanding of the courage of Rabbi Yoḥanan ben Zakkai. For Berdichevsky, ben Zakkai made a cowardly choice in not joining the Zealots defending Jerusalem. For Schwartz and Goldstein, ben Zakkai's decision to submit to the Romans showed a brave trust in divine intervention that allowed the Jewish people to live on. While, like Schwartz and Goldstein, Feinstein praises ben Zakkai for courageously acting to ensure Jewish survival, Feinstein discourages belief in a God who intervenes in history and applauds ben Zakkai for taking responsibility rather than waiting for God (see part IV below).

Whereas Berdichevsky saw heroism in fighting to defend physical territory rather than seeking to study Torah, in part V of the selection below Feinstein reverses this equation. For him, Yoḥanan ben Zakkai showed courage in fleeing Jerusalem so that Torah, rather than land, could become "the territory of Jewish life." Feinstein is by no means opposed to Jews controlling physical territory or fighting to defend it, but he admires the Rabbis who refused to valorize the Maccabees' battles and, with chutzpah, instead insisted that the spiritual task of Torah study could "illuminate a dark and cruel world."

Edward Feinstein, *The Chutzpah Imperative* (2014)

I. The dictionary defines *chutzpah* as "unmitigated effrontery or impudence; gall; audacity; nerve." . . . The word *chutzpah* . . . is found in Talmudic literature. There, it also means "arrogant" or "insolent." But in the ancient texts, *chutzpah* has a second definition. It refers to irrepressible strength, irresistible boldness. The Jerusalem Talmud declared that the Land of Israel, despite all its devastation, remains irrepressibly fertile. The term used is *chutzpah* [JT *Ta'anit* 4:5]. Likewise, the Talmud recognized that in every generation, there are certain human beings prepared to stand up in the face of any power, even God, to champion life, demand justice, and appeal for compassion. These special souls are said to display "chutzpah even in the face of heaven — *chutzpah afilu kelapei shemaya*" [BT *Sanhedrin* 105a].

Chutzpah, in this definition describes a rare quality of moral courage. This chutzpah is at the heart of Judaism. Chutzpah suggests the revolutionary conception of the human condition and our relationship to God offered by the Jewish tradition. The chutzpah of Judaism insists on the significance of human life, the possibilities of human goodness, and the depth of human responsibility to the world. It proclaims the dignity of being human and the possibilities of redemption. The message of Judaism is chutzpah.[59]

II. At the beginning of our people, Abraham was called by God: "Be a blessing. . . . And blessed in you shall be all the families of the earth" (Genesis 12:2–3). This is the perennial project of Jewish existence. It is the message and meaning of Jewish life. At this moment of history, we are called again. The Jewish people has a mission in the world. As the world becomes a global community, facing global dilemmas, we are called to teach chutzpah. We are called to overcome the allure of the ancient myth of moral surrender. We are called to reassert the Bible's ideal of human possibility and responsibility. It is the only way to muster the moral courage and imagination to meet the threats to our future.[60]

III. [In interpreting the story of the Binding of Isaac] the Rabbis of the midrash . . . [teach that] obedience to God is expressed not in silent submission, but in the protest of an Abraham who expects more from God. . . . Abraham is the father of chutzpah, a chutzpah expressed in the moral courage to stand before any authority and demand justice. Even God. The God Abraham taught us to worship not only tolerates this challenge, but cherishes it. For Abraham's God, the expression of chutzpah is itself a form of worship.[61]

IV. Rabbi Yochanan ben Zakkai . . . made a separate peace with the Roman authorities and was permitted to establish an academy near the town of Yavneh. . . . Had Yochanan ben Zakkai told his generation to sit and wait for God's redemption, had he told them to anticipate an imminent return to Temple and priests and sacrifice, holding fast to the way things had always been, we would never have survived the catastrophe of destruction in 70 CE. Within a generation, Jewish life would have disappeared. It takes a special courage to recognize that the moment demands something new. This is especially true for a culture that so reveres its past. It takes luminous creativity to conceive and shape and realize the new. And it takes deep wisdom to recognize what must change and what must remain unchanged. These qualities of leadership are the secret components of Jewish survival. At their common foundation lies the conviction that it is a human prerogative to set the terms of our covenant with God, and it is our responsibility to make a home for God in the world. This is the chutzpah of the Rabbis.[62]

V. Hanukkah celebrates the greatest military victory achieved by the Jewish people since Joshua conquered Canaan, and the only victory until the 1948 Israeli War of Independence. But the Rabbis chose this message ["Not by might, not by power, but by My Spirit . . ." (Zechariah 4:6)]. This people's power is not in military might, nor in political control, but in the life of the spirit. . . . For the Rabbis, Hanukkah celebrates the miracle of light—the persistent power of Torah's light to illuminate a dark and cruel world. Yochanan ben Zakkai fled the defense of Jerusalem to establish the academy of Yavneh. . . . Torah became the territory of Jewish life. The heroic spirit of chutzpah was sublimated into the life of learning.[63]

4.10. COURAGE TO RESIST VIOLENCE AND SEXISM

In section 2.9, we encountered Rabbi Amy Eilberg's teaching that when one is in conflict, one should refuse to view the other as an enemy and instead affirm the other as a whole human being. In part I of the text below, also from Eilberg's book *From Enemy to Friend: Jewish Wisdom and the Pursuit of Peace*, we see an expanded discussion of the importance of restraining one's animosity and defending the dignity of all human beings.

Eilberg returns us to the text from *Mishnah Avot* invoked by Cohen, Schwartz, and Goldstein that defines a hero, a person of courage, as one who conquers one's desire. Eilberg shares Cohen's goal to move beyond courage as a "merely national virtue" and to see it as a "humanitarian virtue," and like Schwartz and Goldstein she urges people to restrain themselves from the impulse to meet violence with violence. But she pushes toward deeper engagement with the other by citing an alternative formulation of *Avot's* teaching, found in the Rabbinic collection *Avot de-Rabbi Natan*, which also includes a second definition of a hero: "one who makes an enemy into a friend."

This teaching, highlighted in the title of Eilberg's book, is crucial to her efforts to push back against models of courage that idealize defeating enemies and conquering cities (as in the excerpts by Heinrich Loewe, Tzevi Yehudah Kook, and Yeshaya Margaliot). For Eilberg, courage is exemplified by those who engage peacefully with their opponents, resisting the instinctual and cultural pressures to view them as enemies and respond to them with violence. Moreover, Eilberg sees great courage in those who refrain from perpetrating damaging verbal attacks on their opponents and who recognize their opponents' strengths as well as their own weaknesses. The model she heralds is diametrically opposed to Margaliot, who saw himself as part of a pure community fighting evil enemies and sought to cultivate the courage to verbally attack and humiliate those enemies.

In part II below (the essay "On True Strength"), Eilberg further develops a nonviolent approach to strength by considering Moses' request (in Num. 13) to those scouting out the Land of Israel to ascertain the strength of the residents there. Drawing on the biblical commentary of Rashi (Rabbi Shlomo Itzhaki, eleventh-century France) and an ancient midrashic tradition that Rashi quotes, Eilberg points out that strength is not defined by "external fortifications." Today as well, those who lack inner strength but who fortify themselves with clenched fists and violent words should not be considered strong. Rather, strength may be found in inner qualities often viewed as "feminine traits" such as empathy, love, and an openness to relationship.

Realizing this, however, requires pushing back against sexist cultural norms that denigrate such traits and praise violent qualities associated with masculinity. Eilberg especially asks her audience to rebut those who, to use Heinrich Loewe's language, idealize "manly courage" demonstrated through physical strength and valor in war.

Amy Eilberg, *From Enemy to Friend* (2014) and "On True Strength" (2022)

I. At times what is required [for peacebuilding work] is the boldness and courage to speak truth and to act. At least as frequently, the peacebuilder's might is expressed in restraining oneself from speaking or acting in harmful ways, or in refusing to rush human processes that inevitably take time. . . .

Let us examine this text: . . . "Who is the greatest of heroes [or, "the most mighty"]? One who conquers one's own impulse (to evil), as it is said, 'Better to be forbearing than mighty, better to master one's own self than to conquer a city' (Proverbs 16:32). . . . And others say, [Who is the greatest of heroes?] One who makes an enemy into a friend" (Avot d'Rabbi Natan 23). The author of this and similar sources calls attention to a paradox of human nature: holding back, refraining from speaking or acting until the time is right, is not passivity. On the contrary, it takes tremendous strength to resist the impulse to do harm when we are frightened and angry, to stop and think before we respond in kind to a verbal attack. It can take all the spiritual force we can muster to scour the contents of our own soul when we would much rather rehearse the outrages committed by the other. The hero's might is apparent; these acts of powerful self-awareness and self-discipline are invisible, yet they frequently demand more rigor than we can muster.

Engaging mindfully with conflict, or helping others to do so, is hardly for the faint of heart. Working skillfully with discord requires courage to stay in the fire of conflict that many would rather flee, to tolerate strong emotion in oneself and others without betraying our own values, and to powerfully oppose parties that are acting in unjust or dangerous ways. Responding wisely and fruitfully in the midst of conflict requires speaking one's truth clearly and compellingly, but without violating the dignity of the other. . . . In the midst of impassioned debate, when it is most difficult, we must strive to recognize both our own weaknesses and the other's strengths.

Insisting on defending the dignity of all parties to the conflict, especially those whom we find threatening and those with whom we profoundly disagree, represents a bold commitment to core values, just when the rubber meets the road. Surely, it is relatively easy to love those who love us back. It is in the presence of an opponent that our moral mettle is most truly tested. When ancient instincts impel us to strike back at our adversary—verbally if not physically—it takes passionate commitment to basic moral principles to refrain. So, too, in intergroup or international contexts, determination to engage the other side without causing additional harm demands a courageous willingness to defy social and international convention that violence is the normal and expected mode of response.

Working for peace is about kindness, love, and humility, but it is also about boldness, courage, and fierce determination to work for the highest good rather than merely for immediate relief of our momentary fear, anger, or frustration. It can be some of the most challenging work we ever do, and the only kind of heroism to which we can aspire on a daily basis.[64]

II. I recently encountered a remarkable piece of Torah commentary on the Biblical story of the so-called "spies," an advance team sent to scout out the Land of Israel before the Israelites were to enter. Moses instructs the spies, "See what kind of country it is. Are the people who dwell in it strong or weak, few or many? Is the country in which they dwell good or bad? Are the towns they live in open or fortified?" (Numbers 13:18–19).

The scouts were sent to bring back a description of the land that would inspire hope in those frightened by the dangers of the conquest to come. (In the end, of course, their report turned out badly for them and the entire Israelite community.)

The information Moses asks them to bring back is telling. What kind of country is it? Are the people strong? Are they numerous? Are their towns fortified? That is to say, how hard will it be for us to conquer them? How much danger will we encounter? Can we be hopeful that we will succeed?

It seems that the hoped-for answer is that the inhabitants of the land are not too strong for us, with God's help, to overcome them. Their cities are not so fortified that we will be turned back. In other words, if they are strong fighters in armored cities, we may not be strong enough to succeed in our campaign against them.

Stunningly, Rashi (quoting a midrash from *Tanḥuma* 6) turns the text on its head. "If they live in open country, they are strong, relying on their own powers. If they live in fortified cities, they are weak" (Rashi, s.v. "strong or weak"). If you see that they need to forcefully defend their borders, there is no need for concern. These people are weak, for they need to rely on external armaments to feel strong. If you see that the inhabitants do not surround themselves with barricades, know that they are confident in their own strength.

Rashi is quoting a paradoxical teaching about strength that is profoundly important for our own lives. In contemporary culture, as apparently in the Torah, external fortifications were considered a sign of strength. Today, perhaps more than ever, those who shout with clenched fists, weaponize their words, and forcefully demean others are considered strong. Those who speak from the heart, with empathy, inviting others into relationship (qualities considered feminine traits), are deemed "weak" and therefore unfit for leadership.

In our relationships with ourselves and others, are we trapped by the old, distorted view that raised voices and rhetorical or physical threats are indicators of strength? Or can we remember (counter to cultural norms) that real strength comes from within, that the strongest power in the universe may well be love? To remember this and embody it in our lives is to push back on powerful sexist conditioning in our culture. Rashi asks us to recognize the deeper truth. As long as we are physically safe, our best strength comes from qualities of soul and the power of human connection.[65]

4.11. WHAT'S HOLDING YOU BACK?

The activist, educator, and organizer Stosh Cotler (b. 1968) has been an advocate for causes including women's rights, Palestinian rights, immigrants' rights, and racial justice. The founder of Open Hand, an organization that trained women and girls in self-defense and violence prevention, in 2005 she began working for Jewish Funds for Justice. Since 2014 she has been CEO of Jewish Funds for Justice's successor Bend the Arc, a progressive organization that seeks to create economic opportunities and secure human rights in the United States.

Encouraging American Jews to cultivate the courage — and the chutzpah — to build a more just society, Bend the Arc's website proclaims: "You've got chutzpah? We've got work to do."[66] The organization additionally identifies one of its five core values as "moral courage," explained in these terms: "We know the fight for justice and equality will not be easy or simple and requires us to take risks and act boldly. We act with integrity and we seek wisdom from our Jewish and social movement traditions to guide us."[67] Following the election of President Donald Trump in November 2016, Cotler released a statement affirming that Bend the Arc would "protest and resist . . . with passion and courage" and "remain true to the values extolled by the ancient prophets, handed down to us by our courageous ancestors, and which have guided our lives and our actions — no matter how unpopular those values may seem or how uncomfortable they may make some of our decisions."[68]

Cotler stood in particularly fierce opposition to Trump's immigration policies. In the November 2017 article excerpted below, she applauds activists who put their lives on the line to prevent the deportation of undocumented immigrants. Most American Jews are unwilling to take such risks, she says, but Jews, the people who stood up to Pharaoh and escaped slavery, must now take risks to liberate all human beings.

The Exodus, in this model, should not inspire calls to divine intervention (as we saw in Yeshaya Margaliot's admiration of Moses' courage in standing up to Pharaoh) but motivate direct human action. And rather than rouse efforts to fight unauthorized foreigners (as with Margaliot's call to fight the "mixed multitude" that infiltrated Jewish communities), the Exodus should provoke efforts to protect undocumented immigrants as part of a necessary "liberation for all people." Though she does not share Hermann Cohen's focus on theology and the virtues of monotheism, Cotler joins Cohen in praising those with the courage to risk their lives for the sake of humanitarian ideals.

Stosh Cotler, "Are Jews Avoiding Anti-Trump Activism out of Fear, or Moral Failure?" (2017)

Last month, I attended a direct action training hosted by Auburn Theological Seminary and Puente Arizona. The organizers described a high-risk action they choreographed that successfully interrupted President Trump's deportation machinery.

Activists approached deportation bus convoys carrying immigrants as they stopped at a light, several literally placing their heads under the front and back wheels of each bus as others approached the front of the bus holding a sign letting the drivers know that if they moved the bus, innocent people would die. These individuals risked their lives to get justice for America's undocumented communities.

I wept. I wondered why most members of my own American Jewish community, by comparison, would not be willing to take anything like that risk to stand up to our nation's most egregious injustices of our lifetimes, when others were risking everything.

I live in a daily state of cognitive dissonance, rage and shame that the community I love, with which I share Jewish tradition and common history, has not found the moral courage to act powerfully, and be a visible partner, in opposition to the real threat Donald Trump presents to our democracy and collective safety.

Since the start of the presidential campaign, for two years, Bend the Arc has been organizing under the banner of "We've Seen This

Before." We saw how Trump scapegoats immigrants, demonizes religious minorities, discredits the free press and incites mob and state violence. We recognized early on, in Trump and Trumpism, the signs of a dangerous, authoritarian leader and his enablers, who by threatening some of us, threaten us all.

We as Jews have seen it before, we swore never to allow it to recur. But yet, right now, only a minority of us are actively resisting.

To those who have been active and visible and vocal: I see you, honor you and I am with you. You sustain me.

But to those who have not showed up, whom I also love: What's holding you back?

Maybe you're not sure where to start? Or what to do? Perhaps it's a denial of the threat to your American Dream? Have the centuries of our collective trauma broken our spirit, are we now convinced that by putting our heads down, this menace will pass us by?

Or are there other, more corrupting reasons? Is it possible that Jewish leaders are unwilling to risk their proximity to power and its accompanying privileges? Is it possible that we're willing to trade the safety and comfort of some members of our community at the expense of so many others who live under daily threat?

Anti-Semitism's specific patterns remind us Jews won't ever be safe or free unless we link ourselves to the freedom and safety of all scapegoated and endangered communities. Pragmatically and ethically, prioritizing our "pseudo-security" over doing the right thing is both shortsighted and morally bankrupt.

I know firsthand that some Jewish communal institutions are choosing not to act out of the concern about losing donors. But ethical imperative aside, that calculation is also wrong. By "winning" this battle, you've lost the war. Young Jews see you and are repelled by your parochialism. You've just sold out the Jewish future you claim to care so much about. . . .

Many Jews are scared; I am too. But that can't prevent us from finding our collective courage to act. Working collectively and cooperatively, we can give each other the strength to engage in brave

communal conversations, advocacy, protest and even civil disobedience to fight back against the ever-looming dangers the Trump
agenda presents. . . .

If we are serious about being a people of justice who lay claim to
a liberation story of escaping slavery as a symbolic liberation for all
people, then we have no other option than to act now. History will
remember us by the choice we make today.[69]

CONCLUSION

Twentieth- and twenty-first-century Jewish thinkers have held considerably diverse perspectives on courage.

Some ideals of courage have related to diverse conceptions of God.
Some Jewish thinkers have seen courage as properly resting on a belief
in divine intervention; others have seen courage as important precisely
because there are no "guarantees of happy endings," as Sherwin Wine
puts it. Some thinkers have seen monotheism as an idea for which one
should courageously die; others have seen monotheism as a fantasy.
Some have seen Abraham's courage in his willingness to give up his
child's life; others have seen courage in Abraham's challenge of the command to sacrifice his child and in his argument with God over Sodom
and Gomorrah.

Differing conceptions of courage also reflect differing conceptions of
nationhood and inclusion. Some thinkers have seen heroism in fighting
one's enemies; others have seen heroism in martyrs who choose not
to fight their oppressors. Some have seen courage in defending fellow
citizens of one's "fatherland"; others have seen courage in risking one's
life to defend those who are not citizens.

Prominent secular Zionists, liberal anti-Zionists, Religious Zionists,
haredi anti-Zionists, and *haredi* Zionists have advanced different attitudes
toward Zionism linked with very different ideas of courage, even as they
have all argued forcefully that Jews must cultivate courage as a virtue.
Some have seen great courage in resisting Zionism, while others have
seen Zionism as the only truly courageous path for Jews to take. Some

Zionists have seen great courage as possible in the Diaspora, whereas others have believed courage is only fully possible in the Land of Israel. Both Zionists and anti-Zionists have praised the courage of violent warriors, and both Zionists and anti-Zionists have insisted that there is no heroism in violence.

Some modern Jewish thinkers have gendered courage as masculine and associate courage with the defense of patriarchy; others, like Amy Eilberg, have challenged patriarchal models of courage, calling upon modern Jews to push back against sexist cultural conditioning. Some models of courage have been linked with physical strength; other models seek to break that link.

Furthermore, we have seen courage connected with the expression of natural desires, and courage connected with the restraint of desires. Those who link courage with self-restraint often imagine self-restraint in very different ways. In the next chapter we will delve into that diversity, as we focus on self-restraint as a virtue in its own right.

5 Self-Restraint and Temperance
(*Shelitah Atzmit/Metinut*)

At least one Rabbinic tradition defines heroism in terms of self-restraint (discussed in chapter 4). Ben Zoma defines the person of courage as the one who "conquers" or "subjugates" (*kovesh*) one's "impulse," "desire," or "[evil] inclination" (*yetzer*).[1] At the same time, many Jews have understood "conquering one's impulse" or "subjugating one's evil inclination" to be a virtue in its own right. This chapter considers varying understandings of this virtue and closely related traits captured by Hebrew words such as *shelitah atzmit* (self-restraint, self-control), *ippuk* (restraint), *metinut* (temperance, moderation), *histapkut* (temperance, contentedness), and *perishut* (abstinence, asceticism).

Ancient Rabbinic sources sometimes describe the "evil inclination" (*yetzer ha-ra*, or simply *yetzer*) as a demon, residing in the human heart, that is entirely evil in nature and must be completely defeated.[2] Over time, another view became widespread among rabbis: that the evil inclination refers to physical appetites (above all, sexual appetites) within the human soul that may be restrained, subjugated, disciplined, trained, tempered, and controlled by the rational/intellectual human spirit. Influenced by a distinction in Aristotelian ethics, some medieval sources distinguish between men who must continually fight to restrain their appetites and those superior individuals who transform and train their desires so that they readily cooperate with reason.[3] Many premodern thinkers describe the study of Torah as key to either restraining or transforming the evil inclination, building on the talmudic maxim that "if this repulsive [inclination] has accosted you, drag it to the study hall" (BT *Sukkah* 52b, *Kiddushin* 30b).[4]

Ancient Rabbinic discourse on self-restraint is concerned with the efforts of men, not women. Torah study, as scholar Michael Satlow has put it, is imagined in Rabbinic literature "as the masculine activity *par excellence*."[5] Self-control is, accordingly, described as a male virtue: as Rabbi Joshua ben Levi puts it in the Babylonian Talmud (*Avodah Zarah* 19a), "Happy is he who overpowers his inclination like a man."[6] Implicit in this statement, Satlow argues, is the assumption that women lack sexual self-control and cannot overpower their inclinations, such that women pose "a particular threat to male self-control."[7] As Judith Plaskow notes in section 5.5 below, traditional Jewish discourse about controlling men's sexual desires often goes hand in hand with discourse about controlling the women who may tempt men.

While Rabbinic texts consistently condemn masturbation, homosexual behavior, and sex during menstruation, among other activities, classical Jewish law is sometimes described as "sex-positive" because of the way that it recognizes the value of sex—within heterosexual marriage, at certain times—not only for the sake of procreation but also to satisfy a wife's right to sexual pleasure (*onah*).[8] But many Rabbinic sources regard even permitted sexual pleasures in a negative light and point to an ideal of abstaining from such pleasures—"sanctifying yourself by abstaining from that which is permitted to you" (BT *Yevamot* 20a). Building on these ancient traditions, Nahmanides defined holiness in terms of abstinence (*perishut*), encouraging men to "minimize sexual intercourse" with their wives to the greatest degree possible.[9]

When it comes to questions of how to restrain appetites for food, Rabbinic traditions present a similar range of views. While Rabbinic kashrut law strictly regulates diet (especially by prohibiting nonkosher meat), many thinkers characterize Rabbinic Judaism as rejecting asceticism (see section 4.2). The Talmud does, after all, teach that one will "have to give an accounting over everything that his eye saw and he did not eat" (JT *Kiddushin* 4:12)—the implication being that God will judge those who abstain from permitted culinary pleasures. But other Rabbinic texts idealize sages who do abstain from pleasures — for example, scholars who "starve themselves" every morning (see section 5.1). *Mishnah Avot* (6:4) describes the life of Torah in these terms: "You will eat bread with salt, you will drink rationed water, you will sleep on the ground, and you will live a life of pain." Maimonides compares satisfying appetites to the disgraceful task of carrying buckets of manure from one place to another, and he urges his audience to reduce their appetites as much as possible.[10]

So too with the acquisition of wealth and possessions: though Rabbinic law places a wide range of restrictions on economic life, Rabbinic Judaism is often described as taking a "positive attitude" toward economic activity[11] and as being generally "life-affirming and this-worldly" (see section 5.7). Still, Rabbinic sources sometimes idealize voluntary poverty and the person who has no possessions — such as the Torah scholar who has no bed but "will sleep on the ground."[12] The Talmud quotes the dictum that "the Holy Blessed One scrutinized all the virtues and found poverty to be the best gift for Israel."[13] Classical musar texts may caution against forms of asceticism that are dangerous to one's health and life, but they urge separation from anything that is not essential for health and life. In the words of Rabbi Moshe Ḥayyim Luzzatto's *Path of the Upright*: "A man should abstain from things in this world which are not absolutely necessary."[14]

The texts included in this chapter respond to these premodern perspectives in diverse ways. On the whole, the voices in the first part of this chapter (sections 5.1–5.4) take a more positive approach to traditions of Rabbinic asceticism and a stringent approach toward human appetites. These Jewish thinkers admire efforts to "crush" (section 5.1), "scorn" (section 5.2), "break" (sections 5.1 and 5.3), and "struggle against" (5.4) basic desires. The voices in the second half of this chapter (sections 5.5–5.10) are less favorable toward asceticism and stress the need to significantly accommodate or honor one's appetites. Yet these thinkers differ in their approaches to concepts of control, discipline, restraint, and subjugation. Some authors appreciate disciplining (section 5.6) and restraining (sections 5.7 and 5.8) certain kinds of desires. One author sees a need to control desires but warns against damaging forms of repression (section 5.9). Another thinker emphasizes awareness of rather than control of desires (section 5.10). And yet another (section 5.5) explicitly rejects control-focused language altogether.

The various selections in this chapter focus on three major areas of human desire — sex, food, and wealth/possessions.[15] Shneur Zalman of Liadi, Ḥayyim of Volozhin, Sherwin Wine, and Sheila Peltz Weinberg (sections 5.1, 5.2, 5.6, and 5.10 respectively) give particular attention to eating. Menaḥem Mendel Lefin, Shalom Noah Berezovsky, Judith Plaskow, and Jay Michaelson (sections 5.3, 5.4, 5.5, and 5.9 respectively) focus on sex. Lefin, Eugene Borowitz and Frances Schwartz, and Lawrence Bush (sections 5.3, 5.7, and 5.8 respectively) address wealth and consumption. Together, all of these sources reveal disagreements among Jews regarding questions of desire and restraint that persist to this day.

5.1. CRUSHING BODILY DESIRES

Shneur Zalman of Liadi (c. 1745–1812) was the founding rabbi of the Hasidic sect known as Chabad (ChaBaD, an acronym for "wisdom, understanding, and knowledge"). The selections below come from his magnum opus the *Tanya*, a book of spiritual guidance for Hasidic men.[16]

Shneur Zalman's view of self-restraint is grounded in his conviction about the uniqueness of the Jewish soul (see section 8.2). Drawing on traditional kabbalistic ideas about the inferiority of non-Jews, he claims that most human beings do not possess "divine souls" and are guided by their "animal souls," characterized by appetites for pleasure as well as pride and other vices. Animal souls come from the demonic, evil "Other Side," also described as the side of the "shells" (*kelippot*, i.e., evil forces) that obscure divine light. Jews, however, have additional, immaterial "divine souls" that are "literally a part of God above."

In parts I and II below, Shneur Zalman contrasts "completely righteous" Jewish men (*tzaddikim*) with "intermediate" men (*benonim*). Very rare men — the righteous — are able to completely annihilate their appetites for pleasure and to "utterly despise the pleasures of this world." More commonly, Jews are able to ascend only to an "intermediate" stage of righteousness wherein their divine souls are sometimes able to control them but more often they are controlled by their animal souls. Those at this intermediate level, or aspiring to reach this level, are particularly in need of virtues of self-restraint so they can fight and defeat the evil appetites that constantly assail them. These appetites are especially difficult to restrain because they are not merely natural but supernatural forces, part of the cosmic evil identified with the demonic Other Side.

Restraining one's bodily appetites, moreover, means not only suppressing appetites for what is prohibited by Jewish law (e.g., nonkosher foods or forbidden sexual activities) but also inhibiting any desire to take pleasure from actions that are permitted by Jewish law (e.g., eating kosher food or engaging in permitted sex). It is possible, however, to eat or engage in sexual activity in a holy way, in service of God (*avodah be-gashmiyut*). Doing so, though, is extremely difficult. One must crush one's appetites for pleasure and partake in activities that help fend off the forces of cosmic evil that animate these appetites — fasting, study, prayer, or (as indicated in the final paragraph of the text below) meditating on the ways in which even the evil material realm is mysteriously encompassed by God.

Shneur Zalman of Liadi, *Tanya* (1796)

I. "A completely righteous man" ... has completely removed the filthy garments of evil, utterly repulsed by the pleasures of this world and by men taking pleasure in gratifying their appetites instead of serving God — for these are drawn from, and flow from, the [evil] shells and the [evil] Other Side. The completely righteous man hates all that is from the Other Side with a complete hatred, because of his great love for God and His holiness ... as it is written, "I hate them with a complete hatred" [Ps. 139:22].[17]

II. [On the other hand,] this is the character trait of the "intermediate" men and their service: subjugating the evil inclination and its [evil] thoughts that rise from the heart to the brain, and completely averting the mind from them, and thrusting it away with both hands. . . . And with each and every thrust, as he thrusts it away from his thoughts, the Other Side in this world is subjugated. . . . Therefore, a man should not be very much depressed or troubled in his heart, even though he must wage this war for all of his life, for perhaps it was for this that he was created, and this is his service: to constantly subjugate the Other Side. . . .

Even with things that are completely permitted, the more that a man sacrifices his evil inclination, even for an hour, intending to subjugate the Other Side in the left part (for example, if he desires to eat, and he delays his meal for an hour or [even] less, and he is immersed in Torah during that hour—as it is stated in the Talmud [BT *Shabbat* 10a] that the fourth hour is when all men eat but the sixth hour is when sages eat, as they would starve themselves for two hours, intending this, even though after the meal they would study for the whole rest of the day as well; or, so too, if he prevents his mouth from speaking words regarding worldly matters that his heart very much desires to express; or, so too, with [restraining] the [evil] thoughts of his mind)—even by the slightest subjugation of the Other Side in this world, the glory and holiness of the Holy Blessed One go forth above, to a great extent.[18]

III. At times, he is unable to wage [this] war with the evil inclination, sanctifying himself with regard to permitted things, because of the heaviness in his heart. Here, the advice is given in the Holy Zohar . . . : "A wooden beam that does not catch fire should be splintered . . . [so too] a body that does not accept the light of the soul within it should be crushed."

The "light of the soul" is the light of the soul and the intellect, which do not shine brightly enough so as to rule over the materiality of the body. Although he understands and contemplates God's greatness in his intellect, this is not grasped and adhered to in his brain so that he can rule over the materiality of the heart, because of the materiality and coarseness [of the brain and heart]. The cause is the coarseness of the [evil] shell that raises itself above the holy light of the [Jewish] divine soul, hiding and darkening its light. He must crush it, and cast it down to the dust, by setting times to cast himself down so that he views himself as despised and repulsive. So it is written: "a broken heart, a broken spirit" [Ps. 51:19] — this is the Other Side, which, for intermediate men, is the man himself. . . .[19]

IV. A great and fierce war is truly required to break one's evil inclination, which burns like a blazing fire, through fear of God. It is like an actual test. Therefore every man, according to his place and level in serving God, must weigh and examine himself, to see if he is serving God in a way appropriate for such a fierce war and test. This is so with regard to [taking positive steps, to] "do good" [Ps. 34:15] — for example, in serving through prayer with intention, truly pouring out his soul before God with all his strength until his soul is exhausted, and waging war against his body and the animal soul within it, which keep him from his intention in fighting the fierce war, and to crush them, and to beat them as into dust, and doing this every day before prayer, morning and evening, and also to exert himself, flesh and soul, during prayer. . . . Anyone who has not arrived at this character trait of waging the fierce war against his body has not yet reached the perspective and value [necessary] for war against the evil inclination, which burns like a blazing fire, so that one may be humbled and broken by fear of God.[20]

V. Because the soul is clothed in the body, it needs a great and fierce exertion, doubled and redoubled. First, there must be the exertion of the flesh, to crush the body and to humble it, so that it will not darken the light of the soul, as was explained above in the name of the Zohar: that "a body that does not accept the light of the soul within it should be crushed" — through penitential reflections from the depths of the heart, as is written there. Second, there must be the exertion of the soul. . . . [One] essential thing is the constant habituation of the mind and thought, so that it always remain fixed in his heart and brain that all that he sees with his eyes—the sky, and the earth and its fullness—are all the outer garments of the Blessed Holy King. In this way, he will always remember their [divine] inner nature and vitality.[21]

5.2. THE LIFE OF TORAH

During the same period that Shneur Zalman of Liadi was a prominent Hasidic leader, Ḥayyim ben Yitzḥak of Volozhin (1749–1821) was a leading rabbi among the *Mitnagdim*, the traditionalist opponents of the Hasidic movement. Though the *Mitnagdim* passionately opposed certain trends in Hasidism, the leaders of both movements voiced fairly similar teachings on self-restraint. Like Shneur Zalman, Ḥayyim was a kabbalist who saw desires for pleasure and material goods as stemming from the demonic Other Side and viewed the task of breaking such desires as difficult because of their supernatural, demonic power.

However, while Shneur Zalman saw self-restraint cultivated through a range of pietistic practices, including Torah study, Ḥayyim and his students proclaimed that Torah study was *the* central arena for the war against the evil inclination and the clear antidote to its temptations.[22] These beliefs would become famously associated with the Volozhin Yeshiva that Ḥayyim founded.

The text below is a commentary on *Mishnah Avot's* description of the life of Torah as involving only bread with salt, rationed water, sleeping on the ground, and pain. Ḥayyim appears to have taken this prescription very seriously, advocating a far more ascetic path than that taught by Shneur Zalman.[23] For Shneur Zalman, eating motivated by gratification of physical appetites was deplorable, but it was possible to eat in a holy way, in service of God; for Ḥayyim, all eating was simply disgraceful. For Shneur Zalman, unlike Ḥayyim, it was possible to affirm the material realm in part because that realm was mysteriously encompassed by God; Ḥayyim's more extreme asceticism may be linked with his stress on divine transcendence.[24] For Shneur Zalman, the material realm was ultimately a vehicle for serving God; for Ḥayyim, the material realm was much more of an obstacle to serving God. As the scholar Allan Nadler has written, the *Mitnagdim* "clearly believed that there could be no inherent spiritual value in the physical act of consumption." Its "true value was merely to provide man with the minimum strength necessary to pursue his religious agenda of Torah study and the observance of *mitzvoth*."[25]

Ḥayyim of Volozhin, *The Spirit of Life* (early nineteenth century)

A man thinks of cleaving to God—and the evil inclination comes and says, "How will you provide for your children, who are crying out for bread, when you are not able to provide it for them . . . ?" And, to this, one should reply, "This is the way of [a life of] Torah: [You will eat bread with salt, you will drink rationed water, you will sleep on the ground, and you will live a life of pain . . ." (*Mishnah Avot* 6:4)].[26]

If you are on the path to approaching God, surely you will know that if you crave sweet delicacies and worldly pleasures, you will be troubled by them all of your days, and you will not be able to avoid them—and when will you engage in Torah study? Thus you should accept upon yourself that you will study, even though you will only have dry bread dipped in water and salt, as well as no garments to protect from the cold. . . .

The truth is that this whole business of eating, whereby man's very existence is dependent upon putting a material thing into his bowels, is a great disgrace to the dignity of a human being. Now surely his soul, the spiritual part [of man], must scorn all of this with utter contempt.[27]

5.3. CONTROLLING THE ANIMAL SOUL

Menaḥem Mendel Lefin (introduced in section 1.1) did not share the severe asceticism of Ḥayyim of Volozhin. Lefin's writings instead stressed moderation, patience, and the orderly and methodical work necessary for controlling desires. But like Ḥayyim of Volozhin, Lefin was deeply opposed to Hasidism in general and the teachings of Shneur Zalman of Liadi in particular. He was particularly galled by what he saw as the irrational teachings and pietistic practices that Hasidic rabbis claimed would effectively repress and control human desires but that only inflamed desires in particularly dangerous and disturbing ways.

In part I of the selections below, from the introductory sections of Lefin's *Book of Moral Accounting*, Lefin voices concern about youth "who are scorched in the fire of fear [of God] when they rush to uproot and quickly eradicate the evil inclination, and to destroy any trace of it within the inner folds of their hearts." As historian Nancy Sinkoff has argued, Lefin here critiques the Hasidic focus on combating the evil inclination through "unbridled emotion and ecstatic worship" (*hitlahavut*) that would evoke deep awe and fear of God and stimulate the supernatural shifts necessary to combat the demonic Other Side.[28]

In section 5.1.IV, Shneur Zalman described cultivating passionate fear of God by "truly pouring out his soul before God with all his strength until his soul is exhausted, and waging war against his body and the animal soul within it" both before and during regular prayer. To Lefin, these passionate efforts to repress and crush desires, as well as Shneur Zalman's vision for how evil thoughts could ultimately be "elevated" and "purified," were irrational and counterproductive — not only deadening the intellects of those who engaged in them but in fact arousing their "animal souls." The most powerful appetites of the animal soul, which Lefin compared to an elephant, would end up trampling the "intellectual soul" of the human being.

What Lefin saw as the higher, rational part of the human soul — the "intellectual soul" or "intellectual spirit" or "human spirit" — was very different from what Shneur Zalman described as the "divine soul." Lefin rejected Kabbalah, including kabbalistic ideas that appetites are linked with supernatural, evil forces that threaten the cosmos or that Jews alone possess supernatural divine souls that are a part of God. For Lefin, seeing Jewish souls as different from non-Jewish souls, or imagining that pietistic customs or ecstatic worship will stimulate shifts in the cosmos, was nonsense — indeed, accepting irrational ideas such as these dulled the human intellect.

Informed by both medieval Jewish and modern European philoso-phy, Lefin advanced a naturalistic view of the human soul, believing that human beings were fully able to overcome their appetites without engaging supernatural forces.[29] He believed that the animal soul was "stubborn" and "stupid" but able to be trained so that it desired only what was physically necessary for the human being, and that one could otherwise "subjugate its remaining strength" to serve the intellectual soul, its proper master. Asserting the mastery of the intellectual soul over the animal soul, conquering its "stubbornness and stupidity," required understanding, cunning, fortitude, patience, and a variety of methods — sometimes harsh discipline and sometimes "gentle words." While Lefin spoke of "breaking [the animal soul's] strength" and "eradicating" its appetites, he also stressed that controlling one's animal soul required understanding and sometimes cooperating with it.

Lefin's *Book of Moral Accounting* offers a particular method for cultivat-ing moral virtue, which he adapted from the *Autobiography of Benjamin Franklin*. The core chapters of his book consider thirteen key character traits; a person was to focus on one each week, taking stock on a ledger each night of how particular virtues were reflected (or not reflected) in one's daily activities, and developing strategies for improvement. This method for spiritual growth, Lefin thought, would compete with the methods advanced by Shneur Zalman and other Hasidic preachers.[30]

In part II below (from his chapter on "frugality," *kimmutz*), Lefin's discussion of "wisdom, understanding, and knowledge" constitutes a direct attack on Shneur Zalman's "Wisdom, Understanding, and Knowl-edge" (=ChaBaD) movement. Like Shneur Zalman and Ḥayyim, Lefin idealized abstinence from worldly pleasures, but he saw Shneur Zalman and other Hasidic leaders as hypocrites who praised self-restraint but in fact encouraged profligacy. They promised Jews that their prayers would be answered if they gave monetary donations to Hasidic masters — but then the masters wasted much of that money on their own elaborate silk robes and jewelry.[31] Rather than squandering wealth on such luxuries that might provide immediate gratification, Lefin urged his audience to "forgo all of the pleasures of this world" and focus on the greater pleasures of the world to come.

In part III (from the chapter on "separation" or "abstinence," *perishut*), Lefin discusses how his male audience might abstain from lustful thoughts. Like Shneur Zalman and Ḥayyim, he sees Torah as a remedy for the evil inclination, though unlike Shneur Zalman he forgoes talk of other remedies, and unlike Ḥayyim he associates Torah study not with pain and hardship but with focus and order. Sexuality, for Lefin, is not inherently evil, though it must clearly be confined to its proper place within heterosexual marriage and its proper purpose in fulfilling the commandments.

Menaḥem Mendel Lefin, *The Book of Moral Accounting* (1808)

I. The man who has understanding and cunning and who controls his spirit can motivate [his appetitive] animal soul for his own good, in accordance with his will. . . . God, who gave man the dominion to utilize the wind to winnow grain, to turn mills, and to move loaded ships across the earth for his benefit and pleasure, also gave him the understanding [*da'at*] to control the "animal soul." . . . He can even command the might of an elephant, and train it to accept the mastery of its owner, to look forward to his stable, and to serve him with all its strength. . . .

For its master, the human spirit, the animal soul [must] only fulfill its physical needs and subjugate its remaining strength to serve its master. The intellectual soul needs to engage in much work, however, to teach discipline to [the animal soul] and various character traits for its whole life. It must humble itself to understand the lowly [animal] soul . . . so that it may learn to discern when it needs to discipline it with whips, and when it needs to conquer its stubbornness and stupidity using gentle words. Moreover, [the intellectual spirit] is itself in constant danger of drowning amid the appetites of the animal soul. . . .

In our era, because of our great sins, there are stories every day of fine people, in the heated time of their youth, who are scorched in the fire of fear [of God] when they rush to uproot and quickly eradicate the evil inclination, and to destroy any trace of it within the inner folds of their hearts. As a result they drown in black bitterness and in the dullness of their understanding—that is, with their intellectual souls dead and trampled by the elephant. . . .

[But through our method of moral accounting] a man can subdue the evil inclination and break its strength, such that even if it demands something for the health of the body, he can deny its request and overcome it, until its appetite is completely eradicated. And then he can fulfill the physical need through considering the counsel of his intellectual spirit.[32]

II. The "wisdom, understanding, and knowledge"[33] praised by the masses are a tapestry of lies, flattery, hypocrisy, misrepresentation, slander, mockery, and so on. Who is [considered] "wise"?[34] One who knows how to profit from the losses of others. . . . And who is [considered] "honored"? One who knows how to squander one's money and the money of others so as to gain honor from their disgrace. This is the path of these "honored" ones: every day, they invent new customs for squandering on clothing, jewelry, and charities that are grander than those of others—so that they can embarrass those who are needy and gain honor for themselves. . . .

[But] "who is [truly] wise? One who can see the future results of an act" [BT *Tamid* 32a]. An animal can see only what is in front of it, and it will follow a bundle of hay that leads it to its slaughter. But the human being was granted understanding to forgo the present for the sake of something more valuable in the future, and [to forgo] something good for the sake of something better, even if it will not come for a long time. Those who are truly wise forgo all of the pleasures of this world for the sake of the future that will come after death. "And who is honorable? One who honors others" [*Mishnah Avot* 4:1]—who is frugal with oneself and benevolent toward others. It is fitting for the righteous and the wise to limit their animalistic pleasures and instead to enjoy the pleasures of the intellectual soul.[35]

SELF-RESTRAINT AND TEMPERANCE

III. Strengthen yourself, so that you may refrain from lustful thoughts, and draw close to your wife only when your mind is free to [focus on] fulfilling the commandment to provide sexual pleasure [*onah*] or the commandment to procreate. . . . [When confronted by thoughts of sin,] one who is in this process of education must be quick to destroy this [thought] that is gestating. . . . When he has introduced some new thought, then he can easily abstain from thoughts of sin with the help of the character trait of "order" and the conclusion of the key phrase [associated with order]: "Let your thoughts be free to focus on what is before you."[36] Our sages of blessed memory have said: "If this repulsive [inclination] has accosted you, drag it to the study hall" [BT *Sukkah* 52b, *Kiddushin* 30b]. And this is the most appropriate advice, as its benefit is immediate, since we may find words of Torah in every place and at all times.[37]

5.4. SEXUAL ABSTINENCE FOR MARRIED MEN

In section 3.5, the Hasidic leader Rabbi Shalom Noah Berezovsky taught that one should nullify one's material self, allow oneself to be wholly possessed by God, and seek no pleasure or benefit for oneself. As his musar book *Netivot Shalom* details, this requires not only restraining desires for that which is prohibited by Jewish law but also "sanctifying yourself by abstaining from that which is permitted to you" (BT *Yevamot* 20a), including one's desires for kosher food or permitted sexual relations. While Shneur Zalman of Liadi used the same language (see section 5.1.III), Berezovsky went farther than Shneur Zalman or Ḥayyim of Volozhin, arguing that pleasure is not permitted unless it is *required* by Jewish law. (In such a case it is not merely "permitted," which implies that you could choose not to experience it; it's an obligation, where you have no choice in the matter.) As Berezovsky put it, "The truth is that nothing is 'permitted'; everything is either an obligation or a prohibition."[38]

When teaching young men how to approach sex with their wives, Berezovsky encouraged them to meet their obligation to have sex with their wives once a month (on *leil tevilah*, the night of a wife's monthly immersion in the *mikveh* following menstruation) but to take as little pleasure as possible from sex and to weep at the prospect of experiencing pleasure. In the text below, distributed to many Slonim Hasidic men after three months of marriage, Berezovsky urged them to look to exemplars in the Hasidic movement who successfully abstained from sex to the greatest degree possible — even, for example, the Hasidic master Avraham "the Angel" (1740–76), who refrained from intercourse with his wife altogether and was willing to risk being denied a place in the world to come for transgressing the normative requirement to engage in monthly intercourse.

Like his fellow Hasidic leader Shneur Zalman, and like Ḥayyim of Volozhin, Berezovsky saw the demonic Other Side, its *kelippot* (shells), and its evil inclination as powerful forces that needed to be battled with great force. Like Shneur Zalman, he saw "Torah study" as an important but insufficient tool for fighting the blazing fire of the evil inclination. But more than Shneur Zalman or Ḥayyim or Lefin, Berezovsky stressed what he saw as the gravest of threats: the temptation to find sexual pleasure within heterosexual marriage.[39] Showing little concern for the pain that the battle against the evil inclination might cause others, he encouraged the married man to risk not only his own life but also the lives of "his wife and family members."

In section 3.5 Berezovsky depicted women passively humbling themselves as their husbands "acquired them." The text below further elucidates Berezovsky's view of men as the active partners in marriage: the obligation to cultivate self-restraint rests on men, who, unlike women, are capable of self-restraint. Berezovsky charges his male reader to act as "a man, and not a woman" — to show the self-restraint that only men are able to achieve.

Shalom Noah Berezovsky, "The Three Months Letter" (1957)

The early Hasidim of the previous generation, whom we were privileged to witness, had shed their sweat and blood in the struggle against permitted pleasures, in just the same way as those who struggle [to refrain from] the most strictly prohibited acts. . . . When someone

149

once said to Rabbi Avraham the Angel, who practiced strict sexual abstinence, that by this he was bound to lose his [share in] the world to come, he replied: "The world to come is worth losing in order to avoid the pleasures of this world." Some of them would weep copiously every *leil tevilah* [the monthly time when sexual intercourse is required].[40] They would repent the required [and permitted sexual act] just as one repents a grave sin, lest their bodies experience physical pleasure. They feared the *kelippah* [evil force, shell] of permission more than the *kelippah* of prohibition. . . . Such was their holiness. And we—what are we by comparison, whose hearts are weak and whose brains are dull?! For when the heart and the brains fail to function, the liver, where lust dwells, takes hold of the body. The boiling, impure blood overflows, and the evil inclination burns like fire, even among those who are engaged in Torah [study] and mitzvot all day long. . . .

One should know how to act as a faithful soldier who is willing to die for the sake of victory, not sparing either his own life or that of his wife and family members. Self-sacrifice, blood, tears, and sweat are required. . . . "Be thou strong therefore, and show thyself a man" [1 Kings 2:2]—a man, and not a woman.[41]

5.5. "TOWARDS A NEW THEOLOGY OF SEXUALITY"

In section 1.6, the American Jewish feminist theologian Judith Plaskow encouraged rabbis to teach about painful, patriarchal aspects of Jewish tradition. In the selections below, Plaskow focuses on what she calls the "energy/control model" of sexuality, the patriarchal view (endorsed by all of the above sources) that sexuality is an evil inclination or dangerous form of energy that must be restrained or controlled.

Plaskow argues that this paradigm is closely linked with two other views: that all proper sexual expression must take place within the confines of heterosexual marriage; and that women's sexuality must be possessed and controlled by men. Since, according to this paradigm, men have the ability to restrain themselves but women do not, men must control women's desires as well as their own. Indeed, what has helped men control their desires, Plaskow argues, is controlling women by keeping them out of sight and within the confines of heterosexual families. In Plaskow's view, this model also diminishes passion and feeling among human beings, damaging not only sexual relationships but also the very capacity to relate with feeling to human beings and to God.

In rejecting the energy/control paradigm and its concept of sexuality as a "separate and alien energy," Plaskow advances the feminist idea that human beings should regard sexuality as part of an empowering erotic energy that provokes our capacity to feel and that "ideally suffuses all activities in our lives."[42] When we repress sexual feelings, we damage this very capacity to feel. Because feeling is essential to knowing and to valuing, we repress our capacity to know and to value. Because feeling is essential to our relations with others, we repress our capacity for positive social relations. Because feeling is essential to spirituality, we repress our capacity to fully love God.

Elsewhere, Plaskow points to Jewish traditions that see erotic energy in positive terms: for example, the biblical Song of Songs appears to value a model of "sensual delight and sexual equality" that may also serve as a model for loving God.[43] As she emphasizes in the selection below, while she does not think that people should act on all of their sexual feelings, have more sex, or embrace an ideology of "free sex," nonetheless sexual feelings should not be controlled or repressed; they must be honored.

Judith Plaskow, "Towards a New Theology of Sexuality" (1989)

An emphasis on control is central to Jewish understandings of sexuality. From the viewpoint of the tradition's "energy/control" model, sexuality is an independent and sometimes alien energy that must be held in check through personal discipline and religious constraints. While the sexual impulse is given by God and thus is a normal and healthy part of human life, sanctified within its proper framework, sexuality also requires careful, sometimes rigorous control in order that it not violate the boundaries assigned it. . . .

While moral norms concerning sexuality generally apply both to men and women, women play a special role in the Jewish understanding of sexuality. They are the ubiquitous temptations, the sources and symbols of illicit desire, the ones whose sexuality threatens even their husbands/possessors with the possibility of illegal action. To speak of control is necessarily to speak of women—of the need to cover them, avoid them, and contain them in proper (patriarchal) families where their threat is minimized if it cannot be overcome. Laws concerning marriage and divorce decrease the danger of women's sexuality by providing for the acquisition and relinquishment of male rights to that sexuality. Marriage brings the "wild and unruly potentialities of female sexuality" under control by designating a woman's sexuality as a particular man's possession.

The control of women's sexuality and its role in the institution of the family, the normativeness of heterosexuality, and the energy/control paradigm of sexuality are all connected pieces of a patriarchal understanding of sexuality. Where women's sexuality is seen as an object to be possessed, and sexuality is confined to heterosexual marriage and perceived as an impulse that can take possession of the self, the central issues surrounding sexuality will necessarily be issues of control. The question then becomes how a positive Jewish feminist discourse about sexuality can move beyond this patriarchal framework, not only rejecting its ethical implications but defining sexuality in fundamentally different terms.

In the past twenty years, feminists have reconceptualized the nature and functions of human sexuality, generating alternatives to the energy/control model that potentially establish our thinking about sexuality on new foundations. Rather than seeing sexuality as a separate and alien energy that can engulf the self, feminists have described it as part of a continuum of embodied self-expression, or as part of a spectrum of erotic energy that ideally suffuses all activities in our lives. . . .

This view of sexuality as part of a spectrum of body/life energy rather than a special force or evil inclination has at least two important implications for understanding the place of sexuality in human life.

First of all, it challenges the value of control by suggesting that we cannot suppress sexual feelings without suppressing our capacity for feeling in general. If sexuality is one dimension of our ability to live passionately in the world, then in cutting off our sexuality, we diminish our overall power to feel, know, and value deeply. While the connection between sexuality and feeling does not compel us to act out all our sexual feelings, it does mean we must honor and make room for feelings—including sexual ones—as "the basic ingredient in our relational transaction with the world."

Second, insofar as sexuality is an element in the embodiment that mediates our relation to reality, an aspect of the life energy that enables us to connect with others in creativity and joy, sexuality is profoundly connected to spirituality, indeed is inseparable from it. Sexuality is that part of us through which we reach out to other persons and to God, expressing the need for relationship, for the sharing of self and of meaning. When we touch that place in our lives where sexuality and spirituality come together, we touch our wholeness and the fullness of our power, and at the same time our connection with a power larger than ourselves. . . .

If we take sexuality seriously . . . as an expression of our embodiment that cannot be disconnected from our wider ability to interact feelingly with the world, then to learn fear and shame of our own bodies and those of others—even when these feelings are intermixed with other conflicting attitudes—is to learn suspicion of feeling as a basic way of valuing and knowing. We should not expect, then, to be able to block out our sexual feelings without blocking out the longing for social relations rooted in mutuality rather than hierarchy, without blocking out the anger that warns us that something is amiss in our present social arrangements, without blocking and distorting the fullness of our love for God.

I am not arguing here for free sex or for more sexual expression, quantitatively speaking. I am arguing for living dangerously, for choosing to take responsibility for working through the possible consequences of sexual feeling rather than repressing sexual feeling and thus repressing feeling in general. I am arguing that our capacity to transform Judaism and the world is rooted in our capacity to be alive to the pain and anger that is caused by relationships of domination, and to the joy that awaits us on the other side. I am arguing that to be alive is to be sexually alive, and that in suppressing one sort of vitality, we suppress the other. The question becomes, then: can we affirm our sexuality as the gift it is, making it sacred not by cordoning off pieces of it, but by increasing our awareness of the ways in which it connects us to all things? Can we stop evicting our sexuality from the synagogue ... and instead bring it in, offering it to God in the experience of full spiritual/physical connection? Dare we trust our capacity for joy—knowing it is related to our sexuality—to point the direction toward new and different ways of structuring communal life?[44]

5.6. SECULAR RATIONAL GUILT AND DIETARY DISCIPLINE

In section 4.8, the Humanistic rabbi Sherwin Wine described pleasure as part of "the real world" that offers opportunity to human beings, pointed to the importance of "passion and emotional power" in providing a foundation for reason, and expressed concern about those who seek to cover up their feelings, while also acknowledging the importance of controlling feelings. In part I of the selection below, we see Wine build on these ideas about passion, feeling, and pleasure, affirming the value of rational self-control and rational guilt while rejecting the ideal of eliminating natural desires.

In Wine's view, one of the failures of traditional religion—well exemplified by the teachings of Shneur Zalman of Liadi, Ḥayyim of Volozhin, Menaḥem Mendel Lefin, and Shalom Noah Berezovsky—is its teaching an impossible ideal of eliminating bodily lusts and then teaching people to feel guilty when they fail to meet this ideal. Wine applauds the psychoanalyst Sigmund Freud (one of many Jewish thinkers who inspired Wine's Jewish Secular Humanism) for pointing to the problems with such guilt and with repressing sexual desires.

Wine distinguishes this "irrational guilt"—feeling guilty about what is simply human nature—from "rational guilt." One should *not* condone all of one's desires, and one *should* feel guilty about failures to act morally. While we cannot hope to eliminate natural desires or feelings, we can tame and discipline them so as to reduce the harms we cause to ourselves and to others.

Part II, a selection from an essay Wine wrote on "dietary laws" among Secular Humanist Jews, exemplifies how Wine appreciated secular efforts to discipline desires. He observes contemporary secular American Jews taking virtues of moderation and self-restraint more seriously than many Orthodox Jews who adopt certain forms of restraint but engage in unhealthy behaviors. To Wine, Orthodox Jews who keep kosher are committing themselves to an antiquated system that they (irrationally) see as divine, while (irrationally) disregarding scientific evidence about what forms of discipline would be healthy for human beings.

Unlike those who eschew the language of "control," Wine embraces such language. And unlike those who simply want to "live and let live" and see no place for judgment and guilt, Wine judges those who make poor choices and seeks to guide them to adopt more rational, scientific, nonreligious forms of self-restraint.

Sherwin Wine, *Staying Sane in a Crazy World* (1990) and "Our Dietary Laws" (1995)

I. Guilt is no longer fashionable. In "liberated" circles it has been the enemy for the past ninety years. . . . The assault on guilt is a passionate response to a world where guilt reigned supreme. In the world of traditional religion sin was an obsession. Almost any desire or pleasure had sinful possibilities. The safest way to live was to resist desire and to avoid pleasure. Since bodily lusts are hard to dismiss, people walked around in a perpetual state of guilt. Only confession and priestly absolution provided any form of relief. The Freudian revolution was a rebellion against this cruel regime. Sexual desire became normal. Repressing it became dangerous. . . .

Guilt turned into a dirty word. It became a symbol of psychic repression. . . . Feeling guilty was now an embarrassment. It was a sign of mental disturbance, a sure indication that you were unable to accept your true feelings and desires. Transcending guilt was now the goal of mentally healthy people. Healthy people never tried to impose their moral standards on others. They lived and let live. They found no significant place for guilt in their lives. Morality was a personal choice. Understanding, tolerance and self-acceptance were to replace the tyranny of the old shame. . . . The battle against irrational guilt turned into the battle against guilt.

[But] guilt is a perfectly normal emotion. Like all human emotions that have survived the test of evolution, it has its place in the human repertory of useful feelings. . . . People who are disposed to too much guilt become either too fearful or too ascetic. Men and women who have no capacity for guilt are emotional defectives and become socio-paths. . . . People without guilt are people without conscience. . . .

Irrational guilt . . . assaults human nature and insists that it be different from what it is. It is uncomfortable with human desire and demands that it disappear. Trying to quench desire is a hard assignment. We can tame our feelings but we cannot dismiss them. Lust cannot be commanded to go away. . . . Irrational guilt, as Freud pointed out, must be unmasked for what it is and then dismissed. It stands in the way of human happiness and survival. Rational guilt, on the other hand, must be cultivated.[45]

II. In this age of scientific nutrition, laissez-faire food consumption has become about as rational as diving from an airplane without a parachute. Every day modern medicine warns us of more and more dangers to our bodies and to our survival. The most delicious pleasures of life are diminished as we surrender to the discipline of health and fitness. Giving up hot fudge for celery may be far more traumatic then giving up pork for mutton.

Recently, I was on a panel with an Orthodox rabbi who was over-weight and a chain smoker. He spent most of his time praising the dietary laws and how they instill a sense of discipline into the daily life of the Jew. Each statement about discipline was punctuated by a long puff of his cigarette, leading up to the finale: a racking cough.

I told him that, from my point of view, tobacco was more dangerous than shrimp, and fried schmaltz was more devastating than lean pork. I also pointed out to him that, when it comes to dietary discipline, no generation of Jews since the Exodus has been more disciplined than the health-craving, weight-watching, pleasure-curtailing secular Jews of modern America.

But we refuse to give ourselves credit for what we do. We are always falling into the Orthodox trap of complaining how discipline has fallen out of Jewish life, of how hedonism with its short-run pleasures and absence of long-run goals has subverted the solid values of traditional Judaism. We fail to see our own stern regimen simply because nobody has bothered to turn it into a divine decree.

Of course Humanistic Jews have dietary laws. They are not the same as the Orthodox. They are not absolute; new evidence constantly forces us to review them. They are not universal; there are different formulas for different physiques. They are not cruel; excommunication or execution seems a harsh penalty for refusing to take care of one's own health. They are not relentless; lapses are only human and moderation makes sense. But they are more than suggestions. They flow from the collective wisdom of the scientific community.

When I teach young children, I have no reluctance to tell them not to smoke tobacco. I believe the evidence is pretty overwhelming that smoking can give them cancer. I do not threaten communal punishment or advocate that their right to smoke in private be taken away. But my responsibility is to encourage them to exercise the discipline that is necessary to their health.

Health is a Jewish value (though not an exclusively Jewish one). It is as important a value as Jewish identity. It needs both information and discipline to make it real.[46]

5.7. RESTRAINT IN AN AGE OF AFFLUENCE

Rabbi Eugene Borowitz (1924–2016) was an influential theologian who taught for many years at the Reform movement's Hebrew Union

College–Jewish Institute of Religion. He is particularly well known for *Renewing the Covenant: A Theology for the Postmodern Jew*, which encourages Jews to reject both Orthodoxy and secularism and instead commit to a personal, covenantal relationship with God informed by both personal autonomy and engagement with Jewish tradition and community.

In *Renewing the Covenant* Borowitz challenges the rationalist view, common among liberal Jews, that "we could tame the beast [the evil inclination] by the full development of our human powers" and instead appreciates what he describes as the view of "the rabbis" — "that we could fend off its attacks by our unremitting effort and discipline coupled with a reliance on Torah's power and God's loving help."[47] Borowitz sees the importance of cultivating self-restraint and discipline, but he is deeply skeptical of rationalist models — such as Sherwin Wine's — that describe human reason as having sufficiently great power to control human drives. In his view, God must play a role as well. Whereas Wine left the Reform movement because it was overly focused on God, Torah, and religious tradition, Borowitz sought to focus the Reform movement more deeply on God, Torah, and religious tradition.

With the educator Frances Weinman Schwartz, Borowitz coauthored *The Jewish Moral Virtues*, a book designed to expose American Jewish readers to a range of traditional Jewish virtues and encourage them "to make musar literature a conscious part of your Jewish self."[48] The selection below, taken from the chapter on *histapkut* (contentedness, simplicity, or temperance), addresses questions of self-restraint regarding wealth and possessions.

Unlike Menaḥem Mendel Lefin (section 5.3), Borowitz and Schwartz do not idealize forgoing all worldly pleasures. Uncomfortable with the "extreme self-restraint" advocated in most classical musar literature, they advance what they term "reasonable self-restraint." As they acknowledge, their notions of frugality have been shaped by living in an affluent society, and they cannot easily condemn themselves or their readers for enjoying luxuries. Further, though Borowitz and Schwartz see simplicity as an important value and invoke the wisdom of the Yiddish saying "Tsu feel iz umgezunt" (Too much is not healthy), they see Judaism as affirming the value of "this-worldly" pleasures. Unlike Lefin, they do not speak of the greater value of immaterial pleasures promised after death; nor do they argue that intellectual pleasures are the greatest pleasures of all.

Eugene Borowitz and Frances Weinman Schwartz, *The Jewish Moral Virtues* (1999)

What a revolution we'd witness in our society if a measure of self-restraint, of being content with what we have, suddenly became an honored American character trait. . . .

[Too often] we become the slaves of our passions. Maybe it's too messianic to hope, mere mortals that we are, that we can consistently dominate our baser side, but it would be absolutely unworthy of us—and certainly a blot on our Judaism—not to try. Maybe we should start by a stiff regimen of impulse control and then revert to the obvious good sense of "Enough already!" . . .

While "delayed gratification," "making do," and "settling" often sound strange to members of the "X" generation, they were staples of wisdom for those who grew up in the aftermath of the Great Depression. Money was truly scarce, though not as limited as in many a shtetl home, where one learned to cope with only two changes of clothing, an "everyday" and a "*yom tov*," special occasion outfit. No wonder our Sephardic folk wisdom said: "Bread for two will also satisfy three" and "When you eat and leave some on your plate, it's like setting a table for two meals" (Ladino proverbs). We like the Yiddish proverb: "Be frugal and you won't need loans," which we update as ". . . and you won't max out your credit cards."

Yet for all of the explicit wisdom we may reap from our tradition, we feel more than a tad uneasy about transmitting all this inspirational *musar* of extreme self-restraint and penny-watching. We sit in our plush studies, using computers costing several thousand dollars. We drive cars not only heated and air-conditioned, but often equipped with multiple speakers, CD players, and portable telephones. Even when sending off our children on their "European experience," with only a backpack to see them through many weeks of travel, we make sure that they carry a credit card, "just in case." We may momentarily be warmed by the ideal of *histapkut* when we hear that our frightfully poor ancestors tried hard to be happy with their lot. But we know that it won't be long before we are again dreaming about owning our own sun-bathed island (or wherever your dream finds you). After all, isn't Judaism life-affirming and this-worldly? Aren't there plenty of texts that urge us to enjoy life? After all, Jacob received his blessing from Isaac, his father, only after bringing him a pot full of savory food (Gen. 27:25). And Esther saved her people from certain death at the hands of Haman after throwing not one, but two banquets and lulling the villain into a wine-soaked, food-satiated smugness (Est. 5:4–8).

The simple truth is that contemporary American affluence has radically altered our notion of *tsu feel iz umgezunt*. We take pride in our own "disposable income," and we consider it an important learning tool to give our children regular allowances, part of which they may spend at their discretion. Perhaps if we followed the notion of spending only to satisfy our needs, we might become like those benefactors we hear about who live in radical self-denial and then give millions to a particular school's scholarship fund or double a museum's already splendiferous collection of paintings. But as numerous commentators have pointed out, only if we show a little self-love can we genuinely love our neighbor as ourselves. But by accepting our somewhat well-to-do status, we have made the problem of living with reasonable self-restraint more complicated. . . .

We quickly admit that opportunity and means do not refute old wisdom—they just increase temptation and make the need for strength of Jewish character all the more important.[49]

5.8. RESTRAINT IN AN ERA OF ENVIRONMENTAL CRISIS

In 2005 the Coalition on the Environment and Jewish Life (COEJL) released the "rabbinical letter" excerpted below, offering a model for how rabbis in the United States might speak to Jews about their responsibilities to protect the environment. Lawrence Bush (b. 1951), editor of the secular *Jewish Currents* magazine, authored the text after consultation with a team of rabbis and Jewish leaders who identified with a range of American Jewish movements (including Conservative, Orthodox, Reconstructionist, and Reform Judaism).[50]

The letter is filled with references to God and Rabbinic texts and concepts, and Bush—a declared secularist—has confessed that he felt "qualms about trafficking in religious imagery." But he decided, "If I can help rabbis guide people towards environmental sanity through the exercise of religious metaphors, I should seize the opportunity. When it comes to our planet's environment, the time is too short for me to be a 'fundamentalist' secularist." Moreover, Bush found much to admire in the traditional Jewish texts regarding restraint and wonder that he explored in the document.[51]

As a result, Bush's secularism here is far more affirming of Rabbinic texts and traditions than Sherwin Wine's. Notably, for example, while Wine derides the laws of kashrut, Bush's letter affirms their value in cultivating restraint.

The excerpts below begin with some of the texts cited in support of environmental protection and restraint. Among them is the line from Shneur Zalman's *Tanya* (section 5.1.V) affirming that "sky, earth and its fullness" lack independent status but are God's outer garments; looking beyond these outer garments will reveal higher aspects of God, just as looking beyond one's material desires will reveal God in God's immateriality. Shneur Zalman was hardly affirming the value of the material realm; in fact, he called for harsh efforts to crush material desires. Bush's letter, however, uses Shneur Zalman's teaching to contend that the material realm should be protected rather than crushed. In this letter, human self-restraint is a virtue precisely because it can help human beings protect the goodness of the material world around them.

The letter is able to draw further support for its vision of restraint by pointing to a range of halakhic obligations that demand self-restraint: the laws that curtail labor on Shabbat; the laws of kashrut that require forgoing certain foods; the laws of *bal tashchit* (alternatively, *lo tashchit*) that restrain economic activity by prohibiting unnecessary damage or waste; the laws of *tza'ar ba'alei ḥayyim* that prohibit causing unnecessary suffering to animals; and a number of other legal principles and values requiring human restraint.

The selection ends with a call to emulate a quality often ascribed to God in kabbalistic tradition: God engages in *tsimtsum*, contraction or "self-withdrawal," so that the universe has space to emerge. Bush's text calls on humans to similarly restrain ourselves from the consumption that is otherwise likely to lead to environmental catastrophe. Forgoing the ascetic models of emulating God championed by the kabbalists Shneur Zalman, Ḥayyim, and Berezovsky, Bush affirms a very different model of emulating God that seeks to protect the material world.

Lawrence Bush et al., "Wonder and Restraint" (2005)

We are moved by psalms of praise and blessing — "You have gladdened me by Your deeds, O Lord; I shout for joy at Your handiwork . . ." (Psalm 92). We have studied the texts of Mishnah and Gemara explicating the Halachic duties derived from the law of lo tashchit, "you shall not waste" (Deut. 20:19). We take to heart the curses of Deuteronomy 28, which chillingly resemble the environmental catastrophes now being predicted by an overwhelming majority of the scientific community: "The Lord will strike you . . . with scorching heat and drought, with blight and mildew . . ." We are inspired by the proclamations of the kabbalists and the Hasidic rebbes — "All that we see, sky, earth and its fullness, are God's outer garment" (Rebbe Shneur Zalman, *Tanya*).

Yet we worry that the same factors of abundance and alienation in modern life that have inured people to the pleading voices of nature could inure them, as well, to these voices of Torah. . . .

Two covenantal responsibilities apply most directly to the environmental challenges of our time. The first demands inwardness, the second, outwardness. The first fulfills the traditional Jewish role as a "holy nation," the second, as a "light unto the nations."

The first, in a word, is *restraint*: to practice restraint in our individual and communal lives. Judaism encourages this sensibility in many of its most fundamental metaphors and mitzvot.

There is the restraint embodied by Shabbat, our central holy day of wholeness and not-producing. There is the restraint expressed through kashrut, dietary consciousness, which gives us an appetite for sacredness instead of gluttony.

There is the restraint expressed as *bal tashchit*, the injunction against wanton destruction that is rooted in the Torah's responses to the environmental ravages of warfare, and as *tza'ar ba'alei ḥayyim*, pity for the suffering of living creatures, requiring us to treat our fellow creatures as sentient beings, not as objects for exploitation.

There is the restraint required to fulfill the demands of *kehillah* — the communal and intergenerational obligations that Judaism applies to our wealth, our private property, our decision-making, and our salvation. In the tradition of Maimonides, modesty and open-handed generosity have long been hallmarks of Jewish life.

There is the restraint implied by *shmirat haguf*, protection of our own bodies, and by *pikuakh nefesh*, the commandment to protect life at nearly any cost. There is the restraint mandated by *s'yag l'Torah*, building a "fence around the Torah," which bids us to err on the side of caution when it comes to matters of life, limb and spiritual integrity, all of which are surely endangered by the destruction of biological diversity and the degradation of the biosphere, most obviously by the catastrophes likely to be induced by global warming.

In the Jewish mystical tradition, it is God who sets the example of restraint by practicing tsimtsum, self-withdrawal, in order to permit the universe to emerge into being. The mystics, drawing upon the Talmud (BT Chagigah 12a), linked this creation story to the appellation Shaddai, usually translated to mean "Almighty," but understood by mystics as the One Who said to the infant universe, "dai," "enough," and thus gave form and boundary to the chaos.

Today, we who are made in the image of Shaddai must emulate this act of tsimtsum if we want our world to persist in health and abundance. Human activity is now as consequential to the Earth and its wealth of species as glaciers, volcanoes, winds and tides, so we cannot persist in the illusion that the world is inexhaustible. Human activity has split the seas, brought down manna from heaven, cured pestilence, built vast tabernacles, so we cannot continue to quake and stammer at the prospect of assuming the responsibility given to us along with our power. Instead, we must transform ourselves from nature's children to nature's guardians by learning to say "dai," "enough," to ourselves.

But not only to ourselves: for the second covenantal obligation that our Earth and our faith require is that we speak out, and speak truth, to the world's leaders. . . .[52]

5.9. GAY LIBERATION

The scholar, educator, and activist Rabbi Jay Michaelson (b. 1971) has written extensively on questions of LGBTQ religious identity. In the Torah commentary from which the selection below is taken, he affirms and envisions gay liberation through a discussion of the Exodus from Egypt, which he describes as "not just a liberation story but an affirmation of love and life."[53]

For Michaelson, Jews who demand sexual repression are speaking like Egyptians. They are failing to grasp the message of Judaism and its Exodus story: "The sweep of the Israelite narrative is unmistakable" in rejecting repression and affirming life. While he acknowledges that "there are contrary voices" in Judaism including "ascetic ones that demand more repression than expression," he insists that "repression of one's basic orientation to love" is not a Jewish value.[54]

His views are in particularly strong contrast with those of Shneur Zalman and Berezovsky. Whereas Shneur Zalman insisted that God requires human efforts to constantly subjugate desire, Michaelson insists that the human impetus to love must not be subjugated to anything else. Whereas Shneur Zalman spoke of crushing the body and its appetites and casting them to the dust, Michaelson teaches that God does not want the heart and its longings to be trampled. Whereas Berezovsky asked men to be willing to die for the sake of victory against the appetite for sexual pleasure, Michaelson affirms life as a supreme value.

Whereas Berezovsky idealized those who engaged in self-sacrifice to achieve holiness, Michaelson rejects "making sacrifices in the name of holiness." Like Judith Plaskow (section 5.5), he sees repression as contrary to holiness, although unlike Plaskow he speaks of "control" in positive terms: "Although control is often a Jewish value, repression of one's basic orientation to love is not."

Jay Michaelson, "Into Life: The Humanism of the Exodus" (2009)

The exodus from Egypt is one from death into life — from a culture that denies this world to one that embraces it. . . .

If we look closely at the basis of liberated sexuality, at its core is a value of life as opposed to death: expression over repression, love over fear, the flowering of human potential over the trampling of it in the name of something else. Obviously, this is not an unmitigated hedonism; the acceptance of one's sexuality does not imply the indulgence in all one's passing lusts or whims. But it is a fundamental affirmation of the goodness of human life and a rejection of the claim that the basic human impetus to love, and to express that love in an embodied way, is to be subjugated to something else.

After all, it is *possible* for a lesbian or gay man to live a heterosexual lifestyle; our ancestors have done it for generations. It just requires repression, deception, double lives, and unethical sexual behavior done "on the side" or "on the sly." A religious fundamentalist would say that this is exactly what God demands — though of course they would phrase it differently: perhaps as "wrestling with my own private demon" or "struggling to serve God" or "making sacrifices in the name of holiness."

This is the rhetoric of death. It is the way of expressing the belief that there is something unworthy about the fundamental structure of this-worldly existence. The heart is wrong. Sexuality is unreliable or evil. And there are more important values than living out one's fundamental truth. . . . [This] is the rhetoric of Egypt. . . .

This rhetoric has become even more prevalent . . . as the scientific evidence of sexuality's innateness has mounted. . . . Many in the antigay camp have shifted their message, from "choice and change" to "cope and repress." After all, they now say, pleasure is not always good, and religion demands sacrifice. . . .

[But] God does not want the trampling of the heart. . . . Although control is often a Jewish value, repression of one's basic orientation to love is not.[55]

5.10. ACCEPTING DESIRES

Sheila Peltz Weinberg (b. 1946) is a Reconstructionist rabbi and meditation teacher. Her writing below builds on the Buddhist teaching that there are five hindrances to proper practice; in Weinberg's rendering, these include sloth and torpor, aversion, doubt, desire and lust, and restlessness. The selection here focuses on desire and lust.

Weinberg points her readers to ways in which these forces inhibit the People of Israel following the Exodus from Egypt. Like Wine, she suggests that improperly directed desires cannot be "repressed" or "fought" but need to be tempered. Unlike Wine (and Borowitz and Schwartz, and Michaelson) she does not advise controlling or disciplining these desires. Rather, she counsels responding to hindrances such as desire and lust by cultivating awareness of them, meeting them with love, and bringing forth other sorts of energy that provide balance and perspective. Her direction to respond to desires for food with love and awareness resembles Plaskow's call for accepting and honoring sexual desires.

"Awareness" is Weinberg's translation of the Hebrew word *da'at*—an important word for thinkers in this chapter including Shneur Zalman and Menaḥem Mendel Lefin. In section 5.3, Lefin spoke of possessing "the understanding (*da'at*) to control the animal soul," seeking "to conquer its stubbornness and stupidity." To Weinberg, by contrast, desire is not "stupid" and *da'at* is not a tool to control desire; it is the awareness that one can reach if one relates to desire *without* seeking control. As she puts it in the text below, "Cultivating the capacity to meet [hindrances such as desire and lust] . . . with wisdom and love actually ends up expanding and freeing . . . awareness." Awareness is freed and expanded precisely to the degree that hindrances are met with a loving, nonjudgmental, and accepting spirit.[56]

Weinberg reads the Exodus as a story of the liberation of awareness. The ultimate liberation of awareness (the Exodus from Egypt) is made possible only through the encounter with hindrances (the descent into Egypt). Thus, for Weinberg, metaphorically being in Egypt is an important part of the journey. Whereas Michaelson views Egypt in entirely negative terms, as a place of death and the repression of desires, Weinberg views Egypt as the place of desire (and other hindrances) that must be met with love and acceptance if liberation is to be possible.

Sheila Peltz Weinberg, "Leaving Egypt Again" (2013)

Five energies ["hindrances," including the hindrance of desire/lust] keep awareness (*da'at*) in exile, in a contracted and limited state. Yet, the worst thing to do is to repress them, fight them, hate them, pretend they are not there. Cultivating the capacity to meet each one again and again with wisdom and love actually ends up expanding and freeing that very awareness. In other words, without the descent into Egypt, the narrow place, liberation does not occur. . . .

The Israelites are great models acting out the hindrance of lust. Who can fault them? They were slaves with no experience exercising independent judgment. Their sense of self-esteem and intrinsic worth has been systematically negated by the system. So it is not surprising that they lust and kvetch and are easily deluded. Right after crossing the sea (Exod. 15:23), they are complaining to Moses: "what shall we drink?" . . . After their thirst is slaked, they imagine how wonderful things are back in Egypt, recalling it in a totally idealized way (Exod. 16:3). When the manna arrives they want to save it until the next day, against Moses' instructions, and of course it rots.

Desire for "what is not" makes it so hard to accept manna, "that which is," the great teacher of trust, patience, gratitude and limits (Exod. 16:20). Then again they thirst for water and their desire turns into doubt and blaming Moses. "And the people thirsted there for water; and the people murmured against Moses, and said, 'why have you brought us up out of Egypt, to kill us and our children and our cattle with thirst?'" In the account in Numbers, we find fantasy merges with desire and doubt: "We remember the fish, which we ate in Egypt free of charge; the cucumbers and the melons and the leeks, and the garlic; but now our bodies are dried up; there is nothing at all save the manna to look at" (Num. 11:5–6). Unable to rest in this moment, in the presence of what is being presented, the Israelites need to wander for forty years in the wilderness.

Awareness is trapped or concealed in the wanting to do and have more, wanting what is not present or possible, wanting what ultimately will not satisfy. . . . Excessive wanting obscures awareness, much like the other hindrances. One could say, it obscures the connection to God's presence. It keeps me dissatisfied and held hostage to my sense of being separate, other, and alone. It obscures joy and connection and reduces my ability to enjoy life as it is, which is not my creation, but a fleeting and precious gift.

In the Passover seder, the bitter herb, *maror*, is often understood as the suffering the slaves endured in bondage. But I would like to see it as a symbol of the energy that balances lust and desire. It reminds me that the end of the sweet is the bitter. I know this when I pursue "too much of a good thing." *Maror* teaches me how greed, lust, and clinging can transform the most pleasant experience into the constriction of suffering. It teaches me the impermanence of pleasure, as well as pain. This profound understanding creates freedom in my mind.[57]

CONCLUSION

Modern Jewish thinkers have advanced diverse views of what constitutes the most virtuous response to human appetites. Some Jewish thinkers have idealized poverty, while others have been comfortable with afflu-ence. Some have viewed sexual desire as the work of the evil inclination, while others have sought to honor and liberate sexual desires. Some have argued that disciplined eating may lead to holiness, or alternatively to health, while others have contended that eating is disgraceful altogether.

When it comes to desire itself, some Jewish thinkers have idealized crushing and destroying desires, while others have argued that desires must be accepted as part of human nature. Some have argued that the repression of desire is central to Jewish tradition, while others have contended that the tradition favors the liberation of desire. Some have seen bodily appetites as demonic; others have acknowledged bodily appetites as problematic; while still others have viewed bodily appetites in positive terms. Some have believed that desires can be controlled; others have been less optimistic about the human capacity for control; and others have eschewed ideals of controlling desire altogether.

Some Jewish thinkers have claimed that Jews have greater control than non-Jews over their bodily appetites, while others have strongly disagreed. Some have thought that God is involved in the work of self-control, while others have not. Some have worried about the effects of unchecked desire on God, while others have worried about the effects of unchecked desire on human mental health, physical health, or the broader environment. Some have counseled restraint out of a desire to protect the natural world, while others have counseled restraint out of a belief that the material world is evil.

To some thinkers, restraint is made possible through gratitude, when we accept "that which is" rather than desiring "what is not" (see section 5.10). But when should we accept and be grateful for things just as they are, and when should we want things to be other than they are? What are the appropriate limits of gratitude? These and other questions about gratitude will be the focus of the following chapter.

6

Gratitude (*Hakarat ha-Tov*)

Gratitude (in Hebrew, *hakarat ha-tov*, "acknowledging the good") might seem to be a relatively straightforward and uncontroversial virtue. Indeed, most human beings agree that it is important to give thanks for the good in their lives. But there is little agreement about how one should acknowledge goods that have no clear source, little agreement about the proper limits and abuses of gratitude, and of course little agreement about what is good. Diverse modern Jews have passionately disputed these issues and have offered various claims regarding the centrality of gratitude to Judaism, the need for gratitude in the face of divine or human power, and the ways in which feelings of gratitude can be abused. Questions of when and whether to show gratitude to those with tremendous power over one's life, but whose goodness is not always self-evident, account for many of the tensions featured in this chapter.

For example, a number of musar teachers—among them Samuel Isaacs (section 6.1), Natan Tzevi Finkel (section 6.4), Alan Morinis (section 6.7), and Shalom Arush (section 6.8)—have emphasized the need to show gratitude to God, informed by premodern traditions that depict God as in control of nature and history. Some thinkers, however, question the virtues of thanking God for terrible misfortune (Harold Kushner, section 6.5) and for good fortune (Mitchell Silver, section 6.6). Lisa Goldstein (section 6.11) expresses the additional concern that a focus on gratitude may inappropriately shut down negative emotions.

Just as assertions about divine power have led to debates about the limits of gratitude, so have claims regarding the power of human institutions. For example, modern Jewish thinkers have argued about gratitude toward the state in the United States, Europe, and Israel/Palestine. Samuel Isaacs (6.1) and Berel Wein (6.9) stress the need to show gratitude toward the state; Simon Dubnov (6.2), Emma Goldman (6.3), Amos Oz (6.10), and Lisa Goldstein (6.11) challenge such assertions. Furthermore, as Oz notes, claims regarding gratitude to the state are often bound up with claims regarding gratitude to God, as when the state is supported by rabbis who claim prophetic inspiration and insist that the state is doing God's work.

6.1. THANKSGIVING FOR AMERICAN EXCEPTIONALISM

The Dutch-born Rev. Samuel Myer Isaacs (1804–78), a leader of Orthodox communities in New York City, advocated for Jews to commit to Jewish observance while also integrating into American society. In 1858 on the occasion of New York's Thanksgiving Day, he delivered a sermon (excerpted below) affirming the value of Jews joining with non-Jewish Americans in "conforming to the will of the authorities" and observing Thanksgiving. Like Jewish preachers in many other U.S. states during the nineteenth century, Isaacs was eager to affirm and encourage his congregation's loyalty to America and to express gratitude for its unparalleled goodness. His words echo those of rabbis in many European nation-states who likewise affirmed the unparalleled goodness of their countries.[1]

Taking gratitude for his theme in honor of Thanksgiving Day, Isaacs noted the importance of gratitude for other regimes (namely, Russia) as well, but above all stressed gratitude for the United States, which "continue[d] to partake so largely of the bounties of heaven." (Isaacs made no mention of the millions of enslaved Black people in the United States, the recent violence in Kansas against opponents of slavery, or the ongoing state violence against Native Americans.) He noted just one dark spot in the world: in Rome, where Vatican authorities had recently baptized and then abducted a Jewish child, Edgardo Mortara. (Isaacs's warning against Rome allowed him to join with the anti-Catholic sentiment uniting many patriotic American Protestant Christians.[2])

Isaacs affirmed in his sermon that tragedies were also God's will. Still, Jewish residents of the United States should be grateful that God had rewarded them with particular blessings rather than treating them like the unfortunate Jews of Rome.

Samuel Isaacs, "Thanksgiving Sermon" (1858)

We should thank God for the enjoyment of national tranquility, holding as we do as a doctrine, that it rests with God in heaven whether nations should be prosperous or suffer the ravages of adversity. It must be to us a source of joy that the land we inhabit, and in whose welfare we are so deeply interested, should continue to partake so largely of the bounties of heaven as scarcely with a parallel in history. We thank Him and praise his name that industry prospers, that no famine has visited our borders, and right earnestly we beseech Him to continue dispensing these blessings to us and to all the inhabitants of the state. . . .

We, as Jews, have every reason to be grateful. Trace back our history—not its golden leaves but its pages crimsoned with blood—and let us contemplate what we have suffered from the virulence of contending factions, when papal power and rude infidelity stood side by side to uproot us, when emperors and monarchs leagued together in dark confederacy to destroy the scion of God's planting. "Come on," said they, "let us cut them off from the nations, so that the name of Israel be no longer remembered." Yet we are here this day, as we are wherever the foot of humanity places its impress, as numerous, as industrious, as faithful, and as happy as at any time since we have lost our Temple. True, there is yet a dark spot which we shall notice in the sequel, but some very dark ones have become burnished; even Russia's autocrat, and we revere him for it, has found out that oppression is wrong, and is now governing two and a half millions of our co-religionists on a much better plan than the system which formed the basis of his predecessor's course.

We say it therefore with a great deal of self-congratulation, that we are at this moment in a better condition than we have been for centuries, and, knowing as we must, that this blessing emanates from the Author of all good, let us thank him, not in empty words only, but from the innermost recesses of our soul, for without this feeling and its utterance we should attribute all to chance. And how utterly dead must be that heart, and clouded the understanding that is thus perverted from its happy path, that considering everything as unguided and unswayed by that unseen yet all-directing Power, whose temple is all space, whose glory was, is, and ever shall remain majestically triumphant throughout nature's work, argues thus blindly. As well might the man cast off on some lonely island, finding a relic of the most exquisite sculpture, exclaim this is the effect of chance, while its mouldering beauties clearly indicate the inventive genius of bygone time. Thank Heaven, those who think thus are not here. . . .

It is not enough to come here this day to thank Him for his continued goodness to the land of our adoption—the home for the houseless, the shelter for the persecuted, the haven of safety for the wayworn traveler. It is not sufficient to pour forth your gratitude this day for the civil and religious liberty you enjoy; from you more is expected. You have to do your utmost to contribute your modicum to aid those who cannot help themselves, who are yet under the ban of degrading servility, who are living in that dark spot of earth where the sun of liberty is not allowed to shine. Need we say we allude to Rome, where the Inquisition, which we imagined had ceased to exist, is yet in full activity? This is the dark spot to which we said we would allude. Let us thank God this day that our glorious republic has no such stain on its escutcheon; if it had, God's blessing would not be so freely scattered throughout its length and breadth.[3]

6.2. JEWISH AUTONOMY, NOT SLAVISH THANKFULNESS

Simon Dubnov (Dubnow, 1860–1941), a historian and political theorist who lived most of his life under Russian rule (in Odessa, Vilna, Saint

Petersburg, and elsewhere), was the foremost theorist of Jewish "auton-omism," which sought Jewish national rights and the establishment of autonomous Jewish communities in the Diaspora. A passionate critic of "assimilated" Jews who surrendered or downplayed their Jewish national identities to integrate into modern nation-states, he also critiqued the common expectation (advocated, for example, in section 6.1) that Jews should show gratitude to states granting them civic rights.

To the contrary, Dubnov wrote (in the letter excerpted below), Jews should instead protest these states' denial of their national rights. As an oppressed people long deprived of their rights, Jews were vulnerable to thinking they were owed less than other peoples and thus tended to show "slavish thankfulness" for any restoration of their rights. But Jews were entitled to the same respect due to all peoples. "The highest principle of all social ethics," Dubnov wrote, is "the idea of the equal value of all nations."

For Dubnov, expressions of gratitude toward those who do not deserve them can be a sign of the vice of servility rather than the virtue of proper gratitude. Self-respect required Jews to protect their independence and resist the pressure to enter into a servile relationship with those possessing greater political power.

Simon Dubnov, "Jews as a Spiritual (Cultural-Historical) Nation" (1898)

It is possible that the non-Jews' demand for Jewish assimilation reflects the conscious, or perhaps unconscious, contempt of the strong for the weak, and a belief that Jewry, enslaved for centuries, must still pay for the "gift" of civic rights (that is, for the return of rights previously taken from them) by renouncing their national individuality. The demands of this sort as well as the submission to such demands repudiate the highest principle of all social ethics: the idea of the equal value of all nations. . . .

To these people we reply: You, gentlemen, regard yourselves as magnanimous and liberal, but how can someone be called magnanimous if, after keeping his innocent neighbor locked in a spiritual prison for many years, he feels at last compelled by an awakened conscience to free that neighbor, and then demands gratitude and self-renunciation from him? ... When Europe is able to make amends for its thousand-year crime against Jewry, then the wrath of the oppressed will be extinguished from our hearts. A feeling of slavish thankfulness for the return of our previously abolished rights, however, will never arise in its place. As a historic and cultural nation, we have proved our capacity to flourish in all possible circumstances, and now we wish for our internal life to freely and independently evolve in a manner that contradicts neither our universal goals nor our civic duties. ... But we will accomplish all of this autonomously and in the context of our own evolution, not out of a desire to convenience, to mimic, or to win the high opinion of our neighbors.[4]

6.3. GRATITUDE AS A SOURCE OF REPRESSION AND TYRANNY

The Lithuanian-born American Jewish anarchist Emma Goldman (1869–1940) was a political activist who supported workers' rights, women's rights, and rights to free expression (among other causes) and advocated revolution against the state, militarism, capitalism, religion, patriarchy, and colonialism. She also "intuited that a successful revolution includes a healthy passion for the inner life," as the writer Vivian Gornick has put it.[5] Goldman's writings consider not only the path to political liberation but also the path of inner liberation, marked above all by a refusal to submit to authority.

The U.S. government deported Goldman to Russia in 1919, and she documented her experiences there in her book *My Disillusionment in Russia*. As she indicates in the selection below, she refused to allow her appreciation of kindnesses shown her by Russia's Bolshevik leadership to stifle her critique of the government's repressive and violent actions.

Like Dubnov, Goldman points out that demands for gratitude can be used to prevent dissent. But unlike Dubnov, who was fighting for Jewish national autonomy within multinational states, Goldman fought against nationalist and statist principles of all sorts. While she had initially hoped that the Bolshevik regime might have some promise, she concluded that like other states it was corrupt, unjust, and preferring its critics to be grateful and silent rather than challenging it. As Goldman's book makes clear, she refused to be silent.

Goldman saw similar dynamics at work in all human relationships. Just as states repressed their citizens by encouraging their gratitude, parents could abuse their children by teaching them to be grateful for their kindness. Goldman, who developed particular concern for the abuse of girls and women in traditional families, was herself abused by her father and accused of ingratitude by her mother.[6]

Goldman's critique of gratitude reflects an anarchist philosophy that emphasized the obligations owed to others out of solidarity with them (see section 9.2) rather than in exchange for past kindness. In contrast to many figures in this chapter, Goldman was also a passionate atheist. She despised the view that a human being was "a mere speck of dust dependent on superior powers on high," and she took special issue with any belief in God that served as "a whip to lash the people into obedience, meekness and contentment." The development of an ethical society, she stressed, depended on the degree to which "man . . . can outgrow his dependence upon God."[7]

Emma Goldman, *My Disillusionment in Russia* (1922)

The conventional conception of gratitude is that one must not be critical of those who have shown him kindness. Thanks to this notion parents enslave their children more effectively than by brutal treatment; and by it friends tyrannize over one another. In fact, all human relationships are to-day vitiated by this noxious idea.

Some people have upbraided me for my critical attitude toward the Bolsheviki. "How ungrateful to attack the Communist Government after the hospitality and kindness she enjoyed in Russia!" they indignantly exclaim. I do not mean to gainsay that I have received advantages while I was in Russia. I could have received many more had I been willing to serve the powers that be. It is that very circumstance which has made it bitter hard for me to speak out against the evils as I saw them day by day. But finally I realized that silence is indeed a sign of consent. Not to cry out against the betrayal of the Russian Revolution would have made me a party to that betrayal. The Revolution and the welfare of the masses in and out of Russia are by far too important to me to allow any personal consideration for the Communists I have met and learned to respect to obscure my sense of justice and to cause me to refrain from giving to the world my two years' experience in Russia.[8]

6.4. SLIGHT INGRATITUDE AS ORIGINAL SIN

The Orthodox rabbi Natan (Nosson) Tzevi Finkel (1849–1927) was a leader of the Musar movement and the spiritual leader of the Slobodka Yeshiva, a traditionalist institution located in the same Lithuanian district in which Emma Goldman was born. But while Goldman fiercely critiqued those who encouraged "dependence on God," Finkel condemned his fellow Jews for even the slightest failures to recognize their dependence on God.

Upholding approaches found in Rabbinic literature and medieval musar literature, Finkel often sought to encourage his students' moral development by reminding them of the harshness of God's judgment—a common approach within the Musar movement through the first half of the twentieth century.[9] He stressed the need for total devotion to God, complete faith in God, and constant gratitude to God.

In the message to his students below, Finkel builds on a talmudic text that condemns the thankless Israelites in the wilderness following the Exodus as "ingrates and children of ingrates," and that links their ingratitude with the ingratitude of Adam, the first human being. As Finkel explains it, the Rabbis of the Talmud appropriately condemn the Israelites even for a slight failure of ingratitude: when God appeared to praise them for their reverence (Deut. 5:26), the people should have gratefully and joyfully proclaimed their dependence on God for their very ability to be reverent.

Finkel explains why, despite their high spiritual level, the Israelites were unable to free themselves of the character trait of ingratitude. This trait has been rooted within the human heart ever since Adam showed slight ingratitude to God, defending his eating from the fruit of the Tree of Knowledge of Good and Evil by blaming "the woman You put at my side" (Gen. 3:12)—the very woman God had given him when he was in need of a spiritual helper. Adam's failure to demonstrate adequate gratitude was the "original sin" for which he was punished in the garden, and (Finkel writes elsewhere) for which God punished human beings with death and many other curses.[10] The tendency toward ingratitude has been passed down through the generations, and Finkel urged his students to be aware of this tendency in themselves and to cultivate greater gratitude toward God.

Natan Tzevi Finkel, *Siḥot ha-Sabba mi-Slabodka* (early twentieth century)

We find in the words of our sages of blessed memory (BT *Avodah Zarah* 5a) that the generation that received the Torah in the wilderness was accused by Moses of ingratitude. Where could one find this character trait in them at the time of the giving of the Torah, when they reached the highest level that human beings are able to reach, such that even the Holy Blessed One himself rejoiced over them and said, "'Who would grant that their hearts would always be such' [Deut. 5:26] before me!," as if to say "This is my delight, and if only it could always be so!"?

But the Talmud says: They should have responded, "You will grant it!"—this would have expressed their feelings of sharing in His joy. This failing is so very slight and obscure that no human being can fully decipher its character.

We are speaking here of the greatest people, who saw and heard the voice of the living God who spoke to them face-to-face, whose corporeality was stripped away, whose hearts were pierced within them—and, nevertheless, our sages did not refrain from attributing a failing of character traits to them and from designating it, in the language of the Torah, as "ingratitude."

Our sages understood, and they called them "ingrates and children of ingrates," and they even understood the secret of the root of this failing, and they taught us to understand that the generation of the wilderness inherited it from their ancestors many generations before, and [in another midrash][11] they found its traces already hundreds of years earlier as the cause of terrible and serious misdeeds, the deeds of the generation of the Flood—and the whole essence of its root was imbibed from Adam, the first human being! And what was the essence of this failing with Adam? Which form did it take at the beginning of its development? For this, it is incumbent upon us to contemplate an entire portion of God's Torah. We read in the portion on the works of Creation: "The Lord God said, 'It is not good for man to be alone; I will make a fitting helper for him'" [Gen. 2:18] ... as a spiritual helper, for Adam needed another possessing "more understanding" [BT *Niddah* 45b], to be helped and guided by her spiritual capabilities, as she would serve as a sort of rabbi or colleague, so that he could reach the fullness of wisdom with her help. ...

[But] when he was accused by God, he defended himself and said, "The woman You put at my side—she gave [the fruit] to me" [Gen. 3:12]. ... In this defense, our sages found one failing, ingratitude and a lack of acknowledgment of God's kindness; this defense sounds like an expression of how there happened to be a bit of something "not good" found in the giving of this helper to Adam. ... This failing became entangled and rooted in his heart, becoming bone of his bones and a quality of his qualities, and then passed on from parents to children, from generation to generation, the cause of many misdeeds that upset the world and its fullness, and even after the passing of thousands of years, and various purifications that purified humanity through a great moral transformation, as the People of Israel were transformed and [in the wilderness] became a "generation of knowledge," with its leader being the master of prophets ... nevertheless, it was not possible for them to be totally free of it. The power of character traits extends this far.[12]

6.5. GOD DOES NOT CAUSE EVIL

Rabbi Harold Kushner (b. 1935), a popular American theologian affiliated with the Conservative movement, is well known for advancing the thesis that God does not have full control over the universe and is not responsible for evil (building on the approach of his teacher Mordecai Kaplan, discussed in section 3.4).

In the selections below from his book *When Bad Things Happen to Good People*, Kushner rejects theologies that teach us to be grateful for evil because God must be trying to teach us something or because God will provide benefit to victims in the world to come. We should see bad things as bad, rather than pretending they are good. Still, he insists that we should thank God for many other things, as the world is "basically good and liveable" despite its tragedies.

Elsewhere in his book, Kushner explicitly rejects the idea favored by Natan Tzevi Finkel (section 6.4) that God punished humanity for sinning in the Garden of Eden. To Kushner, the so-called "punishments" are in fact natural consequences, "the painful consequences of being human rather than being a mere animal."[13]

One such consequence is the human power to make moral choices: human beings can defy God's will and cause great pain. But, Kushner points out, the power to make moral choices is also something to be grateful for, as it allows human beings to bring greater goodness into our imperfect world.[14]

Whereas Finkel and Samuel Isaacs (section 6.1) also acknowledged human free will, their discussions of gratitude were predicated on the assumption that God is ultimately in control of what happens in the world. Isaacs, for example, inveighed against those who failed to show proper gratitude because they attributed events to mere "chance." Kushner, however, holds that it is a virtue to be grateful to God for the good, but human beings should not thank God for all the tragedy caused by human free will, the impersonal forces of nature, or simple bad luck.

Harold Kushner, *When Bad Things Happen to Good People* (1981)

We have all read stories of little children who were left unwatched for just a moment and fell from a window or into a swimming pool and died. Why does God permit such a thing to happen to an innocent child? . . . Is it to make the parents more sensitive, more compassionate people, more appreciative of life and health because of their experience? . . . The price is still too high, and the reasoning shows too little regard for the value of an individual life. I am offended by those who suggest that God creates retarded children so that those around them will learn compassion and gratitude. Why should God distort someone else's life to such a degree in order to enhance my spiritual sensitivity? . . .

When all else fails, some people try to explain suffering by believing that it comes to liberate us from a world of pain and lead us to a better place. I received a phone call one day informing me that a five-year-old boy in our neighborhood had run out into the street after a ball, had been hit by a car and killed. . . . In the eulogy, the family's clergyman had said, "This is not a time for sadness or tears. This is a time for rejoicing, because Michael has been taken out of this world of sin and pain with his innocent soul unstained by sin. He is in a happier land now where there is no pain and no grief: let us thank God for that." I heard that, and I felt so bad for Michael's parents. Not only had they lost a child without warning, they were being told by the representative of their religion that they should rejoice in the fact that he had died so young and so innocent, and I couldn't believe that they felt much like rejoicing at that moment. They felt hurt, they felt angry, they felt that God had been unfair to them, and here was God's spokesman telling them to be grateful to God for what had happened. Sometimes . . . we try to persuade ourselves that what has happened is not really bad. . . .

[But] God does not cause our misfortunes. Some are caused by bad luck, some are caused by bad people, and some are simply an inevitable consequence of our being human and being mortal, living in a world of inflexible natural laws. . . .

[Still,] God has created a world in which many more good things than bad things happen. . . . In the Jewish tradition, the special prayer known as the Mourners' Kaddish . . . praises God for having created a basically good and liveable world. By reciting that prayer, the mourner is reminded of all that is good and worth living for. There is a crucial difference between denying the tragedy and insisting that everything is for the best, and seeing the tragedy in the context of a whole life, keeping one's eye and mind on what has enriched you and not only on what you have lost.[15]

6.6. VALUABLE FUNCTIONS OF GRATITUDE AND GOD

In his book *A Plausible God: Secular Reflections on Liberal Jewish Theology*, philosopher Mitchell Silver analyzes and praises theologians who, like Kushner and Mordecai Kaplan, reject the traditional "old God" endowed with personhood, agency, goodness, will, and omnipotence. To Silver, such theologians have done well to develop ideas of a "new God"—a God without personhood, agency, will, intentions, desires, or control over the universe. The new theologians have in common, as their "baseline," the idea that "God is whatever there is in nature that makes good things possible." Silver refers to this conception of God as the "baseline God" in the selection below.

A secularist who prefers not to use God-language at all (in contrast to Kushner, who confidently uses such language), Silver nevertheless sees good reasons to be sympathetic to Jews who believe in the "new God," especially because God-language can help human beings express the valuable moral emotion of gratitude. So long as one realizes that God does not actually cause things to happen in the universe, there is even utility in invoking the language of divine "graciousness" (seemingly an "old God" concept) since that language can encourage a sense of gratitude. Silver's secularism, with its affirmation of God-language, is clearly very different from the atheism of Emma Goldman, which focused on rejecting outright what Silver calls "the old God."

Silver thinks the most important recipient for our gratitude should be not God but those persons, communities, and institutions that have actually created what we are grateful for. One should "attribute those goods to the source from whence they really came."[16] But he acknowledges (contra Samuel Isaacs) that much is due to chance, and when "no human agency is due ultimate thanks for our fortune," it is appropriate to give thanks to God. Gratitude, after all, must have an object, and speaking of God allows for such expression.

Silver shares Harold Kushner's concerns about gratitude for misfortune. But, unlike Kushner, he also stresses the moral dangers of showing gratitude for good fortune. As he notes below, gratitude for the good that happens to us as individuals is in tension with various virtues and values. Like Emma Goldman, Silver sees how a focus on gratitude may silence just criticism. It may also encourage us to believe that we are separate selves in ways we are not. Furthermore, gratitude for our own good fortune when others suffer misfortune is incompatible with humility, justice, and social solidarity. It would seem that truly just forms of gratitude are incompatible with expressions of complete gratitude amid injustice.

Mitchell Silver, *A Plausible God* (2006)

Gratitude is an important moral emotion. It is right to acknowledge benefits conferred and to be appreciative of life's goods. However, many of life's most valuable goods are not attributable to friends, family, neighbors, or any human institution. Even when a good is attributable to the generosity of a friend, the friend and her generosity themselves are unaccounted for. If we feel ourselves fortunate, especially undeservedly fortunate, the urge to give thanks seems a laudable disposition. Should not this disposition have an outlet? To whom can we offer thanks for all of our undeserved, unattributable good fortune? We need an addressee for our thank-you notes, lest we get out of the habit of sending them. God is the addressee. Giving thanks to God allows us both to show that we are thankful and reminds us that we should be thankful. The habit of gratitude deepens.

Why is gratitude a laudable attitude? First, it keeps us humble. It is an implicit acknowledgement that much of our good fortune is unearned. This acknowledgement strengthens egalitarianism. While we thank others for all sorts of things, the paradigmatic ground for thanks is receipt of a gift. Gifts are not given in payment of services. We do not intentionally cause their coming to us. They just come. There is no moral reason that they should not have come to others. We are grateful that they came to us and mindful that others are no less worthy of them, which is a good thing to be mindful of.

Gratitude also involves a sense of obligation. Indeed, a typical expression of gratitude is, "I am indebted to you." When we are in debt, we must repay, so the feeling of gratitude inclines us to "give something back." If we are grateful for our fortunate status in the world, it is only natural that we should want to make the world a more fortunate place. A grateful attitude presages a giving attitude. If we need God to give thanks, and giving thanks fosters gratitude, and gratitude fosters egalitarianism and a sense of social obligation, then "God" has justified its place in our lexicon.

Do we need God to give thanks? Only if the expression of gratitude requires that *someone* be thanked and that we believe that no *human* agency is due ultimate thanks for our fortune. If *someone* must be thanked, then we must be thankful to God, for God is all that is left. There is no need, however, to turn to God if gratitude is not transitive or if it can take impersonal forces as its object. Can we be thankful, and express our thankfulness without being thankful to anyone or anything, not even to a posited anonymous benefactor?

I think not. At the heart of gratitude is the sense of indebtedness and that requires a creditor. For similar reasons, I do not think that impersonal forces are fit objects of gratitude. One cannot feel that one owes something to a benefactor whose beneficence was unintentional and who, moreover, has no goals, no concerns, and no desires and is completely indifferent to repayment.

This last point, of course, rules out the [impersonal] baseline God as an object of gratitude. Still, if the baseline God can intellectually establish "God's place" in our vocabulary, belief in it may be justified because perhaps "God" can then be used as an image to animate our feelings and expressions of gratitude. *Of course, the God of our verbal image is the old God,* intentionally gracious and bounteous; the image just helps us to have the right, grateful attitude toward the world by providing an auditor for our thanksgivings. When asked to reflect on the actual nature of reality, we drop the image and replace it with the respectable baseline God. . . .

If there is a downside to cultivating gratitude for the beneficial accidents of nature, it is one that might particularly trouble the ["new God"] theologians. Gratitude for good fortune reinforces the sense of a separate self. There is something unseemly about the sole survivor of a plane crash thanking God for his survival. Why should he not, with as much justice and more morality, condemn God for leaving his dead fellow passengers unrescued? Why should I thank God for my children's health rather than curse God for the millions of children suffering from terrible diseases? Why even feel blessed for my peaceful, free life while others are tortured, enslaved, and warred upon? This grateful attitude rests on a vision of myself as significantly separate from others. . . . Insofar as "God" is a heuristic to express gratitude, it is in tension with one of its other major expressive functions—a means of expressing connectedness.[17]

6.7. SEEK THE GOOD IN ALL THAT HAPPENS

Alan Morinis (b. 1949) is the founder of the Mussar Institute, an organization that has done significant work to revive the legacy of the historic Musar movement (represented in this chapter by Natan Tzevi Finkel, section 6.4) especially among twenty-first-century non-Orthodox North American Jews. Morinis's interest in musar literature and musar-focused practices was sparked by his encounter with two contemporary ultra-Orthodox musar teachers in Far Rockaway, New York: Rabbi Yechiel Perr and his wife Rebbetzin Shoshana Perr. As Morinis mentions briefly in the selection below, Shoshana Perr's family had been deported from Poland to

Siberia in 1941, which they understood as an act of divine harshness; but their family soon realized it was an act of divine compassion, a "blessing in disguise," as being in Siberia protected them from being slaughtered along with the Nazis' six million other Jewish victims.[18]

Morinis accepts the teaching of the Perrs (and of Rabbi Akiva, as he explains) that God controls what happens in the universe; and he urges readers to consider reasons to be grateful even for events that seem disastrous. One should consider how God acts "for the good" not only in this world but beyond this world, such as by delivering recompense for one's deeds in the world to come.

Morinis's teachings stand in particularly stark contrast to Kushner's conviction that God is not responsible for the Holocaust and that preachers should not urge gratitude for the promise of otherworldly rewards. And whereas Kushner and Silver exhort readers to distinguish good from bad and to express gratitude only for the good, Morinis encourages readers to admit that they themselves are not able to judge what is good and what is bad. He suggests that there is goodness in all that happens. Though he also warns against an overly optimistic Pollyannaism, he urges his readers to seek out the good in the darkest of life's situations.

Morinis's caution helps distinguish his position from that of Natan Tzevi Finkel (section 6.4), who spoke more stridently on moral failure and harsh divine judgment;[19] and Shalom Arush (section 6.8, to come), who insists, with no reservations, that all suffering is for the best.

Alan Morinis, *Everyday Holiness* (2007)

We cheer for the good that happens to us and mourn for the bad, but are we really in a position to pass such clear judgment as to which is which? How certain can we be that something that happens to us is really for our good, and something else bad? A story about the sage Rabbi Akiva says this perfectly. He used to say, "A person should always make it a habit of saying, 'Whatever the All-Merciful does, He does for the good.'" He backed this up with a story from his own experience.

Once, Rabbi Akiva was walking along the way accompanied by a rooster, a donkey, and a lamp. He came to a certain place and looked for room at the inn, but he was turned away. When that happened, he said, "Whatever the All-Merciful does, He does for the good." So he went with his rooster, donkey, and lamp and spent the night in an open field. The wind came and put out the lamp, a weasel came and ate the rooster, a lion came and ate the donkey. He said, "Whatever the All-Merciful does, He does for the good." On that very night, a marauding troop came to that town and took into captivity everyone in the town. Rabbi Akiva was spared.[20] Had his rooster crowed, had the donkey brayed, had the light glowed, he would have been discovered.

The message is clear. How can we evaluate what is happening right now when we don't know what will happen next? It's only against the contours of that bigger picture that we can grasp the meaning and direction of our present circumstances. Only then can we possibly know what is good and what is bad—and even then we can't really be sure because events continue to unfold. "Did I not tell you?" Rabbi Akiva concluded. "Whatever the All-Merciful does, He does for the good."

It isn't hard to find real-life examples of terrible things that befell people that turned out in the end to be "blessings in disguise." What spared my teacher Mrs. Perr's family from destruction in the Holocaust was the "disaster" that occurred when the invading Russians exiled her family from Poland to Siberia early in World War II . . . [taking] them out of the path of the Nazis. . . .

Though there is great spiritual value in seeking the good in everything that happens, we have to be careful not to set ourselves up to being too much of a Pollyanna. All we want is to affirm that in everything that happens there is the possibility of good, if only we could perceive it, and while it may not be visible now, perhaps in time we'll see the bigger picture. And perhaps that bigger picture will include dimensions that are beyond this world and beyond our known experience, as the Jewish tradition affirms repeatedly in telling us that the real recompense for our lives is not in this world but in the World-to-Come.[21]

6.8. EVERYTHING IS GOOD

The Moroccan-born Israeli rabbi Shalom Arush (b. 1952), affiliated with the Breslov Hasidic sect devoted to Naḥman of Bratslav (see sections 2.2 and 3.2), is the founder of a group of educational institutions known as Chut Shel Chessed (Thread of Kindness) Institutions, many of which spread Breslov teachings to students from secular backgrounds. Arush has given particular attention to musar — to helping his students develop virtues, especially *emuna* (faith), as explained in his book *The Garden of Emuna*, and *hakarat ha-tov* (gratitude), as addressed in *The Garden of Gratitude*. While the selection below comes from the latter book, Arush's conception of *emuna* is also central to his concept of gratitude.

Arush requires that his students believe, without a doubt, that God directs all that happens on earth with exacting precision, and that everything God does is perfectly good. Given this, human beings must be grateful for everything God does for them, including when God (through His human agents) causes immense suffering and abuse. Emma Goldman noted that parents may use gratitude to justify their abuse of their children; Arush provides a theology of gratitude that could justify such abuse. Although he acknowledges that abusive parents may be punished for their misdeeds, he also asks victimized children to be grateful for the ways in which their parental abusers serve as agents of God's will. He counsels that victims will suffer less when they shun resentment and accept their abuse with gratitude.

Arush largely agrees with Alan Morinis but lacks Morinis's moderation. Whereas Morinis affirms that "in everything that happens there is the possibility of good," Arush is certain that everything that happens is undoubtedly, intrinsically good. Whereas Morinis advises his readers to question their ideas of good and bad, Arush affirms that God wants people to banish the concept of "bad" entirely from their minds.

Shalom Arush, *The Garden of Gratitude* (2010)

Complete emuna [faith] in Hashem [God] means that we believe — without any doubt — that He directs and observes each of us individually with exacting precision, and He sees what we don't see. In short, complete emuna gives us the peace of mind that Hashem is doing everything for our ultimate good, regardless of the fact that this is not revealed to us at the time. Therefore, a person should tell himself, "I understand that my suffering is seemingly very bad. I even feel tremendous pain. My tribulations seem unbearable, but I believe that they're all for the best, despite the fact that I don't see how." . . .

Hashem doesn't make mistakes. Abusive parents are sticks in His hands. The victim of the abuse was judged in the most exacting way in the Heavenly court. On the other hand, the parents who sinned — if they do not repent — will certainly be severely punished for causing their child pain instead of giving him warmth and love. . . . But the victimized child must know that his parents are God's rods of reproof and should not resent them. . . .

We must believe that all our suffering is for the best and thank God for it. This mitigates the suffering. When we accept everything — even excruciating situations like parental abuse — with emuna and love, and thank God for all suffering, we sweeten the entire situation and do not suffer. Thus, the main reason for our suffering is lack of emuna.

It is highly likely that a victim of child abuse was still small when he suffered the abuse. At that point, he did not have the intellectual capacity to understand that everything is from God. The problem is that he perpetuated his anger and resentment for all the years he was abused. Every time those memories of abuse enter his mind, he feels pain and anger once again. Why? Because he still has not acquired the belief that there is nothing but God, and that this is what God wanted. Even more, that everything is for the best and that we must thank Him for everything. He must believe that God willed him to grow up in this abusive situation for his eternal good. . . .

In truth, there is no bad in the world. Everything is good. A person who has emuna knows that all of life's hardships are intrinsically good. The entire concept of *bad* comes from the fact that the person wants Hashem to fulfill her desires and requests. When that does not happen, she feels bad. But when a person's desire is to live in congruence with Hashem's desires, then the concept of *bad* no longer exists.[22]

6.9. GRATITUDE FOR THE STATE OF ISRAEL

The U.S.-born Israeli rabbi Berel Wein (b. 1934) is best known as the author of many books and recordings that narrate the history of the Jewish people. An advocate of Orthodox "Religious Zionism," the approach that sees the modern State of Israel as possessing redemptive significance, Wein has campaigned for American Jews to emigrate to Israel. He is a critic of the United States, which he describes as having "lost its moral footing," "hateful of its own heritage," and "hostile to Torah values and to a Jewish way of life."[23] Wein views Israel, by contrast, as a miraculous fulfillment of biblical prophecy (see part II).

In the essay excerpted in part III, Wein focuses on Palestinians who have benefited from Israeli Jewish leadership and American Jewish generosity but he believes have not shown sufficient gratitude. To make his case, he condemns Palestinian leaders in Gaza who have objected to the Israeli blockade of the Gaza Strip and the growing poverty in Gaza but have not shown sufficient gratitude for efforts by Jewish donors and the Jewish state to support them. As evidence, he contends that Palestinians "completely and willfully" destroyed greenhouses gifted to them in 2005, though in fact Palestinian looters caused limited damage to these greenhouses, which were subsequently protected by Palestinian security forces.[24]

The essay as a whole implies that some Israeli Jews may be guilty of insufficient gratitude as well, but Wein's focus is on angry and ungrateful Palestinians. Targeting a minority group unpopular with one's readers is a tried-and-true strategy when one is affirming the goodness of one's own group, as we saw when Samuel Isaacs targeted the "dark spot" of Catholic Rome (section 6.1). Wein might also sound like the non-Jewish Europeans discussed by Simon Dubnov (section 6.2) who asked for Jews to do away with their grievances and instead show proper gratitude to the states that granted them civic rights. Emma Goldman would charge that Wein is encouraging Israel's leaders to do what all other states do: silence their critics, especially those of minority status who can be viewed as threats to the state.

Berel Wein, "Gratitude" and "Saying Thank You" (2010-18)

I. One of the cardinal principles of Judaism is gratitude—the necessity and ability to say thank you. Someone who is *kafuy tova*—unappreciative of what he or she has and ungrateful to the extreme—is deemed to be a sinner, if not in deed certainly in attitude. The Talmud in its inimitable fashion states that a living person should always refrain from complaint....[25]

II. I do not understand how one cannot be grateful for living in a time when the Jewish state in the Land of Israel has been miraculously established and successfully taken root.... Any modicum of a sense of gratitude certainly teaches that we should be inordinately grateful for having seen before our very eyes the fulfillment of many of the predictions of the great prophets of Israel.[26]

III. It is difficult to make peace with people who do not have within themselves any sense whatever of the necessary proprietary emotion of gratitude towards others for help rendered to them....

Is it not unseemly to take sustenance and benefits galore from the State and yet curse and revile it at the very same moment?[27]

6.10. RABBIS WHO PLAY GOD

The Israeli novelist, short-story writer, and essayist Amos Oz (1939–2018) strongly advocated for an independent Palestinian state alongside the State of Israel. His remarks below, made upon receiving an honorary doctorate from the Hebrew Union College–Jewish Institute of Religion in Jerusalem in 1988, responded to Sephardi Chief Rabbi Mordechai Eliyahu's comments a few weeks earlier regarding the ingratitude of Palestinian Arabs for Jewish beneficence.[28]

Eliyahu's remarks were very similar to Wein's (section 6.9) but went beyond Wein's in one respect: depicting the beneficence of Jewish Israelis and the Jewish state toward Arabs in language traditionally used to describe God. The Bible portrays God as the one who "raises the weak from the dust and lifts the poor from the dirt" (1 Sam. 2:8; Ps. 113:7), and Eliyahu describes himself, his fellow Israelis, and the Jewish state as doing the same. To Oz, the implication is intentional: Israel is doing God's work and should be shown the same sort of gratitude owed to God.

Oz also points out that Eliyahu seems to claim to embody God himself, making his confident judgment on the ingratitude of Palestinians as if he was prophetically inspired. For Oz, rabbinical pronouncements like these pretend to represent "the best Jewish tradition" but in fact represent the worst aspects of Jewish tradition, with their assumptions that Jews often embody God's attributes, that great rabbis have ready access to God's will, and that God's will demands militant nationalism, supremacism, fanaticism, or all of the above.

Oz, a passionate secular humanist Jew and a passionate Zionist, is particularly incensed by Orthodox Jews' claims of moral high ground while they distort what he regards as authentic Judaism and authentic Zionism. American money has helped support the flourishing of Israeli Orthodoxy—and Oz shows no eagerness to be grateful for funding that has "actually reduced our ethics, perhaps, to garbage." Arabs have been no less ungrateful than Israeli Jews, who have also been recipients of significant monetary gifts, particularly from America. When we call for gratitude, his remarks suggest, we should be mindful of the political and theological dimensions of our words.

Amos Oz, "He Raises the Weak from the Dust and Lifts the Poor out of the Dirt" (1988)

Several weeks ago, the Holy Spirit suddenly descended upon Israel's Chief Rabbi [Mordechai] Eliyahu, whereupon he made a normative declaration of his own, in keeping with the spirit of ancient Israel and the best Jewish tradition: "We," said the venerable rabbi, "lifted the

Arabs from the dirt and they," he added sadly, "are not even grateful."
This is indeed a weighty conundrum in Judaism. Who now "raises
the weak from the dust and lifts the poor from the dirt"? And who
is ungrateful? Well imagine, my esteemed professors, how the earth
would shake if some anti-Semitic cardinal or archbishop in America
should dare to say that "we Americans lifted those Jews from the dirt
and they, alas, are not grateful." ... And in such a case, the sin of the
archbishop would still be less than that of the venerable rabbi. The
truth is that vast sums of American money have gone to improve the
material situation of both Jews and Arabs in Israel, even though the
enormous funds have actually reduced our ethics, perhaps, to garbage.... For the venerable Rabbi Eliyahu, the Israelis, incredibly, have
become the Holy One, blessed be He Who lifts the poor ungrateful
Arab out of the dirt. But I say to you that before there is peace, and
particularly after there is peace, we will have to lift our own humanity
out of the dirt. We will have to lift out of the dirt Judaism and Zionism,
both of which have come so close to falling captive to their distorters.[29]

6.11. BE THANKFUL, AND BE SAD OR ANGRY, TOO

This chapter began with Samuel Isaacs's 1858 "Thanksgiving Sermon" (6.1)
and concludes with Thanksgiving gratitude in a very different American
political context 158 years later. Rabbi Lisa Goldstein (b. 1965) writes
immediately following Donald J. Trump's election as the forty-fifth
president of the United States and "the sharp spike in acts of hatred
in its wake." Whereas in 1858 the American Orthodox rabbi Isaacs had
urged his fellow Jews to focus on the glories of the United States, in
2016 Goldstein, an American Reform rabbi directing the Institute for
Jewish Spirituality, urges her fellow Jews "to be thankful" (in Hebrew,
le-hodot) for what is good but also "to acknowledge" (again, le-hodot) what
is difficult and unpleasant. While we may almost always find something
to be thankful for (even if it is just "being alive"), we should also allow
ourselves to feel sad and angry in response to all that is wrong in the
world, political and otherwise.

Goldstein's rabbinical vision is deeply engaged with politics while simultaneously attentive to the individual's overall well-being. She builds on ideas we saw earlier in this chapter regarding the appropriateness of negative emotions. Simon Dubnov (section 6.2) objected to extinguishing "the wrath of the oppressed" from Jewish hearts until Europe had made amends for its crimes against them; Emma Goldman (section 6.3) urged crying out against injustice; Harold Kushner (section 6.5) denounced preachers who urged parents to negate their feelings of sadness and anger and rejoice even at the death of their children. Goldstein warns her audience against letting a focus on gratitude shut down "negative" emotions like grief, sadness, anger, and fear—which, she emphasizes, have spiritual value. Sometimes, she says, "they have important messages for us that we urgently need to listen to so that we can respond with wisdom and compassion where it is most needed."

With her emphasis on honoring the fullness of emotional experience, Goldstein's approach contrasts with that of Berel Wein (section 6.9), who cautioned Palestinian Arabs against anger; Shalom Arush (section 6.8), who warned against being angry at God's choices; and Natan Tzevi Finkel (section 6.4), who taught that the People of Israel should have regulated their emotions to better express joy in responding to God's joy. To Goldstein, connection with God depends less on getting one's emotions perfectly right than on acknowledging the value of the richness of human emotional experience.

Lisa Goldstein, "Giving Thanks. Telling the Truth" (2016)

I have to confess: my initial gut reaction to Thanksgiving this year was one of constriction. I am one of the many Jews who were dismayed at the results of the election and at the sharp spike in acts of hatred in its wake. I feel called to act. Sitting and giving thanks seemed out of resonance. I needed to consider the situation more thoughtfully.

I know that cultivating gratitude as a stance towards life is itself a spiritual practice. Gratitude as a *middah*, or desirable way of being in the world, doesn't have to depend on external factors. Certain kinds of prayer practice, gratitude journals and yes, even Thanksgiving, are ways of helping us remember our many blessings that we often take for granted. And this kind of remembering brings more joy and spaciousness to our lives.

And there's a shadow side to this practice. Occasionally I hear from people who are facing something truly difficult in their life. As they are telling me about their pain, they stop themselves and say, "Oh, but I have so much to be grateful for. Other people have so much more to worry about than I do. My little problem doesn't really matter."

In these cases, gratitude isn't really being cultivated as a stance towards life. It is being used to shut down an unpleasant feeling. The implication is that if we use spiritual practice effectively, we will never experience any "negative" emotion. But this is not realistic. The book of Ecclesiastes reminded us during Sukkot that there is a time for the difficult, unpleasant experiences too. And sometimes the "negative" emotions, such as grief, anger and fear, have important messages for us that we urgently need to listen to so that we can respond with wisdom and compassion where it is most needed.

The Hebrew word, *lehodot*, gives us a marvelous insight about this tension: It means to give thanks but it also means to tell the truth, to acknowledge what is real. This word teaches us that when we look deeply at our experience, even a difficult and unpleasant experience, and investigate the full truth about it, we will almost always find something to be grateful for, even if it is simply the fact that we are alive and that that is a miracle.

But it also teaches us what my colleague Lisa Zbar calls "the spiritual practice of AND." We can give thanks AND be sad or angry or afraid at the same time. This AND that are both true. And if both are true, then we can honor the fullness of our experience. We can be with the difficult emotions and discern the appropriate action to address them. And we can be with the gratitude that sweetens our lives and helps us respond from a place of abundance.[30]

CONCLUSION

As modern Jews have debated theology and politics, questions about showing gratitude have been deeply contentious as well. Many thinkers have warned against improper conceptions of gratitude that blind people to injustices and prevent the exercise of other important virtues. Others have counseled letting go of concerns about injustice and focusing on appreciating goodness to a greater degree.

Amid the debates about God, the state, the family, emotions, and the proper response to injustice, different approaches emerge to the question of where goodness may be found. At one extreme is Shalom Arush's contention that we should be grateful for everything because everything, even hideous abuse, is good; on the other hand, Emma Goldman warns how gratitude can easily lead to abuse.

Theology plays an important role in these debates. Goldman, a staunch atheist, rejects Jewish traditions that ask for continual gratitude to God; Arush champions a Hasidic theology that stresses God's goodness and power over all events. Similar theological convictions will intersect with ideas about moral virtue in the following chapter, on forgiveness.

7

Forgiveness (*Salḥanut*)

A number of the tensions regarding gratitude (chapter 6) have parallels with tensions regarding forgiveness. Just as some have argued that being a grateful person requires the acceptance of harm, some have argued that being a forgiving person requires accepting harms and those who have caused them. Just as some have argued that being overly grateful shows servility and a lack of self-respect, some have argued that being overly forgiving shows these same vices. And just as some have warned that gratitude can be abused by those in power, some have warned that forgiveness may be linked with the abuse of power.

This chapter also reflects tensions regarding forgiveness found in ancient Rabbinic texts. Those texts sometimes indicate that an ideally forgiving person will forgive unconditionally, even when an offender has not engaged in repentance.[1] For example, the Talmud records that the ancient sage Mar Zutra forgave all who harmed him when he climbed into bed each night, reciting: "I forgive all who have pained me" (BT *Megillah* 28a).[2] Another statement, printed four times in the Talmud,[3] teaches that when people cede their rights to retaliation and offer forgiveness, God in turn forgives them. As one possible translation of the text would have it, God "forgives [*ma'avir*] all sins of whoever cedes [*ma'avir*] one's rights"[4]—the implication being that one should forgive rather than demand justice. Jewish thinkers who encourage unconditional forgiveness, such as Tzevi Elimelekh Shapira (section 7.2), often encourage Jews to imitate such divine forgiveness. In this model, scholar

Louis Newman points out, "unconditional forgiveness meets the offender more than halfway," emphasizing mercy and representing "an offer to restore the moral standing of the offender as a gift."[5]

But many classical Rabbinic texts indicate that forgiveness should be granted only after an offender has repented appropriately—acknowledging wrongdoing, asking forgiveness, and providing appropriate restitution. In this model, Newman has written, "the moral response is to 'undo' the immoral behavior by reasserting the demands of conventional morality and requiring the offender to restore the world to the state it was in (as much as possible) prior to the offense."[6] Thus, for example, a well-known Mishnah sets the conditions for forgiveness as including not only restitution but seeking forgiveness: "Even though a person gives [monetary compensation] to one [whom he has shamed], he is not forgiven until he asks [explicitly for forgiveness] from him [whom he has shamed]."[7] Another Mishnah (referenced by Emmanuel Levinas, section 7.4) suggests that God will not forgive a person on Yom Kippur, the Day of Atonement, unless that person has first appeased the one who has been harmed: "The transgressions of man toward God are forgiven him by the Day of Atonement; the transgressions against other people are not forgiven him by the Day of Atonement if he has not first appeased the other person."[8] This text suggests a different model of imitating God: just as God forgives only those who properly repent by appeasing those whom they have harmed, so too people should forgive only those who have engaged in such repentance.

Other Rabbinic texts present portraits of great Rabbis who were particularly demanding and refused to grant forgiveness to those who sought it. One talmudic story (BT *Yoma* 87a–b), also cited in section 7.4, tells of how Rabbi Hanina refused to forgive his colleague Rab despite Rab's repeated efforts to appease him. Another group of talmudic texts question whether certain honored men may "forgo the honor" due to them—or "forgive dishonor" against them, as it might be translated—and they are unanimous that a king cannot be so forgiving of dishonor.[9] One statement suggests that a rabbi may not forgive dishonor, though all voices in these talmudic texts agree that a father can forgo the honor due to him. The question is not asked regarding mothers or other women, suggesting that the male rabbis quoted in the Talmud agree that women are not expected to demand honor or withhold forgiveness.

Still other Rabbinic texts suggest that there are clear limits to mercy with certain sinners. In one midrash,[10] Rabbi Simeon ben Lakish is quoted as saying that "one who becomes merciful when he should be cruel, in the end he is cruel when he should be merciful"—or, as Cynthia Ozick renders it in section 7.5, "whoever is merciful to the cruel will end by being indifferent to the innocent." Other texts suggest that some people are unable to repent and therefore cannot be forgiven. One Mishnah teaches that "all who cause the masses to sin" cannot repent,[11] perhaps because the effects of causing widespread sin cannot be repaired. By this logic, other sins for which restitution cannot be made—for example, murder—would also be unforgivable. And one Rabbinic text suggests that divine forgiveness is for the People of Israel alone (seemingly because of the limited repentance possible for those who are not part of Israel),[12] prompting Shapira (section 7.2) to declare, "There is no repentance for the nations of the world—it is only for Israel."

Rabbinic texts inform only some of the Jewish thinkers addressing forgiveness in this chapter. Other thinkers do not engage with these Rabbinic traditions, and some explicitly look outside what is commonly thought of as Jewish tradition. Hannah Arendt (section 7.3) draws inspiration from Jesus of Nazareth, who famously asked God to forgive those who crucified him, "for they know not what they do." Marc Ellis (section 7.6) cites the feminist Christian theologian Carter Heyward. Jacques Derrida (section 7.7) refers to the "Abrahamic heritage" of Judaism, Christianity, and Islam.

Much of modern Jewish discourse about forgiveness has centered on facing the horrors of the Holocaust, and the sources below reflect this focus. A number of thinkers challenge the idea that perpetrators of genocide may be forgiven, though they discuss forgiveness in very different ways. Arendt, for example, writes of evils that cannot be forgiven but heralds the virtue of forgiveness more generally; Cynthia Ozick, by contrast, urges readers to see the brutality of forgiveness and the virtues of vengeance in the wake of the Holocaust.

Three sources consider expectations of forgiveness placed upon women, especially within contexts of marriage and divorce. Urging forgiveness for the sake of *shalom bayit* ("peace at home" or "family harmony"), Eliezer Papo (section 7.1) expects wives to be forbearing even when subjected to violent abuse. To Susan Schnur (section 7.8), preaching forgiveness to women is often a kind of harassment and may facilitate abuse. Finally, Shalom Arush (section 7.10) encourages women to forgive their ex-husbands for the harms they committed—a reflection of the persistence of patriarchal expectations.

7.1. PEACE AT HOME THROUGH FORGIVENESS AND FORBEARANCE

Eliezer Papo (1785–1828) was the rabbi of the Ottoman town of Silistra (modern-day Bulgaria) and a noted author of books on halakhah and musar. His popular musar book *Pele Yo'etz* (Wondrous adviser) covers a wide range of virtues. In chapters devoted to "one's rabbi," "the love of sons and daughters," and "the love of husband and wife," Papo urges his readers to be generally forgiving, as it is "fitting for a person to forgive every other person, and to seek mercy, so that no one be punished because of him."[13] Repeatedly citing the talmudic dictum of the ancient sage Raba that "[God] forgives all sins of whoever cedes his rights," Papo promises that God will reward the one who patiently overlooks another's sins, cedes rights to retaliation, and forgives.[14] Victims may appropriately pardon offenders even when they have seen no signs of repentance, for example by reciting at bedtime a liturgical formula of forgiveness (building on the talmudic prayer of Mar Zutra): "I forgive and pardon anyone who has angered or vexed me or sinned against me. . . ." Certainly, when "his Jewish brother comes to ask forgiveness," a Jew should "immediately agree to forgive, granting complete forgiveness."[15] Papo's stress here appears to come from his belief in the need for solidarity among Jews.

Elsewhere in his book, Papo notes that different relationships among Jews may require different approaches to forgiveness. He refers to the talmudic principle that while a king may not forgo his honor (such that one cannot be forgiven for dishonoring a king), a rabbi or a father may forgo honor (forgiving someone who dishonors them). Expanding on this, he suggests that while dishonor may be forgiven, a rabbi or father may not be forgiving with a more extreme offense—namely, humiliation (*bizayon*). The Talmud singles out relationships with fathers and rabbis as exceptional; Papo indicates that one should be more forgiving in other sorts of relationships.

For example, husbands and wives are expected to "forgive one another, nullifying their wills for the sake of peace at home [*shalom bayit*]." Papo points to the importance of "peace at home" by noting that even God is willing to go to great measures for the sake of such peace. According to the Talmud (BT *Nedarim* 66b), the *sotah* ritual to test a wife's fidelity requires the erasure of God's name, but God is willing to even suffer the erasure of the divine name for the sake of *shalom bayit*; so too, spouses should be willing to go to great lengths to forgive one another. Elsewhere Papo urges the husband whose wife is "difficult" to refrain from anger and "endure everything for the sake of peace at home."

Yet in Papo's patriarchal approach, the expectations of forbearance for men and women are very different. The selection below calls for women to be "forbearing" even when they are abused and raped. While Papo does not explicitly require that women forgive the worst forms of abuse, he nonetheless counsels them to suffer and accept all abuse as God's will. Papo's approach reflects profound sexism as well as a theology that God is responsible for all that happens.

Eliezer Papo, *Pele Yo'etz* (1824)

There are senseless wives who argue with their husbands over their failure to provide for the needs of their home. But this is utter stupidity in any case. If the husband is poor and cannot provide, it should be sufficient that he has pain, pressure, shame, and embarrassment that he cannot provide, which he cannot reveal to his wife; the wife needs to be reasonable and not add pain to his pain. . . . And if God expands her husband's capacities and he is nevertheless stingy in providing for the needs of the home, or delays doing so for some other reason, why should it matter to her? Whatever he provides, she should serve him, and he will eat. If he should say to her, "Why did you not make me the delicacies that I love?" she may say to him, "How can I make them from what you have not provided?" If she argues about clothing, jewelry, and pleasures, this is "futile and pursuit of wind" [Eccles. 1:14], for "better a dry crust with peace [than a house full of feasting with strife]" [Prov. 17:1]. And if God's great name, "written in sanctity" [BT *Nedarim* 66b], is permitted to be erased for the sake of peace at home, how much more so must a husband and wife forgive one another, nullifying their wills for the sake of peace at home.

The wife needs to consider that perhaps her husband is not as wealthy as she thought and that he does not want to tell her that he cannot provide, lest he incur bad luck, and reasons such as this that he may have should be sufficient for not fulfilling her desire. . . . So too, the wife needs to consider that when her husband seems angry at her for nothing, perhaps he has had some disappointment in the marketplace, and he spoke to her in this way out of his abundant anxiety and anger—as people say, "He will quarrel with his wife, whatever his capacities." She needs to forbear, and not to anger him, and not to cause him more pain. . . . And a woman who has fallen into the fate of being with a husband who is truly evil and wicked, who beats and curses and preys on her and rapes her—she should accept the judgment of heaven upon herself, and forbear, and not cease to atone for her soul, for great will be her reward in the world to come.[16]

7.2 THE MODEL OF DIVINE FORGIVENESS

Rabbi Tzevi Elimelekh Shapira of Dinov (1785–1841) was an influential Hasidic leader in Galicia and Hungary, noted for his fierce opposition to the Haskalah and related modernizing trends. Like Eliezer Papo, Shapira urged his audience to give up their anger and forgive those who sinned against them. The selection below stresses the model of ideal forgiveness offered by God.

Shapira describes God as ready to forgive in response to human repentance. He depicts God as infinitely forgiving, open even to the repentance of the person who continually sins. There is no implication that God will forgive unconditionally, without at least some sign of repentance, but neither is there an implication that repentance is terribly difficult for God's children. In offering forgiveness, God will meet an offender more than halfway.

Shapira implies that Jews should model their own forgiveness on God's forgiveness, even though no human being can be as forgiving as God. To the greatest degree possible, a Jew "will be merciful and will cede his rights, pardoning and forgiving anyone who angers him." Just as God meets the offender more than halfway, God's children should "cede their rights" and meet their repentant neighbors more than halfway.

For Shapira, though, only a small portion of human beings can qualify as "repentant neighbors." Building on a classical midrash that points to the limits of divine forgiveness toward non-Jews, Shapira teaches (in part II of the selection below) that those who are not Jewish are unable to repent before God. He explains this conclusion with reference to the talmudic principle that one cannot be forgiven for dishonoring a king, whereas one can be forgiven for dishonoring a father; since for non-Jews God is like a king, non-Jews who offend God's dignity cannot be forgiven. God is, however, like a father for Jews, and therefore willing to forgo His children's offenses.

Shapira doesn't spell out the implications of this for human ethics, but he appears to join Eliezer Papo in stressing that Jews should be forgiving of their fellow Jews. It would seem that Jews need not be so forgiving of their non-Jewish neighbors, who are limited in their ability to repent.

We should bear in mind, however, that Shapira does not believe that all who appear to be Jewish are in fact part of the true People of Israel (a view also articulated in section 4.5 by a follower of Shapira's great-great-grandson Ḥayyim Elazar Shapira). In his fierce opposition to the Haskalah, and especially its efforts to learn from non-Jewish sources,

Shapira famously depicted modernizing Jews as the *erev rav*—the non-Israelite "mixed multitude" that joined the Israelites when they came out of Egypt.[17] Those who have committed such grave sins have taken themselves out of the category of Israel. And since they are no longer "God's children" who are readily forgiven by God, they cannot easily repent, as true Israelites can. As Shapira puts it in another passage, God will judge the People of Israel with mercy, but grave sinners "will not be judged in accord with the standards of Israel, for they have sought to imitate the nations of other lands."[18] For Shapira, then, there is no virtue in forgiving modernizing Jews.

Tzevi Elimelekh Shapira, *Benei Yisakhar* (early nineteenth century)

I. If a mortal has good character traits, he will be merciful and will cede his rights, pardoning and forgiving anyone who angers him.

Nonetheless, when the one who angers him does so continually, day after day, even a good man's good traits of mercy will cease, and he will not want to forgive again. There are many different variations of this, including with the man who is most merciful and most patient.

But, even in this case, every mortal character trait has its limit, for being mortal, he has a limit and an end, and so all of his traits are limited—in contrast to the character traits of the Blessed God, for He is without limit or end, and all of His character traits are without limit. . . . He will certainly accept your repentance, at any time whatsoever. Even if you have gone very far astray, He is good and forgiving, and He will pardon and forgive and provide atonement.[19]

II. There is no repentance for the nations of the world—it is only for Israel.[20] Our ancient sages gave us a reason, that "though a king may forgive his being dishonored, the dishonor is not forgiven." Thus by law there is no repentance—but this is only for the nations of the world, as God is called a "king" only for them, as it is written "God reigns over the *nations*" (Ps. 47:9) and "Who would not revere You, O King of the *nations*?" (Jer. 10:7).

This is not so for Israel, of whom it is written, "You are children of the Lord your God" (Deut. 14:1)—God is a "father" for us (BT *Kiddushin* 32a), and when a father forgives his being dishonored, the dishonor is forgiven. Therefore, there *is* repentance for Israel.[21]

7.3. UNDOING THE PAST FOR THE SAKE OF THE OTHER

The German-born political theorist Hannah Arendt (1905–75) fled Nazi Germany, later lived in Paris, was imprisoned in the Gurs Internment Camp, and finally immigrated to the United States. She is best known for her critical studies of totalitarianism.

Like the next six figures profiled in this chapter, Arendt was the sort of modern Jew whom Shapira would have harshly condemned. Generally described as a secular Jewish thinker, she was decidedly uninterested in learning from the classical Jewish sources Shapira and Papo viewed as essential and divine.[22] Rather, in her discussions of forgiveness, Arendt turned to a Jewish figure whom Shapira and Papo would have viewed as completely alien to authentic Jewish tradition: Jesus of Nazareth.

In so doing, Arendt joined many other modern Jewish thinkers who rejected Christianity but appreciated Jesus's teachings. Arendt, however, held that Jesus's insights were by no means "religious"—they could be understood "in a strictly secular sense." She explicitly rejected the idea (voiced by Shapira, section 7.2) that the power of forgiveness may be derived from God.

In her book *The Human Condition*, excerpted below, Arendt holds that forgiveness is a social virtue. One who forgives for the sake of another "undoes" what that person has done, miraculously changing the past and freeing the other from the consequences of wrong action.[23] Because of the social character of the virtue, Arendt does not think it is possible to "forgive" oneself. But forgiving the other also benefits the one who forgives, above all by offering "freedom from vengeance." Although the appropriately forgiving person need not reject all forms of punishment for all crimes, such a person must renounce the right to vengeance.

Arendt views most wrongdoing as appropriately met with forgiveness because its evil consequences are not intended. People are often thoughtless, shaped by their social conditions, and, with rare exceptions, not willfully intending the evil consequences of their deeds; hence, most deeds may be labeled as "trespasses" and may be forgiven.

But Arendt does not embrace unconditional forgiveness. There are rare examples of "willed evil," including the "radical evil" she herself had been exposed to. Jesus, she notes, did not counsel forgiving such offenses; rather, he hoped for just retribution. Human beings may not be capable of adequately punishing such radical evil—could the willful engineers of the Holocaust ever be adequately punished?—and such offenses that cannot be fully punished by human courts also cannot be forgiven.

Arendt has been criticized for taking an overly forgiving attitude, particularly toward the philosopher Martin Heidegger, her mentor, friend, and onetime lover who became a member of the Nazi Party and never apologized for his Nazism. Arendt reconciled with him after World War II; her apparent forgiveness may reflect her commitment to forgiving trespasses, even without repentance, for the sake of the person being forgiven. As the excerpt below concludes, "Forgiving and the relationship it establishes is always an eminently personal (though not necessarily individual or private) affair in which *what* was done is forgiven for the sake of *who* did it."[24]

Hannah Arendt, *The Human Condition* (1958)

The possible redemption from the predicament of irreversibility—of being unable to undo what one has done though one did not, and could not, have known what he was doing—is the faculty of forgiving. . . . Without being forgiven, released from the consequences of what we have done, our capacity to act would, as it were, be confined to one single deed from which we could never recover; we would remain the victims of its consequences forever, not unlike the sorcerer's apprentice who lacked the magic formula to break the spell. . . . [Forgiving] depend[s] on plurality, on the presence and acting of others, for no one can forgive himself. . . . Forgiving . . . enacted in solitude or isolation remain[s] without reality and can signify no more than a role played before oneself.

The discoverer of the role of forgiveness in the realm of human affairs was Jesus of Nazareth. The fact that he made this discovery in a religious context and articulated it in religious language is no reason to take it any less seriously in a strictly secular sense. . . . It is decisive in our context that Jesus maintains against the "scribes and pharisees" first that it is not true that only God has the power to forgive, and second that this power does not derive from God—as though God, not men, would forgive through the medium of human beings—but on the contrary must be mobilized by men toward each other before they can hope to be forgiven by God also. . . .

Crime and willed evil are rare, even rarer perhaps than good deeds; according to Jesus, they will be taken care of by God in the Last Judgment, which plays no role whatsoever in life on earth, and the Last Judgment is not characterized by forgiveness but by just retribution (*apodounai*). But trespassing is an everyday occurrence which is in the very nature of action's constant establishment of new relationships within a web of relations, and it needs forgiving, dismissing, in order to make it possible for life to go on by constantly releasing men from what they have done unknowingly. Only through this constant mutual release from what they do can men remain free agents, only by constant willingness to change their minds and start again can they be trusted with so great a power as that to begin something new.

In this respect, forgiveness is the exact opposite of vengeance, which acts in the form of re-acting against an original trespassing, whereby far from putting an end to the consequences of the first misdeed, everybody remains bound to the process, permitting the chain reaction contained in every action to take its unhindered course. In contrast to revenge, which is the natural, automatic reaction to transgression and which because of the irreversibility of the action process can be expected and even calculated, the act of forgiving can never be predicted; it is the only reaction that acts in an unexpected way and thus retains, though being a reaction, something of the original character of action. Forgiving, in other words, is the only reaction which does not merely re-act but acts anew and unexpectedly, unconditioned by the act which provoked it and therefore freeing from its consequences both the one who forgives and the one who is forgiven. The freedom contained in Jesus' teachings of forgiveness is the freedom from vengeance, which incloses both doer and sufferer in the relentless automatism of the action process, which by itself need never come to an end.

The alternative to forgiveness, but by no means its opposite, is punishment, and both have in common that they attempt to put an end to something that without interference could go on endlessly. It is therefore quite significant, a structural element in the realm of human affairs, that men are unable to forgive what they cannot punish and that they are unable to punish what has turned out to be unforgivable. This is the true hallmark of those offenses which, since Kant, we call "radical evil" and about whose nature so little is known, even to us who have been exposed to one of their rare outbursts on the public scene. All we know is that we can neither punish nor forgive such offenses and that they therefore transcend the realm of human affairs and the potentialities of human power, both of which they radically destroy wherever they make their appearance. Here, where the deed itself dispossesses us of all power, we can indeed only repeat with Jesus: "It were better for him that a millstone were hanged about his neck, and he cast into the sea."

Perhaps the most plausible argument that forgiving and acting are as closely connected as destroying and making comes from that aspect of forgiveness where the undoing of what was done seems to show the same revelatory character as the deed itself. Forgiving and the relationship it establishes is always an eminently personal (though not necessarily individual or private) affair in which *what* was done is forgiven for the sake of *who* did it.[25]

7.4. FORGIVENESS IN THE TALMUD

Like Arendt, the philosopher Emmanuel Levinas (1906–95) was a Jewish thinker who also studied with and admired the teachings of Martin Heidegger, also lived in Paris in the 1930s, also survived internment in a Nazi camp in France, and also wrote penetratingly about issues of forgiveness after the Holocaust. Levinas, like Arendt, wrote about forgiveness acting on the past, but rather than claiming that forgiveness miraculously "undoes" the past, he asserted that forgiveness makes it *as if* the past has been undone—"*as though* that instant had not passed on."[26] And while Arendt drew inspiration from Jesus of Nazareth, Levinas drew on the Babylonian Talmud, a source that informed much of his writing.

The selection below, from one of Levinas's "talmudic readings," begins with the Mishnah's ruling that "the transgressions of man toward God are forgiven him by the Day of Atonement; the transgressions against other people are not forgiven him by the Day of Atonement if he has not first appeased the other person" (*Yoma* 8:9). It follows, as Levinas understands it, that interpersonal forgiveness should be granted when an offender has appeased the victim by admitting fault, seeking forgiveness, and engaging in the repentance required for reconciliation. The Gemara, the discussion of the Mishnah, also cites Raba's dictum that one will be forgiven if one forgives, "ceding his right" to retribution against an offender. The implication is that one should forgive a repentant offender (and that one who forgives then deserves to be forgiven in turn). Whereas Papo (section 7.1) read the same dictum as addressing divine forgiveness, Levinas interprets Raba's dictum solely in terms of human forgiveness.

As Levinas discusses in the selection below, the Gemara also brings the story of a renowned sage, Rabbi Hanina, who refuses to forgive his colleague Rab despite Rab's repeated efforts to appease him. The key portion of the story, as printed in Levinas's work, is as follows:

Rab was commenting upon a text before Rabbi. When Rab Hiyya came in, he started his reading from the beginning again. Bar Kappara came in—he began again; Rab Simeon, the son of Rabbi came in, and

Rab again went back to the beginning. Then Rab Hanina bar Hama came in, and Rab said: How many times am I to repeat myself? He did not go back to the beginning. Rab Hanina was wounded by it. For thirteen years, on *Yom Kippur* eve, Rab went to seek forgiveness, and Rab Hanina refused to be appeased. . . . And why did Rabbi Hanina act this way? Didn't Raba teach: One forgives all sins of whoever cedes his right? The reason is that Rabbi Hanina had a dream in which Rab was hanging from a palm tree. It is said: "Whoever appears in a dream, hanging from a palm tree, is destined for sovereignty." He concluded from it that Rab would be head of the academy. That is why he did not let himself be appeased, so that Rab would leave and teach in Babylon [BT *Yoma* 87a–b].[27]

What can be learned about the virtue of forgiveness from this story? In his discussion below, Levinas rejects the possibility that Rab Hanina feared Rab's designs on his own position, and he considers how Rab Hanina's refusal to forgive might otherwise be justified. He weighs the suggestion that perhaps forgiveness is never possible because the offender may always be harboring unconscious, aggressive desires. As such, Levinas raises the question: Is forgiveness truly a virtue?

He ultimately indicates that forgiveness may be a virtue but nonetheless it is particularly problematic to forgive offenders who are fully conscious of their aggressive desires and fail to repent for them. From this perspective, it was best for Rab Hanina not to forgive Rab because Rab failed to repent for the sins that he was very conscious of; all the more so, Levinas says, he cannot readily forgive Martin Heidegger, who knowingly supported Nazism and failed to repent. For Levinas, Heidegger's sins must not be viewed as mere "trespasses," as they may have been by Arendt. Though Levinas is open to forgiving Germans who did acknowledge and repent for their complicity with Nazism, forgiving Heidegger is inappropriate.

Later in his talmudic reading, Levinas admires the "savage greatness" of a biblical text that describes "retaliatory justice" (2 Sam. 21) and the Talmud's treatment of that text (BT *Yevamot* 58b–59a). He concludes (as shown below) with the determination that the Talmud supports a right for human beings to demand retaliatory justice (the law of talion, i.e., "an eye for an eye"), yet the People of Israel prefer forgiveness rather than claiming this right. To be a member of the People of Israel is to prioritize mercy and forgiveness and to cede one's right to retaliation.

Like Shapira, Levinas distinguishes between the People of Israel and other people. But, unlike Shapira, Levinas does not define "Israel" by means of ontological distinctions between nations or halakhic rules determining Jewish identity. Rather, he indicates that *anyone* who responds to the other with appropriate humility, justice, compassion, and forgiveness is part of Israel. Those who are too demanding of their rights to retaliate cannot be recognized as part of Israel; those who cede their rights are known as "Israel." The People of Israel need not forgive unrepentant Nazis, but they must be merciful, forgo vengeance, and be open to repentance.[28]

Emmanuel Levinas, "Toward the Other" (1963)

There can be no forgiveness that the guilty party has not sought! The guilty party must recognize his fault. The offended party must want to receive the entreaties of the offending party. Further, no person can forgive if forgiveness has not been asked him by the offender, if the guilty party has not tried to appease the offended. . . .

But how could Rab Hanina have been so harsh as to refuse thirteen times to grant the forgiveness that was humbly sought of him? He refused thirteen times, for on the fourteenth *Yom Kippur*, Rab, unforgiven, left to teach in Babylon. Rab Hanina's attitude is even less understandable, given the teaching of Raba: "One forgives all sins to whoever cedes his right." Whoever cedes his right behaves, in fact, as if he had only obligations and as if well-ordered charity began and ended not with oneself but with the other. Didn't Rab Hanina's intransigence put Rab in the position of the one to whom all sins will be forgiven?

The Gemara's explanation of Rab Hanina's behavior makes me ill at ease. Rab Hanina had a dream in which Rab appeared, hanging from a palm tree. Whoever appears thus in a dream is destined to sovereignty. Rab Hanina could foresee the future sovereignty of Rab, that is to say, his becoming head of the academy. (Is there another sovereignty for a Jew?) Thus, Rab Hanina, having guessed that Rab would succeed him, preferred to make him leave. A petty story!

This makes no sense. Our text must be understood in another way. I worked hard at it. I told my troubles to my friends. For the Talmud requires discourse and companionship. Woe to the self-taught! Of course one must have good luck and find intelligent interlocutors. I thus spoke of my disappointment to a young Jewish poet, Mrs. Atlan. Here is the solution she suggests: Whenever we have dreams, we are in the realm of psychoanalysis and the unconscious. . . . Now, in the story that is troubling us, what is at stake? Rab recognizes his fault and asks Hanina for forgiveness. The offended party can grant forgiveness when the offender has become conscious of the wrong he has done. First difficulty: the good will of the offended party. We are sure of it, given the personality of Rab Hanina. Why then is he so unbending? Because there is another difficulty: Is the offender capable of measuring the extent of his wrongdoing? Do we know the limits of our ill will? And do we therefore truly have the capacity to ask for forgiveness? No doubt Rab thought he had been a bit brusque in refusing to begin his reading of the text again when Rab Hanina bar Hama, his master, came into the school. But Rab Hanina finds out through a dream more about Rab than Rab knew about himself. The dream revealed Rab's secret ambitions, beyond the inoffensive gesture at the origin of the incident. Rab, without knowing it, wished to take his master's place. Given this, Rab Hanina could not forgive. How is one to forgive if the offender, unaware of his deeper thoughts, cannot ask for forgiveness? As soon as you have taken the path of offenses, you may have taken a path with no way out. There are two conditions for forgiveness: the good will of the offended party and the full awareness of the offender. But the offender is in essence unaware. The aggressiveness of the offender is perhaps his very unconsciousness. Aggression is the lack of attention *par excellence*. In essence, forgiveness would be impossible. . . .

But perhaps there is something altogether different in all this. One can, if pressed to the limit, forgive the one who has spoken unconsciously. But it is very difficult to forgive Rab, who was fully aware and destined for a great fate, which was prophetically revealed to his master. One can forgive many Germans, but there are some Germans it is difficult to forgive. It is difficult to forgive Heidegger. If Hanina could not forgive the just and humane Rab because he was also the brilliant Rab, it is even less possible to forgive Heidegger. Here I am brought back to the present, to the new attempts to clear Heidegger, to take away his responsibility. . . .

The Talmud teaches that one cannot force men who demand retaliatory justice [*justice du talion*] to grant forgiveness.[29] It teaches us that Israel does not deny this imprescriptible right to others. But it teaches us above all that if Israel recognizes this right, it does not ask it for itself and that to be Israel is to not claim it.[30]

7.5. FORGIVENESS CAN BRUTALIZE

As part of a symposium published in 1969, the American novelist, short-story writer, and essayist Cynthia Ozick (b. 1928) responded to a question raised by Holocaust survivor Simon Wiesenthal: Was he right to have refused to grant forgiveness to a dying and not-obviously-repentant Nazi for his crimes against other Jews? Her answer, and those of other authors, were published in Wiesenthal's book *The Sunflower*.

Like Hannah Arendt and Emmanuel Levinas, Ozick rejects the idea that it is a virtue to be unconditionally forgiving; some crimes are so evil that they cannot be forgiven. But Ozick has fewer positive things to say about forgiveness than Arendt and Levinas, and she has many more positive things to say about vengeance. Unlike Levinas, Ozick claims the right to retaliate, and unlike Arendt, for whom forgiveness offers release from vengeance, Ozick proclaims the right to retaliation as "vengeance." While she sees forgiveness as a virtue in response to ordinary trespasses—as with a child who can be forgiven for muddying a carpet—she forcefully warns against forgiveness when dealing with crimes whose effects cannot be reversed and "washed away." Such crimes must be met with vengeance, which she defines not as retaliating against evil with further evil but as "bringing public justice to evil . . . by making certain never to condone" or "even appearing to condone it." For Ozick, human beings must demand justice, and when they forgive they must be extremely careful not to condone evil, to forget evil, to negate the rights of victims, or to claim that history can be reversed and undone.

Cynthia Ozick's Response in *The Sunflower* (1969)

Often we are asked to think this way: vengeance brutalizes, forgiveness refines.

But the opposite can be true. The rabbis said, "Whoever is merciful to the cruel will end by being indifferent to the innocent." Forgiveness can brutalize.

You will object, "Only if it seems to condone. But forgiveness does not condone or excuse. It allows for redemption, for a clean slate, a fresh start; it encourages beginning again. Forgiveness permits renewal."

Only if there is a next time. "I forgive you," we say to the child who has muddied the carpet, "but next time don't do it again." Next time she will leave the muddy boots outside the door; forgiveness, with its enlarging capacities, will have taught her. Forgiveness is an effective teacher. Meanwhile, the spots can be washed away.

But murder is irrevocable. Murder is irreversible. With murder there is no "next time." Even if forgiveness restrains one from perpetrating a new batch of corpses (and there is no historical demonstration of this in Nazi Germany), will the last batch come alive again?

There are spots forgiveness cannot wash out. Forgiveness, which permits redemption, can apply only to a condition susceptible of redemption.

You will object: "If forgiveness cannot wash away murder, neither can vengeance. If forgiveness is not redemptive, surely vengeance is less so, because vengeance requites evil with an equal evil, thereby adding to the store of evil in the world."

But that is a misunderstanding. Vengeance does not requite evil with evil; vengeance cannot requite, repay, even out, equate, redress. If it could, vengeance on a mass murderer would mean killing all the members of his family and a great fraction of his nation; and still his victims would not come alive.

What we call "vengeance" is the act of bringing public justice to evil—not by repeating the evil, not by imitating the evil, not by initiating a new evil, but by making certain never to condone the old one; never even appearing to condone it.

"Public" justice? Yes. While the evil was going on, to turn aside from it, to avoid noticing it, became complicity. And in the same way, after three or four decades have passed and the evil has entered history, to turn aside from it—to forget—again becomes complicity. Allowing the evil to slip into the collective amnesia of its own generation, or of the next generation, is tantamount to condoning it.

You will object: "Here you are, naming vengeance as public justice because it does not condone evil. But forgiveness too does not condone evil. It doesn't matter that it may sometimes appear to; the fact is it doesn't. And you have already demonstrated that there are some evils forgiveness cannot wash away. Yet now you say that vengeance, like forgiveness, neither condones nor washes away the evil. How, then, do vengeance and forgiveness differ?"

In this way: forgiveness is pitiless. It forgets the victim. It negates the right of the victim to his own life. It blurs over suffering and death. It drowns the past. It cultivates sensitiveness toward the murderer at the price of insensitiveness toward the victim. . . .

It is forgiveness that is relentless. The face of forgiveness is mild, but how stony to the slaughtered. . . .

I discover a quotation attributed to Hannah Arendt: "The only antidote to the irreversibility of history is the faculty of forgiveness." Jabberwocky at last. She is the greatest moral philosopher of the age, but even she cannot make a Lazarus of history.[31]

7.6. REVOLUTIONARY FORGIVENESS

The American theologian Marc Ellis (b. 1952) has written extensively on Israeli-Palestinian relations, Jewish-Christian relations, and justice and peace studies. He is best known for his criticism of the State of Israel's treatment of Palestinians and his criticism of modern Jews who associate Judaism with Israeli state power.

In the selection below, Ellis seeks to build on Hannah Arendt's concept of forgiveness. Like Arendt, he draws on insights from a Christian source—in his case, the feminist Christian theologian Carter Heyward. While Ellis rejects ideas of unconditional forgiveness associated with some forms of Christianity, he appreciates Heyward's concept of "revolutionary forgiveness," which stresses forgiveness as part of an effort to bring justice to the world. Ellis argues that Jewish tradition affirms this very concept of forgiveness, for (as he puts it elsewhere) "in the Jewish tradition forgiveness cannot be asked for and accepted by God without a justice action plan. What is forgiveness without justice?"[32]

Like many post-Holocaust Jewish thinkers, including Arendt, Levinas, and Ozick, Ellis objects to notions of forgiveness that fail to recognize atrocities and ignore claims to justice. Revolutionary forgiveness, by contrast, recognizes the past, encourages critical thinking about justice, and ensures a just future.

Ellis sees decision-making around forgiveness as fraught with moral dangers. On the one hand, refusals to forgive can diminish self-critical reflection. Ellis supports the Jewish refusal to forgive perpetrators of the Holocaust, but he warns that the accompanying focus on the unique atrocities of the Holocaust may prevent Jews from seeing ways in which they too have engaged in atrocities amid the creation and defense of the State of Israel. On the other hand, forgiveness can diminish self-critical reflection, as when Jews forgive Christians for their antisemitism but their reconciliation leads them to ally against new enemies—for example, Palestinian Muslims—and thereby to perpetuate new injustices.

Ellis also warns that acts of forgiveness can become acts of self-interested deal-making, as when Jews forgive Christians on the condition that they support the interests of the State of Israel and ignore Palestinian rights. Elsewhere in his writings, Ellis criticizes Levinas (section 7.4) for sometimes seeking alliances along these lines—reconciling with "civilized" European Christians while warning against Palestinians and others whom Levinas viewed as insufficiently civilized.[33] From Ellis's perspective, forgiveness that seeks such reconciliation is far from the virtue of true—that is, revolutionary—forgiveness.

Marc Ellis, *O, Jerusalem!* (1999)

Carter Heyward, a Christian theologian, has emphasized the need for forgiveness as a way of embarking on a path toward justice and reconciliation. Heyward terms this "revolutionary forgiveness," a process of forgiveness in which the righting of the wrong that has been done is given priority. The righting of wrong is itself a process of self-discovery and change and becomes, with the act of forgiveness, a way of viewing the world as it is transformed in confession and justice.

In this journey, healing takes place within and between those who were once strangers and enemies. The vision of a just future is essential to enable forgiveness to realize its authenticity and reach its revolutionary potential. For without the movement toward justice forgiveness is simply a piety without substance and leaves the world as it is. Freeing the future, of course, means a forgiveness that interacts critically with the past and seeks to minimize what originally gave offense in the first place.

In her philosophical writings, Hannah Arendt has also written about forgiveness as a way of entering public life with an orientation toward the future. Her caution about forgiveness is important. For Arendt, some crimes in the public realm are so heinous that they exist outside the framework of the human. They, therefore, cannot be forgiven.

One thinks of the Holocaust in this regard, and here the challenge is simply to forge a path beyond the terrible nature of that atrocity. The tragedy of the Holocaust is exacerbated by the generation after the tragedy not because it refuses to forgive but because, by holding up that tragedy, self-critical reflection is diminished. The community chose a path that to some extent replicates what violated the community in the past. Instead of embarking on a new venture, the Jewish community seeks survival and security in the most obvious ways: territorial and national sovereignty.

The consequences for the Palestinian people are obvious, and the cycle of pain and suffering continues. One may argue that the pain of the Holocaust is extended to the Palestinians while the healing that Jews pursued through empowerment has been illusory. It may be that the cycle of dislocation and death continued by Jews after the Holocaust has increased the trauma of the Jewish people. Creating a future that anticipates the replication of the past is more than a refusal of forgiveness for an unforgivable event. Rather it extends the unforgivable act to another people not responsible for the original injury.

The trap is obvious and one that Arendt knew only too well: life cannot be defined by the unforgivable or lived indefinitely within its shadow. The task is to move on with those who will journey with you, but first the desire to move internally must be manifest. Carrying the Holocaust as a sign of distinction is a recipe for isolation and mistrust. Trust cannot be earned within the context of an event beyond even the ability to punish, nor can healing be achieved.

Forgiveness is less a definitive act than a posture of critical reflection and openness to a future beyond the past. Arendt stresses that the act of forgiveness itself is a realization of the complexity and limitations of life, as well as a release from grief. Forgiveness has future consequences for identity, culture, and politics that cannot be known in advance. Insofar as forgiveness is possible within the movement of a new solidarity, the shared history of the adversaries remains so, but in a new configuration.

In the West, the example of Jews and Christians after the Holocaust exemplifies this process. Once bitter adversaries, a new relationship of trust and mutuality has emerged. The transformed relationship is multifaceted and may involve, among other things, a solidarity against new "enemies." Clearly part of the Jewish-Christian relationship in the present is an agreement to share the spoils of Western capitalism; in some quarters Jews can be elevated into full participation in the white and Western domination over other races and cultures. Forgiveness here is a deal to resolve one injustice and unite to perpetuate further injustices with a clear conscience. The other disappears to create a different other, more convenient and more important in the present. Still the new relationship may develop a critical matrix from which Jews and Christians can recognize a constantly evolving estrangement.

The task, then, is to be vigilant in recognizing that resolution of one enmity may lead to still another projection of otherness. Could such a forgiveness, a revolutionary forgiveness whose path is justice, give birth to an Israel/Palestine where values formed in the Jewish and Palestinian exile help create a political structure that gives voice to those values?[34]

7.7. PURE FORGIVENESS

The Algerian-born French Arab-Jewish philosopher Jacques Derrida (1930–2004) is best known for developing an approach to analyzing texts and institutions known as "deconstruction" (or "deconstructionism"). Derrida has described this approach as emerging, in part, in response to the horrors of the Holocaust, which called into question the rational philosophical traditions of Europe.[35]

In his discussions of forgiveness, Derrida idealized what he described as "pure" forgiveness, which cannot be conditional in any way, prompted by anyone or anything, or aiming at any goal (as he puts it below, any "finality"). As he explained elsewhere, such "pure or unconditional forgiveness must be the event or the act of a grace that cannot be commanded. There shouldn't be a duty to forgive or a duty not to forgive."[36]

In fact, for Derrida, forgiveness merits to be called forgiveness only when it forgives someone who is guilty, who has not repented, and whose crimes are "unforgivable" and irreversible. Challenging the French-Jewish philosopher Vladimir Jankélévitch's claim that "forgiveness died in the death camps"—i.e., one cannot forgive the perpetrators of the Nazi genocide—Derrida agrees that the perpetrators of the Nazi genocide are unforgivable but asserts that this is precisely where pure forgiveness is possible.[37]

In tension with Arendt (section 7.3), who linked forgiveness with redemption, Derrida rejects the idea that forgiveness can serve a goal of any sort of redemption. And whereas Arendt, Levinas, Ozick, and Ellis saw forgiveness as dependent on repentance and argued that we cannot forgive the most serious ("unforgivable") atrocities, such as those willfully committed by Holocaust perpetrators, Derrida claims that in fact forgiveness is possible *only* in such situations.

Derrida notes that this may seem unintelligible—as he puts it below, "forgiveness is mad" and "must remain a madness or the impossible." But, he claims, just as the idea of conditional forgiveness is embedded within the "Abrahamic" (Jewish, Christian, Muslim) heritage, so too the unintelligible idea of unconditional forgiveness is inscribed within that heritage. He describes this idea elsewhere as "a demand for the *unconditional*, gracious, infinite, aneconomic forgiveness granted to the guilty as guilty, without counterpart, even to those who do not repent or ask forgiveness."[38]

Derrida is an apparent atheist, but this description of "gracious," "infinite" forgiveness seems to allude to "Abrahamic" concepts of divine forgiveness. As the philosopher Marguerite La Caze has argued, Derrida appears to challenge Arendt's claim that forgiveness is a human matter and suggests "that pure forgiveness somehow goes beyond the human."[39] If so, this would seem to place Derrida in an odd partnership with Tzevi Elimelekh Shapira (section 7.2), the other figure in this chapter to make such a claim. Shapira, however, would be horrified by Derrida's atheism and his rejection of traditional Judaism (including his failure to acknowledge the superiority of Jews and Judaism).

Like Ellis (section 7.6), Derrida is deeply concerned by how forgiveness may be abused by those in power. When sovereigns issue claims of forgiveness for strategic or political reasons, as when war criminals are pardoned for the sake of "social and political health,"[40] such "forgiveness" has little to do with "pure forgiveness." But whereas Ellis speaks of conditional forgiveness as revolutionary precisely because of its political potential, Derrida seeks to detach forgiveness from power altogether, and his model of "mad" unconditional forgiveness dismisses all pragmatism aimed at justice.

Such madness would surely offend all thinkers profiled in this chapter who highlight the importance of repentance and are concerned with matters of justice. Ozick (section 7.5), for one, would see Derrida's forgiveness of the unforgivable as negation of the victims' suffering and rights. Derrida seems to admit that pure forgiveness will indeed be offensive—and yet, somehow, in its very offensiveness, forgiving the unforgivable represents an extraordinary ideal of virtue toward which human beings should aspire.[41]

Jacques Derrida, "On Forgiveness" (2001)

I shall risk this proposition: each time forgiveness is at the service of a finality, be it noble or spiritual (atonement or redemption, reconciliation, salvation), each time that it aims to re-establish a normality (social, national, political, psychological) by a work of mourning, by some therapy or ecology of memory, then the "forgiveness" is not pure—nor is its concept. Forgiveness is not, it *should not be*, normal, normative, normalizing. It *should* remain exceptional and extraordinary, in the face of the impossible: as if it interrupted the ordinary course of historical temporality. . . . Forgiveness forgives only the unforgivable. . . .

[Vladimir Jankélévitch argues that] forgiveness will no longer have meaning where the crime has become, like the Shoah, "inexpiable," "irreparable," out of proportion to all human measure. "Forgiveness died in the death camps," he says. Yes. Unless it only becomes possible from the moment that it appears impossible. Its history would begin, on the contrary, with the unforgivable. . . .

Imagine . . . that I forgive on the condition that the guilty one repents, mends his ways, asks forgiveness, and thus would be changed by a new obligation, and that from then on he would no longer be exactly the same as the one who was found to be culpable. In this case, can one still speak of forgiveness? This would be too simple on both sides: one forgives someone other than the guilty one. In order for there to be forgiveness, must one not on the contrary forgive both the fault and the guilty *as such*, where the one and the other remain as irreversible as the evil, as evil itself, and being capable of repeating itself, unforgivably, without transformation, without amelioration, without repentance or promise? Must one not maintain that an act of forgiveness worthy of its name, if there ever is such a thing, must forgive the unforgivable, and without condition? And that such unconditionality is also inscribed, like its contrary, namely the condition of repentance, in "our" ["Abrahamic"] heritage? Even if this radical purity can seem excessive, hyperbolic, mad? Because if I say, as I think, that forgiveness is mad, and that it must remain a madness of the impossible, this is certainly not to exclude or disqualify it. It is even, perhaps, the only thing that arrives, that surprises, like a revolution, the ordinary course of history, politics, and law. . . . Pure and unconditional forgiveness, in order to have its own meaning, must have no "meaning," no finality, even no intelligibility. It is a madness of the impossible. . . .

What makes the "I forgive you" sometimes unbearable or odious, even obscene, is the affirmation of sovereignty. It is often addressed from the top down, it confirms its own freedom or assumes for itself the power of forgiving. . . . What I dream of, what I try to think of as the "purity" of a forgiveness worthy of its name, would be a forgiveness without power: *unconditional but without sovereignty*. The most difficult task, at once necessary and apparently impossible, would be to dissociate *unconditionality* and *sovereignty*.[42]

7.8. GENDERING FORGIVENESS

The American Reconstructionist rabbi Susan Schnur (b. 1951) is a clinical psychologist and longtime editor of the Jewish feminist magazine *Lilith*. The selection from her writing below gives particular attention to the ways in which forgiveness is praised during Rosh Hashanah and Yom

Kippur, when the male-written High Holiday liturgy stresses forgiveness and when male scholars have often stressed forgiveness as a virtue.

Schnur argues that a stress on forgiveness is necessary for males, who are socialized to be unforgiving (and also not to ask for forgiveness). But given that females are socialized to be forgiving, even "to forgive the unforgivable," they do not need to be harassed about the virtues of forgiveness. Rather, women need to be supported in doing what is more difficult for them: not forgiving, when that is appropriate; and, also, forgiving themselves. Whereas Arendt (section 7.3) declared that it was not possible to forgive oneself, for Schnur, self-forgiveness is not only possible but deeply important for many women.

As Schnur explains, girls are often socialized to be forgiving "for *shalom bayit* [for family harmony]," and concerns for *shalom bayit* lead domestic-violence victims to tolerate abuse. Schnur fiercely rejects the approach of figures like Eliezer Papo (section 7.1), who instructed women to be forgiving and thereby tolerate abuse in just this way. Hating offenders may in fact be the best response, she points out, and emotional resolution may not require giving up resentment: "Maybe we need to not forgive because hating this person who has traumatically victimized us is the way we feel most deeply safe. . . . Having Judaism support us in our authentic journey towards emotional resolution would be a deeply religious experience."

While some Jewish thinkers discussed above seem to pay no regard to gender, Schnur points out that teachings on forgiveness may be received very differently by those of different genders. "Forgiveness, in and of itself," she insists, "is a gendered issue."

Susan Schnur, "Beyond Forgiveness" (2001)

Forgiveness, in and of itself, is a gendered issue. In the seasonal Jewish work of "forgiveness" that confronts us during the Days of Awe, this means that male liturgists and scholars through the ages have formulated their ideas about forgiveness in relation to male, not female, character—and males, as most of us can attest, typically struggle with the kinds of feelings that get aroused through both the granting of forgiveness (an act that can feel shamefully sissified) and the requesting of it (that can feel craven, too). As two college-aged males in a recent workshop on gender put it, "Asking somebody to forgive you is a blow to your self-esteem. It makes you feel vulnerable and undefended, like a girl." Added the other, "It's worse than asking for directions."

Indeed, 'I did something wrong' is much harder for most males to say than it is for most females—for good reasons. As children, males are shamed about their perceived "weaknesses," and, as psychotherapists can attest, shamed children generally grow up to be people who find it extremely difficult to apologize. Also, most Dads don't do much apologizing, so that becomes the model passed on to their sons.

The statements "I'm sorry" and "I forgive you," then—the *mene mene tekel ufarsin* of the High Holiday season—fundamentally are meant to correct for male socialization. They are pro-social codewords meant to restore connection and interpersonal harmony. In my congregation the kids sing, "Let's be friends, make amends, now's the time to say 'I'm sorry'" (a ditty, with plaintive hand motions, that continues, "*please* say you'll forgive me" and "take my hand and I'll take yours"), front-loading, of course, the social harmony theme of the Days of Awe. The in-your-face incantations of the season—"I'm sorry" "I forgive you"—*need* to be in your face if you're a guy, as they are in opposition to almost all other behavioral injunctions and must transcend them. Asking for and granting forgiveness are, if you will, religious trump cards, an eleventh commandment that sanctions, for men, doing pro-social things without suffering shame.

Which brings us to female socialization, and the fact that women are systematically steered towards maintaining connections, even at great personal cost. If you imagine, say, King Solomon's adjudication in relation to the two mothers who both claimed rights to the same baby ("cut the child in half"), and you change the parents into dads—well, the story kind of fizzles, it just doesn't have the same emotional oomph, which derives not only from the mothers' ferocity of attachment when they first come to see Solomon, but, more viscerally, from the real mother's willingness to sacrifice herself, as it were, for this child. That's, in particular, the part that deeply resonates as female.

We females, indeed, know that we say "I'm sorry" to a fault—even when we're the ones being victimized! Forgiving is easy for us; it's *not* forgiving that's the struggle. We are over-socialized to stay connected, to "make peace," to make sure nobody is offended, to forget to ask if we ourselves are offended. Indeed, this is perhaps the core of our gender socialization.

To give a favorite example—some years ago in Baltimore, the American Cancer Society received hundreds of calls from women who had been led into having a conversation with a man who claimed he was from the Society but whose questions, as the interviews went on, became increasingly sexually harassing. Later interviewed for an article, the women uniformly said that what distressed them the most was not, in fact, the guy's obscenities, but their own response. They couldn't switch gears fast enough. They heard themselves saying, politely, to their horror, "I'm sorry, but I really have to go now. I'm afraid I have to hang up."

And in studies that examine how gendered norms become internalized in children, most men report that they learned what it means to be a male through being told things like "Boys don't cry" and "You go right back out there and beat the shit out of that kid." Women, on the other hand, learned what it means to be female through another set of shibboleths: "Be the bigger person," "Let it go," "Don't be so sensitive," "Let bygones be bygones," "You're more mature than your brother, let him have his way," "He doesn't mean it." All of these speak to the issue of forgiveness. Classically, we are the ones asked to make the concessions, to forgive the unforgivable, to sacrifice ourselves for the greater cause. In ultra-Orthodox Jewish families, girls internalize the message, "Do it for *shalom bayit* [for family harmony]," a phrase that domestic-violence victims in this community invoke to explain why it takes them significantly longer (than non-religious women) to report abuse. . . .

In the theological abstract, then, mandating "forgiveness" at this penitential season—that is, having male scholars and liturgists enshrine forgiveness as moral canon for their world of male worshippers and their male God—is a corrective, necessary response to the demands of the male ego in conflict with the communitarian goals of society. But asking women to enact compulsory forgiveness is an injury of a whole different color. Where's our spiritual corrective? . . .

Judaism's liturgy and theology need to support women in our work towards responsible *not* forgiving, when that's appropriate, so that we can come to believe that the world, indeed, *won't* explode as a result of our failure to "make constant nice-nice." Maybe we need to *not* forgive because Mom did—over and over—and it ruined her life. Maybe we need to *not* forgive because hating this person who has traumatically victimized us is the way we feel most deeply safe. For many of us, *not* forgiving is more difficult than forgiving, and having Judaism support us in our authentic journey towards emotional resolution would be a deeply religious experience.

Or, if we're "attached" (after all, that's what we do) to the canonical idea of forgiving, maybe we can try something refreshingly new this High Holiday season: forgiving *ourselves*. For many martyring women, this would definitely count as extremely high-level forgiving. Exhorting people to forgive, to put it another way, might be an important civilizing prod for men, but it's harassment for some women, a victimization dished out from our religious *heym* (home), from the very place that we need also to feel embraced and understood and, indeed, forgiven.[43]

7.9. FORGIVENESS REDEEMS YOUR INNER LIGHT

Karyn Kedar (b. 1957), an American Reform rabbi, is the author of *Bridge to Forgiveness: Stories and Prayers for Finding God and Restoring Wholeness*, from which the selection below is taken.

For Kedar, forgiveness is a gift to oneself rather than to others. Through forgiveness we "reinvigorate our energy and optimism," "regain a sense of life's purpose," and restore our "sense of wholeness" and "inner light." As she explains elsewhere, the light created on the first day of Creation exists "as goodness within the core of humans," as the soul that is "eternal, divine, and powerful." That light can be diminished with "every offense, every bit of criticism, every attack." But forgiveness brings back that light: "Forgiveness is light restored."[44]

Echoing Ozick (section 7.5), Kedar refuses to "forgive and forget" and thereby condone genocides and other evils. And yet, unlike Ozick, she stresses that forgiveness is nonetheless ideal, because, she insists, forgiveness need not be about the offender at all. Like Arendt, she sees how forgiveness offers liberation for the one who forgives—though unlike Arendt she does not stress liberation for the one who is forgiven.

One might conclude that, for Kedar, forgiveness is not primarily an altruistic, moral virtue. It might seem in line with the approach found in "much contemporary self-help literature," according to scholar Louis Newman: "an increasingly popular view according to which forgiveness is a gift to the one who forgives, essentially an act of self-care."[45] And yet Kedar conceives of this self-care as making altruistic moral goodness possible. Forgiveness allows for a release that then enables us to "live with goodness and love."

Karyn Kedar, *Bridge to Forgiveness* (2007)

Forgiveness is like a bridge. It carries you over an expanse to the side of life that is softer, kinder, easier to bear. It is a shift of perspective, a new way of seeing our world, a different way of experiencing our inner life. If life is really a journey, then forgiveness is a main avenue, a path to life renewed. And along the way, there are stepping-stones to carry you through: loss, anger, acceptance, forgiveness, learning, and restoration. With each step, a new perspective is gained.

Forgiveness is often understood as an act of unselfish, unconditional love, an act in which we learn to "forgive and forget," maybe even to "turn the other cheek." That is not what is described in this book. After bearing witness to evil such as the Holocaust, genocide, and other acts of terror, we search for a new paradigm. There should be no forgetting of evil acts, no condoning of offense, sin, hatred. To forget is to run the risk of allowing these evils to happen again. Yet at the same time, to hold within us the horror and pain of every offense diminishes our lives. Resentment, anger, and fear must be released from within us so that we may restore our inner light, regain a sense of life's purpose, and reinvigorate our energy and optimism, so we can live with goodness and love. . . .

Forgiveness is a spiritual state, a way of being in the world that is sustainable with work and practice. Forgiveness can be about the other, but not necessarily. It can be about reconciling with whoever has offended you. But not necessarily. It is always about finding what you have lost, restoring a sense of wholeness, redeeming your inner light. It is always about an internal process of loss and acceptance, pain and understanding, anger and blessings, love and faith regained. . . .

While you do not, cannot, forgive evil, you must shift your focus from the offender, and the offense he or she committed, to the deep and undying desire to regain equilibrium and control over your life. Forgiveness is not what you grant another person. Rather, it is a state of mind. Forgiveness is actually a decision about how to live. Forgiveness is regaining control over your life.[46]

7.10. FORGIVENESS AND FAITH IN DIVINE PROVIDENCE

In section 6.8, the Breslov Hasidic leader Rabbi Shalom Arush, extolling gratitude as a great virtue, asked victimized children not to resent their abusive parents but instead be grateful for the ways in which abusers serve as agents of God's will. That text implied that victims should forgive their abusers as well. When Arush writes directly about forgiveness, he asks victims to do just that.

The discussion below, from his book *Women's Wisdom* (addressed to "women only"), focuses on forgiving an ex-husband after a divorce. Earlier, when discussing marriage, Arush echoes the teachings of Eliezer

Papo (section 7.1), advising female readers to "lovingly accept whatever suffering they suffer from their spouse"; if the husband seeks to placate her, she should "be flexible and accepting no matter what" and "assure him that she is appeased and that she forgives him."[47] When she disagrees with her husband over financial matters, she should "be patient" and "strengthen her faith in the importance of marital peace [*shalom bayit*]."[48] In the event of a divorce, she "needs to forgive him even if he hurt her," accepting that any abuse stemmed from God (who controls all that happens in the world).

Such forgiveness should be unconditional. The ex-husband need not first repent, admit fault, or seek forgiveness; rather, Arush urges his reader to have *emunah* (faith) that all pain caused by God was for the best, and to forgive the offending ex-husband for everything. Like Papo (section 7.1), forbearance is linked with an acceptance of God's will, but Arush more explicitly links forbearance and the virtue of forgiveness.

By contrast, Arush's parallel volume addressed to men speaks more generally of the obligation of ex-spouses to forgive and does not emphasize the ex-husband's particular duty to be forgiving.[49] Arush's work offers a clear example of the patriarchal male tendency, identified by Schnur (section 7.8), to especially preach the virtues of forgiveness to women.

Shalom Arush, *Women's Wisdom* (2010)

A divorced couple must do everything in their power to make peace and forgive one another for all that transpired between them before the divorce. With continued hard feelings—bitterness, anger, and hatred in their hearts against each other—neither will succeed in building a new life. These negative sentiments will only bring harsh judgments against them, for transgressions between people are harder to atone for than those committed against God.

Therefore, a woman should not be obstinate in her anger, even if it is justified. Her wrath will not only hurt her ex, but herself as well, and will prevent her from building a new life for herself.

The woman may feel that her husband alone was to blame for the divorce. Since she was the hurt party, it is unfair that she should be punished for her unwillingness to forgive. However, she must realize that any suffering and sorrow she suffered was given to her through Divine Providence, either as a wake-up call for her to do *teshuva* [to repent] or as an absolution for her sins. She needs to forgive him even if he hurt her. Her unwillingness to do so is a great flaw in her *emuna* [faith], and separates her from Hashem. This separation will inevitably prevent her from properly building a new life for herself.

Remember that whoever hurt you was chosen to serve as Hashem's "stick" because of his own sins. The sorrow you suffered is from Hashem, according to His judgment. It was given to you fairly because of your transgressions. If you continue to refuse to forgive your ex-husband, you are saying that the pain you have suffered is not from Hashem, but rather from the man you were married to. That is absolute heresy. Therefore, find emuna—and forgive him![50]

CONCLUSION

Modern Jewish discourse around forgiveness has been filled with disagreement. Many of these tensions regard questions of whether, and when, forgiveness should be conditional and whether, and when, it is a virtue to be unconditionally forgiving.

Most thinkers in this chapter point to circumstances in which one should not be forgiving, and Jewish concerns about being overly forgiving are especially heightened after the Holocaust. But ideals of unconditional forgiveness persist even in the contemporary era, whether animated by theology (as with Shalom Arush) or a vision of an extraordinary ideal (as with Jacques Derrida).

Such views generally emphasize mercy rather than justice. But many Jewish traditions regarding forgiveness emphasize the need to restore justice to the world, and many thinkers are troubled by constructions of forgiveness that overlook concerns of justice. Hannah Arendt stresses that radical evil cannot be forgiven, and Cynthia Ozick warns of the dangers of ignoring or forgetting victims when perpetrators have not been brought to justice. Emmanuel Levinas delineates the depth of repentance that may be required before forgiveness, and Marc Ellis observes how acts of forgiveness can diminish the self-critical reflection necessary for ensuring justice in the world. Susan Schnur examines how forgiveness demanded of women may lead to systemic domestic abuse and other harms, and Karyn Kedar cautions that forgiveness may allow evils to happen again.

Still, these very thinkers who warn against unjust forgiveness do believe that forgiveness is a virtue in certain contexts. Arendt stresses the need to liberate people from vengeance and the consequences of their actions, and Ozick points to cases where forgiveness can be an effective teacher. Levinas maintains that being part of the People of Israel requires a preference for mercy and forgiveness, and Ellis warns that those who refuse to forgive may fail to see their own offenses. Schnur views forgiving others as "an important civilizing prod for men" and forgiving oneself as vital for women. Finally, Kedar sees forgiveness as providing the forgiver newfound freedom, energy, and spiritual purpose.

Different approaches to forgiveness may reflect authors "talking about quite different things, but using the same terminology to describe them," as Louis Newman has put it.[51] But even when modern Jewish thinkers are ostensibly talking about the same moral quality, they have significant disagreements about how and when it is a virtue and how consequential it should be for moral development.

8

Love, Kindness, and Compassion
(*Ahavah/Ḥesed/Raḥmanut*)

The virtues of altruistic love, kindness, and compassion—commonly expressed in Hebrew as *ahavah* (love), *ḥesed* (love, kindness, or loving-kindness), and *raḥmanut* or *raḥamim* (compassion or mercy)—have been the subject of significant tensions among modern Jewish thinkers, as can be seen in previous chapters. In the discussion of humility, for example, Shalom Noah Berezovsky (section 3.5) condemned those who loved themselves and therefore had no room for loving their fellow Jews (or God), while Rebecca Alpert (section 3.7) taught that we "can only learn to love our neighbors if we learn to love ourselves," an idea echoed by Eugene Borowitz and Frances Schwartz in their discussion of self-restraint (section 5.7). Reflecting on gratitude, Emma Goldman (section 6.3) pointed to ways in which kindness can be a tool of power and enslavement. When considering forgiveness, some thinkers emphasized mercy, while Cynthia Ozick (section 7.5) condemned those who are merciful to the cruel.

The present chapter builds on some of these tensions. We will see debates about the relationship of altruistic love and self-love (sections 8.3 and 8.4), claims about power justified in the language of lovingkindness (section 8.6), and a response to the sort of rhetoric invoked by Ozick (section 8.8). Tensions also emerge over whether these virtues ought to be considered dangerous; how difficult and demanding love should be; who deserves love, kindness, and compassion; and how people of different identities — Jewish or non-Jewish, male or female — may best express these virtues.

Many biblical and classical Rabbinic texts speak of love, kindness, or compassion. Widely cited passages include Leviticus 19:18, "love your neighbor as yourself" (or "love your fellow as yourself," as it is sometimes translated), which Rabbi Akiva is said to have defined as "the great principle" (or "a great principle") of the Torah (JT *Nedarim* 9:4); the verse's Aramaic rephrasing, "Do not do anything to your fellow that is hateful to you," which Hillel the Elder is said to have viewed as summarizing "the whole Torah" (BT *Shabbat* 31a); and the related biblical commandment to "love the stranger as yourself" — for example, "Love the stranger, for you were strangers in the land of Egypt" (Deut. 10:19). While biblical authors viewed the stranger as a non-Israelite, Rabbinic texts came to view the stranger as a convert to Judaism, understanding the commandments to love both neighbor and stranger as commandments to love fellow Jews.[1] On the other hand, some classical Rabbinic texts appear to speak of love of human beings more generally, as when Hillel the Elder describes the ideal of "loving [God's] creatures and drawing them close to Torah" (*Mishnah Avot* 1:12).

When dealing with one's fellow Jews, some Rabbinic texts focus on aiding one's enemy and turning a relationship of hatred into one of love. Thus, for example, *Mekhilta de-Rashbi* (23:4) describes "curbing your inclination [*yetzer*], in order to make one who hates you [your enemy] into one who loves you [your friend]." Explaining the commandments in Leviticus 19:17 to not "hate your brother in your heart" but nonetheless to "rebuke your kinsman," Sifra specifies that one may repeatedly rebuke and even "curse, strike, or slap" your kinsman — so long as you do not hate "in your heart" or cause embarrassment to the other.[2] Some sources depict rebuke as an expression of love, in line with a statement attributed to Rabbi Yosi ben Hanina: "Any love without rebuke is no love."[3]

The Talmud also speaks of compassion for sinners. In BT *Berachot* 10a, Beruriah counsels her husband Rabbi Meir not to pray for the death of "sinners" but for the death of "sins"; she punctuates Psalms 104:35 so that it no longer reads "Let sinners die" but rather "Let sins die."

In Beruriah's formulation, one should "pray for compassion for them, that they will repent." Other talmudic texts regarding sinners, however, are less focused on compassion. In BT *Pesachim* 113b, Rav Naḥman bar Yitzḥak teaches that despite the Torah's general rule not to hate one's fellow Jew, when it comes to sexual (and perhaps other) sins, it is in fact "a commandment to hate" the sinner; Rav Ashi adds that one may inform a teacher so that the teacher will also hate the sinner. In another passage (BT *Shabbat* 116a), Rabbi Yishmael justifies hatred of heretics by quoting a line from Psalms (traditionally attributed to King David): "I hate them with a complete hatred" (Ps. 139:22).

At the same time, Rabbinic texts sometimes depict the Jewish people as uniquely capable of altruistic love and other nations as incapable of such love. In BT *Bava Batra* 10b, a series of Rabbis explain the verse "the lovingkindness of the nations is sin" (Prov. 14:34) as showing that the kindness of non-Jews is motivated by desires for self-glorification and power. By contrast, true descendants of the Patriarch Abraham—that is, true Jews—are sometimes described as distinguished by their compassion: "With anyone who has compassion for [God's] creatures, it is known that he is of the seed of our father Abraham; with anyone who does not have compassion for [God's] creatures, it is known that he is not of the seed of our father Abraham" (BT *Beitzah* 32b).

Premodern Jewish literature particularly linked Abraham with love, kindness, and compassion, and kabbalistic literature heightened Abraham's connection with the divine quality of *ḥesed*.[4] The opening of the daily standing prayer, the *Amidah*, associates *ḥesed* with all three of the Patriarchs (Abraham, Isaac, and Jacob), describing God as "recalling the lovingkindness of the Patriarchs" (though it may be alternatively understood as speaking of "the lovingkindness [shown by God] to the Patriarchs").[5] Other Rabbinic traditions allude to the lovingkindness of the Matriarchs Sarah, Rebecca, Rachel, and Leah, especially in their roles as mothers, wives, and sisters (see section 8.7).

Other premodern texts depict God as an exemplar of love. Classical liturgy often makes use of the biblical description of God showing compassion "as a father has compassion for his children" (Ps. 103:13).

Many texts build on the description of God having "mercy upon all of His works" (Ps. 145:9), as with one midrash that describes how "the Holy One has compassion for animals just as He has compassion for humans."[6] Building on a reference in the book of Proverbs to the "Torah of lovingkindness" (31:26) spoken by a "woman of valor," some texts link lovingkindness with the experience of Torah study.[7] These texts are interpreted in various ways in the selections below, reflecting the diverse views of love, compassion, and kindness in modern Jewish ethics.[8]

8.1. SEEING THE OTHER IN THE IMAGE OF GOD

Naphtali Herz (Hartwig) Wessely (1725–1805) was a scholar, poet, and leader of the German Haskalah (Jewish Enlightenment) movement. The author of a volume devoted to musar, *The Book of Character Traits* (*Sefer ha-Middot*), Wessely also discussed virtues and vices in his commentary (*Biur*) on the book of Leviticus, edited by Moses Mendelssohn, from which the selection below is taken.

Wessely advocated for Jews to integrate socially, politically, and economically into the societies in which they lived, and he encouraged them to love all human beings, including their non-Jewish neighbors. His stress on love for all human beings may be seen as part of his effort to promote moral concern across lines of difference.

At the same time, Wessely cautioned against overstating one's obligations of love. Responding to scholars who insisted that the biblical commandment to "love your neighbor as yourself" meant that one should be as concerned for others as one is naturally concerned for oneself, Wessely noted that no one could possibly express such love. One cannot be constantly concerned for the needs of all other human beings—or, even, all other Jews—to the extent that one is concerned for oneself, and in any case emotional engagement with other people cannot be commanded. Moreover, a classical Rabbinic teaching, attributed to Rabbi Akiva, advises that when having to choose between one's own life and the life of one's fellow, one may prioritize one's own life. One need not sacrifice one's own life on account of love for the other.

Instead, Wessely asked his readers to understand the commandment to love their fellows as requiring each of them to see the common humanity shared by others. Here, the virtue of love ordained by the Torah is the virtue of seeing all others as also created in God's image, and thereby respecting their interests and feelings. Above all, one must generally avoid causing "pain or humiliation to any human being," following Hillel's admonition in the Talmud: "Do not do to your fellow that which is hateful to you."

Grounded in his vision of love, Wessely offers a Golden Rule–based approach to morality whereby the only pain that one can inflict on another is the pain that one would welcome inflicted upon oneself (e.g., being lovingly rebuked, in helpful ways, when one does something wrong).

Naphtali Herz Wessely, Commentary on Leviticus (1781)

"Love your neighbor as yourself" (Lev. 19:18): if the intention [of this verse] was in accordance with the understanding of the biblical commentators of blessed memory that one should love every human being as one loves oneself, it would be very surprising that [God] would command something of which no soul is capable. It is not possible for a human being to love another, especially one who is a foreigner, as one loves oneself. Nor is it possible to command love or hate, which a human being cannot control. . . .

Furthermore, if this [interpretation] were right, one would need to grieve over the sorrow of every other just as for his own sorrow, and he would not live his life, as there is no moment in which one does not see or hear of a Jew's misfortune. And so too with the idea that the good that one would need to do for the other should be all that one does for oneself—this is also an absurd idea. I have also seen the statement of Nahmanides, of blessed memory, that "'Love your neighbor as yourself' is an exaggerated expression, as a human heart is not able to accept that one must love one's fellow *as* one loves one's self; and, furthermore, Rabbi Akiva has already taught that 'your life takes precedence over the life of your fellow' [if there are limited resources and only one can survive, as taught in BT *Bava Metzia* 62a]." . . .

The [true] interpretation is: love your neighbor, for he is like you, equal to you, similar to you, for he was also created in the image of God, and he is a human being like you. And this includes all human beings, for they were all created in [God's] image, and Rabbi Akiva says that this is the general principle of the Torah, and Rabbi Akiva himself restated this principle in the Mishnah: "Beloved are human beings, for they are created in [God's] image" (*Mishnah Avot* 3:14). Even if one behaves wickedly, one is [still] created in the likeness of God, with self-governance and choice, able to choose the good. . . .

Hillel the Elder came and [correctly] interpreted the matter: "Do not do to your fellow that which is hateful to you" [BT *Shabbat* 31a]— that, in any case, you should not do anything to him that you would be sorry to have done to you. This is a clear truth: it is forbidden to you to cause pain or humiliation to any human being, whether a righteous person or a wicked person, except through proper judicial procedure or through giving loving rebuke to turn someone to the good. Just as the Torah ordains death for one who spills the blood of [any] human being, whether a wise person or a fool, whether a righteous person or a wicked person, and gives the reason as "for God made the human being in [God's] image" (Gen. 9:6)—so too for the matter of "not doing to your fellow that which is hateful to you" [the commandment applies to all human beings, for they are in God's image].[9]

8.2. LOVE FOR UNIQUE JEWISH SOULS

In section 5.1, Chabad-Lubavitch Hasidism founder Rabbi Shneur Zalman of Liadi offered a vision of how one should hate whatever is within the domain of materiality, evil, and impurity known as the "Other Side," while loving God and the purity within God's domain. "The completely righteous man hates all that is from the Other Side with a complete hatred, because of his great love for God and His holiness . . . as it is written, 'I hate them with a complete hatred' [Ps. 139:22]." The selections below, from Shneur Zalman's *Tanya*, further explore how to relate to God and to the Other Side with reference to the virtues of love, kindness, and compassion.

In part I, Shneur Zalman teaches that Jews are the only human beings who possess souls connected to God's holiness; other human beings possess only souls that come from the Other Side and its "impure shells." The commandment to love one's neighbor appears to stem from the fundamental command to love God; to the degree that one finds God within Jewish, divine souls, one is commanded to love those souls.

Alongside their divine souls, Jews also have souls that come from the Other Side. As indicated in part II, one may hate the evil and material aspects one sees within one's fellow Jew while still loving the "divine soul" that animates him. The "direct and easy path" to such love is to hate the material realm — including the body — and view it as repulsive, while loving the spiritual realm in which the divine souls of all Jews are united. Ideal love does not culminate in concern for the physical needs of particular others but in transcending the physical realm and joining the united souls of Israel in love with the One God ("the One within the One" as Shneur Zalman puts it).[10]

As such, Shneur Zalman asserts that Hillel's formulation about not doing "to one's fellow that which is hateful to you" is fundamentally a teaching about the unity of the Jews, the supremacy of the soul over the body, and the supremacy of the Jews over other nations. Each Jew must love all other Jews (and not do what is hateful to them) precisely because of the divine soul that links them all, even when that divine soul may seem hidden by the repulsive and evil human body. Thus, he counsels, one must love even Jewish sinners who are "far from God's Torah and from serving Him" and therefore are better described as mere "creatures" than fully actualized human beings. By no means have such "creatures" forfeited their divine souls; these can still be uncovered.

Shneur Zalman teaches this with reference to Hillel's emphasis in *Mishnah Avot* (1:12) on "loving [God's] creatures and drawing them close to the Torah." To him, this text signifies the importance of loving even those uneducated sinners who can be rebuked, educated, and drawn close to Torah. While Wessely also spoke of the value of showing love by rebuking sinners, Shneur Zalman's language is notably more paternalistic. Love, for him, is particularly found in the moments in which elites reach out to the ignorant, rebuke them for their sins, and teach them what they truly need.

As the end of the selection indicates, however, some Jews have "no portion in the God of Israel" because they are heretics (a label that Shneur Zalman would no doubt apply to most of the other authors profiled in this chapter). Heretics appear to have forfeited their divine souls such that there is nothing to love within them, and it is fitting to "hate them with a complete hatred." Shneur Zalman also follows the talmudic teaching that it is a commandment to hate unrepentant Jewish sinners in certain circumstances: when they are learned in Torah ("his colleague in Torah and commandments") and when they have already been rebuked for their wrongdoing but have not changed their ways. When such sinners brazenly and deliberately reject the Torah to the point that they no longer have a "portion in the God of Israel," they may be hated. Hatred would also seem proper toward non-Jews, who are not created in God's image and lack divine souls. And, for Shneur Zalman, the commandment to "love one's neighbor as oneself" clearly requires cultivating love for Jews, not for non-Jews.

Further, in Shneur Zalman's view, non-Jews are incapable of true love for others. Non-Jewish souls "have no goodness in them whatsoever," as attested by the talmudic teaching that "all the charity and lovingkindness done by the nations of the world is only for their own self-glorification" (BT *Bava Batra* 10b). Love, here, is a uniquely Jewish character trait: in its full form, at least, it can be cultivated only by Jews and directed toward other bona fide Jews.

Shneur Zalman of Liadi, *Tanya* (1796)

I. Rabbi Hayyim Vital [has taught us] ... that in every Jew, whether righteous or wicked, there are two souls, as it is written, "The souls that I made" [Isa. 57:16]—referring to two souls. There is one soul that is from the "side of the shells" [that conceal holiness and purity], the [impure] "Other Side." . . . All of the evil characteristics come from [this soul] . . . but also the good character traits that are innate in the nature of each Jew come from it, such as compassion and lovingkindness. For in the case of the Jew, this soul comes from the shell-that-can-be-illuminated, which also has goodness within it. . . .

But this is not the case with the souls of the [other] nations of the world, which come from the other, impure shells, which have no goodness in them whatsoever, as is written in [Rabbi Ḥayim Vital's book] *Etz Ḥayim* (49:3): all the good that the nations do is done for selfish motives. And so the Talmud [BT *Bava Batra* 10b] comments on the verse "the lovingkindness of the nations is sin" [Prov. 14:34]—that all the charity and lovingkindness done by the nations of the world is only for their own self-glorification, etc.

The second soul [unique] to a Jew is literally a part of God above. . . .[11]

II. Viewing one's body as despised and repulsive, and restricting one's joy to the joy of the soul: this is the direct and easy path for fulfilling the commandment to love your fellow Jew, whether great or small—for one's body is seen as repulsive and disgusting, while who can know the greatness and excellence of the [Jewish] soul and spirit, with their root and source in the living God? They all match, and there is one Father for them all. And therefore all Jews are called brothers, literally, as the source of their souls is in the one God, and it is only their bodies that are distinct. Therefore, there can be no true love and brotherhood among those who make their bodies their primary focus and their souls secondary; there is only [love] that is dependent upon a [material] thing.

And this is what Hillel the Elder said regarding the fulfillment of this commandment: "This is the whole Torah, and the rest is commentary," etc., for the foundation and root of the whole Torah is that one raise the soul very high above the body, reaching the essence and root of all worlds, and bringing down the light of the blessed Infinite One [*Ein Sof*] upon the community of Israel . . . so that in the source of the souls of all Israel, the One [Israel] is within the One [God]. . . .

As for the statement in the Talmud that when one sees his fellow sinning, "it is a commandment to hate him," and also to tell one's teacher so that he will hate him [BT *Pesachim* 113b], this applies to the one who is his colleague in Torah and commandments, when one has already fulfilled the commandment to "rebuke your kinsman" [Lev. 19:17]—one who is with you in Torah and commandments but has nevertheless not repented of his sin (as is written in *Sefer Haredim*).

But when he is not one's colleague and one is not close to him, Hillel the Elder said, "Be among the disciples of Aaron, loving peace and pursuing peace, loving [God's] creatures and drawing them close to Torah" (*Mishnah Avot* 1:12)—meaning that even those who are simply called "creatures," for they are far from God's Torah and from serving Him, must be brought in with strong cords of love. With all that, perhaps, one can draw them close to the Torah and service of God. Even if one does not, one has not lost the reward for loving one's fellow.

Even those who are close to him, whom he has rebuked, but who have not repented of their sins, and it is a commandment to hate them—it is also a commandment to love them. Both responses are correct: hatred with regard to the evil within them, and love with regard to the goodness hidden within them, the divine spark that is within them that animates their divine soul. One should also awaken compassion in one's heart for [the divine soul], for it is in exile amid the evil of the Other Side, which, in wicked people, overpowers it. And compassion cancels out hatred and awakens love, as is known from the verse "Jacob [compassion] redeemed Abraham [lovingkindness]" [Isa. 29:22].

David said, "I hate them with a complete hatred" [Ps. 139:22] only with regard to heretics who have no portion in the God of Israel (as is stated in BT *Shabbat* 116a).[12]

8.3. THE EXTENT OF LOVE

Rabbi Simḥah Zissel (Broida) Ziv (1824–98), a leader of the Musar movement in Lithuania, emphasized the commandment to love one's neighbor as oneself. Like Wessely (and unlike Shneur Zalman), Simḥah Zissel often stressed that the virtue of love must extend to all human beings, Jewish or not. He also agreed with Wessely that loving and showing concern for others in the same way that one loves oneself is a divine ideal no human being can actually reach—but, unlike Wessely, he insisted that God commands human beings to aspire to this ideal nonetheless.

Whereas Wessely saw the biblical phrase "as oneself" as an adjectival phrase, teaching you that your neighbor is like you, Simḥah Zissel understood "as oneself" as an adverbial phrase, teaching the extent to which one is commanded to love. In part I, Simḥah Zissel teaches that one should accustom oneself to be concerned for others just as one is naturally concerned for oneself or one's own family.

For Simḥah Zissel, there is no "direct and easy path" for cultivating the virtue of love (as Shneur Zalman had written); there is only a slow process of gradually accustoming oneself to become more responsive to the needs of others. But as he indicates in part II, love can still be cultivated in less demanding ways: through refraining from harm to others (following Hillel's teaching "not to do anything to your fellow that is hateful to you"); and through small gestures that build bonds of partnership and concern within a political community, such as greeting one's fellow in the marketplace.[13]

In part III, Simḥah Zissel describes the Patriarchs Abraham and Isaac as exemplars of love and compassion for even the most wicked of people such as the inhabitants of Sodom (Gen. 18) and Isaac's son Esau (Gen. 25,27). Simḥah Zissel clearly does not think that one should forgo punishing such sinners, but he does demand compassion for them. He does not speak of an "Other Side" that contains no goodness at all and that must be hated; rather, Simḥah Zissel insists that a little goodness may even be found in a figure like Esau. As one midrash notes, Isaac saw that Esau possessed one good quality (honoring his father) and so, as Simḥah Zissel sees it, Isaac was therefore able to love even his wicked son. Though he understands that (contrary to the plain meaning of the biblical text) Isaac must have shown a greater love for his good son, Jacob, he praises Isaac for showing Esau the bit of love that Esau deserved, proportionate to the bit of goodness that Esau possessed.[14] In doing so, Simḥah Zissel indicates, Jacob demonstrated the virtue of love more clearly than his wife Rebecca, for Rebecca failed to love Esau at all. Simḥah Zissel also finds inspiration for loving sinners in the midrashic tradition that God rebuked the angels who celebrated while the Egyptian army was drowning, and in the story of Beruriah teaching her husband to pray with compassion for the death of "sins" rather than "sinners."

Despite this invocation of a woman's teaching, however, we see in part IV how Simḥah Zissel considered the love shown by fathers superior to the love shown by mothers. This teaching is grounded in the biblical comparison of God's compassion to the compassion of a father: "As a father has compassion for his sons, so the Lord has compassion for those who fear Him" (Ps. 103:13). Simḥah Zissel indicates that a mother's love is inferior because it focuses on meeting a son's physical needs, whereas a father's love is properly directed toward what is infinitely more important: the son's eternal soul. While part I shows the importance of love expressed in providing for physical needs (food and clothing), and parts II and III demonstrate the importance of extending concern to non-Jews, including non-Jewish sinners, part IV reveals that Simḥah Zissel saw the ultimate love as focused on the spiritual-intellectual needs of the Jewish, male soul.[15]

That love for the soul, notably, also requires a certain amount of cruelty to the body. Simḥah Zissel recommends that a father demonstrate love by striking his son "with cruel blows." Here, the father's efforts to discipline the son's body constitute acts of kindness because they will contribute to moral and spiritual reform, ultimately leading to "unending eternal goodness" for the soul in the world to come. Physical abuse can thereby be countenanced for the sake of love.

To Simḥah Zissel, such a model of love is justified in part because God's love is sometimes expressed through cruelty. Simḥah Zissel is building on the ancient Rabbinic tradition that sees God as expressing love by causing physical suffering to beloved human beings whose souls will ultimately be rewarded in the world to come. It is appropriate to imitate this harsh aspect of divine love, he teaches, just as he stresses (in parts I and III) the importance of imitating divine generosity and mercy.

Simḥah Zissel Ziv, *Writings of the Alter of Kelm* and *Wisdom and Musar* (late nineteenth century)

I. We are warned to slowly, slowly accustom ourselves to the character trait of generosity to such an extent that one gives charity in the way that one gives to one's children, to whom one does not give because of the commandment of charity but in the way that one puts food in one's own mouth: a human being finds joy whenever he is able to please his family with clothes and food and drink. A human being needs to accustom oneself to the character trait of generosity in this way, to such an extent that he finds joy in helping and providing for the poor, as if they are truly part of his family. . . .

And this is as the matter of "loving your neighbor as yourself." . . . One should love one's neighbor as one loves oneself, for a human being does not love himself to fulfill the commandment of loving [God's] creatures, but rather loves himself naturally. Thus . . . the warning is given to a human being that he should accustom himself to the character trait of loving God's creatures, slowly, slowly, until he naturally loves the other, and naturally rejoices in the good of the other, just as he naturally rejoices in his own good and the good of his children, rather than to fulfill a commandment, for then his love would not be complete. His love will be complete only if he loves naturally. And this is the goal of the commandment and the desire of the Blessed One in commanding "loving your neighbor as yourself," and in this way one will come to resemble the Blessed One.[16]

II. The prime foundation in a person's life should be instilling in his heart true love of human beings, whatever religion they may be, because the entire political community is a partnership. . . . One should become habituated to always think that everyone is making preparations for each other—in order that love of [God's] creatures, whether Jewish or not, can be implanted in his heart. Thus we find with Rabbi Yoḥanan ben Zakkai, that no one outdid him in greeting others, even the non-Jew in the marketplace (BT *Berachot* 17a). For he outdid everyone—in order to habituate himself to the love of God's creatures. And thus we understand the intent of Hillel: "Do not do anything to your fellow that is hateful to you" (BT *Shabbat* 31a). . . .[17]

III. Our father Abraham, peace be upon him, walked in the ways of God, the Blessed One, and he learned from [God's] behavior with the world, and he commanded his descendants to also walk in God's ways. He learned from [God's] behavior at Sodom how one should act with the wicked: that one should even have compassion for the wicked, and that one should seek [compassion] for them in prayer. For he understood why the Holy Blessed One revealed [his plans] to him—so that he would seek [compassion] on their behalf in prayer. . . .

[Some] would decree that one should not be merciful to the wicked. But, in truth, this is not true; rather, one must be merciful to the wicked as well. [As God objected to the singing angels when the Egyptians were drowning in the Sea of Reeds,] "The works of my hands are drowning, and you are singing?" (BT *Sanhedrin* 39b). [And as Beruriah taught, Psalms 104:35 says,] "Let sins die. Is 'sinners' written? No, 'sins' is written" (BT *Berachot* 10a). And here God said, "'Should I hide' (Gen. 18:17) this teaching from Abraham? Rather, I will tell him, and he will understand, that my intention is for him to pray for the wicked as well, and to seek compassion for them. . . ."

It is the nature of the human being that, when faced with his enemy, he will turn his eye away from the goodness that is in him, and not see it at all. But this is not so with the Holy Blessed One. Esau was wicked, and he had only one good quality, [honoring his father], as is taught in the midrash[18]—and one can see how great a reward was given to him and his descendants for a long time afterward. And from this, a human being can learn to walk in the ways of God, the Blessed One. And this is what God, the Blessed One, wanted to tell our father Abraham, peace be upon him, with the matter at Sodom: to teach the ways of His compassion. . . .

And so we come to explain the matter of Isaac's love for Esau. . . . Isaac our father, peace be upon him, walked in the ways of his father Abraham, having compassion for the wicked, and not turning one's eye from the little goodness found within them. Therefore [Isaac] "loved Esau" (Gen. 25:28) as well—and there is no intent to reject Jacob, only [to show] that Isaac loved Esau as well, and [he loved] Jacob all the more so . . . whereas Rebecca loved only Jacob and did not love Esau at all. . . .

On account of [Esau's] one good quality, [Isaac] had a little love even for his older son, for he had learned from his father Abraham, peace be upon him, to have compassion even for the wicked and to seek their goodness.[19]

IV. This was a pearl [of wisdom] taught by my father, my rabbi and teacher of blessed memory, explaining [the verse] "as a father has compassion for his sons" (Ps. 103:13). A mother has compassion for her son's body but not for his soul. . . . On the other hand, a father has compassion for his [son's] intellect and not for his [material] nature. [The father's] compassion is so very great, therefore he has mercy for that which is so very great—the soul, for it is eternal. . . . Therefore, he should strike [his son] with cruel blows, so that there may be unending eternal goodness for him [in the world to come]. And this is the compassion of a father, not a mother, and thus [we refer to God as] "our father," meaning that He has unending compassion for us, for God is good to all, and all the more so to his sons.[20]

8.4. THE DANGERS OF COMPASSION AND LOVE IN PUBLIC LIFE

Hannah Arendt (introduced in section 7.3) wrote extensively about morally and politically dangerous understandings of compassion, love, and pity. For example, in her 1963 book *Eichmann in Jerusalem*, she noted the ways in which Nazi leaders developed pity for themselves, focusing on the hardships they themselves endured ("What horrible things I had to watch . . . !") while ignoring the horrors they were inflicting on their victims.[21] In her book *On Revolution*, published the same year, she laid out her concerns with compassion in politics, including that compassion is exclusive, directed at whomever one is partial toward.

In a selection from that book below (part I), Arendt describes compassion as responding to individuals whose suffering is perceived by one's eyes and ears. Compassion requires joining with suffering individuals, but as Wessely indicated, our capacity to do this is limited, and so compassion is necessarily partial. As Arendt argues, identification with suffering individuals clouds our judgment, causing us to lose perspective and to ignore the broader picture that is so essential for ensuring justice within a political community.

Unlike Simḥah Zissel Ziv, Arendt does not think that expressions of love can be foundational for political communities; nor does she envision, like Shneur Zalman, the unity of Jewish souls. Rather, for Arendt, politics requires acknowledging, from a respectful distance, the diversity of human beings within a community. Politics requires distance from the needs of particular individuals so that one can see multiple perspectives, hear multiple voices, and establish institutions that can judiciously negotiate the multiple claims and arguments made by human beings. Compassion, and love more generally, are dangerous in part because they "abolish the distance" and seek immediate, direct action—including, often, violence. As scholar Margaret Canovan writes about Arendt's thought in this regard, compassion "leads those who profess it to take to violence in a vain attempt to demonstrate their own sincerity."[22] One of Arendt's key examples is how the compassion that animated the French Revolution gave way to the Reign of Terror.

Arendt's concerns about compassion and love in Jewish communal politics are evident in her 1963 letter to Gershom Scholem, excerpted in part II below. Scholem had claimed that Arendt's *Eichmann in Jerusalem*, filled with strong criticisms of many Jews, revealed her lack of love for the Jewish people (*Ahabath Israel*, in the transliteration below); Arendt replies that indeed she cannot love any group, for love can only be applied to particular individuals. Moreover, she raises her concerns about love that is directed toward one's own group, suggesting how "love of the Jewish people" readily leads to chauvinism and the desire to conceal truths—such as those she was revealing—that seem damaging to the Jewish people.

At the same time, Arendt views compassion as "an entirely admirable quality in personal relations," Canovan has written. "Her argument is not concerned to deny the goodness of compassion, but only to consider what happens when it moves out of the sphere of direct, face-to-face personal relationships and becomes entangled with politics."[23]

Hannah Arendt, *On Revolution* and Letter to Gershom Scholem (1963)

I. Compassion, by its very nature, cannot be touched off by the sufferings of a whole class or a people, or, least of all, mankind as a whole. It cannot reach out farther than what is suffered by one person and still remain what it is supposed to be, co-suffering. Its strength hinges on the strength of passion itself, which, in contrast to reason, can comprehend only the particular, but has no notion of the general and no capacity for generalization. . . .

Compassion, . . . not unlike love, abolishes the distance, the in-between which always exists in human intercourse. . . . Because compassion abolishes the distance, the worldly space between men where political matters, the whole realm of human affairs, are located, it remains, politically speaking, irrelevant and without consequence. In the words of [Herman] Melville, it is incapable of establishing "lasting institutions." . . .

Talkative and argumentative interest in the world is entirely alien to compassion, which is directed solely, and with passionate intensity, towards suffering man himself; compassion speaks only to the extent that it has to reply directly to the sheer expressionist sound and gestures through which suffering becomes audible and visible in the world. As a rule, it is not compassion which sets out to change worldly conditions in order to ease human suffering, but if it does, it will shun the drawn-out wearisome processes of persuasion, negotiation, and compromise, which are the processes of law and politics, and lend its voice to the suffering itself, which must claim for swift and direct action, that is, for action with the means of violence.[24]

II. Let me begin . . . with what you call "love of the Jewish people" or *Ahabath Israel* [*ahavat Yisra'el*]. . . . You are quite right—I am not moved by any "love" of this sort, and for two reasons: I have never in my life "loved" any people or collective—neither the German people, nor the French, nor the American, nor the working class or anything of that sort. I indeed love "only" my friends and the only kind of love I know of and believe in is the love of persons. Secondly, this "love of the Jews" would appear to me, since I am myself Jewish, as something rather suspect. I cannot love myself or anything which I know is part and parcel of my own person. To clarify this, let me tell you of a conversation I had in Israel with a prominent political personality [Golda Meir] who was defending the—in my opinion disastrous—nonseparation of religion and state in Israel. What [s]he said—I am not sure of the exact words anymore—ran something like this: "You will understand that, as a Socialist, I, of course, do not believe in God; I believe in the Jewish people." I found this a shocking statement and, being too shocked, I did not reply at the time. But I could have answered: The greatness of this people was once that it believed in God, and believed in Him in such a way that its trust and love toward Him was greater than its fear. And now this people believes only in itself? What good can come out of that?—Well, in this sense I do not "love" the Jews, nor do I "believe" in them; I merely belong to them as a matter of course, beyond dispute or argument.

We could discuss the same issue in political terms; and we should then be driven to a consideration of patriotism. That there can be no patriotism without permanent opposition and criticism is no doubt common ground between us. But I can admit to you something beyond that, namely, that wrong done by my own people naturally grieves me more than wrong done by other peoples. This grief, however, in my opinion is not for display, even if it should be the innermost motive for certain actions or attitudes. Generally speaking, the role of the "heart" in politics seems to me altogether questionable. You know as well as I how often those who merely report certain unpleasant facts are accused of lack of soul, lack of heart, or lack of what you call *Herzenstakt* [sympathy]. We both know, in other words, how often these emotions are used in order to conceal factual truth. I cannot discuss here what happens when emotions are displayed in public and become a factor in political affairs; but it is an important subject, and I have attempted to describe the disastrous results in my book *On Revolution* in discussing the role of compassion in the formation of the revolutionary character.[25]

8.5. THIS LOVE IS YOURSELF

Whereas Arendt devoted significant attention to developing a concept of the political that would not be guided by standard ethical virtues such as love and compassion, Emmanuel Levinas (introduced in section 7.4) sought to develop a concept of the ethical that was distinct from the realm of politics but that would nonetheless challenge that realm. Like Arendt, he emphasized respect for difference, but unlike Arendt he invoked God, the Bible, and radical ideals of self-sacrifice.

Levinas often focused on the virtues of responsibility to the other (see section 9.9), but at times he used the language of love to describe this responsibility. One example of this, printed below, comes from a 1975 interview at the University of Leiden in which Levinas was asked whether moral experience can be "translated as an experience of the other as identical to oneself," which would seem to correspond to the biblical commandment to "love your neighbor as yourself."

In his response, Levinas considered the limits of the biblical translation of Martin Buber and Franz Rosenzweig, which seemed to follow Wessely in understanding the biblical commandment to stress the equality of the neighbor in relation to the self ("love your neighbor, he is like you"). For Levinas, this was an inadequate understanding. Far from emphasizing the symmetrical and equal relationship between the self and the other, one should see the "dissymmetry" and unequal relationship whereby the other always has priority over the self. Unlike Wessely, who pointed to the talmudic teaching attributed to Rabbi Akiva that "your life takes precedence over the life of your fellow," and Simḥah Zissel, who affirmed that love should bring you to treat the other as well as you treat yourself, Levinas taught that the life of your fellow takes precedence over your own. As he said in another interview, "My duty to respond to the other suspends my natural right to self-survival."[26]

For Levinas, love requires vulnerability, self-sacrifice, recognizing one's infinite responsibility, and giving the other priority over oneself. He sees the priority of the other as the very essence of the Bible — "the Bible *is* the priority of the other in relation to me."

With this priority in mind, Levinas reads the commandment to "love your neighbor as yourself" quite differently from others in this chapter. In the passage below he offers a series of possible translations, all of which prioritize the other over the self. Indeed, one's very self is constituted only with reference to love and responsibility for the other, as "it is this love of the neighbor which *is* yourself."

For Levinas, responsibility is not limited to one's own people. Rather, all human beings are commanded to be responsible for all other human beings, and to prioritize the other. "I am in reality responsible for the other even when he or she commits crimes. That is for me what is essential in the Jewish conscience," Levinas once explained. "But I also think that this is what is essential in the human conscience: all men are responsible for one another, and 'I more than anyone else.'"[27]

Levinas joins most other figures in this chapter in rejecting Shneur Zalman's ethnocentric focus on God's unifying presence exclusively within Jewish souls. For Levinas, God does not reside within souls as their point of likeness; rather, God is known only in the commandment to be ethical, and God's commandment is heard only from the face of the other, who must be seen as a unique human being. Levinas, scholar Robert Gibbs writes, "replaces the notion of 'like loves like' with the keen awareness that I love a unique person, unique to such an extent that that person must be radically other from me."[28]

Emmanuel Levinas, *Of God Who Comes to Mind* (1975)

What does "as yourself" signify? Buber and Rosenzweig were here very perplexed by the translation. . . . They translated it, "love your neighbor, he is like you." But if one first agrees to separate the last word of the Hebrew verse, *kamokhah* ["as yourself," "like you"], from the beginning of the verse, one can read the whole thing still otherwise. "Love your neighbor; this work is like yourself"; "love your neighbor; he is yourself"; "it is this love of the neighbor which is yourself." Would you say that this is an extremely audacious reading? Yet the Old Testament supports several readings and it is when the entirety of the Bible becomes the context of the verse that the verse resounds with all its meaning. . . . Now, in the entirety of the book, there is always a priority of the other in relation to me. This is the biblical contribution in its entirety. And that is how I would respond to your question: "Love your neighbor; all that is yourself; this work is yourself; this love is yourself." *Kamokhah* does not refer to "your neighbor," but to all the words that precede it. The Bible is the priority of the other [*l'autre*] in relation to me. It is in another [*autrui*] that I always see the widow and the orphan. The other [*autrui*] always comes first. This is what I have called, in Greek language, the dissymmetry of the interpersonal relationship. If there is not this dissymmetry, then no line of what I have written can hold. And this is vulnerability. Only a vulnerable I can love his neighbor.[29]

8.6. FIGHTING WITH LOVE FOR A
THEOCRACY THAT LOVES THE JEWS

The contemporary Israeli Chabad Hasidic rabbi Yitzchak Ginsburgh (b. 1944) is known for his militant Jewish supremacism, his endorsement of Jewish terrorism, and his fierce support for Israeli efforts to settle and control Palestinian territories.[30] Grounded in the approach of Shneur Zalman's *Tanya* (section 8.2) as well as other later Chabad teachings, including those of his own teacher, Rabbi Menachem Mendel Schneerson,

Ginsburgh asserts that "love your neighbor" refers to the love of one's fellow Jew and that Jews possess a divine soul that makes them superior to non-Jews. Yet the emphasis of his teaching is somewhat different than Shneur Zalman's, reflecting the shift within Chabad Hasidism during the latter half of the twentieth century from political quietism to a much more politically activist approach.[31] Following Schneerson, Ginsburgh's writings stress the necessity of establishing a Torah-ruled theocracy in Israel and extending Jewish sovereignty over the entire Land of Israel (including, for the time being, the Palestinian West Bank territories, though eventually including land from the Nile to the Euphrates and beyond).[32] We can see below how, for Ginsburgh, moving toward these goals is the best possible expression of love for one's fellow Jews.

The selection comes from the chapter on lovingkindness (ḥesed) in Ginsburgh's book *Tikkun ha-Medinah*, translated into English as *Rectifying the State of Israel*, in which Ginsburgh lays out a program for the rectification (*tikkun*) of the State of Israel and of the world. Ginsburgh's multistage program corresponds to various channels of divine energy (*sefirot*). First, rectification requires developing intellectual clarity about the three ideas (corresponding to upper *sefirot*) that Ginsburgh sees as essential truths for all human beings to understand: the Torah is completely authoritative; all Jews must live in Israel, settling all of the land and building a kingdom guided by all of the Torah; and Jews are superior to non-Jews. But the heart of the work of rectification requires repairing "our emotional makeup," beginning with love for others, the "most essential emotion."[33]

Rectifying one's capacity for love, Ginsburgh teaches, requires loving what God loves: the Jewish people as well as the Torah and the Land of Israel. For the people to thrive, Jews must establish a kingdom in the Land of Israel that will be governed by Torah—a theocracy. Aware that some readers may fear the idea of theocracy, Ginsburgh assures them that a proper theocracy will be ruled by lovingkindness, as "the whole Torah is a 'Torah of lovingkindness'" (Prov. 31:26). Also sensing that readers may raise questions about the ethics of his vision for expelling non-Jews from the Land of Israel, he explains how expulsions are a sign of love. Ensuring every Jew a share in the land expresses the deepest love, whereas allowing foreigners to possess any part of the Promised Land would be a betrayal of love.

Ginsburgh also cautions, at the conclusion of the selection below, that lovingkindness also requires a certain level of "might" (*gevurah*). Though kabbalistic traditions describe "might" as a quality in tension with lovingkindness, a key theme in Ginsburgh's book is that, in line with traditional kabbalistic discourse, every trait should also include all other traits (a process that Ginsburgh calls "inter-inclusion"). Thus, within lovingkindness, we can also find "might." For example, as Ginsburgh puts it elsewhere, "the might necessary to eradicate terrorism" is fundamentally located within lovingkindness—it reveals, above all, a love for the Jewish people.[34] So too, the expulsion of non-Jewish Palestinians who do not support Jewish sovereignty, "though outwardly forceful in nature, depends upon an intensification of loving-kindness."[35]

The dynamic here seems to illustrate what Hannah Arendt observed (section 8.4): love can lead to chauvinism, clouded judgment, and violence motivated by sincere compassion, as perpetrators of violence develop compassion for themselves while lacking it for their victims. We can also see an inversion of Levinas's vision of "the entirety of the Bible": for Ginsburgh, the essence of the Torah is not about the priority of the other but precisely about the priority of the Jewish people.

Yitzchak Ginsburgh, *Rectifying the State of Israel* (2002)

To truly love the Creator is to love all that He loves. In particular, dearest to Him of all His creations is His chosen people, Israel. And so, in particular, to love God is to love Israel. Thus, the actual stages of the rectification process begin with the act that most reflects the love of the Jewish people, innate in the heart of every Jew. The love of the Jewish people entails, as well, the love of the Torah and the love of the Land of Israel. The Torah is "our life and the length of our days."[36] Together with the study and the observance of the Torah, the longing of our people to return to the Promised Land and build there our communal life as a [theocractic] "kingdom of priests" (Exodus

257

19:5–6) and "a light unto the nations" (Isaiah 49:6) is what has kept us alive over thousands of years of exile. . . .

(As we shall see, instituting a theocracy is predicated on making the values of Judaism dear to all Jews and dispelling the myths that make them fear the Torah's vision of government. The whole Torah is a "Torah of lovingkindness" [Proverbs 31:26]: all its ways are "ways of pleasantness" and all its paths are "paths of peace" [Proverbs 3:17].)

To love another soul is to love, of course, its source of life and nest of life. And so, the love of the Jewish people entails the love of the Torah and the love of the Land of Israel. . . .

Whoever truly loves the Jewish people and the Land of Israel, the Jewish homeland, seeks to pair these two loves—to join the nation to its land. In the Israel of today, national rectification must begin with a declaration of love for the people and the land and an affirmation of the unequivocal bond of love between them. This implies that the taking of possession of any part of the Land of Israel by a foreigner is a betrayal of one's beloved. Thus our first act of rectification must be to declare Jewish sovereignty over the entire Land of Israel. . . .

Practically speaking, love of the people and the land and the marriage between them translate into settling the whole land with Jews. Granting every Jew a share in the Land of Israel expresses the deepest love of the people. . . . In order for the bestowal of this gift to succeed, after we have formally declared that the land belongs exclusively to the Jewish people, we must make every effort to settle the land by as many Jews in as many places as soon as possible. . . . To do so requires, at the spiritual level, the manifestation of the inter-inclusion of the attribute of might [*gevurah*] . . . within the attribute of loving-kindness [*ḥesed*]. We must be fast and forceful in expressing our deepest love for our people.[37]

8.7. THE LOVE OF OUR MOTHERS

Jews have often viewed the Patriarchs Abraham, Isaac, and Jacob as exemplars of lovingkindness and described God as "recalling the lovingkindness of the Patriarchs" in the opening paragraph of the daily *Amidah* prayer. In recent decades some Jews have added references to the Matriarchs Sarah, Rebecca, Rachel, and Leah to that paragraph of the *Amidah*. Einat Ramon (b. 1959), the first Israeli-born woman to be ordained as a rabbi and the former dean of the (Conservative) Schechter Rabbinical Seminary in Jerusalem, argues that this addition should direct our attention to the lovingkindness of the Matriarchs.

Ramon points to midrashic traditions that allude to the lovingkindness of Sarah, Rebecca, Rachel, and Leah. These midrashim, she notes, generally focus on the Matriarchs providing for the physical needs of their dependents, especially in birthing and raising their children and running their homes. Ramon sees this legacy of lovingkindness as continued by more recent generations of Jewish mothers, who have also conveyed their love through "physical acts of caring, beyond normative expectation," while often focusing their energies beyond the confines of their families. The association between maternal love and physical acts of caring led Simḥah Zissel Ziv to suggest that maternal love was inferior to paternal love; for Ramon, by contrast, the attention to physical nurturing is a sign of the great virtue of the Matriarchs and of later mothers.

And yet, as Ramon indicates in the selections below, there are serious problems with idealizing this model of maternal lovingkindness. The idea that the virtue of lovingkindness demands continual physical acts of caring, beyond normative expectation, toward one's family and also beyond, is a formula for enslavement. The construction of maternal virtue in exclusively physical terms has often left women uneducated, unable to participate in communal intellectual and spiritual life, barred from positions of authority, and too burdened to express their love through writing and teaching. In fact, such barriers to engagement and expression contributed to the devaluation of physical care provided by women.

Ramon argues that the practice of recalling the Matriarchs in the *Amidah* can help contemporary Jews honor a legacy of domestic nurturing while at the same time bringing this legacy into the public realms women have historically been unable to access: communal prayer; the public work of repairing the world (*tikkun olam*); and studying and teaching Torah, particularly the "Torah of lovingkindness" (Prov. 31:26).

But while the book of Proverbs speaks of a "woman of valor" with a "Torah of lovingkindness," that woman is trapped within a patriarchal world. Contemporary women should be able to teach a "Torah of lovingkindness" free from patriarchy: speaking publicly and acting with lovingkindness in response to physical *and* intellectual and spiritual needs. For Ramon, the midrash on the book of Psalms (*Midrash Tehillim*) that describes the continual study of Torah as an experience of divine lovingkindness supports the idea that, for a contemporary "woman of valor," "her personal, domestic, and daily acts of loving-kindness appear as an expression of her learning." In Ramon's feminist reframing, the virtue of lovingkindness may be expressed in a variety of contexts and in response to a variety of needs.

Einat Ramon, "The Matriarchs and the Torah of Hesed (Loving-Kindness)" (2005)

Invoking the matriarchs in the *Amidah* reflects the presence of God in their deeds of loving-kindness, as described in the stories of Genesis and in the various midrashic texts, paralleling and complementing the memory of the acts of loving-kindness reflected in the stories of the patriarchs. . . .

As it was for the matriarchs, the founders of the nation, so it was for our mothers of the recent past and the present: loving-kindness was their daily bread and the Torah of their lives. Their deeds on behalf of their congregations, their people, and humanity were an expansion of their daily maternal activity within their families, whose essence was loving-kindness — acting on behalf of others, through physical acts of caring, beyond normative expectation. . . .

Burdened with safeguarding the sanctity of everyday life, our foremothers were denied the requisite education and authority and the practical possibility of recording their religious experiences and ethical insights on paper. The ongoing performance of deeds of loving-kindness, then, has had an enslaving aspect, insofar as it limited the realms of female expression over the generations, binding women to their homes and preventing them from actively participating in the intellectual and spiritual life of the people. Their generosity became taken for granted, devoid of elevated ethical significance, and as a result they became anonymous righteous women, lacking in identity and uniqueness, and nameless because they had been erased from national memory.[38]

This female experience distanced many Jewish women in recent generations from their female genealogy, and from the need to seek it out. The feminist journey through the pages of the Talmud and midrash is not only a matter of illuminating the scraps of testimony to the religious-ethical world of women that can be seen by peering over the patriarchal wall. It also signifies a coming to terms with our dialectical relationship with our mothers and with the "domestic" value system that they represent. For women who aspired to the realms of Torah, prayer, and *tikkun olam*, that system was seen as entailing the confinement of female experience within the four cubits of home and kitchen. Now that those realms have finally been opened to us, the greatness of the matriarchs, feeding their children and all who dined at their tables, goes unacknowledged. By recalling the loving-kindness of the matriarchs in the *Amidah*, we seek to integrate the two sides of Jewish feminism: striving for Torah, prayer, and *tikkun olam*, and valuation of the acts of loving-kindness associated with domestic nurturing. Invoking their names endows the maternal greatness of the mother with religious and public recognition, grounded in our mature, critical, and loving stance.[39]

Women—mothers, far and near—perhaps experienced the presence of God not so much in shofar blasts, thunderclaps, lightning, wind, and earthquake (Ex. 19:16, I Kings 19:12), nor in a still, small voice, but in the loving-kindness that lessens the depth of sorrow and exalts the joy of existence. This is the "Torah of loving-kindness" on the tongue of the "woman of valor" (Prov. 31:26). Yet even the "woman of valor" was trapped in a patriarchal mold, dependent as she was upon the exalted status of her husband (Prov. 31:33); awaiting his approval and that of her sons (31:28; daughters, of course, are not mentioned); and ultimately being serenaded with this song by the "head of the family" every Sabbath eve.

At the same time, the verse "Her mouth is full of wisdom, her tongue with the Torah of loving-kindness" (Prov. 31:26) breaks, in effect, the patriarchal pattern of thinking that confines the woman to the home, drawing her out into the realm of Torah and wisdom. Her deeds of loving-kindness in and outside the home are expressed in the Torah that she teaches. The midrash on Psalms supports this reading, interpreting the verse "God's loving-kindness never ceases" (Ps. 52:3) as referring to "a person who busies himself with loving-kindness towards God all day, namely Torah, as it is written, 'Her tongue with the Torah of loving-kindness'" (Midrash Tehillim 52:6). An interpretation appearing in the Talmud holds, by contrast, that "The term 'Torah of loving-kindness' refers to Torah for its own sake" (BT Sukkot 49b), thus reifying the hierarchical dichotomy between "for its own sake" and "not for its own sake," between the scholars and the common folk (including women, denied the opportunity to learn and teach). The midrash on Psalms 52, on the other hand, elucidates the deep meaning of the Torah of the woman of valor, a Torah in which her personal, domestic, and daily acts of loving-kindness appear as an expression of her learning.[40]

8.8. LOVE, COMPASSION, AND THE TORAH OF NONVIOLENCE

Lynn Gottlieb (b. 1949), another pioneering Jewish feminist and the first woman ordained as a rabbi in the Jewish Renewal movement, is cofounder and coordinator of the Shomer Shalom Network for Jewish Nonviolence, an organization that seeks to promote nonviolent understandings of Torah and train *shomrei shalom* (practitioners of nonviolent peace stewardship). She lays out the principles that guide her vision in her book *Trail Guide to the Torah of Nonviolence*.

By Gottlieb's understanding, love and compassion that promote nonviolence are at the heart of the classical Rabbinic tradition, and this provides contemporary Jews with a precedent for further developing the tradition to be even more committed to nonviolence. The Rabbis of the Talmud developed a series of strategies for suppressing, annulling, or rereading biblical texts and rituals that promote violence, she contends. In part, they "developed approaches that invalidated or hemmed in sections of the text which did not accord with their view that, 'One who is not compassionate cannot truly be of the seed of Abraham our father'" (BT *Beitzah* 32b).[41] While the Rabbis were somewhat limited in how far they could go in promoting nonviolence, as they felt bound by tradition and divine authority, contemporary Jews may be liberated from these constraints and press even further toward developing a Torah of nonviolence.[42]

To Gottlieb, this ongoing process should be grounded in seven *middot* (principles and virtues), among them that one should "love your neighbor as you love yourself; do not do to others that which is hateful to you." In part I below, from her discussion of this *middah*, Gottlieb stresses how the commandment to love one's neighbor applies to all human beings, and how the heart of the obligation is found in the commandment to "love the stranger, for you were strangers in the land of Egypt." Gottlieb here offers a teaching common among late twentieth- and early twenty-first-century Jewish thinkers, who have similarly understood "the stranger" as the non-Jewish outsider (rather than the convert to Judaism, per classical Rabbinic texts). Emmanuel Levinas, for one, also described the obligation to love the non-Jewish stranger as core to his understanding of ethics.[43]

Furthermore, Gottlieb stresses that the commandment to love applies even to one's enemies, a point also made by Simḥah Zissel Ziv (section 8.3). Elsewhere in her writing, Gottlieb refers to other traditions also cited by Simḥah Zissel, including the story of Beruriah teaching her husband not to pray for the death of sinners.

In the selection below, Gottlieb turns to a classical Rabbinic reading of verses in Exodus 23 that stress helping one's enemy. In one Rabbinic formulation, this is an opportunity to overcome one's evil inclination ("drive," in Gottlieb's translation) and turn the one who hates you ("your enemy") into one who loves you ("your friend"). Gottlieb reads this counsel as applying not only to enemies from among one's people but to any enemy on earth.

Here, Gottlieb is not focused on identification with the other or self-sacrifice for the sake of the other, but rather on the more easily attainable goal of fair treatment. For Gottlieb, "love is equivalent to fair treatment of every human being, which includes the effort to accommodate basic needs."

Part II comes from Gottlieb's discussion of another *middah*, that one should "conscientiously object to and resist structural violence and war," which Gottlieb contextualizes with reference to the struggle between compassion and cruelty. Pointing to examples of how Jews have failed to show proper compassion for non-Jewish Palestinians during the Israeli-Palestinian conflict, she addresses "the blatant racism" of Chabad approaches (sections 8.2 and 8.6) and related perspectives popular among Israeli settlers—especially those, like Yitzhak Ginsburgh, who work with "deepest love" to support the forceful Jewish occupation of the whole Land of Israel.

To Gottlieb, though, cruelty may be perpetuated not only by those who forcefully advocate for "holy war" but also by those who advocate for "just war" against those whom they view as "cruel enemies." She points to the teaching that "one who is not compassionate cannot truly be of the seed of Abraham our father." Those she is rebuffing would no doubt respond by quoting the midrashic source (referenced by Cynthia Ozick in section 7.5) condemning those who "become merciful when one should be cruel."

Part III comes from a section of Gottlieb's book that describes archetypes of creativity and leadership, based on models of biblical women but using trans- and nonbinary language "to honor the revolution in thinking about gender as a new element in the history of nonviolence."[44] Among these archetypes is the *kallah*, often translated as "bride" but, in Gottlieb's understanding, the wholehearted, empathic person who shows compassion "for perself" and who extends one's circle of compassion to include others, even those with whom one is in conflict. This model for love, more than any other in this chapter, stresses compassion for oneself that transcends the gender binary.

Lynn Gottlieb, *Trail Guide to the Torah of Nonviolence* (2013)

I. The word *ahavah* (love) incorporates *rachamim* [compassion] and *hesed* [generosity and altruism]. We are commanded to love ourselves, our neighbors, the stranger, and even those who we consider our enemies.[45] [...]

A *shomeret shalom* [practitioner of nonviolent peace stewardship] interprets the obligation to love your 'neighbor' as a universal principle that applies to all human beings, regardless of religious, ethnic, cultural, gender or national identity. This interpretation is supported from the inclusion of *gerim* (strangers) in the biblical obligation. "Love the stranger, for you were strangers in the land of Egypt" (Deut. 10:19). In this usage *ger* references non-Israelites, immigrants, foreign residents and strangers.[...]

Every human being, whether they are known to you or not, must enjoy fair treatment. Love is equivalent to fair treatment of every human being, which includes the effort to accommodate basic needs.[46] [...]

The Torah teaches us that no person or nation exists outside the circle of love's obligation, including people we may consider our enemies. Exodus 23:4, for example, states, "When you encounter your enemy's ox or donkey wandering, you must take it back to him." Furthermore, "When you see the ass of someone who hates you lying helpless under its load, however unwilling you may be to help it, you must give him a hand with it" (Exodus 23:5).[...]

Turning enemies into friends is a religious obligation that requires much personal effort. We are asked to curb the impulse to seek revenge and refrain from hurting those who hurt us. The work of curbing our impulse to hurt others means we must strive to heal our own wounds so that we do not let our grief and rage impel us to harm others. "If you have curbed your drive in order to make your enemy

your friend, I promise you that I will make your enemy your friend"
(Mekhilta de-Rashbi, 23:4).[47]

II. In the current period, Jews are living with the results of our collective decision to support Israel's military prowess and promote
militarism among the Jewish people. The secular and religious movements continue to fashion a Jewish narrative framework that justifies
militarism; the settler movement's ideology that non-Jews have no
right to an existence in the holy land and their presence occurs only
by the largess of Jews who permit them to live there, is supported by
Israeli military policy. Adherents of The Elder Rav [Abraham Isaac]
Kook and [the settler movement] Gush Emunim, as well as [the] late
Rabbi Menahem Mendel Schneerson and members of Chabad along
with many other so-called religious settlers believe that non-Jews
are a lesser class of human beings. Laws of mercy and kindness do
not apply to them. The following opinion of Rav Kook illustrates
this attitude. "The difference between a Jewish soul and souls of
non-Jews—all of them in all different levels—is greater and deeper
than the difference between a human soul and the souls of cattle."
[. . .] One cannot ignore the blatant racism inherent in much of the
religious nationalism which fuels Israeli militarism.

Contemporary religious settlers justify acts of cruelty on the basis
of a single passage in the works of the mediaeval sage Nachmanides
that the conquest and settlement of the Land of Israel falls under
the category of obligatory wars and "is *a positive commandment for
all generations* obligating every individual, even during the period of
exile." Under the framework of 'holy war' Barukh Goldstein massacred twenty nine Muslims in prayer at the Tomb of Abraham, Yigal
Amir assassinated Yitzhak Rabin and many settlers feel justified in
perpetrating all manner of horrendous acts against Palestinians.
Settler violence has been on the rise for decades.

Even those who do not use the language of 'holy war' nor consider
themselves 'extremists,' nonetheless, frame the Palestinian Israeli
conflict in the language of just war.[. . .]

The assumptive principle that motivates such thinking is the notion that there is no alternative to military defense when it comes to the protection of Jewish national sovereignty and security. How else can we understand the battle protocol given by the Chief Military Rabbi Brigadier General Avi Ronzki in a pamphlet he distributed through his office to Israeli troops implicitly sanction[ing] the killing of civilians by urging soldiers to "show no mercy." "When you show mercy to a cruel enemy you are being cruel to pure and honest soldiers."[. . .] His [advice] contradicts Talmudic teachings such as the one found in Beitzah 32b, "One who is not compassionate cannot truly be of the seed of Abraham our father."[48]

III. Active nonviolence is a path of whole-heartedness and empathy. The word *kallah* is often translated as bride. The root of *kallah* is wholeness. In the context of *hitorrarut* [awakening to nonviolence within] it means a whole hearted person who strives to walk in peace with perself. Sit in a quiet place and imagine standing under a peace canopy. Imagine you are standing opposite yourself. Wish yourself the blessing of compassion and peace.[. . .] A peace canopy can also be a place where you invite your community to stand with you.[. . .] Invite those you consider your beloved community. Those who are in the next circle of connection. Continue to extend the connection to those with whom you are in conflict or struggle.[. . .] What would have to happen in order to invite them into the circle?[49]

8.9. LOVE FOR NONHUMAN ANIMALS

Many of the texts and traditions invoked by Gottlieb have also been central to the teachings of the Open Orthodox rabbi Shmuly Yanklowitz (introduced in section 1.9). Yanklowitz's writings on combating xenophobia and aiding non-Jewish immigrants and refugees, for example, repeatedly invoke the memory of slavery in Egypt and cite the commandment to "love the stranger."[50] He describes Beruriah as a "feminist hero" for her commitment to learning and her compassion.[51] Though unlike Gottlieb he is not a pacifist and he identifies as a Zionist, he shares a number of Gottlieb's moral concerns regarding Israel, describing contemporary Religious Zionism as "fundamentally flawed, directionless, and even broken in many ways."[52] Furthermore, like Gottlieb he invokes the teaching that "one who is not compassionate cannot truly be a descendant of our father Abraham." For Yanklowitz, this indicates that "a Jew is expected to be obsessed with compassion"—toward human beings as well as toward other sentient beings.[53]

Most of the figures profiled earlier in this chapter (except for perhaps Simḥah Zissel Ziv)[54] have written little about the welfare of nonhuman animals, but to Yanklowitz, the mass suffering of animals who are raised on factory farms for their meat, milk, or eggs is "one of the greatest ills of our time." In the selection below, he addresses those Jews who ignore obligations toward animals and support contemporary factory farming systems that unnecessarily torment animals. Indeed, as he notes in the introduction to the essay from which the text below is excerpted, some Jewish communities view the consumption of meat as a religious obligation and even as a "cultural necessity" and look down upon vegetarians as having a "holier than thou" attitude.

Yanklowitz asks Jews who are skeptical of veganism or vegetarianism to consider Jewish traditions that can motivate love for animals, such as a midrash that describes how "the Holy One has compassion for animals just as He has compassion for humans." He also points to Jewish ideas of reincarnation, which break down "the strict distinction between *self* and *other*; between human and animal"; if humans can see their past or future reincarnation, they can come to love the animal not just because they are "like yourself" but "because they are yourself."

Yet even as Yanklowitz wants readers to consider how love for animals may flow from a recognition of how humans and animals are the same, he also wants them to consider how love may flow from a recognition of human and animal differences. The selection below ends with a teaching from the Musar movement's Rabbi Shlomo Wolbe that, echoing Levinas's teachings, urges us to avoid our self-centered impulse to identify the other with ourselves and instead urges us to see the other as "precisely other, different from us in essence." Here applying Wolbe's teaching regarding human-human relations to human-animal relations, Yanklowitz suggests that the work of musar may help us to cultivate love for animals, and in fact "resonates most deeply, when it comes to our obligation toward animals, precisely because of the otherness that emerges alongside our sameness."[55]

Shmuly Yanklowitz, "Mussar and Loving Animals" (2018)

The mass suffering of animals in factory farming is one of the greatest ills of our time. It requires an urgent response that is not only just but loving. . . . Exploring how the ethos of loving non-human animals is deeply-rooted in traditional Jewish thought is indispensable for contemporary moral growth. . . .

We learn that God is compassionate to all and, thus, we are to emulate this compassion. . . . While some people might only be concerned with compassion for other humans, the rabbis teach that this is not the Divine approach: "If a person traveling by ship encounters a great storm, he will throw his possessions and livestock overboard in order to save the passengers. He does not have the same degree of compassion for his animals and possessions as he does for other human beings. However, the Holy One . . . has compassion for animals just as He has compassion for humans. As it states, '[God's] mercy is upon all [God's] works (Psalms 145:9)'" (Midrash Tanḥuma, Noaḥ 6). . . .

[Or] one might be motivated by the Kabbalistic teaching regarding *gilgulim* (reincarnation) where we see that there is a breakdown in the strict distinction between *self* and *other*; between human and animal. We are concerned for an animal because we *are* an animal. Human anatomy, biology, and behavior are predictable to that of animals, to the point where in a past life, we were an animal; in a future life, perhaps we will be an animal. We understand the biblical instruction to "love another like yourself" more as "love another because they are yourself."

Or consider a theology where all beings have a Divine purpose and therefore dignity and value: "There is nothing superfluous in the universe. Even flies, gnats, and mosquitoes are part of creation and . . . serve a Divinely-appointed purpose" (Bereshit Rabbah 10:7). This is not a love based on reciprocity; it's love based upon empathy. As Rabbi Samson Raphael Hirsch explains: "Compassion is the feeling of empathy which the pain of one being of itself awakens in another; and the higher and more human the beings are, the more keenly attuned are they to re-echo the note of suffering which, like a voice from heaven, penetrates the heart" (*Horeb* 17:125). . . .

But this spiritual work is not easy. On this, the great 20th century *mussar* teacher Rabbi Shlomo Wolbe explains: "We see ourselves in the other, as if every person we encounter is simply a mirror in which we see ourselves! That is to say: we have not yet freed ourselves from the self-centered perspective to see that the other is not identified with us. The other is precisely other, different from us in essence, and it is incumbent upon us to focus on the way the other differs from us and see that which the other needs, not that which we need!" (*Alei Shur* 2:6)

It is impossible to understand another's trauma and impossible to grasp the extent of another's suffering. But we can create spaces to listen, to cultivate empathy, and to respond to their needs. And Rav Wolbe teaches here that we must start with transcending the self: getting beyond the idea that because we know our own needs that we truly understand the needs of another. There is a strong case to be made for the commonalities between humans and animals. But there is also a strong case to be made for our otherness. The work of mussar is to see the gap in our commonalities as the space for our work of empathy, to transcend our needs toward understanding the needs of the other. Indeed, the work of mussar resonates most deeply, when it comes to our obligation toward animals, precisely because of the otherness that emerges alongside our sameness.[56]

CONCLUSION

All of the thinkers in this chapter see love, kindness, and compassion as important virtues, but many of them disagree profoundly about their character and application.

Some Jewish thinkers have emphasized love for fellow Jews, while others have stressed love for all humans or all sentient beings.

Some thinkers have characterized love as incredibly demanding and even requiring self-sacrifice, while others have characterized love for others as compatible with self-love or the pursuit of self-interest.

Some thinkers have viewed self-love as a virtue, while others consider it a vice, and still others as an impossibility.

Some concepts of love require recognizing the similarity or unity between the one who loves and the one who is loved; other concepts of love require recognizing otherness and difference.

Some more paternalistic approaches reflect certainty about what the other needs; other concepts of love stress the unique choices of diverse individuals.

Some thinkers link love and compassion with violence; others link love and compassion with nonviolence.

Some patriarchal models associate ideal love with masculinity. Challenging these models, other models of love uplift matriarchs and still others transcend the gender binary.

Some thinkers have integrated love and compassion as key elements of politics; other thinkers have characterized love and compassion as inappropriate virtues within the political realm.

And Jewish thinkers have linked love, kindness, and compassion with a gamut of theological perspectives, ranging from the view that God is uniquely found within Jewish souls to the view that God is known only through the commandment to be ethical.

While many modern Jewish thinkers have viewed love, kindness, and compassion as virtues, they have often disagreed on what love, kindness, and compassion are like. These disagreements often reflect very different ideas about proper human relationships, including very different ideas about responsibility for others. Many of the tensions in this chapter will surface in the following chapter, on solidarity and social responsibility.

9

Solidarity and Social Responsibility (*Arevut/Aḥarayut*)

Like the other virtues discussed in this volume, virtues of solidarity (typically, standing in unity with others) and social responsibility (typically, taking responsibility for others for the sake of the common good) can be understood in many different ways. Solidarity is often understood as joining with others *across lines of difference*,[1] and most of the sources in this chapter do speak about one's obligation to stand with and take responsibility for others who are different from oneself—but those differences may be very broad or very narrow. While the majority of thinkers emphasize solidarity with and responsibility for diverse human beings regardless of their national or religious identities, others stress solidarity and responsibility as part of state-building and thereby emphasize relationships with those sharing a common national/state identity (sections 9.1, 9.7); and some emphasize solidarity with and responsibility for diverse Jews rather than non-Jews (sections 9.3, 9.5, 9.7). In one text (9.3), solidarity and responsibility extend only to the select group of Jews whom the author sees as potentially faithful to the covenant—though he calls upon virtuous Jews to follow the biblical example of Moses, reaching out across lines of difference in the Jewish community and taking responsibility for those Jews who are not grave sinners.

Different views of the character of Moses serve as models for these different approaches to solidarity and responsibility. For Yisroel Friedman (section 9.3), Moses shows great wisdom in standing in solidarity with his people, in refusing to accept the rebel Korach as part of his people, and in calling for Korach to be "annihilated" (Num. 16). To Natan Tzevi Finkel (section 9.4) and Yosef Yitzḥak Schneersohn (section 9.5), Moses offers a model for taking responsibility for all Jews, even serious sinners. For David Ben-Gurion (section 9.7), Moses' mantle of leadership appears to have been transferred to the Israel Defense Forces, which will help build a new model of Jewish solidarity. For Amanda Mbuvi (section 9.11), Moses helps the People of Israel draw strength from their diversity, including from the "mixed multitude" that has often been viewed as alien to the true People of Israel. In direct contrast to Friedman's Moses, who draws sharp lines and encourages violence against those who are not a part of the community, Mbuvi's Moses is linked with an approach that refuses to engage in "ideological or physical violence against those who don't fit."

Many authors in this chapter draw on Rabbinic texts as well as biblical traditions. Friedman, for example, is animated by a Rabbinic principle articulated in the Babylonian Talmud (*Shevuot* 39a): *kol Yisra'el arevim zeh la-zeh*, "all of Israel are responsible for each other" (or "all Israel takes care of Israel"). In Rabbinic literature, the phrase generally indicates that all of Israel—that is, the entire Jewish people—are guarantors for each other, such that they may be punished for the sin of one Jew if they had the power to prevent that sin but failed to do so.[2] The Jewish people are mutually responsible (*arevim*) to prevent each other from sinning, and insofar as one should strive to internalize this responsibility, one may speak of the virtue of "mutual responsibility" or "solidarity" (*arevut*). A related talmudic text (BT *Sotah* 37b, introduced by Emmanuel Levinas, section 9.9) brings a debate about just how far this mutual responsibility goes. By one interpretation, the debate is between those who think that each Jew is responsible for other Jews' fulfillment of the commandments and those who think that each Jew is also responsible for ensuring that every other Jew is "responsible for the responsibility"—responsible for ensuring that every other Jew takes on the responsibility for other Jews' fulfillment of the commandments. These sorts of Rabbinic traditions inspire the thinking of other authors including Natan Tzevi Finkel (section 9.4), Yosef Yitzḥak Schneersohn (9.5), Abraham Joshua Heschel

(9.8), and David Jaffe (9.10). On the other hand, Hannah Arendt (9.6) and David Ben-Gurion (9.7) reference the Rabbinic concept of mutual responsibility but discredit it as inadequate to meet twentieth-century political challenges.

Some of the discussions in this chapter build directly on ideas of love and kindness in the previous chapter. Echoes of Chabad Hasidic ideas regarding the unique bonds of love joining all Jews (section 8.2) and the importance of coercing other Jews to accept the Torah (section 8.6) appear here in the assertions of another Chabad Hasidic leader, Yosef Yitzḥak Schneersohn (section 9.5). Echoes of the Musar movement leader Simḥah Zissel Ziv's teaching that God demands an extremely high level of compassion for others, even for the wicked (section 8.3), emerge here in the teaching of his student Natan Tzevi Finkel (section 9.4). Hannah Arendt's respect for human diversity and her sense that patriotism requires "permanent opposition and criticism" (section 8.4) inform her thinking on solidarity (section 9.6). And Emmanuel Levinas builds on his idea that "there is always a priority of the other in relation to me" (section 8.5) in discussing "infinite responsibility" (section 9.9).

A number of the broad political disagreements that have shaped approaches to virtue in previous chapters also play a significant role in this chapter. Among these are different views of various modern nationalisms that are sometimes seen as sources of solidarity and other times seen as undermining solidarity. This chapter begins with the views of Murād Farag (section 9.1) and Emma Goldman (section 9.2), each of whom develops visions of solidarity in response to the claims of modern nationalisms.

9.1. A UNIFIED, COLLECTIVE EGYPTIAN SOUL

The lawyer, theologian, and writer Murād Farag (Faraj) (1866–1956) was a reformist leader of the twentieth-century Jewish community of Karaites (a minority Jewish group that rejects the authority of Rabbinic traditions) in Egypt. In his writing, Farag called for solidarity among Karaites; at the same time, he also called for solidarity between Karaite

Jews and Rabbanite Jews. His efforts included a campaign to reverse the communities' mutual bans on intermarriage between them. Traditional leaders in the two Egyptian communities, both of whom regarded the other as having abandoned true Israelite identity, rejected his call.[3]

Farag also worked for solidarity at the national level, joining with many Egyptians in seeking their country's liberation from its British colonial rulers. An advocate of liberal Egyptian nationalism, he envisioned Egypt becoming an independent, secular liberal state that would guarantee equal rights to Muslims, Christians, and Jews. These diverse communities could be "passionately united internally and externally," he hoped, by their patriotic commitment to the state, affirming themselves as "one family whose members cannot be separated from each other, or like partners in an indivisible property."[4] "We are all nationalist Egyptians," he declared.[5] Echoing the views of many other Jews who supported Jewish integration into a variety of nation-states throughout the nineteenth and twentieth centuries, Farag saw how Jews could develop a sense of solidarity that would allow them to feel part of the state, and how non-Jewish Egyptians could develop a sense of solidarity that would allow them to accept Jews as fellow citizens.

Farag was certainly aware, however, of obstacles to unity. In the series of articles written in 1908 excerpted in the selection below, he was particularly troubled by discriminatory practices within Egyptian Muslim communities. For example, many Muslims refused to greet Christians or Jews with the salutation "Peace unto you" (*Alsalam aleikum*), as "to them, neither the Christian nor the Jew qualifies to have peace bestowed upon them."[6] Like Simḥah Zissel Ziv, who saw greetings of peace as foundational to establishing unified political communities (section 8.3.II), Farag viewed basic gestures such as these as foundational to political life, and he urged Egyptian Jews, Christians, and Muslims alike to overcome their mutual distrust and extend wishes of peace to all others regardless of religious identity.[7]

Egyptian nationalism could remedy communal tensions, he argued, because nationalism creates powerful bonds of fraternity and patriotism. Enmity can be ended "only if we change ourselves to live for the nation.

To become a unified, collective soul—we must all be sincere toward one another." "Sincerity" in this context may refer to sincere dedication to a common cause; as another translation puts it, "In order for there to be a single soul, it is necessary for the individual souls to be dedicated to that which they share among one another."[8] Achieving solidarity, for Farag, requires internal work: the changing of hearts and minds, and the reorientation of religious passions so they do not stand in the way of the unifying nationalist cause.

Notably, a few years earlier Farag had expressed particular admiration for the patriotic unity found in the United States—the very model of patriotism that Emma Goldman (section 9.2) condemned. Farag admired how in the U.S., as in France and other countries, "unity of will and word" led to national independence, prosperity, power, and dominion. Any well-functioning nation, like any other well-functioning group, is like a body that requires all of its organs to work together, he explained. The sort of unity achieved by powerful nations may inspire other nations, as well as other communities (e.g., the Jewish community, or the Karaite community in particular) to work toward greater solidarity.[9]

Murād Farag, "The War for Our Nation" (1908)

A nation or [constitutional] monarchy is always in need of a bond created by nationalism, particularly when it includes people who are believers in different religions or affiliates of different doctrines. If people in Egypt were to be armed with religions or doctrines, they would kill each other. By killing I do not mean taking lives but the killing of fraternal passion and national feeling in peoples' souls; nothing is more evil than that. . . .

If we wish to have our own home, it can be ours only if we change ourselves to live for the nation. To become a unified, collective soul—we must all be sincere toward one another. This sincerity is seen in the expulsion from the community of anything that stands in its way in the religious realm. . . .

We are like warriors for the nation. Yet this war is neither systematic nor based on a solid foundation. The worst thing about this war is the lack of confluence, meaning that we are not united in rallying around the same purpose. In doing so, we are very much like the army—convergent in body but divergent in heart. It is hearts, rather than bodies, that should first be brought together. . . .

Nothing is greater than people from all religions and doctrines coming together in friendship to become Egyptians in the true national sense of the word. One nationality that knows for itself only one homeland shall work together to identify a nationality overruling any other national allegiance, so that we are all called Egyptians—a word of the heart that is not different from that of the tongue.[10]

9.2. REPLACING PATRIOTISM WITH INTERNATIONAL SOLIDARITY

The year 1908 saw the publication not only of Murād Farag's ardent call to nationalism but also the Jewish anarchist Emma Goldman's ardent condemnation of nationalistic discourse and vision for the downfall of all state powers.

In section 6.3, Goldman pointed to the ways in which gratitude may be used to silence dissent. Goldman rejected the idea that one should submit to state power out of gratitude for the ostensible benefits provided by a state. Rather, solidarity with those who are oppressed worldwide demands that one revolt against those in power to establish a more just order.

Here, in her essay "Patriotism: A Menace to Liberty," Goldman addresses nationalistic discourse, especially in the United States but also in other countries. Her essay lays out key features of her approach to international solidarity while condemning "patriotism and its bloody spectre, militarism."[11]

In sections of the essay not included below, Goldman describes patriotism as a vice grounded in superstition. It is like religion in this respect, but it is "far more injurious, brutal, and inhumane than religion."[12] Patriotism, created by lies regarding the superiority of one's nation, justifies attacks on other nations, causing immense bloodshed and suffering.

Governments seek to cultivate patriotism in schools, where "youthful minds [are] perverted to suit the government," taught to see their nation as superior, and induced to cheer for their countries in war or become soldiers themselves.[13]

Below, Goldman emphasizes that soldiers in particular must be reeducated to turn away from these lies about nationalism and war. At the same time, all people must be taught to reject the vice of patriotism in favor of the virtue of solidarity with oppressed people across international lines. Those united in solidarity must reject militarism and capitalism, turn to anarchism, and refuse to be divided by religion, nationality, gender, race, or class.

In contrast to other thinkers in this chapter, Goldman did not stress the virtue of solidarity among Jews. In fact, she criticized her fellow Jewish anarchists for being "still too Jewish" when they primarily engaged with Yiddish-speaking Jews while neglecting broader audiences.[14] Nonetheless, Goldman herself did not neglect Jewish audiences during the period in which she wrote this essay; she regularly spoke to both Jewish and non-Jewish audiences on these themes. And when she addressed her fellow Jews, she exhorted them to stand firm in rejecting Judaism, capitalism, and all forms of patriotism, and to join in solidarity with oppressed people all around the world.

Emma Goldman, "Patriotism: A Menace to Liberty" (1908)

Thinking men and women the world over are beginning to realize that Patriotism is too narrow and limited a conception to meet the necessities of our time. The centralization of power has brought into being an international feeling of solidarity among the oppressed nations of the world; a solidarity which represents a greater harmony of interests between the workingmen of America and his brothers abroad than between the American miner and his exploiting compatriot; a solidarity which fears not foreign invasion, because it is bringing all the workers to the point when they will say to their masters, "Go and do your own killing. We have done it long enough for you."

This solidarity is awakening the consciousness of even the soldiers, they, too, being flesh of the flesh of the great human family. . . . What we need is a propaganda of education for the soldier: anti-patriotic literature that will enlighten him as to the real horrors of his trade, and that will awaken his consciousness to his true relation to the man to whose labor he owes his very existence.

It is precisely this that the authorities fear most. It is already high treason for a soldier to attend a radical meeting. No doubt they will also stamp it high treason for a soldier to read a radical pamphlet. But then, has not authority from time immemorial stamped every step of progress as treasonable? Those, however, who earnestly strive for social reconstruction can well afford to face all that; for it is probably even more important to carry the truth into the barracks than into the factory. When we have undermined the patriotic lie, we shall have cleared the path for that great structure wherein all nationalities shall be united into a universal brotherhood—a truly FREE SOCIETY.[15]

9.3. SINNERS BEYOND THE HOLY COMMUNITY

Rabbi Yisroel Friedman of Chortkov, Galicia (1854–1933) was the leader of Chortkover Hasidic communities in Galicia, in Vienna (where Friedman transferred his court after the outbreak of World War I), and elsewhere in Europe. He was also a prominent leader of Agudat Israel (Agudas Yisroel, the Union of Israel), a non-Zionist *haredi* Orthodox political movement founded in 1912. He hailed Agudat Israel as allowing Jews "to unite and be like one man with a common aim," committed to Torah and faith, obedience to proper rabbinical authorities, and defense against the poisonous influence of non-Jews and non-Orthodox Jews alike.[16] Like Farag and Goldman, Friedman was deeply engaged with politics and with promoting solidarity, but he thought about politics and solidarity in radically different terms.

Friedman saw Agudat Israel as the governing body that would unify the true "community of Israel" (*klal Yisra'el*), and he saw all Jews claiming a place within the community as obligated to support the organization.

No Jew, he wrote, "has the right to remain outside our camp and ignore our demand to participate in building and strengthening the walls of the Torah."[17] Friedman viewed himself and his fellow rabbinical authorities as obligated to save the souls of Jews who failed to heed this demand, taking on particular responsibility to bring back to "our camp" those Jews who seemed tempted by secular institutions, non-Orthodox ideas, and even dangerous heresies concocted by Satan such as secular Zionism. Even within his own family, Friedman could find Jews who might be tempted to remain "outside our camp," such as his nephew Abraham Joshua Heschel (section 9.8). It is said that when Friedman heard that his nephew was pursuing secular learning, he summoned him to his court to persuade him to abandon such pursuits and remain within the fold.[18]

Friedman saw himself as living in the times of the "birth pangs of the Messiah," in a world dominated by satanic forces to which Jews were spiritually vulnerable. In this era, Jews who sampled foreign wisdom would quickly adopt heretical ideas and render themselves *hefker*, "without belonging" in the People of Israel. He acknowledged that not all Jews could be saved: some would cease to be a part of Israel. "When young men study foreign wisdoms," he wrote, "they immediately forsake God's Torah and become without belonging [*hefker*]."[19]

Friedman did not, of course, see the threat of being cut off from one's people as a uniquely modern threat. After all, the written Torah spoke of "being cut off from one's people" as punishment for a range of sins, including sex during menstruation, performing labor prohibited on Shabbat, eating or drinking on Yom Kippur, and eating leavened products on Passover; and Rabbinic tradition described the rebellious Korach (Num. 16) as "taking himself out" and separating himself from the People of Israel. But Friedman, during his tumultuous era that he thought marked the eve of redemption, observed increasing numbers of Jews committing such grave sins and even acting like Korach.

In the selection below, working from a kabbalistic theology that sees the People of Israel as connected by their shared "divine souls" (see section 8.2), Friedman describes Jewish souls as all carved from the same "mountains of holiness," bestowing a unique bond of solidarity and mutual responsibility. One's personal Jewish soul is not merely one's own; its merits provide merit for other Jewish souls, just as its sins lead to punishment for other Jewish souls. Those who commit grave sins, however, lose their divine souls entirely, becoming mere flesh; they are no longer in a relationship of solidarity with other Jews, and the virtue of mutual responsibility (*arevut*) no longer applies to them. This was the case with the heretic Korach, who relinquished his divine soul, rendering himself *hefker* such that his former people no longer needed to be responsible for him.

Indeed, in Friedman's reading, part of Moses' virtue is his very recognition that Korach is now outside of the community. God appears not to recognize this at first, as God tells Moses and Aaron to "separate yourselves from this community so that I may annihilate them in an instant" (Num. 16:21)—seemingly threatening to annihilate almost the entire community of Israel (except for Moses and Aaron) for their failure to prevent Korach's sins. But, as Friedman understands it, when Moses protests—"When one man sins, will You be wrathful with the whole community?" (Num. 16:22)—he is pointing out that Korach is merely "one man," an individual who is no longer connected to "the whole community," such that he alone can be violently annihilated. Yes, the faithful community must be held responsible for all those who are still within the community, for the People of Israel "are responsible for each other." But they cannot be held responsible for solitary individuals who commit such grave sins that they are cut off from their people. As Friedman concludes, God agrees with Moses, recognizing that the virtue of mutual responsibility applies only to those who are committed to the community.

Yisroel Friedman, *Ginzei Yisra'el* (1927)

It is known that all of Israel are responsible for each other [*kol Yisra'el arevim zeh la-zeh*] (BT *Shevuot* 39a) and also that all of Israel are in the fellowship [of observance; *kol Yisra'el ḥaverim*] (BT *Ḥagigah* 26a). Why? Because the Holy Blessed One and the Torah and Israel are one (Zohar, Aḥarei Mot 73), and as the souls of Israel are carved from the mountains of holiness, each and every one is connected to his fellow. Therefore they are responsible for each other, and so they can provide merit for each other, and thus their good deeds are numerous.

But this is only if he does not commit a grave sin. If he does sin, and is guilty of sins about which it is said that "he will be cut off from his people," then he will be separated from his people and they will not protect him with their merit, because he will have been separated from them.

And this was the case in the controversy with Korach, as he made himself without belonging [*hefker*] to such an extent that he left the community of Israel [*klal Yisra'el*], and [their merit] did not provide further protection. This is the intention of *Targum Onkelos*, that "Korach took" [Num. 16:1] means "he took himself" — out of the community of Israel. The midrash [BT *Sanhedrin* 109b] hints at this in saying that he "took a bad deal for himself" — for he separated himself from the good, and had no portion of the supernal divine soul [*neshamah*] at all, but only a soul [*nefesh*] of flesh. And so when the Holy Blessed One said, "Separate yourselves from this community so that I may annihilate them in an instant" [Num. 16:21], the argument and recommendation [to God] of our teacher Moses was: "It is true that all of Israel are responsible for each other — but this applies only when the sinner has a portion of the [divine] soul, and then you are 'the God of the souls' [Num. 16:22]. But Korach, who left the community, and for whom only flesh remained — what connection did he have to the community of Israel? He became an individual person, and the community of Israel did not have any responsibility [*arevut*] for him. And so, 'When one man sins, will You be wrathful with the whole community?' [Num. 16:22] God forbid that you would do this!" And the Holy Blessed One agreed.[20]

9.4. RISKING YOUR LIFE IN SOLIDARITY WITH SINNERS

In section 6.4, Musar movement leader Rabbi Natan (Nosson) Tzevi Finkel declared that it was appropriate for Adam, and also the Israelites, to be condemned even for slight sins. Similarly, Finkel argues in the text below, it was appropriate for Noah and Abraham to be condemned for their slight sins of insufficient solidarity with the wicked people of their generations.

Drawing on Rabbinic traditions, Finkel makes it clear that Noah was deeply faithful to God, urging the rest of his generation to repent even as they mocked him. But Noah had insufficient empathy for these wicked people; he failed to risk his life in challenging God's judgment and seeking mercy for them. Abraham clearly improved on Noah's performance, risking his life by challenging God and praying to save the innocent people of Sodom; but even this was insufficient, as Abraham failed to also pray on behalf of the guilty. Finkel points to a passage from the Zohar that presents both Noah and Abraham as inferior to Moses, who stood in solidarity with the guilty Israelites following their idolatrous worship of the Golden Calf and pledged his own life on their behalf, telling God to "please wipe me out of your book" (Exod. 32:32). Although Noah did well in taking responsibility to rebuke his fellows, and Abraham did well in risking his life to save the righteous, Finkel concludes that it is right to criticize these biblical heroes for failing to reach the level of Moses.

Finkel was a student of Simḥah Zissel Ziv, and some of Simḥah Zissel's ideas seen in section 8.3 are reflected in Finkel's teachings about Noah, Abraham, and Moses. Like his teacher, Finkel believed that God is exceedingly demanding, harsh, and exacting. Finkel also emphasized the need to be concerned for the wicked and to pray on their behalf. Simḥah Zissel had made the case that Abraham learned at Sodom "that one should have compassion for the wicked, and that one should seek [compassion] for them in prayer"; Finkel saw Abraham as learning the same lesson, even though he concluded that Abraham did not go far enough in his compassion.[21]

The Musar movement approach that Simḥah Zissel developed and Finkel furthered had much in common with the approach of Yisroel Friedman (section 9.3). Finkel and Friedman were contemporaries and, like Friedman, Finkel played an important role in creating a *haredi* model of Jewish identity that would encourage Torah and faith, demand obedience to rabbinical authority, and stand in staunch opposition to non-Jewish and non-Orthodox ideas. But Finkel's teaching deemphasized the value of separating from the wicked.[22] In fact, he sometimes stressed that the wicked had significant potential for goodness within them. Thus, in his own discussion of Korach, Finkel did not emphasize the gravity of Korach's sins—in fact, he taught, Korach was guilty of only a minor sin, though of course people should be punished even for minor sins—or the need to separate from Korach. Rather, Finkel noted Korach's good qualities and taught that Moses was correct to seek to engage with Korach in the spirit of brotherhood.[23] For Finkel, solidarity with all human beings is clearly a virtue, and all of us have room to grow further toward the ideal of solidarity achieved by Moses.

Natan Tzevi Finkel, *Or ha-Tzafun* (early twentieth century)

As our sages of blessed memory tell, Noah built the ark in public for one hundred and twenty years, and he rebuked the people of his generation, telling them that God would bring a flood to the world, so that they would repent. But they regarded him with contempt and made fun of his words.[24] He did not heed their words, and he rebuked them further, and sought to get them to repent. But he was accused of not risking his life in praying for them as our father Abraham prayed for the people of Sodom. . . . [Noah] did not reach the level of sharing in the sorrow of human beings, risking his life as our father Abraham did, and he did not pray for them. . . .

Our sages of blessed memory also drew a line between Noah and Moses. . . . Noah was accused of not risking his life for the people of his generation, and of not telling God that it would be better for him to also be wiped out, together with all the people of the world, than for [God] to bring the Flood—as Moses did, in saying "Please wipe me out of your book" [Exod. 32:32]. . . . [Abraham] did not fulfill his obligation completely, on the level of Moses, as our sages of blessed memory taught:

Noah did not do anything . . . for the benefit of the righteous or for the benefit of the wicked. Abraham sought justice appropriately, that the innocent should not die with the guilty, but he was not perfect, as he did not request mercy for both [the innocent and guilty]. But who did act perfectly, as is appropriate? Moses, since when the Holy Blessed One said, "They have been quick to turn from the way" [in worshipping the Golden Calf], even though they had all sinned, Moses did not budge from there until [God] said, "I forgive." And given this, there was never a person in the world who defended his generation like Moses, the faithful shepherd.[25]

How very subtle are the accusations against the greatest and most perfected human beings, that with their highest virtues there is further room to seek higher, without end.[26]

9.5. WE ARE RESPONSIBLE FOR AWAKENING THE OTHER JEWS

Rabbi Yosef Yitzḥak Schneersohn (1880–1950) was a leader of the Hasidic Chabad-Lubavitch dynasty founded by Shneur Zalman of Liadi (sections 5.1, 8.2). Like Shneur Zalman and many other Hasidic thinkers—including Yisroel Friedman—Schneersohn saw Jews as uniquely connected to the Divine and uniquely obligated to care for fellow Jews, including Jewish sinners, with whom they shared a common divine soul. Like Shneur Zalman and Friedman, he also believed that grave sinners could cut themselves off from the holy community of Israel. Yet one factor especially distinguished Schneersohn's approach: his particular zeal for reaching out to Jewish sinners who had abandoned their Jewish ritual obligations (e.g., observance of Shabbat and holidays, daily prayer, and refraining from sex during menstruation).

Like Friedman, Schneersohn believed he was living in the "birth pangs of the Messiah," the tumultuous era just before the Messiah's arrival characterized by God's particularly harsh punishments in response to sin. He wrote the proclamation excerpted below in May 1941, after having escaped the Nazis in Europe and settling in the United States, where he saw a second catastrophe unfolding. Just as the Jews of Europe were being killed physically by the Holocaust's "stormy fire," the Jews of America were being killed spiritually by the "silent fire" of assimilation, faithlessness, impurity, and indifference to Jewish law — forces that destroyed Jewish souls. These two simultaneous tragedies indicated that the final redemption was truly imminent, and yet that redemption would come only when a majority of Jews thoroughly repented, accepting "authentic" Torah and faith.

As he indicated in his introduction to the proclamation (not included below), Schneersohn was appalled that Jews all around him held the vain hope that "the Jewish people will be saved through the victory of world democracy." Jews who placed their faith in human political projects and military power, who supported foolish ideologies such as Zionism or called for Jewish armies to fight in World War II, were adopting "the greatest heretical idea," namely "that Jews are like all the nations." Such Jews thought that taking responsibility for other Jews required political and military strategies of the sort that might help other nations; they failed to realize that the only path to assuming responsibility for one's fellow Jews was the path of "penitent return and prayer."[27]

Rather than aligning himself with Agudat Israel as Yisroel Friedman had, Schneersohn created his own organization, Maḥaneh Yisrael ("camp of Israel" or "army of Israel"), described by scholar Gershon Greenberg as "an eschatological movement intent upon stopping the growing catastrophe by means of total religious commitment."[28] All Jews, Schneersohn believed, were obligated to join this organization, and to stand in solidarity in defense of Torah and faith against the evil forces that encouraged Jews to think of themselves as an ordinary nation like other nations.

Schneersohn's proclamation effectively put himself in the place of Moses at the time of the Exodus from Egypt, echoing Moses' desire to lead "our young and our old" (Exod. 10:9) away from a place of impurity and to form a holy "army of Israel" (Exod. 14:19) that would be protected by God. Just as Moses instructed his people to purify themselves so that the "angel of destruction" (Exod. 12:23) would not visit their homes, so too Schneersohn counseled his fellow Jews to "choose life" and the path of repentance so they would not be destroyed by contemporary angels of destruction. Just as Moses enlisted the faithful to take responsibility to awaken and save their fellow Jews, so too Schneersohn directed his followers: "You and we are responsible for all the other Jews, and you and we must be the first to awaken ourselves and to awaken others!" As he observed, the world was filled with Jews who were "born to the Torah and to faith" but needed to be awakened and brought back to this true inheritance.

Like several other thinkers in this chapter, including Natan Tzevi Finkel, Schneersohn described self-sacrifice as a vital component of responsibility. As he noted in another proclamation, the prophets conveyed the urgency of God's message and took responsibility for their people even though they were "ridiculed and mocked," "treated terribly," forced to endure "plenty of suffering," and were not even "certain about their own lives."[29] Schneersohn urged his fellow believers to likewise engage in "tremendous self-sacrifice"—not by joining a human army, but rather by joining him in the true "army of Israel" and enduring whatever suffering that choice might entail.

Yosef Yitzḥak Schneersohn, Proclamation on Repentance (1941)

It must be explained to the Jewish masses that without penitent return one cannot expect the redemption! . . . The angel of destruction has come to obliterate everything that is bad and traitorous in the world. . . . We must now have an awakening in the name of purity of heart, purity of thought, purity of the house, purity of the yeshivah, and purity of family in the sense of bringing back the children who have been born to the Torah and to faith! Now we must tell the young generation about the new festival for the Lord and "we will go with our young and with our old" [Exod. 10:9]. And every Jewish house that does not want to be visited by the angel of destruction, heaven forbid, must be purified of all forty-nine gates of impurity and filled with authentic holiness! . . . Without the readiness of the majority of the whole Jewish people to become the only holy people, to go out to greet the Messiah, we will, heaven forbid, not be any better in the eyes of the angel of destruction than any other nation. . . .

The first ones who must respond are the believers and also those children of believers who still remember what Judaism meant for their parents. You and we are responsible for all the other Jews, and you and we must be the first to awaken ourselves and to awaken others! . . . Let us carry on tremendous self-sacrifice to show that we will truly rectify our betrayal until now of Torah and faith. . . . We call on all Jews to join the camp of Israel (*Maḥaneh Yisrael*), which is, with God's help, being organized for this task! . . . The community of Israel will be blessed with the complete redemption very speedily in our day. With this outcry we intend only to warn every Jewish individual that he should not, heaven forbid, be an exception![30]

9.6. JEWISH SOLIDARITY, HUMAN SOLIDARITY, AND POLITICAL ACTION

Hannah Arendt (sections 7.3, 8.4) offered the sort of approach to solidarity and responsibility in the face of the Holocaust that particularly alarmed Yosef Yitzḥak Schneersohn. Whereas Schneersohn emphasized responsibility to awaken Jews to Torah and faith, Arendt had little interest in "Torah" and instead sought to awaken Jews to political action. Whereas Schneersohn condemned those who focused on worldly political strategies, Arendt urged her fellow Jews to see "their responsibility to take their political fate into their own hands." Whereas Schneersohn was a fierce anti-Zionist, Arendt was a Zionist, and whereas Schneersohn was appalled by the idea of a "Jewish army," Arendt was a passionate advocate for establishing a Jewish army that, under Allied command but independent of any nation, would battle the Nazis. Whereas Schneersohn demanded that Jews separate themselves from non-Jews, Arendt promoted human solidarity across national, ethnic, and religious lines. Whereas Schneersohn emphasized that Jews were a Chosen People with unique divine souls, and condemned those who taught that Jews were like all other peoples, Arendt wrote that "Jews are a people like every other people."[31]

Arendt opposed all doctrines of Jewish uniqueness. She was a particularly harsh critic of David Ben-Gurion (section 9.7), who encouraged secular ideas of Jewish uniqueness and the falsehood that "all Gentiles were alike" in their hatred of Jews. Arendt, by contrast, sought to promote a Zionism that saw "the Jews as a people among peoples, a nation among nations, a state among states."[32]

Additionally, whereas Ben-Gurion saw unity and solidarity among Jews as foundational to what would become the State of Israel, Arendt objected to nation-states that cultivated national or ethnic solidarity and failed to emphasize plurality. In section 8.4.II, Arendt raised the concern that notions of mutual love among Jews could shut down criticism; she affirmed only the sort of patriotism that would allow for "permanent opposition and criticism."[33] Elsewhere, she warned against Jews who viewed political unanimity as an ideal, as "to hold different opinions and to be aware that other people think differently on the same issue shields us from that Godlike certainty which stops all discussion and reduces social relationships to those of an ant heap" — and which "tends to eliminate bodily those who differ."[34]

Arendt's notions of solidarity were also bound up with her ideas of reason and human dignity. Criticizing the role of compassion in politics (section 8.4.I), she recommended that political action, guided by the impartial and reasoned principle of solidarity, focus on human dignity and "establish deliberately and, as it were, dispassionately a community of interest with the oppressed and the exploited."[35] She warned that people should not be carried away by their emotions, and she particularly cautioned against "pity," a sentiment of sorrow in the face of mass suffering that condescended rather than respected those who suffered, and thereby failed to encourage responsible action to alleviate that suffering. Perversely, in fact, pity could perpetuate and sometimes glorify suffering: "Without the presence of misfortune, pity could not exist, and it therefore has just as much vested interest in the existence of the unhappy as thirst for power has a vested interest in the existence of the weak."[36]

In part I of the selections below, Arendt further shows how condescending attitudes are incompatible with responsible action. Surveying

Jewish history, she concludes that the principle of *kol Yisra'el arevim zeh la-zeh* — "all Israel takes care of Israel," in the translation below — often failed to encourage responsibility. In modern European Jewish communities, responsibility for other, less fortunate Jews was claimed as the virtue of the parvenu (the newly rich social climber, accepted by non-Jewish society), and particularly as the virtue of wealthy and powerful Western European Jews. Yet their claims of responsibility were proven tragically false.

Writing in 1942, amid the devastation of the Holocaust, Arendt is clear that Jews must adopt a new model of responsibility. Responsibility must not only be a virtue for shepherds seeking to protect their sheep; rather, it should be a widespread virtue that leads to political action. Jewish solidarity requires respecting diverse Jewish interests and joining together to defend them politically — but without demanding that all Jews be united by a common leader, a common ideology, or (certainly) any common faith. As Arendt concludes, the Nazi violence being unleashed against Jews will not automatically lead to a new conception of solidarity, but it does provide the opportunity for developing one.

In another article she wrote in 1942, excerpted in part II, Arendt condemns opponents of a Jewish army under Allied ("United Nations") command and demands solidarity that respects Jews' capacity for political action. Arendt opposed "suicidal" politics of any sorts — elsewhere in her writings she opposed Jews who rejected alliances with other nations but were committed to "fighting at any price" on their own[37] — yet she was also opposed to the idea that Jews should *not* join other nations in taking up arms against the Nazis. She argued that a Jewish army would help ensure Jewish survival as well as Jewish dignity — "Jews could be combatants on equal terms instead of being mere victims," as scholar Margaret Canovan has written[38] — and she asked other nations to stand in solidarity, "shoulder to shoulder with Jews," in fighting the Nazi regime.

In part III, Arendt writes in defense of the Christian theologian Paul Tillich, who had cautioned American Jews against adopting an anti-German racism that would parallel German antisemitism. While some Jews saw Tillich as failing to show solidarity with them, Arendt insisted on the priority of human solidarity that requires opposition to racism of any kind. As she put it in another 1942 article (not included below), all peoples must be "united in solidarity against those who claim racial superiority and the right to dominate."[39] True friendship with oppressed Jews required respecting their perspectives, but not necessarily supporting all their stances. For example, one need not support Jewish perspectives shaped by a "slave mentality," as when experiences of slavery and oppression had led Jews to dream of enslaving and asserting their superiority over others.

Hannah Arendt, *The Jewish Writings* (1942)

I. The world in which we live is full of sorcery, magic, and ordinary hocus-pocus. Rising like irregular boulders out of the chaos of ancient and hyper-modern superstitions—brewed by despair and spread like advertising around the world by machine guns—are yesterday's truths, almost sunk in the mire. And a few of those truths have also been included in sorcery's great book of despair disguised as science. Except that they have been able to convince the masses in direct proportion to their loss of political effectiveness.

Among the distorted truths with a real capacity for duping even reasonable people is the old adage, *All Israel takes care of Israel*. For who in this most devastated of worlds does not wish to hear the call of solidarity with an open heart, and who does not wish to belong to some sort of mutual insurance society? In the period before emancipation, when there was still an autonomous Jewish congregation, the whole congregation took care of paying to the state or the prince the taxes and debts of each of its individual members. The ghetto was one great mutual insurance company.

Over the course of the seventeenth and eighteenth centuries, court Jews assumed this task, inasmuch as their power in the congregation was based on wealth and relationships with princes, and their position at court was based on their belonging to world Jewry and to international connections arising from that fact. Out of the democratic organization of a pariah people there grew the plutocratic regime of a doubly powerful class of parvenus. They assumed responsibility for those to whom, and to no one else, they owed their wealth, power, and what, for the time, were unlimited opportunities. And the people willingly let themselves be ruled by them, for the people owed them their security, their chances of rising in society, and a new self-awareness. For if antisemites still smell a Rothschild in every door-to-door salesman, one ought not forget that for more than a hundred years every door-to-door salesman thought of himself as a future Rothschild. *All Israel took care of Israel.*

At the height of their power — in the wake of the failed revolution of 1848 and under the rule of Napoleon III — after the founding of the Alliance Israélite Universelle,[40] Western Europe's Jewry dared to claim this adage as its own motto. They lived in the proud illusion of a people who were united and governed by it and to whom it would guarantee, on the basis of international monetary transactions between nations, security and upward mobility. They believed themselves powerful enough for all Jews, because they were rich enough to assume the responsibility of taking financial care of all Jews. It was a splendid time, when businessmen still dreamed of national unity and monetary transactions still provided them with a sense of political power.

Reality, however, very quickly began to look a bit more shabby. All Israel took care of each other's tickets to the borders of their own land and guaranteed governments that uninvited guests, whose money no longer protected them in their own country, would vanish without further ado or expense; and if this did not happen voluntarily out of concern for their own security, those same governments adopted very unpleasant practices to remind Israel of its chosen motto and to interpret it in new ways. Until finally the Nazis used barbed wire to turn their version of Jewish solidarity into reality — into ghettos that made no distinction between rich and poor, between Western and Eastern European Jews.

Let us not be taken in by magic charms. The All Israel Insurance Company has gone bankrupt. Jewish solidarity would be a fine thing if it were backed up by the people's awareness that it is their responsibility to take their political fate into their own hands. You can use the catchword of solidarity to induce a people to complain of its rags or to establish a "blood brotherhood."

Solidarity does not arise simply out of a common enemy, because there is no such thing as a solidarity of fear; one cannot depend, you see, on frightened people. The Jewish solidarity of our fathers had much in common with the peaceful and profitable practice of keeping sheep in a herd; the wolf likes to scatter the herd, not keep it together. A common enemy can only *awaken* solidarity—and in the exact same measure as it awakens the desire to join together in defense, instead of running and scattering.[41]

II. Just as a man who is threatened with murder should not trust a friend who suggests suicide as a way out of his predicament, Jews should not trust friends who try to convince them that collective suicide is the best way to ensure their collective security. What we demand of the United Nations [Allies] is nothing more than that it show the same solidarity with us that many European peoples under the pressure of the Nazis' terror machine have already shown us. We do not want promises that our sufferings will be "avenged," we want to fight; we do not want mercy, but justice. . . . Mercy without justice is one of the devil's most powerful accomplices—it claims outrage and sanctions the structures that the devil has created. Freedom, however, is not a reward for sufferings endured and one does not accept justice as if it were crumbs from the table of the rich. . . . The real criterion for the justice of this war will be seen in the degree to which other nations are prepared to fight their, our, and humanity's battle shoulder to shoulder with Jews.[42]

III. It is very difficult to be a friend of an oppressed people. It is doubly difficult when one has never been one of the oppressed. It is very sad to learn that every slave has a tendency to dream of owning slaves and that the oppressed masses—however passionately their sufferings plead the cause of freedom—learn the language of freedom only slowly and with difficulty. . . .

Friends of the oppressed will always end up in conflict with the oppressed themselves. Every great friend of the Jews has had trouble with the Jews—and it is in these very conflicts that the Jewish people have been able to tell their genuine friends from false patrons. . . . We Jewish patriots, who have been forced for so long to do battle against both slave owners and a slave mentality, will greet that person as our friend and ally who directly or indirectly helps us to eradicate the madness of racial superiority and to restore the humanity, the solidarity of the human race.[43]

9.7. STATE-FOCUSED RESPONSIBILITY AND UNITY

David Ben-Gurion (1886–1973), the first prime minister of the State of Israel, widely viewed as the leading founding father of the country, was clearly opposed to all of the aforementioned approaches to solidarity and responsibility. Leading the Zionist effort to unite the Jewish people in a new state, an effort he viewed as the greatest and most significant project in Jewish history, Ben-Gurion opposed not only the traditionalist, exilic, non-Zionist Judaism promoted by figures like Yisroel Friedman, Natan Tzevi Finkel, and Yosef Yitzhak Schneersohn; he fiercely opposed efforts by figures like Murād Farag to integrate Jews into other states, efforts by figures like Hannah Arendt to form a binational Arab-Jewish federated state and welcome dissenters' perspectives, and certainly efforts by figures like Emma Goldman to reject state power altogether.[44] Ben-Gurion fought for a secular state with a clear Jewish majority that reflected the unique vision of the Jewish people and had very limited trust in other nations. He emphasized Jewish unity and the need to bow to the authority of the new Jewish state.

In seeking to found an independent Jewish state, Ben-Gurion resolved not to repeat the errors that had led to the downfall of past Jewish regimes. In particular, he was determined not to let Jews within the state become overly divided. In his view, Jewish independence during the First Temple period had lasted for only a short while because "we were always divided and quarreled among ourselves." So too, the downfall of the Second Jewish Commonwealth was in part because "the Jews did not know how to unite." Throughout many difficult crises in Jewish history and into the present day, Ben-Gurion lamented, Jews had displayed a "lack of talent to act as one entity in which a single member bends his will to that of the majority."[45]

Now, however—under his leadership—the Jewish people could develop a new and unifying moral consciousness, characterized by patriotic "statism," dedication to state sovereignty, and a sense of unity and civic responsibility. To describe this consciousness, Ben-Gurion invented the Hebrew adjective *mamlakhti* ("state" or "state-focused") and the noun *mamlakhtiut*, which generally conveyed the civic virtue of being state-focused.[46] In Ben-Gurion's view, citizens needed an internal moral orientation toward the state; the state needed to be "internalized inside people's hearts, souls, and consciousness."[47]

In the selection below, Ben-Gurion also describes the virtue of civic responsibility by speaking of *aharayut mamlakhtit*, "state-focused responsibility." He insists that this virtue will be very different from the sense of responsibility instilled by Jewish leaders in previous centuries. Yes, they had taught that "all of Israel are responsible for each other," and they had urged Jews to pray and to engage in acts of lovingkindness on behalf of their brethren—but, exiled in foreign lands and lacking independent political power, they were unable to fathom the levels of responsibility it would take to build a just political community. Even when they thought messianic redemption was imminent, as Yosef Yitzḥak Schneersohn did (section 9.5), they demanded that all Jews take responsibility for ensuring the redemption by engaging in ritual commandments, thereby "depending on miracles and supernatural forces from beyond."

Like Schneersohn (and unlike many other Zionists, such as Arendt), Ben-Gurion used messianic language and often described redemption as imminent, but he insisted that "redemption must come from within ourselves."[48] Redemption would be realized only to the degree that Jews fulfilled their *mamlakhti* political responsibilities: engaging in state-building, cultivating a commitment to the state, unifying the Jewish people under state authority, and developing an army that would defend the state.

For Ben-Gurion, the task of cultivating appropriate virtues for the new Jewish state required the establishment of a new, unified *mamlakhti* educational system (replacing systems developed by political parties, which he saw as too divisive). It also necessitated the establishment of a new armed forces (that would replace various prestate militias): the Israel Defense Forces (IDF), "an educational force for national unification" and "the crucible of national unity." The IDF would not only defend the country but serve to bridge the many political and ethnic divides within the new state, training citizens to feel a sense of brotherhood, mutual responsibility, solidarity with other Jews, and commitment to the Jewish state.[49]

The selections below come from a November 1951 speech to Israel's Journalists' Association—an audience not always entirely sympathetic to Ben-Gurion's vision. Ben-Gurion evinces concern that the Jews gathered together in the new state, shaped by the conditions of exile, might not yet have the capacity for a *mamlakhti* sense of solidarity and responsibility. Still, he expects that the "exceptional" people will learn, in time: "It is not possible that the suffering that has come upon us has been in vain."

Like other thinkers in this chapter, Ben-Gurion mentions both Korach and Moses. Korach serves as a symbol of inappropriate dissent (as he did for Yisroel Friedman). Moses is the redemptive leader whose mantle of leadership has now been inherited by the IDF (who, like Moses, stood victorious by the shores of the sea in the final battle of the 1947–49 War of Independence). The Jewish people, Ben-Gurion hopes, will be guided by their newly responsible leadership to overcome inappropriate dissent and discover a new sense of state-focused responsibility and brotherhood.

David Ben-Gurion, Speech to the Journalists' Association (1951)

It is not even clear if the Jewish people has the capacity for the state-focused [*mamlakhtit*] responsibility that the state has imposed upon it. This is perhaps a bitter paradox, but it is true: for generations, there is nothing that the Jewish people yearned for as much as a Jewish state—and there is nothing that the Jewish people is as unprepared for as a Jewish state. The state needs to struggle not only with objective difficulties and external enemies but also—and perhaps especially at this time—with internal difficulties and stumbling blocks, and it is not possible to tell which is greater. A people that has lived for hundreds and thousands of years in foreign countries, in wandering, in dependence on the kindness of strangers, that has not had to take responsibility for itself and its destiny, and that has depended on miracles and supernatural forces from beyond—this people cannot transform overnight into a state-focused [*mamlakhti*] people that knows how to bear the burden of responsibility that independence imposes upon any people, for independence increases and exacerbates responsibility rather than reducing and alleviating it. "All of Israel are responsible for each other"—this principle was also operative in our lives during the period of exile, and it endures for us. But the mutual responsibility of those scattered in exile, built on acts of lovingkindness for their oppressed brothers, is insufficient for a free nation that requires collective power, shared political responsibility, and a unifying historical will. . . .

I have no delusions regarding the Jewish people. I understand, as it seems to me, its flaws and shortcomings and weaknesses—not only those that are shared with other nations but also those unique to it. I do not read only the newspapers of our day; I have also read the newspapers that appeared in the days of Korach. . . . With regard to enmity and opposition and hatred and envy, we have not brought about much that is new in our era; and the exiles who have been gathered in our state are not helping to increase Jewish brotherhood and solidarity at this time. Nevertheless!—we need to believe in this exceptional people! Is there another nation that is capable of such a long journey on the stage of history, from the Red Sea in the era of our teacher Moses to the Red Sea in the era of the Israel Defense Forces? We have learned much on this long journey, and it is not possible that the suffering that has come upon us has been in vain.[50]

9.8. IN A FREE SOCIETY, ALL ARE RESPONSIBLE

In January 1967, Rabbi Abraham Joshua Heschel (introduced in section 2.6) delivered a prayer for peace during a mobilization of Clergy and

Laymen Concerned about Vietnam, an interfaith organization he had cofounded in 1965.[51] That prayer and Heschel's further discussion of the Vietnam War would be printed two years later in *Vietnam: Crisis of Conscience*, which Heschel coedited along with Catholic scholar Michael Novak and Protestant scholar Robert McAfee Brown to persuade American Christians and Jews to pressure the U.S. government to end the war. "Responsibility is the essence of being a person, the essence of being human," Heschel insisted, "and many of us are agonized by a grave crisis of responsibility" marked by the inability to stop the killing of innocent people in war. He beseeched Americans to take responsibility to help end the war, understanding that "Vietnam is a personal problem. To speak about God and remain silent on Vietnam is blasphemous."[52] In the selection below, Heschel makes the point that all Americans are responsible for the atrocities committed by their government. Americans must stand in solidarity alongside the people of Vietnam, and indeed stand in solidarity with all human beings in opposition to the arrogance and cruelty of war.

Significantly influenced by the Chortkover and Ruzhin Hasidic dynasties within which his father grew up,[53] Heschel joined his uncle, Yisroel Friedman (section 9.3), in teaching about divine-human unity and the interconnection of human souls, but he rejected key aspects of Freidman's perspective. Whereas Friedman taught of the unity of the divine souls of faithful Jews "carved from the mountains of holiness," Heschel taught that all souls—across oceans, and across religious boundaries—are united by God's concern and presence. "There is no other way to feel one with every man . . . except in feeling one with him in a higher unity: in the one concern of God for all men," he wrote.[54] Moreover, he saw all human beings united by "the presence of God" and "the presence of a soul," such that every encounter with another human being must begin with sensing "the kinship of being human, solidarity of being."[55] God is in unity with all people, such that God suffers whenever human beings suffer and all human beings are afflicted whenever other human beings are afflicted. In God's presence, the boundaries between different selves dissolve such that the suffering inflicted on anyone should be felt by everyone. God shares in this suffering, but God depends on human beings to alleviate it. In other words, for Heschel, human beings are ontologically alike—all human beings possess souls carved from the mountains of holiness—and nobody is cut off from the worldwide community of solidarity and responsibility.

Interestingly, Heschel, who would have agreed with Emma Goldman (section 9.2) about extremely little (especially given her opposition to God and religion), here shares her concern about militarism in general and American militarism in particular. Goldman feared that citizens indoctrinated with "the patriotic lie" would support their country in war or become soldiers themselves, and Heschel was similarly alarmed by how "the lords of the flocks issue proclamations, and the sheep of all nations indulge in devastations." As Goldman hoped that her readers would awaken to the "real horrors" of war, Heschel hoped that his readers would awaken to the "ongoing nightmare." And as Goldman hoped for an international feeling of solidarity whereby workers would refuse the militaristic visions of their masters, Heschel similarly hoped that people worldwide would stand in solidarity, united by "the refusal of the conscience to accommodate to the arrogance of military power."

Abraham Joshua Heschel, "The Moral Outrage of Vietnam" (1967)

Since the beginning of history evil has been going forth from nation to nation. The lords of the flocks issue proclamations, and the sheep of all nations indulge in devastations. . . .

At this hour Vietnam is our most urgent, our most disturbing religious problem, a challenge to . . . every one of us [as] an individual. . . .

Most of us prefer to disregard the dreadful deeds we do over there. The atrocities committed in our name are too horrible to be credible. It is beyond our power to react vividly to the ongoing nightmare, day after day, night after night. So we bear graciously other people's suffering.

O Lord, we confess our sins, we are ashamed of the inadequacy of our anguish, of how faint and slight is our mercy. We are a generation that has lost the capacity for outrage.

We must continue to remind ourselves that in a free society, all are involved in what some are doing. *Some are guilty, all are responsible....*

At this moment praying for peace in Vietnam we are spiritually Vietnamese. Their agony is our affliction, their hope is our commitment....

The encounter of man and God is an encounter within the world. We meet within a situation of shared suffering, of shared responsibility.

This is implied in believing in One God in whose eyes there is no dichotomy of here and there, of me and them. They and I are one; here is there, and there is here. What goes on over there happens even here. Oceans divide us, God's presence unites us, and God is present wherever man is afflicted, and all of humanity is embroiled in every agony wherever it may be.

Though not a native of Vietnam, ignorant of its language and traditions, I am involved in the plight of the Vietnamese. To be human means not to be immune to other people's suffering....

What is it that may save us, that may unite men all over the world? The abhorrence of atrocity, the refusal of the conscience to accommodate to the arrogance of military power.[56]

9.9. INFINITE RESPONSIBILITY FOR THE OTHER

The virtue of recognizing infinite responsibility for the other and giving priority to the other rather than to oneself, as noted in section 8.5, stood at the heart of Emmanuel Levinas's ethics. A sense of responsibility for the other is "what is essential in the Jewish conscience," Levinas wrote, and so too "this is what is essential in the human conscience: all men are responsible for one another, and 'I more than anyone else.'"[57]

Levinas joins Heschel in teaching that all human beings are responsible for the lives of all other human beings, but whereas for Heschel, "moral sentiments originate in man's sense of unity, in his appreciation of what is common to men,"[58] for Levinas morality stems from the recognition that the other is not the same as I am but is precisely "other." Heschel finds human unity through the "higher unity" of "the one concern of God for all men,"[59] whereas Levinas rejects the notion of a personal God who feels concern and instead detects the trace of God on the face of the other who is distinctly different.[60] And Levinas, far more than Heschel, stresses the need for self-sacrifice unto death for the sake of fulfilling the infinite obligations each of us owe to the other. "I am responsible for the Other without waiting for reciprocity, were I to die for it," as Levinas put it in one interview. "I am responsible for a total responsibility, which answers for all the others and for all in the others, even for their responsibility. The I always has one responsibility *more* than all the others."[61]

In the text below, Levinas interprets the debate in the Babylonian Talmud (*Sotah* 37b) about the extent of responsibility borne by each of the Israelite men who followed Moses in the wilderness. In the Talmud, Rabbi Mesharsheya explains that while Rabbi Simeon ben Judah believes that every Israelite is responsible for every other Israelite's fulfillment of the commandments, Rabbi Judah the Patriarch believes that every Israelite is also responsible for ensuring that every other Israelite takes on the responsibility of which Rabbi Simeon speaks. Every Israelite is not only responsible for every Israelite, but responsible for the responsibility of every Israelite. According to Rabbi Judah the Patriarch, any Israelite is liable for failing to take responsibility, to the degree that one is able, to ensure that every other Israelite takes responsibility for every other Israelite.

Traditionalists such as Friedman, Finkel, and Schneersohn (sections 9.3, 9.4, and 9.5, respectively) would understand this passage as addressing not only interpersonal ethical responsibilities (in Hebrew, *bein adam la-ḥaveiro*) but also ritual responsibilities that concern the private relationship between the individual and God (*bein adam la-makom*). Schneersohn's message in section 9.5 most explicitly shows an embrace of the level of responsibility demanded by Rabbi Judah with regard to ritual (with Schneersohn's sense of responsibility to ensure that his fellow Jews assume the responsibility to awaken their fellow Jews to their ritual responsibilities). Levinas's focus, by contrast, is on interpersonal responsibilities.

Furthermore, Levinas is not exclusively concerned with obligations of and for Jews but with the obligations of and for human beings in general. He interprets Rabbinic language regarding the Israelites' responsibility for other Israelites to refer to human beings in general. "Israelites" are not members of a particular religious/ethnic/national group but are, rather, any and all human beings who take on responsibility for other human beings. To the degree that human beings accept the divine law requiring them to stand in solidarity with other human beings, they are worthy of being called "Israel" because they are worthy of being called "human." The phrase "all of Israel are responsible for each other" should, then, be translated as "all human beings are responsible for each other."

Levinas, moreover, goes further than Rabbi Judah the Patriarch's injunction that one is responsible for ensuring that others are responsible: Levinas describes that responsibility as *infinite*. Among his core convictions is that the individual is responsible "more than anyone else." Responsibility is always asymmetrical: I am always called to take on a higher level of responsibility than my fellow. If others are responsible for my responsibility, then I must be responsible for their responsibility for my responsibility. In turn, they must be responsible for my responsibility for their responsibility for my responsibility, and these levels of responsibility expand infinitely, for all human beings. To Levinas this aspirational ideal defines our humanity, however impossible to fulfill it may be.

Emmanuel Levinas, "The Pact" (1982)

[According to Rabbi Simeon ben Judah in the name of Rabbi Simeon,] within this Covenant each person finds himself responsible for everyone else. . . . The Israelites, more correctly described as men participating in a common humanity, answer for each other before a genuinely human law. . . .

[But according to Rabbi Judah the Patriarch] one is not only responsible for everyone else, but responsible also for the responsibility of everyone else. . . .

A moment ago, we saw ... something resembling the recognition of the Other, the love of the Other. To such an extent that I offer myself as guarantee of the Other, of his adherence and fidelity to the Law. His concern is my concern. But is not my concern also his? Isn't he responsible for me? And if he is, can I also answer for his responsibility for me? *Kol Yisrael 'arevim zeh lazeh*, "All Israel is responsible one for the other," which means: all those who cleave to the divine law, all men worthy of the name, are all responsible for each other.

This must also mean that my responsibility includes the responsibility taken up by other men. I always have, myself, one responsibility more than anyone else, since I am responsible, in addition, for his responsibility. And if he is responsible for my responsibility, I remain responsible for the responsibility he has for my responsibility. *Ein ladavar sof*, "it will never end." In the society of the Torah, this process is repeated to infinity; beyond any responsibility attributed to everyone and for everyone, there is always the additional fact that I am still responsible for that responsibility. It is an ideal, but one which is inseparable from the humanity of human beings. In the Covenant, when it is fully understood, in the society which fully deploys all the dimensions of the Law, society becomes a community.[62]

9.10. SIGNIFICANT SACRIFICES IN SOLIDARITY WITH STRANGERS

David Jaffe (b. 1965) is an American Open Orthodox rabbi who, like Shmuly Yanklowitz (sections 1.7, 8.9), identifies with Orthodox models of observance while often challenging conventional Orthodox ideas and practices. Jaffe describes himself as deeply shaped by Orthodox movements such as Hasidism (particularly the ideals of passion and yearning for God in the teachings of Naḥman of Breslov) and the Musar movement (particularly its model of "step-by-step guidance for ethical and moral development").[63] Jaffe has also been deeply shaped by politically progressive visions for social change developed by non-Jews such as Rev. Martin Luther King Jr. and by non-Orthodox Jews including Abraham Joshua

Heschel. Indeed, in one message calling Jews to take responsibility for addressing global issues (e.g., "climate change, income inequality and violent, identity-based conflict"), he has invoked Heschel's teaching that "some are guilty, while all are responsible." And he has argued that musar and Hasidism, along with other forms of Jewish wisdom, "offer the guidance and practices for taking this responsibility in a way that . . . honors the dignity and sovereignty of all people."[64]

In the text below, Jaffe draws inspiration from a contemporary non-Orthodox Jewish leader, Stosh Cotler, responding directly to Cotler's article on courage in this volume (section 4.11). Writing on the occasion of Martin Luther King Jr.'s birthday, and focusing on how to best protect undocumented immigrants in the United States who are subject to deportation, Jaffe looks to aspects of King's model of a nonviolent disobedience campaign as well as two Orthodox Jewish sources: the methods for personal and communal transformation developed by Musar movement founder Israel Salanter and the teaching on self-sacrifice by Musar movement leader Natan Tzevi Finkel seen above (section 9.4).

In his introduction to the selection below, Jaffe quotes Stosh Cotler's description of activists placing their heads under the front and back wheels of a bus being used to deport immigrants. Jaffe admits that he "would not be willing to risk my life like this." His initial reaction is that "risking one's life in this way is not Jewish," given the traditional Jewish focus on "choosing life," "guarding your well-being," and "not relying on miracles." But Jaffe goes on to acknowledge that Jewish sources, including Finkel's discussion of Moses, do support sacrificing one's life in solidarity with one's people.

In the version of this text first published in 2018, Jaffe showed some openness to viewing self-sacrifice as an ideal. In a newly revised version of the text below, however, he concludes that one should not sacrifice one's life out of solidarity with others. Rather, he calls for other "significant sacrifices for solidarity beyond what most Jews are doing to this point"—specifically, sacrifices of financial resources, privilege, and time—in order to uphold the Torah's commandment to love the stranger. Whereas Finkel speaks of harsh judgments against those who fail to fully put their lives on the line, Jaffe is open to many ways that Jews can sacrifice resources in solidarity with others.

Jaffe's vision of solidarity also differs from Finkel's in a number of other ways. While Finkel avoided active involvement in political affairs, Jaffe is a social and political activist. Whereas Finkel showed his admiration for prayer directed at God, Jaffe shows his admiration for action directed at oppressive government authorities. (His emphasis on direct action draws on models developed by activists including Emma Goldman, though unlike Goldman, who supported violent direct action when necessary, Jaffe is dedicated to nonviolent direct action.)

Moreover, Jaffe's commitment to developing relationships with non-Jewish "strangers" goes far beyond what Finkel encouraged. While Finkel did envision solidarity stretching beyond the Jewish community—he admired Abraham's risking his life for innocent residents of Sodom—Jaffe stresses the importance of forming real relationships with people who are oppressed. Solidarity requires seeking out those in need, hearing their stories, getting to know them, and supporting them in a wide variety of ways.

For Jaffe, cultivating relationships along these lines is essential for establishing a relationship based on solidarity rather than pity. Like Hannah Arendt, Jaffe is concerned about privileged people who relate to the oppressed with condescending pity rather than deep respect. His ideal activists are "constantly revisiting their own privilege and real relationship with the oppressed group." He similarly guides his readers to engage in the sort of deep introspection about privilege that goes beyond what Salanter or Finkel ever counseled. Finkel, for example, did not expect Abraham or Moses to question their own privilege and ways in which they might be condescending toward the Sodomites or Israelites.

But Finkel's depictions of Abraham and Moses remain sources of inspiration for Jaffe. These characters, as imagined by the Musar movement, show the importance of making tremendous sacrifices for the sake of others. Thus, Jaffe says, the Musar tradition can teach us how to build the deep commitment necessary to fulfill the requirement to stand in solidarity with all who are oppressed.

David Jaffe, "Is Putting One's Life on the Line to Stand Up to Oppression a Jewish Value?" (2022)

In the center of our master narrative we have the example of Moses, willing to give his life in solidarity with his people. Rabbi Natan Tzevi Finkel, the founder of the Slobodka school of Musar (d. 1927) and trainer of several generations of Jewish leaders, writes that neither Noah nor Abraham were on the spiritual level of Moses. Why not? When confronted with the destruction of the world, Noah never argued for, or prayed for, the world to be saved. He went about his business building an ark, as God instructed him, but he didn't challenge God. Abraham challenged God for not acting justly and potentially killing the righteous with the wicked in Sodom. Abraham fought for, and prayed for justice—this was better than what Noah did. But only Moses actually put his own life on the line for the people. When God said (after the golden calf) that God was going to destroy the people and start again with Moses, Moses responded, "if you are not going to forgive them, then take my life also." This powerful act of solidarity with his community convinced God to back down and forgive the people. Rabbi Finkel challenges us to live at that level of empathy and self-sacrifice.

Furthermore, putting one's life at risk to act righteously in the face of oppression also has its place in Jewish legal tradition. *Kiddush ha-Shem*, "Sanctifying the Divine Name," is the public display of righteous behavior by Jews, including offering one's life to do the right thing. This concept is well-established in Jewish legal codes. Among others, Maimonides codifies that one is to die rather than violate certain Torah prohibitions such as murder, idol worship, and incest. In a time of oppression, when the oppressor demands violation of the commandments, martyrdom extends to even minor mitzvot. The medieval Crusade Chronicles document multiple incidents of entire Jewish communities sacrificing their lives rather than undergo forced conversion to Christianity.

Willingness to make the ultimate sacrifice is, indeed, a Jewish sensibility. However, it is a sensibility that is carefully limited. The weight of our 2000-year-old rabbinic tradition leans against this type of dramatic martyrdom and exhorts us to "Live by the commandments and not die by them." Thus, the challenge Cotler poses to our community raises the additional question of whether it is appropriate and ethical to expand the concept of putting one's life in danger beyond several core commandments and beyond deep solidarity with our own Jewish community. This is a serious question that deserves careful consideration.

In a time of oppression, when Jews are being forced to violate Jewish law, it is a mitzvah to sacrifice oneself rather than violate the law. In a very graphic way this communicates to all that there are values greater than life itself. Perhaps we can expand this idea to the contemporary situation and say that in times of social oppression, when core Jewish principles like "Love the stranger" are being violated by cruel public policies toward undocumented immigrants, it is our responsibility as a community that believes deeply in these principles, and stands in solidarity with these vulnerable people, to be willing to make significant self-sacrifice to oppose these hurtful policies.

However, I do not think we can expand the obligation of Kiddush Hashem to permit sacrificing our lives themselves, for at least two reasons. The first is that seventy-five years after the Shoah and loss of one-third of the world's Jewish population to genocide, the balance of *halakhah* must be towards preserving life. Second, there is something so shocking and extreme about giving one's life that it can make the many, many other necessary forms of self-sacrifice seem unimportant. The Shema calls on us to "Love the Lord your God with all your heart, all your soul and all your resources." My response to Cotler is that social oppression that violates Jewish law calls on us to have radical empathy (all your heart) and risk sacrificing our financial resources and privilege (all your resources), but to stop short of sacrificing our actual lives. This formulation still calls on us to make significant sacrifices for solidarity beyond what most Jews are doing at this point.

To be willing to make these sacrifices takes a tremendous sense of fidelity to the commandments and solidarity with the people suffering. Preparation for giving up privilege, social standing, time and financial well-being will require building a deep commitment to the commandment to love the stranger impacted by unjust laws. It is in building this inner commitment that the Musar tradition has much to offer by way of practical wisdom. Rabbi Israel Salanter, the founder of the 19th century Musar movement, developed a method of personal and communal transformation based on deeply internalizing ethical precepts through study, reflection, emotional catharsis and action. We can apply this method to our preparation for putting ourselves on the line to fight injustice.

The first stage is intellectual and, in the case of fighting the oppression of undocumented immigrants, would involve deep study of the Torah concept of loving the stranger. This could be done through traditional study of Biblical and Rabbinic sources as well as learning as much as possible about the actual current immigration system, its policies and its effect on actual people. In some ways this is similar to the research stage of a Non-Violent Disobedience campaign. (According to Dr. Martin Luther King, Jr., "In any nonviolent campaign there are four basic steps: collection of the facts to determine whether injustices exist; negotiation; self-purification; and direct action.")

The second stage is affective and would involve deeply integrating the teachings above. This involves relating the teachings to one's own family and collective experience as strangers. This could be accomplished through talking with relatives and studying the actual history of the Jewish immigrant experience. It also includes doing the emotional work involved in feeling one's own vulnerability as a "stranger" and where one was mistreated personally and mistreats others. This work can be done in carefully constructed, supportive group environments that encourage deep introspection and emotional catharsis.

The affective stage also involves developing real solidarity with people suffering now. This can be done through a combination of learning about real stories of contemporary undocumented immigrants and forming real relationships. This stage includes engaging in increasingly

challenging levels of action to stand up against the oppressive policies. Activists can start with driving an undocumented person to an
appointment, then accompanying them to a meeting, making a visit
to a detention center, then engaging in a street protest, then risking
arrest in a non-violent direct action that interrupts the deportation
machine. These engagements need to be framed within a group process
in which the activist is constantly revisiting their own privilege and
real relationship with the oppressed group to develop solidarity, rather
than pity and sympathy. No one should be accepted for an action that
risks significant sacrifice without already participating in many other,
less intense, forms of support and solidarity. Organizers will need to
be thoughtful about the risk levels different people are taking based
on their race, age, and other demographic factors.

This process of cognitive and affective preparation for significant
acts of solidarity can help develop a cadre of Jews ready to act boldly
for our values. Ethical concerns about encouraging people to risk their
resources and financial and physical security need to be seriously
debated. If we determine that this moment indeed calls on us to take
such a bold stand, we have the spiritual technologies from our rich
Jewish tradition to prepare well for the call.[65]

9.11. RESISTING THE PATH OF PHARAOH

Biblical scholar Amanda Beckenstein Mbuvi (b. 1976), vice president for
academic affairs at the Reconstructionist Rabbinical College, is an expert
on questions of identity and community, especially with reference to the
books of Genesis and Exodus. She describes her interest in identity and
community as shaped by her own experiences as an interracial African-
American Jew who has struggled with "racial impostor syndrome—a
set of insecurities that arise among those whose bodies, families, or
predilections don't correspond to their normative sense of what it means
to be a member of a group to which they putatively belong."[66]

In her 2016 book *Belonging in Genesis: Biblical Israel and the Politics of
Identity Formation* and elsewhere, Mbuvi considers the ways in which

Genesis subverts conventional notions of stable national, racial, or religious identities and communities. Israelite identity is determined by relationship to God, she explains, and all of humanity and all of creation are connected both within family trees (described by the genealogies of Genesis, beginning with Gen. 2:4) and in relationships of "blessed interdependence." Genesis, Mbuvi put it in one essay, "situates human diversity within a family tree that links not only all humanity, but also all creation in a single network in which the fruitfulness of any branch depends on the well-being of the entire tree."[67] Mbuvi challenges those who would describe the People of Israel as the "only holy people" (to use Yosef Yitzḥak Schneersohn's language) and, indeed, all whose conceptions of solidarity depend on stable notions of communal identity.

In 2018 scholars from ten traditions convened at the Parliament of the World's Religions–University of Chicago conference that marked the twenty-fifth anniversary of the publication of the Global Ethic, the Parliament's interfaith declaration that lays out a set of core values shared by the world's religious and ethical traditions.[68] In the paper Mbuvi delivered at the conference, "*Avadim Hayinu*: An Intersectional Jewish Perspective on the Global Ethic of Solidarity," Mbuvi considered the ways in which Passover seder practices encourage identification with the outsider and ways in which the Exodus narrative shows the People of Israel as strengthened by diversity.[69]

The short essay printed below builds on the themes of Mbuvi's longer paper, emphasizing the contrast between God's and Pharaoh's respective visions for solidarity. Pharaoh views outsiders as pests, and he wields "ideological or physical violence against those who don't fit" within his exclusive community. By contrast, according to the vision of God reflected in the book of Exodus, people should not make sharp distinctions regarding who is and is not within the community. Hence, Exodus embraces ambiguity when it depicts the identities of Moses (born to Hebrews but raised by an Egyptian princess) and of the midwives Shiphrah and Puah (who may be Hebrews or Egyptians). Furthermore, Exodus depicts solidarity between the People of Israel and the ostensibly non-Israelite "mixed multitude" (Exod. 12:38) who escape Egypt with them. Moses and the People of Israel are called to follow a path that embraces "God's vision of blessed interdependence": one that sees diversity and complicated identities as sources of strength.

In section 4.5, Yeshaya Asher Zelig Margaliot depicted the mixed multitude as representing demonic evil that must be fought and excluded from the People of Israel. Mbuvi acknowledges the long-standing tradition of viewing the mixed multitude in a negative light, which is upheld by traditionalists in this chapter. Though the selections above did not mention the mixed multitude, Yisroel Friedman (section 9.3) depicted Moses as similarly drawing sharp lines and encouraging divine violence against those who are not part of the true community of Israel; and Yosef Yitzḥak Schneersohn (section 9.5) invoked an image of Moses warning that divine violence would befall those who did not join his particular approach to Torah. To Mbuvi, however, calls for violence or ideological conformity are more representative of Pharaoh's approach to solidarity than God's. Moses, in her view, is in fact a "mixed multitude" of an individual himself, "able to speak for a group with whom he has a fractured history" — championing solidarity even with those who are perceived as threats or who do not easily fall into line.

Amanda Mbuvi, "Choosing Solidarity" (2022)

Exodus, the story through which Israel emerges as a people, depicts a contest between God and Pharaoh in which each's claim to worship is rooted in a different conception of solidarity. God and Pharaoh both call communities into existence and summon them to action, but do so on the basis of contrasting notions of what it means to be authentically human that have divergent implications for relating to "others." The conflict between them does not end when the people of Israel leave Egypt. Depicting Pharaoh's dominion as a state of mind as well as a political polity, Exodus invites us to choose to live into our liberation as people of God even as Pharaoh's worldview remains a potent temptation.

As conceptualized by the Torah, being authentically human refers to living into a kind of spiritual wholeness and health that fulfills the intention of the existence of the human species. Exodus revisits elements from Genesis, with words and images associated with creation reappearing in a different light. Readers trained by Genesis will recognize its interconnected vision of blessed life in the descriptions of the people of Israel in Exodus. But in Pharaoh's world of competition, the same features lead to the characterization of the people of Israel as pests. Rather than distinguishing between better and worse ways of living into one's humanity, Pharaoh's version of authentic humanity distinguishes between those humans who count and those who matter less, or not at all. It applies different rules to those within the group than to those without, demanding violence against those perceived as a threat.

Exodus does not neatly sort the people who live with these distinct ways of conceptualizing and constituting community into one camp or the other, as illustrated by the ambiguity surrounding the identity of the midwives. The text identifies Shiphrah and Puah as "midwives to the Hebrews" (1:15), leaving open the question of whether they themselves are Hebrew or whether they are Egyptians who work with Hebrews. Regardless of the answer, they, like everyone in the book, are impacted by both the exercise of the power of Pharaoh and the power of God. They receive Pharaoh's command to kill Hebrew babies, and they must answer to him when they do not comply because they have chosen a course of action rooted in fear of God rather than fear of Pharaoh (1:17). By prominently featuring this choice by midwives who are Egyptian or who even might be, Exodus foregrounds the question of where the Egyptians will find blessedness—as people of this Pharaoh or as people of God?

Likewise, those who are part of the people of Israel can opt for Pharaoh's way of interpreting the world, as illustrated by the various ways of characterizing the "mixed multitude" that went up with the people of Israel from Egypt (12:38). In Hebrew, "mixed multitude" (erev rav) resembles the name for the fourth plague (arov). Some of the ancient sages saw this parallel as indicating that the mixed multitude constituted a cancer on the people. Accordingly, they blamed this group for instigating the negative episodes in the wilderness. In this view, the series of punishments served to cleanse the people by expunging those who were never really Israelites. However, the linguistic link between the plague and the multitude could be read in the opposite direction. Following the pattern in which the same words have different meanings for the people of Pharaoh and the people of God, the use of the same root would indicate that the diversity experienced as a plague by the people of Pharaoh does not present a problem to the people of God, and may even be a source of strength.

The solidarity between the people of Israel and the mixed multitude reflects their common plight, but fully leveraging that commonality requires more than a shared dislike of being oppressed. For the exodus to accomplish more than creating a new version of Pharaoh's dominion with different people in charge, it must be accompanied by the embrace of God's vision of blessed interdependence. Genesis presents that vision as part and parcel of creation, predating the existence of the people of Israel, which in its earliest manifestation (the call of Abraham) does not enter the picture until several chapters later. Accordingly, the Genesis vision of blessed interdependence naturally encompasses the mixed multitude of Exodus whether or not its members become the people of Israel. The alliance with the mixed multitude illustrates the potential for partnerships that transcend the covenantal particulars that constitute the people of Israel's distinctive identity. Envisioning unity across difference, it avoids the exclusiveness of false universals that achieve their scope through ideological or physical violence against those who don't fit.

Moses illustrates these dynamics on the individual level. His reluctance to take on the assignment at the burning bush may not have been rooted in concerns about his faculty of speech per se, but rather about his ability to speak for a group with whom he has a fractured history. Like a transracial adoptee,[70] Moses is born to Hebrews but raised by an Egyptian princess. Accordingly, when God addresses Moses from the burning bush, the reference to "your ancestors" is not obvious. As an adoptee and an emigre living with his wife's family, Moses may not know which ancestors are meant without further clarification.

Rather than resolving the ambiguities of Moses' identity, God offers companionship on the journey (3:12). This response resembles the call of Abraham in that each of them gets called into an identity best characterized as being the one with God, an identity that also entails occupying a liminal space with regard to conventional kinds of identity. Occupying this position leads Moses to a distinctive way of being in the world and equips him especially well to call the people of Israel into the new way of life of the Sinai covenant. A mixed multitude of an individual, he exemplifies the way in which the people of Israel draw strength from diversity.[71]

CONCLUSION

All of the thinkers in this chapter support joining with others across lines of difference for the sake of the common good, yet they think about solidarity and responsibility in very different ways.

Some stress the value of solidarity with and responsibility to others who are very different than they are, while others stress the value of solidarity with people who are similar in many respects.

Some stress conformity to particular ways of thinking or acting, while others stress the need to recognize difference and include diverse perspectives.

Some emphasize solidarity and responsibility as part of state-building, while others raise deep concerns about state-building projects.

Some emphasize the value of supporting responsible uses of violence, while others raise concerns about the use of violence.

Some imagine God's presence linking the Jewish community in solidarity, others imagine God's presence linking all human beings in solidarity, while still others emphasize human-to-human solidarity exclusive of God.

Some stress the Jewish people's responsibility for the faith of their fellow Jews, while others stress Jews' responsibility for ensuring justice. And those who do invoke justice employ very different concepts of it, some of which are tied to notions of God and Torah while others are not. We will delve deeper into disagreements about justice in the following chapter.

10

Justice and Righteousness
(*Tzedek*)

Concerns for justice infuse this volume. Some thinkers have pointed to connections between justice and virtues such as courage (chapter 4) and solidarity (chapter 9). Others have pointed to tensions between justice and virtues such as gratitude (chapter 6) and forgiveness (chapter 7). This chapter builds on some of those discussions while also considering other ways in which justice may be cultivated as a virtue.

This chapter is oriented around the Hebrew word *tzedek*, which most (though not all) thinkers understand as "justice." So translated, *tzedek* generally refers to a disposition to act rightly or fairly in relation to others. It may involve distinguishing right from wrong, following principles of fairness, giving people what they need or deserve, showing appropriate care and concern for those who are particularly disadvantaged, being appropriately impartial, acting appropriately in relationship to law, or some combination of these.[1]

Other thinkers understand *tzedek* as "righteousness," which may be understood even more broadly as referring to virtuousness in general, beyond interpersonal ethics. This usage is employed, for example, in the Rabbinic concept of the *tzaddik*—"the righteous man" who plays a unique role in sustaining the world.[2]

A passage in the biblical book of Deuteronomy that commands the pursuit of *tzedek*, while also using a second Hebrew term for "justice," *mishpat*, animates some of the discussion below. In its original context, the passage stresses behavior that is proper for a judge: "You shall not judge unfairly [*lo tateh mishpat*]: you shall show no partiality [*lo takir panim*]; you shall not take bribes, for bribes blind the eyes of the discerning and upset the plea of the just [*tzaddikim*]. Justice, justice [*tzedek, tzedek*] shall you pursue, that you may thrive and occupy the land that the Lord your God is giving you" (Deut. 16:19–20; see also Deut. 1:17). As discussed in section 10.3, Deuteronomy describes God with similar language, giving particular attention to justice for those who are most disadvantaged in society: God "shows no partiality [*lo yisa fanim*] and takes no bribe, but upholds justice [*mishpat*] for the fatherless and the widow, and loves the stranger, providing him with food and clothing" (Deut. 10:17–18).

One well-known midrash discussed below describes *tzedek* as playing a key role in the creation of the first human being. Personifications of Peace and Truth argue that God should not create humans, but personifications of *Tzedek* and *Ḥesed* (kindness or love) argue in favor of creation, pointing to the righteous/just and kind/loving deeds humans will perform.[3]

Still, another classical Rabbinic tradition, also invoked below, seems to caution against too much *tzedek*, quoting Eccles. 7:16: "Do not be overly righteous" (or "overly just"). A midrash cited in the Talmud (BT *Yoma* 22b) imagines this warning directed at Saul, the first king of ancient Israel, as he questions (and fails to implement) God's command to slaughter all the Amalekites (1 Sam. 15:3). As the midrash imagines it, Saul points to the Torah's concern about bloodshed, exemplified in its commandment to engage in a ritual killing of a heifer as atonement for an unsolved murder (Deut. 21:1–9), and to the presumed innocence of the Amalekite children and animals, whom God has also commanded him to slaughter. But God admonishes him not to be "too righteous" or "too just." In a parallel text in Ecclesiastes Rabbah (7:25), God warns: "Do not be more of a *tzaddik* than your Creator," and the text invokes Rabbi Simeon ben Lakish's dictum, "One who becomes merciful when he should be cruel, in the end he is cruel when he should be merciful" (see section 7.5). Some modern Jewish thinkers (see sections 10.4 and 10.8) have appealed to this tradition when criticizing views of justice that they see as merely human and out of line with the divine will.

10.1. THE RIGHTEOUSNESS OF THE *TZADDIK*

Hasidism is largely distinguished by its concept of the *tzaddik*, the charismatic male rabbinical leader who provides a unique link between God and the Jewish people (see sections 1.2, 2.2, 3.2, 5.1). The *tzaddik* ("the righteous man," as it is translated below, or "the just man") also possesses exceptionally high levels of *tzedek* (righteousness or justice).

These ideas are grounded in classical Rabbinic descriptions of the *tzaddik* as possessing unique power to sustain the world and in kabbalistic depictions of the *tzaddik* as an embodiment of the aspect of God (*yesod*) that emanates divine grace to the world. Early Hasidic sources accept this model while also stressing the *tzaddik*'s social role as an authoritative leader of the Jewish community who should be financially supported and whose teachings should be obeyed.[4]

Perhaps the most influential figure in shaping Hasidic concepts of the *tzaddik* was Rabbi Elimelekh Weissblum of Lizhensk, Galicia (1717–87).[5] His posthumously published volume *No'am Elimelekh* (1788) explained passages from the Torah in light of the concept, perhaps offering a sort of handbook for those aspiring to this role.[6]

In the three brief selections from that volume below, Elimelekh signals the importance of the character trait of righteousness in the development of the righteous leader.

Part I discusses the *tzaddik* in his role as a social leader. Although Elimelekh views the *tzaddik* as in a state of constant communion with the Divine and as fundamentally distinct from other Jews, he sees the *tzaddik* as also called to interrupt his contemplation and to "lower his level" by engaging with lowly, sinful, ordinary Jews.[7] Elimelekh indicates that the *tzaddik* must forge a connection with sinners by acting at least somewhat similarly to them—engaging in, to use the language of the Talmud, "a sin committed for the sake of God" (*averah lishmah*). Thus, for example, the *tzaddik* may relate to a liar by engaging in lying himself—though, Elimelekh is careful to explain (building on traditions seen in section 1.2), he would engage only in permissible lying. He argues that human existence depends on championing the value of righteousness (*tzedek*) over the value of truth, drawing on the midrashic tradition that at the dawn of Creation, only Righteousness, and not Truth, sanctioned the creation of human beings. The implication is that the *tzaddik*, the embodiment of righteousness, should be able to tolerate lying human beings in ways that Truth cannot. The righteous man knows that it was good that human beings were created despite their sins, and that the task of the righteous is to engage with sinners and even to descend to their level in the hopes of eventually raising them from their sin.

In part II, Elimelekh describes how righteousness is displayed when one gives financial support to a *tzaddik*. The word *tzaddik*, importantly, is related to the word for charity, *tzedakah*, here translated as "righteous charity"; and *tzedakah* is the same Hebrew word as the character trait of *tzedek* with the addition of one final letter. That missing Hebrew letter represents the aspect of God and the People of Israel (*malkhut*) that is presently cut off from the body of God; righteous giving to the *tzaddik*, however, moves the world toward redemption by joining these aspects of the Divine together.[8] When one gives righteously to the authority figure described as the embodiment of righteousness in the world, righteousness itself is brought to a higher level—and, the text indicates, this giving allows divine abundance to flow into the world. The *tzaddik* will distribute the charity with ideal justice, and this display of righteousness enables other divine gifts—"abundance, blessing, mercy, life, children, sustenance, and peace, without end"—to miraculously flow (through the *tzaddik*) into the world.

We see here a justification of the economic arrangement whereby Hasidim offer monetary donations (*pidyonot*) to Hasidic masters in exchange for promises of blessing.[9] As seen in section 5.3.II, Menaḥem Mendel Lefin was appalled that Hasidic masters spent these donations on luxuries for themselves. For his part, Elimelekh acknowledges that a *tzaddik* may spend such charitable donations for his own benefit—not for luxuries but "to benefit himself in order to provide sustenance and a livelihood." The *tzaddik* who does so is still a *tzaddik*, still a righteous man, but because he intends to only receive rather than to give, he is "feminine," in contrast to the superior "masculine" man who receives *tzedakah* only with the intent of giving it to others. (There is no possibility for a woman to be a *tzaddik* in this model.[10])

In part III, Elimelekh's approach to a biblical verse often invoked in Jewish discussions of justice—"You shall not judge unfairly. You shall show no partiality" (Deut. 16:19)—strikingly points to an ideal of *tzedek* as "righteousness" rather than to concerns about interpersonal justice that otherwise dominate this chapter. Reflecting a tendency among Hasidic teachers to understand biblical commandments as referring to internal spiritual struggles,[11] Elimelekh understands the commandment regarding judging others fairly to refer to a process of internal cultivation of a "righteous" personality. Specifically, he urges a focus on God and warns against "alien thoughts" and "improper sights and imaginings"—language that generally connotes thinking sexually of women, who constitute a distraction to the God-focused, righteous male personality.[12]

Elimelekh Weissblum of Lizhensk, *Noam Elimelekh* (1788)

I. "A sin committed for the sake [of God is greater than a commandment not performed for the sake of God]" [BT *Nazir* 23b]: the righteous man needs to lower his level in order to break the foolishness of the lowly person by performing a sin for the sake [of God]. For example, with someone who is accustomed to lying, the righteous man must act similarly in order to break it. Of course, God forbid, the righteous man would not lie, but we do find that our sages of blessed memory [BT *Bava Metzia* 23b] permitted [lying about] one's studies [etc.]. Or similarly, a righteous man may say that he is not a righteous man and this would be a lie, for he is a righteous man, but he is performing a sin for the sake [of God] in order to break the liar's strength. We find in the Talmud: "Truth said, 'Let [man] not be created, for he is all lies.' Righteousness [*Tzedek*] said: 'Let him be created [because he acts righteously].'"[13] This is the meaning of the verse, "I proclaimed righteousness in a great congregation" [Ps. 40:10]—that when there is a great congregation, it is impossible that there would not be one liar among them, but the righteous man will raise him up from his foolishness and lying, by lowering himself down to him, to a state similar to his. This is like the proclamation [agreeing] with Righteousness, for it was good that it said that [man] should be created.[14]

II. There is . . . the righteous man [*tzaddik*], and there is righteousness [*tzedek*]. When the righteous man receives righteous charity [*tzedakah*], he joins the final letter ("hey") to the character trait of righteousness . . . so that it becomes [truly] righteous charity [*tzedakah*], and the world is filled with all goodness: abundance, blessing, mercy, life, children, sustenance, and peace, without end—emanating in abundance due to the righteous man who accepted the righteous charity, and through him it continues to emanate to the entire world, sufficiently for each according to his needs. . . . [On the one hand,] there is the righteous man who, when he receives righteous charity, does not think of the benefit to himself, but only intends that it emanate abundant goodness to all Israel. . . . And this righteous man is called "masculine," even though he is a "receiver," for his sole intent and request is to emanate abundance [for others]. . . . [On the other hand,] there is the righteous man who receives righteous charity but who also intends to benefit himself in order to provide sustenance and a livelihood, and this one is called "feminine," as his intent is also to be a "receiver."[15]

III. "You shall not judge unfairly. You shall show no partiality" [literally, "You shall not recognize faces"] [Deut. 16:19]. It is written, "You shall have no other gods before me" [literally, "before my face"] [Exod. 20:3]. We must explain thus: The blessed Creator is known as the "face" of everything, because everything has a part of godliness that gives it existence and life. And if, God forbid, a man thinks an alien thought, or looks at something improper, he drives [God's] face away; the alien thoughts and improper sights and imaginings are called "other gods," and this is the meaning of "You shall have no other gods [before my face]," and this is the meaning of "You shall not recognize faces."[16]

10.2. SUBJECTIVE AND OBJECTIVE JUDGMENT

Whereas Elimelekh was a prominent figure in one early modern pietistic movement, Hasidism, Rabbi Israel Salanter (Israel Lipkin of Salant, Lithuania, 1810–83) was the prominent founder of another modern pietistic movement, the Musar movement (see sections 1.4, 2.4, 6.4, 8.3, 9.4). Salanter's Musar movement had some commonalities with Hasidism. Both were traditionalist movements that encouraged a focus on inner piety, defended the authority of Jewish law, and produced significant works of musar literature; both were also sectarian movements that challenged established communal frameworks and generated new pietistic practices.[17]

But unlike Elimelekh and other Hasidic leaders, Salanter adopted a generally naturalistic model of psychological change that did not require battling metaphysically evil forces. He also rejected the Hasidic concept of a charismatic *tzaddik* who would embody the Divine, work miracles, effect metaphysical changes in the cosmos, and serve as an intermediary between God and Israel. Notably, while Hasidic leaders such as Elimelekh imagined that the *tzaddik* was generally free from sin (other than the requisite "sinning for the sake of God"), Salanter generally emphasized that even a supremely righteous person was filled with sin.[18] His movement greatly encouraged self-criticism and questioning the righteousness of those who claimed to be righteous (see especially sections 6.4 and 9.4). For Salanter, the most righteous individuals are those who are best skilled at self-criticism and so best able to uncover sinfulness within their souls.[19]

As Salanter indicates in the selection below, it is almost impossible to purify one's soul so that one may be governed by abstract reason alone. "Soul-forces" (*koḥot ha-nefesh*) — emotions, desires, and undisciplined sense perceptions — easily cloud the objective powers of reason.[20] Even the very process of reflecting on character traits, while necessary for purifying one's soul, inevitably involves the emotions. A rabbinical judge, making determinations about Jewish law—i.e., about God's will—must strive to judge with the greatest rationality and objectivity possible but must know that complete objectivity is virtually impossible.[21]

Still, Salanter indicates, a judge has properly fulfilled the obligation of "pursuing justice" (redifat ha-tzedek) if he continually "dedicates heart and soul to purifying one's thoughts in accordance with one's knowledge." The Torah's commandment to "pursue justice" (tzedek tzedek tirdof, Deut. 16:20) may be fulfilled through such dedication. Even though a judge's judgment will not be perfectly, objectively true, it may be considered "true" and one may say to the judge, "God is with you in the judgment" (2 Chron. 19:6). One should, moreover, have "faith in the sages" (Avot 6:6) who pursue justice in this way, deferring to the legal rulings of sage rabbis despite their subjectivity.[22]

This dedication to "faith in the sages" that admits the subjectivity of the sage is rather different from Elimelekh's faith in the true tzaddik, which does not appear to admit the subjectivity of the tzaddik; but Salanter nonetheless joins Elimelekh in encouraging deference to certain rabbinical authorities. In the conclusion of the selection below, Salanter also imagines an ideal of perfectly true, abstract judgment that can be carried out by a human being—a king of Israel such as David who is also a prophet and is likened to an angel. Though it may be almost impossible for human beings to judge with the pure rationality of the angels, Salanter indicates that it is not totally impossible. This seems close to Elimelekh's ideal of the tzaddik, though for Salanter it does not appear that such a king will again exist until the days of the Messiah (the righteous future king descended from David).

While Salanter elsewhere focused on other aspects of justice, especially giving tzedakah to those in poverty,[23] his vision of the pursuit of justice for judges is an especially original contribution to modern Jewish discourse regarding justice as a virtue.

Israel Lipkin Salanter, "The Light of Israel" (1862)

When reflecting deeply on a character trait, it is almost impossible to completely purify reason and to strip away the soul-forces from [one's reason]. . . . It is [only] the angels, who are purely rational, who are free from the influence of the soul-forces. And so their consciousness of what is "good" and "evil" becomes a consciousness of what is "true" and "false." . . . And so we have the statement in scripture [addressed to King David]: ". . . my lord the king is like an angel of God, understanding everything, good and evil" (2 Sam. 14:17). . . .[24]

[Our Rabbis] speak of . . . "faith in the sages" (*Mishnah Avot* 6:6) [as one of the essential virtues for acquiring Torah]. . . . One should follow and implement the ruling of one who is a great decisor and uses evidence and proofs, to nullify one's own opinion in deference to his, even if [the decisor's] words are simply emerging from his judgment. . . .

Our Rabbis of blessed memory warned (BT *Sanhedrin* 7a): "A judge should always imagine himself as if a sword rests between his thighs, and hell [*Geihinnom*] is open beneath him." They offered this warning . . . for monetary cases, where the inclination [to bias] is very common. Nonetheless, if a person dedicates heart and soul to purifying one's thoughts in accordance with one's knowledge, this is truly the pursuit of justice that God seeks. This is the "truth" of the case [according to which a judge should judge], the definition of truth in legal judgment. . . .

Perhaps this is part of the meaning of the teaching of our sages of blessed memory (BT *Sanhedrin* 6b): "Perhaps a judge will say: 'Why should I take on such trouble?' But the Torah says: '[God] is with you in the judgment' [2 Chron. 19:6]—one only has to judge based on what one's eyes see." Even after one has purified one's thought [as best one can], one cannot be certain whether one's soul-forces still interfere. But it will be "what one's eyes see," and it will be justice for him, even though it will come about not by means of general, abstract reason but, rather, by means of the personal assemblage of one's soul-forces.

But with the king, who is elevated above all his people, his judgments are defined as the truth—"true truth"—offering demonstration, as [was said of King David] ". . . my lord the king is like an angel of

God, understanding everything, good and evil (2 Sam. 14:17)." That which would be a matter of "good" among the people is a matter of "truth" with the king—as with the angels....[25]

10.3. JUSTICE BEFORE LOVE

The German-born rabbi Kaufmann Kohler (1843–1926) became a prominent leader of Reform Judaism in the United States, serving as the longtime president of Hebrew Union College. Kohler polemically argued that justice was the highest principle of ethics and the essence of God.

Kohler's polemic was especially directed against Christianity, which, in his view, devalued justice and proclaimed "love" without justice as its central moral principle—while often committing cruel injustices against others, including the Jews.[26] In part III of the text below, excerpted from Kohler's 1918 book *Jewish Theology*, he contrasts the Church's historic embrace of love, which without the guidance of justice is easily "swayed by impulse and emotion and is often too partial," with Judaism's emphasis on impartial, rational justice as its central principle.[27] Kohler's praise of rationality resembles Salanter's praise of rationality in certain ways, although Salanter would have been appalled by Kohler's Reform Judaism. In the passage from Salanter above, the pursuit of justice upheld the authority of traditional Jewish law; for Kohler, by contrast, the overriding principle of justice often required the reform of Jewish law.

In part II, Kohler contrasts cultures on a "low cultural plane," those that see the defense of law as the core of justice, with what he considers the high-level culture of Judaism, which defends not law but the rights of any oppressed human being. At the same time, Kohler believes that Judaism avoids the error of perverting justice for the sake of love or compassion. This path emulates the description of God's justice in Deut. 10:17–18. Representing the ideal of impartiality, God "regardeth not persons" (alternatively, "shows no partiality") "nor taketh bribes" (Deut. 10:17); and, above all focused on ensuring fair justice for those who are weak and oppressed, God "executes the judgment of the fatherless and the widow" (Deut. 10:18).

Notably, Kohler borrows and reverses rhetoric used by some Christian leaders, both in ranking cultures (for them, showing the superiority of Christianity) and also in praising "manly" religion (for them, Christianity).[28] For Kohler, society and religion at their best should be governed by the masculine virtue of reasoned justice rather than by love, which may "effeminize society." Judaism is therefore an admirably manly religion, whereas Christianity is disturbingly feminine. As scholar Sarah Imhoff has written: "Love, which Kohler associated with Christianity, was an emotion, and it was therefore partial and particular. And emotions and the particular were both coded feminine. Justice, in contrast, was impartial, rational, and universal, each of which was coded masculine. Unlike a love-centered society, one centered on justice would not be effeminate and particularist, but would be universal—treating every person alike and making the same ethical demands of all."[29] Thus Kohler joined Elimelekh in masculinizing justice, while describing the feminine in a very different way.

Kohler also linked his passion for justice with his opposition to Political Zionism. In part I, from an address delivered in November 1915, Kohler hopes that Jews will promote justice and righteousness wherever they live and not merely "in the confines of the little territory of Palestine." While Kohler did support Jewish settlement in the Land of Israel, he rejected Political Zionist calls for Jews to focus their attention on their own interests in their own land. For Kohler, such Zionism contradicted the mission of the Jews to spread their ideals of justice and righteousness throughout the world.[30]

Kaufmann Kohler, "Israel's Mission in the World" (1915) and *Jewish Theology* (1918)

I. You must with all your power resist evil and assert your own right as well as that of others, because justice is the foundation of God's throne, and without it the whole social structure totters and falls. Here, then, is the scope and mission of the Jew. Not in an especial State of his own, but in the very midst of the nations among which he lives, must he, as he did under far less propitious conditions in former ages, battle for justice and righteousness as the true basis of social and private ethics, as the foundation of the world. . . . Not in the confines of the little territory of Palestine [but] wherever the Jew lives, he must do his share to turn the earth into a mountain of God, the seat of righteousness and disinterested love.[31]

II. It cannot be denied that justice is recognized as a binding force even by peoples on a low cultural plane. . . . [In many cultures] the maintenance . . . of the status quo is considered justice by the law, whatever injustice to individuals may result. But the Jewish idea of justice is not reactionary; it owes to the prophets its position as the dominating principle of the world, the peculiar essence of God, and therefore the ultimate ideal of human life. They fought for right with an insistence which vindicated its moral significance forever, and in scathing words of indignation which still burn in the soul they denounced oppression wherever it appeared. The crimes of the mighty against the weak, they held, could not be atoned for by the outward forms of piety. Right and justice are not simply matters for the State and the social order, but belong to God, who defends the cause of the helpless and the homeless, "who executes the judgment of the fatherless and the widow," "who regardeth not persons, nor taketh bribes" (Deut. 10:17–18). Iniquity is hateful to Him; it cannot be covered up by pious acts, nor be justified by good ends. "Justice is God's" (Deut. 1:17). Thus every violation of justice, whether from sordid self-seeking or from tender compassion, is a violation of God's cause; and every vindication of justice, every strengthening of the power of right in society, is a triumph of God.

Accordingly, the highest principle of ethics in Judaism, the cardinal point in the government of the world, is not love, but *justice*. Love has the tendency to undermine the right and to effeminize society. Justice, on the other hand, develops the moral capacity of every man; it aims not merely to avoid wrong, but to promote and develop the right for the sake of the perfect state of morality. . . . Social life . . . must be built upon the firm foundation of justice, the full recognition of the rights of all individuals and all classes. It can be based neither upon the formal administration of law nor upon the elastic principle of love, which too often tolerates, or even approves certain types of injustice. Judaism has been working through the centuries to realize the ideal of justice to all mankind. . . .[32]

III. Love as a principle of action is not sufficiently firm to fashion human conduct or rule society. It is too much swayed by impulse and emotion and is often too partial. Love without justice leads to abuse and wrong, as we see in the history of the Church, which began with the principle of love, but often failed to heed the admonitions of justice. Therefore justice is the all-inclusive principle of human conduct in the eyes of Judaism. Justice is impartial by its very nature. It must right every wrong and vindicate the cause of the oppressed. . . . Justice is the requisite not only in action, but also in disposition,[33] implying honesty in intention as in deed, uprightness in speech and mien, perfect rectitude, neither taking advantage of ignorance nor abusing confidence. . . .[34]

10.4. IDEALS OF JUSTICE IN THE SOUL

Like Kohler, Rabbi Abraham Isaac Kook possessed a strong sense of the greatness and mission of the Jewish people. In section 4.4, Kook insisted that Israel drew strength from the presence of God that rested, uniquely, within their souls; in section 8.8, Lynn Gottlieb pointed to Kook's racism in differentiating between Jews and non-Jews.

In part I of the selections below, Kook celebrates the great "ideals of justice" resting within the Jewish soul. These ideals have been "latent," awaiting their full expression; Zionism will be the vehicle for their expression. Kook sees the Zionist cause as just, and guided by divine providence. In the future, he believes, Zionism will establish a uniquely just state that will nurture the Jewish soul and reflect its greatness.

At the same time, as seen in part II, Kook describes state-building as a morally fraught enterprise, as politics intensifies the strength of the evil inclination. Nonetheless, justice can be cultivated on a collective level, within a Jewish state, so long as the state is built on the foundations of Torah.

In part III, from his writings on human-animal relations,[35] Kook holds that a natural sense of justice—including an often deeply concealed sense of justice toward nonhuman animals—is implanted within all human beings. In the messianic era, that sense of justice will be able to flourish: human beings will become vegetarian, returning to the vegetarianism of the Garden of Eden (Gen. 1:29). But while eating meat is a "moral defect," human beings have been permitted to eat meat ever since the time of the Flood (Gen. 9:2–3). As such, "the virtue of recognizing justice for animals" (or, one might translate, "recognizing the rights of animals") is "not at all appropriate" for the current era.

How might this virtue be inappropriate for the present time but appropriate for times of greater enlightenment? Kook believes that in the present era of corruption, a focus on justice toward animals will lead people to neglect justice toward human beings. All human beings have some "natural hunger for justice," but the wicked will satisfy that hunger with kindness to animals, freeing them to engage in grave injustices against human beings ("slaughtering human beings without mercy").

Kook appears to view a focus on justice for animals in the present day as the dangerous sort of "overrighteousness" the book of Ecclesiastes warned about—akin to when, according to midrashic tradition, the prophet Samuel condemned King Saul for not (immediately) slaughtering King Agag and the best of the Amalekites' flocks: "Do not be overly righteous and do not act too wise" (Eccles. 7:16).

Abraham Isaac Kook, "The Rebirth of Israel," "A Kingdom of Priests," and "Streams in the Negev" (early twentieth century)

I. It is a fundamental error to turn our backs on the only source of our high estate and to discard the concept that we are a chosen people. We are not only different from all the nations, set apart by a historical experience that is unique and unparalleled, but we are also of a much higher and greater spiritual order. Really to know ourselves, we must be conscious of our greatness. Else we shall fall very low. Our soul encompasses the entire universe, and represents it in its highest unity. It is, therefore, whole and complete, entirely free of all the disjointedness and the contradictions which prevail among all other peoples.... Our past is a great one, and our future is even greater, as is evidenced by our striving for the ideals of justice that are latent in our souls. This great force inspirits our present and gives it full life.[36]

II. We can see that individuals can grasp basic issues of human morality that can be guided by the natural sense of justice ... but mankind as a whole has not yet found consensus on what constitutes moral obligations for public policy (or even for political factions). Thus, we know that the individual's evil inclination becomes doubly powerful in collective politics, to such an extent that concepts of good and evil, justice and iniquity are completely lost in the political turmoil and the boiling cauldron of the state that is "like the troubled sea" [Isa. 57:20].... [But] state power is derived from the essence of the foundation of holiness, which is latent within the depths of the collective Jewish soul, before the turmoil of life in the world can mark out the erasure of justice and the loss of morality.... In our [Zionist] movement, in which we feel our national, societal flowering, we are obligated to raise its moral level and its connection to the foundation of our holiness through the power of our sacred Torah, the Torah of life, the source of justice, the fountain of truth.[37]

III. The cruel philosophies ... have not managed, nor will they manage, with all their sophistry, to change the character of the natural justice that the Creator of the human being has implanted within him. And even though, with regard to animals, it is like the gleam of a faint and dim ember buried under a very great heap of ashes, it is nevertheless impossible for them to negate what is felt in every sensitive heart: it is a universal moral defect that mankind does not fulfill the fine and exalted sentiment of refraining from taking the life of living beings for human needs and pleasure....

The permission given to eat meat that emerged after the Flood was not intended ... to be put into practice forever, for how would it be possible for such an honored and enlightened moral condition to pass away, after it had already been observed? Rather, the divine wisdom saw that the human being had fallen from his moral condition, and until the blessed and enlightened time of returning to this level, awakening to true moral consciousness, this moral virtue of recognizing justice for animals was not at all appropriate for him. . . . If the moral obligations of humans to animals were fully put into practice in an era lacking moral perfection, this would cause great evils and hinder the development of human morality. . . . For the human feeling for the good and right seeks to fulfill its task, sometimes even knocking on the doors of the hearts of the wicked of the earth, who must seek to alleviate their natural hunger for justice, the foundational desire that maintains the world. Sometimes [this feeling] may find a wicked tyrant who chooses a moral issue and rejoices in acting with justice in order to alleviate the regret and moral remorse that naturally surges within him. If showing oneself to be kind toward animals was a widespread way to satisfy the desire for justice fixed within human beings . . . we would encounter a great mass of wicked people who would seek prey like wolves of the steppe [Zeph. 3:3], slaughtering human beings without mercy—and when their moral remorse would bother them, they would comfort themselves with their kindness to animals. . . .

What form of life would be appropriate for moral characteristics such as these [ideals of justice toward animals], such that these glorious ideals would not be a leap outside the system and would not be a case of "Do not be overly righteous and do not act too wise"? It is clear that moral values such as these will not be appropriate for human beings until [human beings] have been perfected, to the height of perfection, in all respects.[38]

10.5. HUNGERING FOR JUSTICE VERSUS KILLING FOR FOOD

The Polish-born American Yiddish writer and Nobel laureate Isaac Bashevis Singer (1902–91) was a passionate advocate of vegetarianism and animal rights, which he understood very differently than Abraham Isaac

Kook.[39] Whereas Kook believed that a focus on justice toward animals could encourage the slaughter of human beings, Singer believed that a neglect of justice toward animals leads to the slaughter of human beings. Whereas Kook warned that a "hunger for justice" might be perversely satisfied with kindness toward animals and cruelty to humans, Singer warned that a "hunger for justice" was neglected when animals were killed for food. Whereas Kook believed that ideals of justice toward animals could be put into place only once human beings had been perfected, Singer believed that the unjust killing of animals had to stop immediately. Whereas Kook believed that God would continue to condone the killing of animals until the messianic age, Singer believed that even if God were to condone killing animals, one had to "protest the ways of God and man."

Beyond this, Kook embraced an Orthodox belief in God and cautioned against taking "a leap outside the system"; Singer rejected Orthodox beliefs about God and sought to question all conventional religious systems.[40]

Isaac Bashevis Singer, Foreword to *Vegetarianism* (1979) and Preface to *Food for the Spirit* (1986)

I. What gives man the right to kill an animal, often torture it, so that he can fill his belly with its flesh? We know now, as we have always known instinctively, that animals can suffer as much as human beings. Their emotions and their sensitivity are often stronger than those of a human being. Various philosophers and religious leaders tried to convince their disciples and followers that animals are nothing more than machines without a soul, without feelings. However, anyone who has ever lived with an animal—be it a dog, a bird, or even a mouse—knows that this theory is a brazen lie, invented to justify cruelty. The only justification for killing animals is the fact that man can keep a knife or an ax in his hands and is shrewd enough and selfish enough to do slaughter for what he thinks is his own good. . . . Even if God or nature sides with the killers, the vegetarian is saying: I protest the ways of God and man. . . . There is only one little step from killing animals to creating gas chambers à la Hitler and concentration camps

à la Stalin—all such deeds are done in the name of "social justice."
There will be no justice as long as man will stand with a knife or with
a gun and destroy those who are weaker than he is.[41]

II. When a human kills an animal for food, he is neglecting his own
hunger for justice. Man prays for mercy, but is unwilling to extend it
to others. Why should man then expect mercy from God? It's unfair
to expect something that you are not willing to give. It is inconsistent.
I can never accept inconsistency or injustice. Even if it comes from
God. If there would come a voice from God saying, "'I'm against
vegetarianism!" I would say, "Well, I am for it!"[42]

10.6. JUSTICE AND PARTIALITY

In the essay below, Rabbi Susan Schnur (introduced in section 7.8)
addresses the subject of justice with particular reference to gender.
Women, she says, may be treated unjustly both by those who proclaim
their impartial allegiance to the law and those who seek to be partial to
women's situations. She suggests that Jewish women, "wise in the ways
of disprivilege," are especially well positioned to see both the dangers
of justice and the dangers of being overly partial.

Framing her essay as a response to the commandment "You shall
not judge unfairly. You shall show no partiality" (Deut. 16:19), Schnur
indicates that while we should not show *excessive* partiality, justice in fact
requires *some* partiality. It would be a mistake to be absolutely partial,
but it would also be a mistake to commit to impartial justice without
tenderness, love, and attachment to particular people, communities, and
institutions. One should not, for example, relate to one's mother only with
impartial justice. So, too, other relationships require love and partiality.

Schnur's embrace of tenderness, love, and attachment to particular
others stands in stark contrast to Kaufmann Kohler's suspicions regarding
tenderness, love, and attachment to particulars (section 10.3); similarly,
her appreciation of partiality as part of justice stands in stark contrast
to Kohler's demand for impartial justice.

Schnur's approach may also be contrasted with that of Israel Salanter (section 10.2). While Salanter puts a premium on the authority of law, Schnur questions unjust laws. Whereas Salanter is troubled by the subjectivity of judgment, Schnur appreciates subjectivity. And whereas Salanter points to the ideal (messianic) king who will judge only with abstract reason, Schnur depicts the ideal (messianic) future as demanding the continuation of a dialectic that integrates reason and emotion, justice and love.

A teaching above by Elimelekh of Lizhensk (section 10.1.III) interprets the same verse from Deuteronomy but understands it in a strikingly divergent way. For Elimelekh the verse is warning against distractions, particularly the sexual distractions presented by women. The methods for preventing such distractions he and other Orthodox Jews have favored have typically included keeping women from participating in public prayer or public leadership—the very methods Schnur points to as examples of injustice. Thus the commandment regarding justice might encourage Elimelekh to unjustly restrict women; Schnur seeks a model that *requires* justice for women.

Susan Schnur, "Justice" (1997)

"You shall not judge unfairly. You shall show no partiality."—Deut. 16:19

The Hebrews, more than any people, cared deeply about justice, and this earned them at times (peculiarly, one might think) a negative reputation. "Those Jews, you know, so narrowly legalistic."

But there's a grain of truth in many accusations, and this one's no exception. Obsessive justice-hunting—untempered by "partiality"—can take on a life of its own, can even lead, oddly, to injustice. Some contemporary halakhic (Jewish legal) stances—in relation to justice for women, for example—are cases in point. For example, a girlfriend of mine was grossly insulted when she was told she was not "allowed" to recite *Kaddish* (mourner's prayer) for her father. In response, the local Orthodox rabbi informed her that law and even custom took precedence over her feelings.

"Partiality," of course, means those loyalties in our lives that cause us to turn a blind eye to justice. Camus, for example, said, "I believe in justice, but I will defend my mother before justice."

Partiality is affirmative action.

Aren't we commanded, indeed, to be always "partial" to our Hebrew God—despite the vagaries of Her justice? And isn't the binding of Isaac powerful precisely *because* Abraham chose partiality to God over justice? And isn't the Jewish *brit* (covenant) itself based on loyalty, not justice?

"All other things on issues being roughly equal," wrote the columnist William Safire, "women should strongly support women until some parity [i.e., equal representation in political office] is reached. Then, secure in a system in balance, they can throw the rascals out, regardless of sex."

But partiality can be misused as a mere slogan and a tool for manipulating public opinion. As both women and Jews, we are wise in the ways of disprivilege, having developed, over centuries, a hard-bitten, doubly earned reality principle. Mercy shmercy, we say (we've too often been the one-way benefactors of it). Only "justice" is to be trusted in this deeply flawed world. Apologists use partiality to explain why women have been exempted and then excluded from daily prayer with a *minyan*. Women are so spiritually elevated, they argue, that we do not *need* to pray at specified hours. Or, our contributions on the home front are so essential that we cannot be spared to lead in the public arena, as well.

Whatever its limits or abuses, Jewish women value partiality as a core element of justice. For who among us would care about justice at all if we didn't, at base, have a certain transcendent attachment to others? We hold justice and partiality in tension, but, in the larger picture, partiality is an essential part of justice.

Jewish women—minorities times two—are ideally suited to model the crucial maturity required by this moral dialectic. In relation to Judaism, we have learned both to criticize and to defend. If we weren't "partial" to it (and to Israel as well), we would be at risk, at times, of throwing the whole thing out. And, on the other hand, if we were *only* partial, then we would court danger. Standing excessively by our institution, our community, our state, our partner—we turn virtue into vice.

We are privileged to have this hard-earned wisdom: Absolute partiality deprives us of our good judgment, but absolute justice deprives us of our human tenderness. We've learned this from our lives.

And so we mold Judaism's brightest future—keeping in balance, always, a love for our parochial selves and a vision of global justice—sometimes one declaring trump, and sometimes the other. It is worthwhile to discuss and infer the "rules of the game," to name criteria for deciding when and to what degree partiality or pure justice should prevail. Yet, in the end, the dialectic is too sophisticated for any calculus.

So when, in the future, some Empress somewhere is found, yet again, to have no clothes, we will be neither exclusively crowd nor exclusively child. Rather, we will hold our two responses in harmonic tension, responding with both justice *and* partiality. Loyal to the Empress, we will not shame Her. Yet we will not collude with Her either. We will speak truth to power—because we share power. Demanding justice, we will also love.

It is a messianic task for which we are perfectly suited.[43]

10.7. A JEWISH LESBIAN VISION OF JUSTICE AND LOVE

The Reconstructionist rabbi Rebecca Alpert's book, *Like Bread on the Seder Plate: Jewish Lesbians and the Transformation of Tradition*, features interpretations of the prophet Micah's three-part precept that "what is good and what the Lord requires of you" is "only to do justice [*asot mishpat*], to love well [*ahavat ḥesed*], and to walk humbly with God [*hatznea lekhet im elohekha*]" (Mic. 6:8). Section 3.7 (when Alpert was introduced) displays how she understands the third portion of the precept, "walking humbly with God," in terms of accepting oneself. In the selection below, Alpert focuses primarily on the first part: "doing justice."

Alpert emphasizes that Jewish lesbians must be treated with justice. Justice for lesbians requires rejecting the authority of halakhah that is central for figures such as Elimelekh, Salanter, and Kook; and it requires Jewish communities to work toward justice for LGBTQ Jews.[44] Furthermore, Jewish lesbians ought to fight for justice for other oppressed communities, including racial minorities and Palestinians living under Israeli occupation.[45]

In the selection, Alpert points to broad elements of justice necessary for all human beings, including providing for basic human needs. Elimelekh also called for satisfying all people according to their needs (section 10.1.II), but rather than asking for charity to be funneled through a righteous male rabbi, Alpert calls for democratic processes and for addressing structural injustices.

The selection makes an especially important contribution to discussions of the relationship between love and justice. Like her fellow Reconstructionist rabbi Susan Schnur (section 10.6), Alpert appreciates both love and justice. Her writing, however, stresses how love denotes "respect not only for those whom we love particularly, but for all humanity." Alpert describes such love as a prerequisite to justice: the emergence of justice requires a climate in which hatred is replaced by loving respect for all people. She goes on to take a stand against those—like Kaufmann Kohler (section 10.3), and also like the feminist philosopher Carol Gilligan—who associate love with feminine approaches to intimate caring, and justice with masculine approaches to abstract reasoning. Alpert sees these associations as mischaracterizing love and justice *and* placing them in opposition rather than showing their necessary interconnectedness. At the same time, she argues against those (like Carter Heyward, introduced in section 7.6) who see justice and love as identical. Building on the language of Micah, Alpert describes justice and love as "separate but connected values."

She also takes issue with those who judge others as "inferior to themselves." Here, she points specifically to the problem of hatred toward those who are viewed as inferior, though elsewhere in her writings she identifies broader dangers in seeing one's own favored group as superior. In one essay she urges readers to "work toward a society that no longer sees difference as a mark of superiority or inferiority, but accepts difference as a normal part of what it means to be human."[46] With concerns such as these, Alpert joins the founder of her movement, Mordecai Kaplan (section 3.4), in pointing to the dangers of the concept of chosenness—a concept that, as seen in this chapter, has shaped ideas of justice promulgated by some Reform Jews (section 10.3), Orthodox Jews (section 10.4), and others.

Rebecca Alpert, *Like Bread on the Seder Plate* (1997)

The commitment to do justice requires us to go beyond our own lives and to look at larger issues in the world around us. In the conception of Micah's precept [to do justice (*asot mishpat*), to love well (*ahavat ḥesed*), and to walk humbly with God (*hatznea lekhet im elohekha*)] . . . these efforts are intrinsically interconnected. We cannot make a choice between accepting ourselves, caring for our circle of loved ones, and doing justice in the world. These efforts must be woven into one framework.

What, then, is the justice that we seek as human beings who are Jewish lesbians? Our goal is to live in a world where every person has what it takes to satisfy basic human needs: food, clothing, and shelter. Where every person has the opportunity for health care, safety, education, and work. Where all people have the opportunity to participate in decisions that affect their lives. Where nations do not make war against one another. And where the planet itself, and all that lives on it, is treated with dignity and respect. These are the goals of a just society.

We cannot begin to envision such a world unless we have created the possibilities within ourselves and our community of working toward this plan. As Jewish lesbians, we begin with the idea that to walk with decency with God is measured by our self-acceptance and willingness to be visible. This is the beginning of justice. For only if we speak out about who we are, can we create the opportunity for justice for ourselves.

JUSTICE AND RIGHTEOUSNESS

But this is insufficient: love is also a prerequisite to justice. In relation to justice *ahavat ḥesed* means respect not only for those whom we love particularly, but for all humanity. This means figuring out how to deal with hatred that is expressed in violent words and deeds. Many acts of violence in our society are perpetrated by those who hate others whom they judge to be inferior to themselves. . . . Only if we remain vigilant against those who hate difference can we begin to speak about *asot mishpat*.

Some feminists have severed the connection between love and justice. In an effort to demonstrate the value of love, feminist philosophers such as Carol Gilligan have posited that a female way of being is to focus more on intimate caring, whereas the masculine approach is to demand abstract justice.[47]

This dichotomized notion demeans both love and justice. It places them in opposition rather than as connected parts of a single obligation as Micah states.

On the other hand, Carter Heyward, a white Christian lesbian theologian, argues that justice is love. In doing justice, one is creating a loving world.[48]

From the perspective of Micah's precept, however, these values are not one and the same. I interpret Micah's precept to make distinctions between loving well and doing justice—seeing them as separate but connected values. . . .[49]

10.8. DO NOT BE OVERLY RIGHTEOUS

Steven Pruzansky (b. 1958) is rabbi emeritus of an Orthodox congregation in Teaneck, New Jersey, and has served in the leadership of the Rabbinical Council of America, the union of Centrist (non-*haredi*) American Orthodox rabbis. A passionate Zionist who has drawn inspiration from the writings of Abraham Isaac Kook (section 10.4), Pruzansky emigrated to Israel in 2020.

Pruzansky is also a passionate preacher of musar who admires Israel Salanter's willingness to affirm the morality of the Torah and reject other moral standards.⁵⁰ But while Salanter was a political quietist whose most controversial actions involved his efforts to introduce musar into Jewish education, Pruzansky has courted controversy largely through his political pronouncements. He has received particular media attention for calling for the destruction of entire Palestinian towns.⁵¹

Below, Pruzansky defends his views with reference to justice and righteousness in the biblical stories of Samson (referred to by his Hebrew name, Shimshon, in Pruzansky's text) and Saul (referred to as Shaul).

In part I, he presents Samson's sense of justice in his fight against the Philistines as a model for the sense of justice contemporary Jews should have as they help Israel combat threats posed by Palestinians. For Pruzansky, just as Samson maintained faith in the justice of his cause in his fight with the Philistines, so too Jews today should maintain a "belief in the justice of our claim to this land." Pruzansky does not speak of justice for Palestinians, who, he says, are like bees (see Judg. 14:8), "a constant source of irritation"—cruel and wicked enemies stirred up by God to send a message to Israel.

For Pruzansky, Samson's killing of enemy Philistines after they murdered his ex-wife and her father (Judg. 15:8) exemplifies "Biblical justice," the sort of justice present-day Jews should cultivate in their fight against wicked Palestinians. Biblical justice requires distinguishing one's own goodness from the cruelty and wickedness of others. Pruzansky condemns Jews who insist on seeing goodness even in Palestinian terrorists, defending and "coddling" them instead of justly punishing them.

Expanding upon this theme in part II, Pruzansky identifies the defense of the wicked as the great sin of Saul, the first king of Israel. According to a midrash (BT *Yoma* 22b), after the prophet Samuel conveyed God's clear message to proscribe the entire nation of Amalek, sparing neither human beings nor Amalekite animals (1 Sam. 15), Saul voiced concern about the moral implications of killing an entire nation, including innocent children and animals, but God admonished him: "Do not be overly righteous." As Pruzansky understands it, when Saul proceeded to kill most of Amalek, he did so reluctantly (and spared Agag and the best of the flock, planning to later complete the killing). Saul thought that God would appreciate his reluctance—but, Pruzansky emphasizes, God did *not* appreciate his reluctance. The prophet Samuel was right to condemn Saul in no uncertain terms (1 Sam. 15:26). Saul committed the grave sin of thinking that his own ethical sensibilities were more important than God's clear will.

Pruzansky blames the Haskalah, the Jewish Enlightenment movement, for encouraging modern Jews to question God's commandments and to rely on moral standards other than God's. Salanter, he says, was right to be hostile to the Haskalah. (The story Pruzansky tells regarding Salanter is apocryphal, but it does capture the spirit of Salanter's strong opposition to the Haskalah.)

For Pruzansky, God's will is clear. He would be appalled by the voices in this chapter (beginning with Kohler) who reject God's law; who are willing to "protest the ways of God" (to use Singer's language); who support criticizing Judaism (to use Schnur's framing); and who take a stand against war and violence in the name of love and justice (as Alpert does) despite God's clear support for war and violence in many situations.

Steven Pruzansky, *Judges for Our Time* and "The Tragedy of Shaul" (2009)

I. Like the Philistines of Shimshon's day, the Palestinians today are like bees. They can (and do) sting us, they are a constant source of irritation—but, ultimately they cannot defeat or even harm Israel. They cannot affect our national lives intrinsically. *That* we can only do to ourselves, if we lose faith, steadfastness, tenacity, and the belief in the justice of our claim to this land. The Philistines then—like the Palestinians today, and like all enemies throughout our history—were simply tools of God to ensure our faithfulness, guarantee that we will pursue our destiny, and secure our commitment to building a holy society based on the laws of the Torah....

[Shimshon said regarding the Philistines,] "As they did to me, so too I did to them" (Judges 15:11). This type of Biblical justice is ridiculed today as primitive and uncivilized, especially by people who live in a world in which thousands and millions of innocents can be brutally exterminated by barbarians who remain unimpeded and unrestrained because of the conscious indifference of those same people. It is a product of a worldview that cannot see good and evil, but sees in every ideology some shade of good and some redeeming value. This moral homogeneity has unleashed the depravity of man rather than contained it, whereas so-called Biblical notions of right and wrong both cultivate virtuous conduct and lead the fight against malevolence in all its forms. But the Biblical model of justice has been suppressed in an environment in which terrorist chieftains are coddled, terrorist murderers are freed from prison to murder again, and—especially—the goodness of good people has been falsely but continuously projected onto the most cruel and vile killers in existence.[52]

II. Shaul is told to "go and destroy Amalek, men, women and children, all their cattle and all their property" (I Samuel 15:3)—to leave absolutely no trace of Amalek at all. He failed.

The gemara in Yoma 22b characterizes Shaul's sin in one pithy expression from Kohelles (7:16): "Do not be overly righteous." Shaul reasoned: If for the loss of one life, the Torah says to bring an eglah arufah [the broken-necked heifer, Deut. 21:1–9] how much more so for many lives? And if man sinned, what did the animals do? And if the adults sinned, what did the children do? Why should they be killed? A heavenly echo admonished: "Don't be overly righteous."

It is a strange phrase, to say the least. We want people to be righteous. What does it mean to be "overly righteous"? What exactly did Shaul do wrong? He killed every living Amalekite, except for their king Agag, whom he planned to kill in front of all Israel. He also kept alive the best of the flock in order to allow people to bring korbanos [sacrifices]. His violation of Shmuel Hanavi's express command was undertaken with the purest motivation.

In his mind, his sin served a greater purpose, fulfilling G-d's Will, but on his own terms. Does that justify his destruction and the destruction of his dynasty, as well as Shmuel's accusation, "You have rejected the word of Hashem" (I Samuel 15:26)?

Shaul's sin is especially jarring to us today because ever since the Haskallah and its infiltration into our world, Shaul has had many kindred spirits and even advocates. Often we hear these questions, overtly or subtly: "Does G-d want us to be robots? Does He not want us to think for ourselves? We were given minds to understand the Torah and to master creation but Man's moral notions have advanced over the centuries."

In the most extensive and pernicious expression of this doctrine, there are Jews who question whether the Torah is the final word on ethics and morality, and posit that there is a greater ethic than the Torah and a higher morality than Hashem's Word. They brazenly claim that where the reigning moral notions conflict with the Torah, the Torah has to give way. They feel they must reinterpret the Torah according to the conventional morality of today (whether in dealing with non-Jews, with our enemies, with women, etc.).

Indeed, what did Shaul do but feel his ethical sensibilities were violated by the particulars of the mitzvah of mechiyas Amalek [blotting out Amalek, Deut. 25:19]? Kill an entire nation and their cattle? So he killed the nation, reluctantly, but stopped short of fulfilling Hashem's Will. For this he was "rejected by Hashem from being king over Israel" (ibid.)? But what did he do wrong? Shaul's kal vachomer [a fortiori argument] seems valid—why kill the innocent? That cannot be G-d's Will!

In the early days of the mussar movement, which sought to revitalize and institutionalize the ethical sensitivities of Jews, the maskilim [Haskallah leaders] thought they had an ally in Reb Yisroel Salanter and asked him to open a modern Rabbinical school in which they would teach mussar along with the ideals of the Haskallah. Reb Yisroel declined, explaining the difference between Haskallah and mussar: "In mussar, we judge people by the standards of the Torah; in Haskallah, you judge people by the standards of Rousseau."

What did Shaul do wrong? What is wrong with using one's mind not only to probe Hashem's wisdom but also to think for oneself? The answer is that the free, independent thinker is not essentially an eved Hashem [servant of God], but, in fact, serves himself, his own thoughts, and his own opinions. He thereby severs the chain of the mesorah [tradition] and becomes disconnected from Sinai. In a real sense, the mesorah must start again with him, and, unfortunately for him, it usually ends with him as well. Every generation then becomes responsible for creating a new Torah, and soon there is no Torah, and Hashem's Voice is drowned out amid the cacophony of Man's own clamoring.

Chazal [our sages of blessed memory] succinctly summarized Shaul's sin: "Do not be overly righteous." "Overly righteous" means substituting our morality for Hashem's, thinking that we can improve the Torah and make it more consonant with our values. When we evaluate each mitzvah and each doctrine of the Sages to see whether it withstands our moral scrutiny, then we are "too righteous" for our own good, and the Torah begins to wither and our commitment wears thin. Rav Yaakov Emden wrote that those Spanish Jews, who were of a philosophical bent, subjecting the Torah to the dictates of their reason, were the first to convert to Catholicism at the beginning of the Spanish Inquisition, whereas those Jews whose emunah [faith] came from the mesorah of their fathers and mothers willingly sacrificed their lives in sanctification of Hashem's name.

Is this anti-intellectualism? Certainly not. Understanding Torah demands a very rigorous intellectual discipline — as well as humility. "Do not be overly righteous" means that just as the Torah attempts to refine our deeds through mitzvos, the Torah also attempts to refine our thoughts through its ideas and values. We cannot just carry out empty performances, and allow our minds to roam wantonly over the barren landscape of modern moral notions. "Do not be overly righteous." If we are "too righteous" we may empty the Torah of its ability to guide and inspire and cease to be the Am Hashem [People of God].

This is Shaul's enduring lesson. Accepting the yoke of heaven means submitting our actions and our thoughts to Hashem's Will. If a particular mitzvah or Torah standard troubles us, then we have to bend ourselves even more (not less) to the Divine Will. We defer to the infinite and eternal Chochmas Hashem [Divine Will].[53]

10.9. JUSTICE AND THE PROPHETIC

In section 7.6, Marc Ellis emphasized that justice is essential to forgiveness. Here, he focuses on what he calls "the prophetic" aspects of justice: the difficulty of being just when one's people are occupying the lands of others, and ways in which Jews can be "a part of the prophetic" by struggling against empire.

In Ellis's book *The Future of the Prophetic*, the source of the selections below, he considers "the prophetic" a gift that ancient Israel gave the world—but he rejects any implication that Jews are a superior people with superior ideas. He joins Alpert in fierce opposition to "claims of difference that might . . . lead to claims of superiority."[54] Indeed, he explains, while the prophets of ancient Israel stood in solidarity with the People of Israel, they were deeply suspicious of the people's goodness. In the present day, those who carry on the prophetic tradition must continue to be suspicious and demand justice for all who are "outcast and marginal." The prophetic voice emerged in ancient Israel to advocate for justice and take a stand against those in power; with the founding of the State of Israel, as Jews have regained power, the prophetic voice has reemerged to critique how Jews use power, especially in their treatment of Palestinians who live under Jewish control in Israel/Palestine.[55]

Seeking justice is central to the prophetic. At the same time, Ellis envisions the prophetic as "probing a deeper level than justice itself." The prophetic is clearly opposed to overly superficial conceptions of justice: those that too easily calculate "needs and wants," that depend on law, that wait contentedly for the unfolding of justice, that fail to center attention on "the outcast and the marginal," or some combination of those. Ellis is suspicious of law, rational analysis, claims to impartiality, and calls for patience.

As such, whereas Kook (section 10.4) asserted that ideal justice will only unfold, under God's guidance, in the future, Ellis insists that the full realization of justice cannot be deferred: "For the prophetic . . . the time is always now." While Ellis might appreciate Kook's discussion of how politics can corrupt one's sense of justice, he would view Kook's own sense of justice as itself deeply corrupted, since Kook saw Jewish law and Zionism as deeply just and paid insufficient attention to issues of justice for Palestinians.

Additionally, though Ellis might appreciate Kohler's critique of law and his impulse to spread ideals of justice for the oppressed worldwide (section 10.3), he would view Kohler's vision of rational, impartial justice as superficial, and his confidence in Jewish prophetic wisdom as troubling.[56] For Ellis, the prophetic must not be satisfied by its own traditions; rather, "the prophet displaces the prophetic so the prophetic can regain its depth."

Ellis would strongly protest against Pruzansky (section 10.8) — his denigration of Palestinians, his sense of justice in the Jewish claim to the Land of Israel, his calls for vengeance, and his assertions of self-righteousness and the righteousness of the State of Israel. Furthermore, Ellis would be troubled by the way Pruzansky, Kohler, Kook, and others in this chapter invoke God. For Ellis, the prophet must stand in solidarity with God but also be suspicious of God. As he notes elsewhere in the book, God-language has become so linked with injustice that "contemporary Jewish prophets speak justice in fiery tones without God. In our time, falling back on God seems too easy, a crutch, somehow unreal, childlike. It would cheapen Jewish history as it unfolds." Ellis suggests, in fact, that it may be more respectful to God to refuse to name God, rather than idolatrously associating God with injustice.[57]

In the selections below, Ellis doubts that most people in the world can be just today. Certainly most Jews cannot be just, as so many Jews tolerate the unjust imperial projects of Israel or the United States (or both). Still, he affirms, Jews can "be part of the prophetic" by engaging in the ongoing pursuit of justice — a process that will never end, as one will never find purity and "there is always another step to be taken."

Interestingly, while Ellis and Israel Salanter are very far apart on most issues, Ellis's framing of the pursuit of justice has some structural similarities to Salanter's discussion (section 10.2). Salanter also regards perfect justice as generally impossible to achieve, though he thinks that those who pursue justice by continually seeking to purify their souls may be trusted to interpret the prophetic tradition. Salanter, like Ellis, advocated deep self-criticism, condemned his fellow Jews for being insufficiently self-critical, and was in turn criticized for ostensible pretensions to higher levels of righteousness than other Jews. Ellis, notably, has been criticized in similar ways: while he calls for suspicion about one's own righteousness, he has been critiqued for his ostensible pretensions to be on a "prophetic" moral level, far above ordinary Jews whom he views as complicit in injustice.[58]

Though he mentions prophetic solidarity with the People of Israel in the selections below, Ellis has tended not to emphasize solidarity with other Jews but rather with Palestinians, who as "the outcast and the marginal" need to be the focus of prophetic attention.[59] Ellis shares Susan Schnur's concerns about standing excessively by one's community or state, as well as her desire to speak truth to power and demand justice (section 10.6). Yet while he speaks of the prophet's solidarity with Israel, Ellis does not emphasize partiality and loyalty to Judaism and the State of Israel as Schnur does. Proclaiming love for and loyalty to the "empress who has no clothes," Schnur promises not to collude with the empress but also not to shame her. She will speak truth to power, but she also seeks to share power rather than condemning all exercises of power. Ellis's prophetic radicalism leaves him much less sympathetic to Jewish exercises of power, and much less appreciative of Jewish love for and loyalty to Israel.[60]

Marc Ellis, *Future of the Prophetic* (2014)

The prophetic is a profound wrestling with the complexities of creation, God, and the human. The prophetic wants justice but the prophetic probes a deeper level than justice itself. The prophetic explores the very heartbeat of the cosmic journey as we experience it on earth. Paradoxically, that heartbeat is supremely earthy. Prophetic hands are dirty. The outcast and the marginal are at the center. They are the ones who experience injustice's cycle of destruction and death. The prophetic is never a theoretical construct. . . . The prophetic views the stakes as higher than a justice of needs and wants. That is why the prophetic sometimes disturbs the prophetic itself. Especially when the prophetic is intoned too easily or is taken on a superficial plane, the prophet demurs. The prophet's suspicion—of the prophetic—is in order. The prophet displaces the prophetic so the prophetic can regain its depth....

The prophet is suspicious of Israel. The prophet is suspicious of the world. The prophet is suspicious of God. The prophet is also connected to Israel, the world, and to God. The prophet is in solidarity with Israel, the world, and God. The prophet is frequently disappointed by all three...

Mainstream Jews think they are for justice, that they remain the conscience of humanity. The betterment of humankind is their credo. Yet the permanent occupation of another people's land makes this claim suspect. Armed with empire, such [a] claim becomes an obvious hypocrisy....

Can a Jew be just? For that matter, can any person with a collective identity be just?... If we simply assume for a moment that because of Israel's oppression of Palestinians, today's Jew cannot be just, where does that leave the prophet and the prophetic? If the prophet isn't just, who is?...

To be just is to seek engagement with others on the same playing field with equal power and possibility. To be just is to engage the complicated intersection of the person and society, and the structures that impact both.

Taking this definition, Jews, at least in America and Israel, are so intertwined with empire and injustice, and benefiting from both, that the initial response has to be: "No, in today's world, a Jew cannot be just." As for the prophetic and the prophet herself in relation to being just and justice, this, too, depends on definitions. Yet, again, using a plain sense of the category, and noting that the prophet and the prophetic are never pure, the initial response has to be: "Yes, in today's world, a Jew and Jews can pursue justice. Therefore, a Jew can be a prophet and Jews can be part of the prophetic."

That is, Jews—with others—within empire can struggle against empire, even as they benefit from it. The measuring rod is whether

> the struggle is real. This is why critical thought is honed within active participation for justice. We know that justice is never fully realized. It is always partial. However, we can never be content with partial practice. There is always another step to be taken. . . . For the prophetic . . . the time is always now. The tension inherent in the prophetic timescape is intense. Justice achieved at another point in time is always too late.[61]

10.10. PURSUING *TZEDEK* IN BLESSED INTERDEPENDENCE

In section 9.11, Amanda Mbuvi described the contrast in the book of Exodus between Pharaoh's exclusive vision of community and God's vision of blessed interdependence that sees diversity as a blessing. Building on that discussion, her short essay on *tzedek*, below, concludes that the proper pursuit of *tzedek* cannot be carried out in a homogeneous group but, rather, requires intimacy with "those who do not see and hear as we do."

Many of the figures quoted in this chapter have shown great confidence in their sense of justice. Mbuvi encourages anyone who sees their understanding of justice as "obvious" to look for their own blind spots and the ways in which their understanding is not obvious. She points to sensory tests that demonstrate individual differences in sensory perceptions: one person hears a sound as "yanny" while another hears the same sound as "laurel"; one person sees a dress as white and gold while another sees it as blue and black.[62] The sensory process "prioritizes some features and filters out others, a process that varies from person to person, with those prioritizing different features arriving at a different assessment of what has been seen or heard." Mbuvi suggests an analogy with moral judgments: shaped by different cultures, circumstances, and experiences, one person may see a clear injustice where another person may not. We are especially likely to have blind spots when we perceive injustices that do not affect us directly. Our judgment can be improved when we come to recognize our blind spots and challenge our "sense of the obvious."

Mbuvi here has much in common with Israel Salanter (section 10.2). Both thinkers are committed to pursuing justice by examining one's inner life and one's own sense of *tzedek*. Both agree that human judgment is subjective and often biased, but that individuals can direct their pursuits accordingly and use their sense perception to make proper judgments "based on what one's eyes see," as Salanter puts it. Mbuvi also joins Salanter in appreciating the pursuit of justice through the proper direction of what Salanter would call the "soul-forces," although, unlike Salanter, she does not idealize judgment that is free from the taint of soul-forces.

Moreover, rather than deferring to great legal decisors and "faith in the sages" who will properly defend "the standards of the Torah," Mbuvi seeks to listen to diverse perspectives both from within and beyond the Jewish people. Jewish efforts to pursue justice should be informed by intimacy with diverse perspectives—from diverse Jews, non-Jews, and perhaps nonhuman beings (as we are linked "to all creation"). Such engagement is not contrary to the Torah but rather serves to enrich the Torah. After all, the Torah itself offers a vision of "blessed interdependence" between diverse communities.

For Mbuvi, God's voice is not "drowned out amid the cacophony of Man's own clamoring," as Pruzansky puts it. Rather, it is strengthened through listening carefully to what might seem like a cacophony but that offers diverse forms of wisdom. Jews have no monopoly on the path to *tzedek*; they are not, as Abraham Isaac Kook imagined, "entirely free of all of the disjointedness and the contradictions which prevail among all other peoples." Rather, all of us, whether Jewish or not, are subject to disjointedness and contradictions. Improving our ability to perceive justice through the contradictions "requires intimacy—being close enough to those who do not see and hear as we do."

Amanda Mbuvi, "Perception and the Pursuit of *Tzedek*" (2022)

Pursuing *tzedek* depends heavily on interpretation—of the traditions through which conceptions of *tzedek* are mediated, and of the circumstances in which they are lived out. The recent proliferation

351

of viral sensory tests like the white/gold or blue/black dress and the yanny/laurel recording reminds us that acts of interpretation are not as clear cut as they may appear. Others may encounter the same thing and come away with a different "obvious" interpretation. Discovering these conflicting interpretations results in recognition of multiple valences where only one had been apparent before. These multiple valences lead to an important insight: the sensory process prioritizes some features and filters out others, a process that varies from person to person, with those prioritizing different features arriving at a different assessment of what has been seen or heard. In a similar way, culture and life experience prompt people to notice or overlook different features of a text or aspects of a situation. Only in a diverse community of interpreters does greater understanding emerge as we become aware of what we habitually filter out and its significance.

Exodus depicts the pursuit of *tzedek* as intimately linked to seeing—as when Yoheved saw that Moses was good (Exod. 2:2), an echo of God's response to creation (Gen. 1:4, 10, 12, 18, 25) that precipitated her decision to defy Pharaoh. Exodus also links *tzedek* to hearing, as when Pharaoh's daughter adopts baby Moses after seeing the basket in the reeds and hearing his cry (Exod. 2:5–6), a rescue echoed when God hears the people of Israel crying out from their slavery; remembers the covenant with Abraham, Isaac, and Jacob; sees the people; and effects their deliverance (Exod. 2:24–25). Likewise, Moses receives his prophetic commission after he responds to the sight of the burning bush and the voice of God (Exod. 3:2–4). Covenant plays an important role, but seeing and hearing are what create agents of *tzedek*, and not just among the people of Israel.

Seeing and hearing sound like simple acts, but culture and circumstances conspire to create blind spots that train us not to see and hear injustice, especially when we are not its victim. As a result, pursuing *tzedek* cannot properly take place in isolation. It requires intimacy—being close enough to those who do not see and hear as we do—to have our sense of the obvious challenged. Being part of a homogenous group is not enough. To know what *tzedek* is and how to live it out, we need to embrace the historical, cultural, and social diversity of the Jewish people, and we need to embrace the Torah's vision of blessed interdependence that embeds us in the network of nurture linking all people to one another and to all creation.[63]

CONCLUSION

Modern Jewish thinkers have deeply disagreed on what it means to be just, righteous, or characterized by *tzedek.*

Some Jewish thinkers have stressed that being just requires impartiality—and other thinkers, partiality.

Some thinkers have prioritized justice over love; others have stressed the interconnectedness of justice and love.

Some thinkers have affirmed that being righteous or just requires obedience to Jewish law; others have challenged the justice and righteousness of particular laws or the importance of law altogether.

Some thinkers have seen the highest levels of righteousness in the giving of charity; others have seen the highest levels of righteousness in efforts to challenge structural injustices.

Some thinkers have seen justice as demanding war and violence; others have seen justice as requiring opposition to war and violence.

Some thinkers have emphasized justice toward Jews; others have emphasized justice toward all human beings; others have emphasized justice toward nonhuman animals.

Some thinkers have emphasized justice toward women; others have seen male righteousness as requiring the exclusion of women.

Some thinkers have seen justice and righteousness as masculine; others have rejected gendering these qualities.

Some thinkers have argued that human beings, or at least certain human beings, can perceive and emulate a divine ideal of justice; others have stressed the difficulty of perceiving divine justice.

Some thinkers have seen justice as demanding obedience to God, even when God's demands may seem unjust; others have argued that the person of justice must disobey God's unjust demands.

Some thinkers have viewed justice as requiring one's obedience to certain Jewish sages, while others have seen justice as requiring one to listen to a broad diversity of voices, whether Jewish or not.

In these and in many other ways, there have been many different conceptions of *tzedek* among modern Jewish thinkers. Individual thinkers may claim that there is a distinctly "Jewish sense of justice" or "Jewish view of righteousness," but listening to the diversity of voices within this chapter makes it clear that Jewish thinkers have not agreed on these matters. Modern Jewish discourse on *tzedek*, as with the other virtues in this volume, has been complex, multivocal, dynamic, and highly contested.

Conclusion

Too often, claims about Jewish ethics depend on inaccurate assertions about the history of Jewish thought. As we have seen in this volume, Jewish thinkers sometimes describe the approach of Jewish ethics to a given virtue as that which agrees with their own perspective, and they describe views with which they strongly disagree as outside of the Jewish tradition. For example, some Jewish thinkers maintain that authentic Jewish tradition values the equal dignity of all human beings and develop notions of humility or justice bolstered by this assertion, whereas other Jewish thinkers maintain that the authentic Jewish tradition recognizes the superiority of certain male Jews over other human beings, bolstering the authority of their own views with reference to this claim. But in truth there has been no consensus among Jewish thinkers about human equality, or any other principle. Nor has there been any consensus on how to best understand humility, justice, or any other virtue. Nor, of course, has there been any consensus among Jews about which Jewish thinkers have the authority to define Jewish ethics in general or the insight to understand any particular virtue. In my view, teachers of Jewish ethics would have stronger arguments if their arguments did not rest on dubious assertions about the consensus of tradition.

The claim that Jewish tradition values the equal dignity of all human beings may be especially tempting for those who want to ensure that Jewish tradition is perceived positively by contemporary readers.

Considering musar texts that value Jews above non-Jews may be particularly fraught when presenting Jewish ethics to non-Jewish audiences. Given the history of antisemitic misrepresentations of Judaism, many teachers of musar have had good reasons to seek to present Judaism as consistently "working through the centuries to realize the ideal of justice to all mankind," to use Kaufmann Kohler's phrase (section 10.3). It may seem inappropriate to teach, for example, the view of Abraham Isaac Kook that Jews are "of a much higher and greater spiritual order" than other nations (section 10.4) or the view of Shneur Zalman of Liadi that non-Jewish souls come from "impure shells, which have no goodness in them whatsoever" (section 8.2) as part of the history of musar. Won't such texts induce non-Jews, and many Jews as well, to think negatively of musar and of Jewish traditions as a whole?

Bringing positive changes to any sort of community, however, requires honesty about that community and the diverse ways its traditions have been constructed. Failing to acknowledge contested histories makes it more difficult to learn from the past. Claims that Judaism simply supports solidarity with all human beings, for example, may encourage contemporary Jews to ignore failures of Jewish solidarity because they are viewed as impossible to associate with Judaism. When we regard certain approaches to ethics as beyond the boundaries of what is possible in our traditions, we may fail to see the possibility that those approaches persist within our traditions, our own communities, and even within ourselves. Moreover, when we choose not to reflect on the perspectives of those who disagree with us, we weaken our own ability to respond to them.

By contrast, I hope that the critical study of the history of Jewish ethics encouraged by this volume can help us to more clearly see the diversity of Jewish approaches and to be more thoughtful about how to respond to others.

Such study of this deeply contested ethical tradition can help us to challenge Jews who claim authority for their views by asserting that Jewish tradition agrees with them.

Such study can focus our attention on problems that partisans might prefer to brush aside, including the ethnocentrism, xenophobia, racism, sexism, and homophobia that can be found within Jewish traditions, as seen throughout this volume.

Such study may help us to deepen our own senses of justice, solidarity, compassion, and other virtues, by challenging us to respond thoughtfully to those who disagree with us.

Such study may even teach us to see troubling ethical impulses within ourselves, as we seek to understand those with whom we disagree and recognize how we may share some of their troubling tendencies.

More generally, the critical study of musar can help us to realize that we have commonalties of perspective, at least to some extent, with people very different from us. By the same token, we may see flaws in the perspectives of those who think more like us. And our study may help us to see the merits of multiple contradictory ways of approaching the same issue.

And, most clearly, such study can help us to understand the diversity of musar traditions that have developed in the past and that continue to shape individuals and communities in our time.

List of Source Texts

Source Acknowledgments

CHAPTER 1

1.1: Menaḥem Mendel Lefin, *Ḥeshbon ha-Nefesh* (Vilna, 1844), 71–73. Translation by Geoffrey Claussen.

1.2: Shlomo ha-Kohen Rabinovich, *Sefer Nifla'ot ha-Tiferet Shlomo*, ed. Avraham Shmu'el Tzevi Hirsch Silberstein (Piotrków, 1923), 23. Translation by Geoffrey Claussen.

1.3: Samuel Holdheim, *Das Religiöse und Politische im Judenthum* (Schwerin, Germany: C. Kürschner, 1845), iv–v, viii. Translation by William Templer. Published by permission of William Templer.

1.4: Elijah Eliezer Dessler, *Strive for Truth*, trans. Aryeh Carmell, vol. 1 (Jerusalem; New York: Feldheim, 1978), 267–71.

1.5: Meir Kahane, *Beyond Words: Selected Writings of Rabbi Meir Kahane, 1960-1990*, ed. David Fein, vol. 4 (1981–85) (Jerusalem: Institute for Publication of the Writings of Rabbi Meir Kahane, 2010), 564–65, 567.

1.6: Judith Plaskow, "Preaching against the Text," in *The Coming of Lilith: Essays on Feminism, Judaism, and Sexual Ethics, 1972-2003*, ed. Donna Berman and Judith Plaskow (Boston: Beacon, 2005), 152–56.

1.7: Daniel Lapin, *America's Real War* (Sisters OR: Multnomah, 1999), 71–72.

1.8: Abigail Treu, "Our Lying Patriarch," Jewish Theological Seminary of America, October 12, 2009, http://www.jtsa.edu/our-lying-patriarch. Reprinted by permission of the Jewish Theological Seminary of America.

1.9: Shmuly Yanklowitz, "Holy Lies? Review of *Changing the Immutable* by Professor Marc B. Shapiro," *Jewish Journal*, June 1, 2015, http://www.jewishjournal.com/socialjusticerav/item/holy_lies_review

_of_changing_the_immutable_by_professor_marc_b._shapiro.
Reprinted by permission of the *Jewish Journal*.

1.10: Emily Filler, "The Honesty of Radical Pessimism." Published by
permission of Emily Filler.

CHAPTER 2

2.1: Baruch Lindau, "Toledot ha-Minim ha-Tiviyim," *Ha-Me'asef* 4 (1788):
211, 212, 218. Translation by Geoffrey Claussen.

2.2: Naḥman of Bratslav, *Sefer Likkutei Moharan*, vol. 1 (Jerusalem, 1975),
5b, 21b–22a, 101b. Translation by Geoffrey Claussen.

2.3: Benjamin C. Gruenberg, *Science and the Public Mind* (New York:
McGraw-Hill, 1935), 5–6, 24–25, 28–29.

2.4: Elijah Eliezer Dessler, *Mikhtav me-Eliyahu*, ed. Aryeh Carmell and
Alter Halpern (London, 1955), 2:142–43, 149; 3:177–79. Translation by
Geoffrey Claussen.

2.5: Joseph Dov Soloveitchik, *Halakhic Man*, trans. Lawrence Kaplan
(Philadelphia: The Jewish Publication Society of America, 1983), 5, 17, 20.

2.6: Abraham Joshua Heschel, *Man Is Not Alone: A Philosophy of Religion*
(New York: Farrar, Straus & Young, 1951), 72–73, 76.

2.7: Danya Ruttenberg, "The Hermeneutics of Curiosity: On Reclamation," in *New Jewish Feminism: Probing the Past, Forging the Future*, ed.
Elyse Goldstein (Woodstock VT: Jewish Lights, 2009), 59–60, 61, 62, 65.

2.8: Jamie Arnold, "The Snake, the Skylight, and the Seeker:
ReCreating Self with Courageous Curiosity," September 4,
2013, http://tikkunmiddotproject.wikispaces.com/file/detail
/erev rosh hashanah sermon on Curiosity 5774.docx. Reprinted by
permission of Jamie Arnold.

2.9: Amy Eilberg, *From Enemy to Friend: Jewish Wisdom and the Pursuit
of Peace* (Maryknoll NY: Orbis Books, 2014), 250–52. Reprinted by
permission of Orbis Books.

2.10: Sandra Lawson, "Curiosity Can Be Invasive and Hurtful." Published
by permission of Sandra Lawson.

CHAPTER 3

3.1: Pinḥas of Polotsk, *Keter Torah* (Jerusalem: Ya'akov Klein, 1896), 20b,
21b–22a. Translation by Geoffrey Claussen.

3.2: Naḥman of Bratslav, *Sefer ha-Middot* (Lubavitch, 1821), 16a–17a. Translation by Geoffrey Claussen, adapted in part from Naḥman of Bratslav, *Sefer Hamidot: The Book of Traits* (ebay hanachal, 2014).

3.3: Aharon Shmuel Tamaret, *Sefer Kenesset Yisrael u-Milḥamot ha-Goyim* (Warsaw, 1920), 16–17, 21, 63–64. Translation by Geoffrey Claussen.

3.4: Mordecai M. Kaplan, *The Future of the American Jew* (New York: Macmillan, 1948), 211, 216, 219.

3.5: Shalom Noah Berezovsky, *Sefer Netivot Shalom*, vol. 1 (Jerusalem: Yeshivat Beit Avraham Slonim, 1982), 1:19–20, 25–26, 88–89, 126. Translation by Geoffrey Claussen.

3.6: Meir Kahane, *The Jewish Idea*, trans. Raphael Blumberg, vol. 1 (Jerusalem: Institute for Publication of the Writings of Rabbi Meir Kahane, 1996), 46–47, 53–54, 55, 57, 273–75, 525–27, 530.

3.7: From *Like Bread on the Seder Plate: Jewish Lesbians and the Transformation of Tradition*, by Rebecca T. Alpert. Copyright © 1997 Columbia University Press. Reprinted with permission of Columbia University Press.

3.8: Jeremy Benstein, *The Way into Judaism and the Environment* (Woodstock VT: Jewish Lights, 2006), 23–24, 106–7.

3.9: Ira F. Stone, "Anavah (Humility)," *Mussar Leadership E-Newsletter* 5, no. 10 (August 4, 2013), Mussar Leadership, Temple Beth Zion–Beth Israel, Philadelphia. Reprinted by permission of Ira F. Stone.

3:10: Ruth Abusch-Magder, "Should a Woman Be Humble?," My Jewish Learning, March 6, 2017, http://www.myjewishlearning.com/rabbis -without-borders/should-a-woman-be-humble. Permission granted by JTA and My Jewish Learning (MJL). May not be reproduced without MJL's permission. More information about MJL is available on its website at https://www.myjewishlearning.com.

CHAPTER 4

4.1: Todd Samuel Presner, *Muscular Judaism: The Jewish Body and the Politics of Regeneration* (London: Routledge, 2007), 194–95.

4.2: Hermann Cohen, *Religion of Reason out of the Sources of Judaism*, trans. Simon Kaplan (Atlanta: Scholars Press, 1995), 436–40. Copyright © 1995, The American Academy of Religion. Reproduced with permission of Oxford Publishing Limited through PLS clear.

4.3: Mikhah Yosef Berdichevsky, *Ba-Derekh*, vol. 2 (Leipzig: Stybel, 1922), 58–59, 61–62, 72. Translation by Geoffrey Claussen.

4.4.I–II: Abraham Isaac Kook, *Orot* (Jerusalem: Degel Yerushalayim, 1920), 5–6, 7, 11. Translation by Geoffrey Claussen.

4.4.III: Abraham Isaac Kook, *Orot* (Jerusalem: Mossad Ha-Rav Kook, 2005), 122–23. Translation by Geoffrey Claussen.

4.4.IV: Abraham Isaac Kook, *Abraham Isaac Kook: The Lights of Penitence, the Moral Principles, Lights of Holiness, Essays, Letters, and Poems*, trans. Ben Zion Bokser (New York: Paulist Press, 1978), 179.

4.4.V: Abraham Isaac Kook, *Ma'amarei ha-Re'ayah*, vol. 1 (Jerusalem, 1988), 190, 193. Translation by Geoffrey Claussen.

4.5: Yeshaya Asher Zelig Margaliot, *Ashrei ha-Ish* (Jerusalem: Breslov, 1921), 61–65. Translation by Geoffrey Claussen.

4.6: Tzevi Yehudah Kook, *Siḥot ha-Rav Tzevi Yehudah*, ed. Shlomo Aviner, vol. 1 (Jerusalem, 1993), 245–46. Translation by Geoffrey Claussen.

4.7: Yoel Schwartz and Yitzchak Goldstein, *Ha-Shoah: Leket Devarim be-Nose Ḥurban Yahadut Eiropah 5700–5705 mitokh Aspaklaryah shel Torah* (Jerusalem: Ha-Mosad le-Iddud Limmud ha-Torah, 1988), 183–84, 192–93. Translation by Geoffrey Claussen.

4.8: Sherwin T. Wine, *Staying Sane in a Crazy World: A Guide to Rational Living* (Birmingham MI: Center for New Thinking, 1995), 152, 265–66. Reprinted by permission of the International Institute for Secular Humanistic Judaism.

4.9: Edward Feinstein, *The Chutzpah Imperative: Empowering Today's Jews for a Life That Matters* (Woodstock VT: Jewish Lights, 2014), xix–xx, 20–21, 56, 61, 77–78, 152.

4.10.I: Amy Eilberg, *From Enemy to Friend: Jewish Wisdom and the Pursuit of Peace* (Maryknoll NY: Orbis Books, 2014), 260–62. Reprinted by permission of Orbis Books.

4.10.II: Amy Eilberg, "On True Strength." Published by permission of Amy Eilberg.

4.11: Stosh Cotler, "Are Jews Avoiding Anti-Trump Activism out of Fear, or Moral Failure?" *Haaretz*, November 22, 2017, https://www.haaretz.com/opinion/.premium-1.824297. Reprinted by permission of Stosh Cotler.

CHAPTER 5

5.1: Shneur Zalman of Liadi, *Likkutei Amarim [Tanya]* (Shklow, 1806), 13b–14a, 35b–36a, 37b, 40b, 63b, 65b. Translation by Geoffrey Claussen.

5.2: Ḥayyim of Volozhin, *Ruaḥ ha-Ḥayyim: Peirush Rabbi Ḥayyim mi-Volozhin le-Pirkei Avot* (Vilna, 1859), 77. Translation of first two paragraphs by Geoffrey Claussen; translation of final paragraph from Allan Nadler, *The Faith of the Mithnagdim: Rabbinic Responses to Hasidic Rapture* (Baltimore: Johns Hopkins University Press, 1997), 87.

5.3: Menaḥem Mendel Lefin, *Ḥeshbon ha-Nefesh* (Vilna, 1844), 3–4, 7–8, 13, 39–40, 62–64, 74, 76. Translation by Geoffrey Claussen.

5.4: Benjamin Brown, "Kedushah: The Sexual Abstinence of Married Men in Gur, Slonim, and Toledot Aharon," *Jewish History* 27, nos. 2–4 (2013): 492–94.

5.5: Judith Plaskow, "Towards a New Theology of Sexuality," in *Twice Blessed: On Being Lesbian, Gay, and Jewish*, ed. Christie Balka and Andy Rose (Boston: Beacon, 1989), 141–44, 147–48. Reprinted by permission of Christie Balka.

5.6.I: Sherwin T. Wine, *Staying Sane in a Crazy World: A Guide to Rational Living* (Birmingham MI: Center for New Thinking, 1995), 206–9, 214. Reprinted by permission of the International Institute for Secular Humanistic Judaism.

5.6.II: Sherwin Wine, "Our Dietary Laws," *Humanistic Judaism* 41, nos. 3–4 (2013): 22–23. Reprinted by permission of the Society for Humanistic Judaism.

5.7: Eugene B. Borowitz and Frances Weinman Schwartz, *The Jewish Moral Virtues* (Philadelphia: The Jewish Publication Society, 1999), 161, 163, 165–67. Reprinted by permission of The Jewish Publication Society.

5.8: "Wonder and Restraint: A Rabbinical Call to Environmental Action," Coalition on the Environment and Jewish Life (COEJL), http://www.coejl.org/news/20060112_rabletter.php. Reprinted by permission of COEJL.

5.9: Jay Michaelson, "Into Life: The Humanism of the Exodus: Parashat Beshalach (Exodus 13:17–17:16)," in *Torah Queeries: Weekly Commentaries on the Hebrew Bible*, ed. Gregg Drinkwater, Joshua Lesser, and David Shneer (New York: New York University Press, 2009), 90–91. Reprinted by permission of New York University Press.

5.10: Sheila Peltz Weinberg, "Leaving Egypt Again: Aging with Awareness," in *Chapters of the Heart: Jewish Women Sharing the Torah of Our Lives*, ed. Sue Levi Elwell and Nancy Fuchs Kreimer (Eugene OR:

Cascade Books, 2013), 157, 162–63. Used by permission of Wipf and Stock Publishers, www.wipfandstock.com.

CHAPTER 6

6.1: Samuel M. Isaacs, "Thanksgiving Sermon," *The Jewish Messenger*, December 3, 1858, 122.

6.2: Simon Rabinovitch, ed., *Jews and Diaspora Nationalism: Writings on Jewish Peoplehood in Europe and the United States* (Waltham MA: Brandeis University Press, 2012), 40–41, 42–43.

6.3: Emma Goldman, *My Disillusionment in Russia* (Garden City NY: Doubleday, Page, 1923), xiii—xiv.

6.4: Natan Tzevi Finkel, *Siḥot ha-Sabba mi-Slabodka*, ed. Yekutiel Cohen, vol. 2 (Jerusalem, 2009), 543–45. Translation by Geoffrey Claussen.

6.5: Harold S. Kushner, *When Bad Things Happen to Good People*, Twentieth Anniversary Edition (New York: Schocken Books, 2001), 34–35, 38–39, 180, 186–87.

6.6: Mitchell Silver, *A Plausible God: Secular Reflections on Liberal Jewish Theology* (New York: Fordham University Press, 2006), 72–75. Republished with permission of Fordham University Press; permission conveyed through Copyright Clearance Center, Inc.

6.7: Alan Morinis, *Everyday Holiness: The Jewish Spiritual Path of Mussar* (Boston: Trumpeter, 2007), 68–69, 71.

6.8: Shalom Arush, *The Garden of Gratitude*, trans. Lazer Brody (Jerusalem: Chut Shel Chessed Institutions, 2011), 112, 217–19, 321–22.

6.9.I: Berel Wein, "Saying Thank You," RabbiWein.com: The Voice of Jewish History, https://www.rabbiwein.com/blog/saying-thank-you -511.html.

6.9.II: Berel Wein, "Gratitude," RabbiWein.com: The Voice of Jewish History, https://www.rabbiwein.com/blog/post-2090.html.

6.9.III: Berel Wein, "Gratitude," RabbiWein.com: The Voice of Jewish History, http://www.rabbiwein.com/blog/gratitude-167.html.

6.10: Amos Oz, *The Slopes of Lebanon*, trans. Maurie Goldberg-Bartura (Boston: Mariner Books, 2012), 212–13, 217–18.

6.11: Lisa Goldstein, "Giving Thanks. Telling the Truth," Institute for Jewish Spirituality, November 23, 2016, http://www.jewishspirituality .org/november-2016-gratitude-e-letter. Reprinted by permission of the Institute for Jewish Spirituality.

CHAPTER 7

7.1: Eliezer Papo, *Pele Yo'etz*, vol. 1 (Vienna: Joseph Schlesinger, 1876), 7–8. Translation by Geoffrey Claussen.

7.2: Tsevi Elimelekh Shapira, *Benei Yisakhar*, vol. 2 (Jerusalem: S. A. Sifrei Kodesh, 2005), 58, 107. Translation by Geoffrey Claussen.

7.3: Hannah Arendt, *The Human Condition* (Chicago: University of Chicago Press, 1958), 237–38, 240–41. Republished with permission of University of Chicago Press; permission conveyed through Copyright Clearance Center, Inc.

7.4: Emmanuel Levinas, *Nine Talmudic Readings*, trans. Annette Aronowicz (Bloomington: Indiana University Press, 1990), 13, 19, 24–25, 28–29. Reprinted by permission of Michaël Levinas.

7.5: Excerpt(s) from THE SUNFLOWER: ON THE POSSIBILITIES AND LIMITS OF FORGIVENESS by Simon Wiesenthal, copyright © 1969, 1970 by Opera Mundi Paris, renewed © 1997 by Simon Wiesenthal. Symposium copyright © 1976, 1997, 1998 by Penguin Random House LLC. Used by permission of Schocken Books, an imprint of the Knopf Doubleday Publishing Group, a division of Penguin Random House LLC. All rights reserved.

7.6: Marc H. Ellis, *O, Jerusalem! The Contested Future of the Jewish Covenant* (Minneapolis: Fortress, 1999), 142–44. Reprinted by permission of 1517 Media.

7.7: Jacques Derrida, *On Cosmopolitanism and Forgiveness*, trans. Michael Hughes and Mark Dooley (London: Routledge, 2001), 31–32, 37, 38–39, 45, 58–59.

7.8: Susan Schnur, "Beyond Forgiveness," *Lilith Magazine* 25, no. 3 (Fall 2001), http://lilith.org/articles/beyond-forgiveness, 19, 45. Reprinted with permission from Lilith magazine—independent, Jewish & frankly feminist. Subscriptions and more at www.Lilith.org.

7.9: Karyn D. Kedar, *Bridge to Forgiveness: Stories and Prayers for Finding God and Restoring Wholeness* (Woodstock VT: Jewish Lights, 2007), 3, 20, 34.

7.10: Shalom Arush, *Women's Wisdom: The Garden of Peace for Women Only*, trans. Lazer Brody (Jerusalem: Chut Shel Chessed Institutions, 2010), 161–62.

CHAPTER 8

8.1: Moses Mendelssohn, ed., *Sefer Netivot ha-Shalom*, vol. 3 (Vilna, 1851), 347–48. Translation by Geoffrey Claussen.

8.2: Shneur Zalman of Liadi, *Likkutei Amarim [Tanya]* (Shklow, 1806), 3b–4a, 43a–44a. Translation by Geoffrey Claussen.

8.3.I: *Kitvei ha-Sabba mi-Kelm: Inyanei Elul ve-Yamim Nora'im* (Benei Berak: Siftei Ḥakhamim, Va'ad le-Hafatzat Torah u-Musar, 1997), 147–48. Translation by Geoffrey Claussen.

8.3.II–III: Simḥah Zissel Ziv, *Sefer Ḥokhmah u-Musar*, vol. 2 (Jerusalem, 1964), 7, 193–95. Translation by Geoffrey Claussen.

8.3.IV: Simḥah Zissel Ziv, *Sefer Ḥokhmah u-Musar*, vol. 1 (New York, 1957), 174. Translation by Geoffrey Claussen.

8.4.I: Hannah Arendt, *On Revolution* (New York: Penguin Books, 2006), 75–77.

8.4.II: Excerpt(s) from THE JEWISH WRITINGS by Hannah Arendt, edited by Jerome Kohn and Ron H. Feldman, copyright © 2007 by The Literary Trust of Hannah Arendt and Jerome Kohn. Used by permission of Schocken Books, an imprint of the Knopf Doubleday Publishing Group, a division of Penguin Random House LLC. All rights reserved.

8.5: Emmanuel Levinas, *Of God Who Comes to Mind*, trans. Bettina Bergo, 2nd ed. (Stanford CA: Stanford University Press, 1998), 90–91.

8.6: Yitzchak Ginsburgh, *Rectifying the State of Israel: A Political Platform Based on Kabbalah*, 2nd ed. (Jerusalem: Gal Einai, 2003), 75–78.

8.7: Einat Ramon, "The Matriarchs and the Torah of Hesed (Loving-Kindness)," *Nashim: A Journal of Jewish Women's Studies & Gender Issues* 10 (2006): 168, 171–73. Reprinted with permission of Indiana University Press.

8.8: Lynn Gottlieb, *Trail Guide to the Torah of Nonviolence* (Paris: Éditions Terre d'Espérance, 2013), 94–96, 128–30, 152. Reprinted by permission of Éditions Terre d'Espérance.

8.9: Shmuly Yanklowitz, "Mussar & Loving Animals!," The Times of Israel, March 13, 2018, http://blogs.timesofisrael.com/mussar-loving-animals. Reprinted by permission of Shmuly Yanklowitz.

CHAPTER 9

9.1: Murād Farag, "The War for Our Nation," trans. Fuad Saleh in *Modern Middle Eastern Jewish Thought: Writings on Identity, Politics, and Culture, 1893–1958*, ed. Moshe Behar and Zvi Ben-Dor Benite (Waltham MA: Brandeis University Press, 2013), 49–51.

9.2: Emma Goldman, *Anarchism and Other Essays* (New York: Mother Earth, 1910), 148, 150.

9.3: Yisroel Friedman, *Ginzei Yisrael*, vol. 2 (Jerusalem: Ezras Yisroel, 1986), 90. Translation by Geoffrey Claussen.

9.4: Natan Tzevi Finkel, *Or ha-Tzafun*, vol. 2 (Jerusalem: Yeshivat Hevron, 1959), 73–74. Translation by Geoffrey Claussen.

9.5: Steven T. Katz, Shlomo Biderman, and Gershon Greenberg, eds., *Wrestling with God: Jewish Theological Responses during and after the Holocaust* (Oxford: Oxford University Press, 2007), 174–75.

9.6: Excerpt(s) from THE JEWISH WRITINGS by Hannah Arendt, edited by Jerome Kohn and Ron H. Feldman, copyright © 2007 by The Literary Trust of Hannah Arendt and Jerome Kohn. Used by permission of Schocken Books, an imprint of the Knopf Doubleday Publishing Group, a division of Penguin Random House LLC. All rights reserved.

9.7: David Ben-Gurion, *Ḥazon ve-Derekh*, 2nd ed., vol. 3 (Tel Aviv: Mapai, 1953), 261–63. Translation by Geoffrey Claussen.

9.8: Abraham Joshua Heschel, "The Moral Outrage of Vietnam," in *Vietnam: Crisis of Conscience*, ed. Michael Novak, Robert McAfee Brown, and Abraham Joshua Heschel (New York: Association Press, Behrman House, Herder & Herder, 1967), 48–50, 52–53, 55.

9.9: Emmanuel Levinas, *The Levinas Reader*, ed. Seán Hand (Oxford: Basil Blackwell, 1989), 224–26.

9.10: David Jaffe, "Is Putting One's Life on the Line to Stand Up to Oppression a Jewish Value?" Original version published January 15, 2018, https://jewschool.com/2018/01/80805/mlk-day -torahfortheresistance-putting-ones-life-line-stand-oppression -jewish-value. Revised version published by permission of David Jaffe.

9.11: Amanda Mbuvi, "Choosing Solidarity." Published by permission of Amanda Mbuvi.

CHAPTER 10

10.1: Elimelekh Weissblum, *Sefer No'am Elimelekh* (Lemberg: A. N. Süss, 1865), 22a, 33b, 59a. Translation by Geoffrey Claussen.

10.2: Israel Salanter, "Or Yisra'el," in *Or Yisra'el*, ed. Isaac Blazer (Vilna, 1900), 87–89. Translation by Geoffrey Claussen.

10.3.I: Kaufmann Kohler, *Hebrew Union College and Other Addresses* (Cincinnati: Ark, 1916), 169–72.

10.3.II–III: Kaufmann Kohler, *Jewish Theology: Systematically and Historically Considered* (New York: Macmillan, 1918), 120–22, 485–86.

10.4.I: Arthur Hertzberg, *The Zionist Idea: A Historical Analysis and Reader* (Philadelphia: The Jewish Publication Society, 1997), 427, 429.

10.4.II: Abraham Isaac Kook, *Ma'amarei ha-Re'ayah*, vol. 1 (Jerusalem, 1988), 174. Translation by Geoffrey Claussen.

10.4.III: Abraham Isaac Kook, "Afikim ba-Negev," *Ha-Peles* 3 (1903): 656, 658–60, 717–18. Translation by Geoffrey Claussen.

10.5.I: Isaac Bashevis Singer, "Foreword," in *Vegetarianism: A Way of Life*, by Dudley Giehl (New York: Barnes & Noble, 1979), vii–ix.

10.5.II: Isaac Bashevis Singer, "Preface," in *Food for the Spirit: Vegetarianism and the World Religions*, by Steven Rosen (New York: Bala Books, 1987), i.

10.6: Susan Schnur, "Justice," in *Lifecycles: Jewish Women on Biblical Themes in Contemporary Life*, ed. Debra Orenstein and Jane Rachel Litman (Woodstock VT: Jewish Lights, 1997), 331–33.

10.7: From *Like Bread on the Seder Plate: Jewish Lesbians and the Transformation of Tradition*, by Rebecca T. Alpert. Copyright © 1997 Columbia University Press. Reprinted with permission of Columbia University Press.

10.8.I: Steven Pruzansky, *Judges for Our Time: Contemporary Lessons from the Book of Shoftim* (Jerusalem: Gefen, 2009), 124–25, 129–30.

10.8.II: Steven Pruzansky, "The Tragedy of Shaul," Rabbi Pruzansky's Blog, March 6, 2009, https://rabbipruzansky.com/2009/03/06/the-tragedy-of-shaul. Reprinted by permission of Steven Pruzansky.

10.9: Marc H. Ellis, *Future of the Prophetic: Israel's Ancient Wisdom Re-Presented* (Minneapolis: Fortress, 2014), 116–18, 343, 361, 366. Reprinted by permission of 1517 Media.

10.10: Amanda Mbuvi, "Perception and the Pursuit of *Tzedek*." Published by permission of Amanda Mbuvi.

Notes

INTRODUCTION

1. For an example of a contemporary Jewish writer speaking of "the Jewish view of forgiveness," see Telushkin, *A Code of Jewish Ethics*, 1:204. For a discussion of "what is really meant by compassion in the uniquely Jewish view," see Morinis, *Everyday Holiness*, 76. On "the Jewish sense of justice," see Elkins and Treu, *Bible's Top Fifty Ideas*, 262; Schwarz, *Judaism and Justice*, 41. For responses to claims such as these, see Dorff and Crane, *Oxford Handbook*, 3, 305; Newman, "Woodchoppers and Respirators," 35–37.
2. See Dan, "Ethical Literature," 525; Tishby and Dan, *Mivhar*, 12.
3. Dan, "Ethical Literature," 525–26; Tishby and Dan, *Mivhar*, 12–13.
4. See Etkes, *Rabbi Israel Salanter*, 260–68; Dan, *Sifrut ha-Musar*, 271.
5. On using this volume in a classroom setting, see Claussen, "Teaching Modern Jewish Ethics," 74–93. On the phenomenon of "musar groups," see Claussen, "American Jewish Revival," 63, 65; Claussen, "Practice of Musar," 14.
6. Dan, *Sifrut ha-Musar*, 265.

1. HONESTY AND LOVE OF TRUTH

1. Maimonides, *Mishneh Torah*, Hilkhot Sanhedrin, 2:7.
2. *Bereshit Rabbah* 65:18, 67:4.
3. The suggestions here follow the standard interpretation in the commentary of Rashi (Rabbi Shlomo Itzhaki, eleventh-century France) ad loc.
4. See Shapiro, *Changing the Immutable*, 282n208.

5. Sinkoff, *Out of the Shtetl*, 134–61.

6. See especially Sinkoff, *Out of the Shtetl*, 147–49.

7. See Stone, *A Responsible Life*, 77–79; Huff, "Toward 'Moral Perfection,'" 33; Padowitz, "Ḥeshbon ha'Nefesh," 112, 115.

8. A proverb, here suggesting that a person won't be able to escape from the consequences of the lie.

9. Lefin, *Ḥeshbon ha-Nefesh*, 71–73 (paragraphs 101–3).

10. Biale et al., *Hasidism*, 336.

11. See Shapiro, *Changing the Immutable*, 281–82.

12. Rabinovich, *Sefer Nifla'ot ha-Tiferet Shlomo*, 23.

13. See Harris, *How Do We Know This?*, 168–71.

14. See Kohler, "Judaism Buried or Revitalised?," *37.

15. See Koltun-Fromm, *Abraham Geiger's Liberal Judaism*, 58–61.

16. Meyer, "Most of My Brethren," 2–3, 13–14.

17. Holdheim, *Das Religiöse*, iv–v, viii.

18. See Solomon, "Rabbi Eliyahu Eliezer Dessler," cv–cxix.

19. See Brown, "Jewish Political Theology," 281–83.

20. Schacter, "Facing the Truths of History," 233–34.

21. Dessler, *Strive for Truth*, 1:267–71.

22. Shaul Magid, "Is Meir Kahane Winning?," *Tikkun*, March 24, 2016, http://www.tikkun.org/is-meir-kahane-winning-reflections-on -benjamin-netanyahu-the-hilltop-youth-and-aipac; Magid, "Kahane Won," *Tablet*, March 15, 2019, https://www.tabletmag.com/jewish-news -and-politics/281388/kahane-won; Magid, *Meir Kahane*; Claussen, "Two Orthodox Approaches," 56–57.

23. Kahane, *Beyond Words*, 2:445.

24. See further Kahane, *Beyond Words*, 4:265, 6:314; 7:149.

25. Kahane, *Beyond Words*, 4:564–65, 567.

26. Tirosh-Samuelson, "Judith Plaskow," 12.

27. Plaskow, *Standing Again at Sinai*.

28. Plaskow, "Preaching," 152–56.

29. On Lapin's connections to the Musar movement, see Claussen, "Legacy of the Kelm School," 169–74.

30. See, e.g., Lapin, *America's Real War*, 14, 141–45.

31. Lapin, *America's Real War*, 12–18.

32. Lapin, *America's Real War*, 71.

33. For Lapin's concerns about misrepresentation, see Lapin, *America's Real War*, 12–13.

34. Lapin, *America's Real War*, 71–72.

35. "Get to know Rabbi Abigail Treu in a Minute(ish)," https://www .youtube.com/watch?v=pdqvHbngAf4.

36. Abigail Treu, "Our Lying Patriarch," October 21, 2009, http://www.jtsa .edu/our-lying-patriarch.

37. See Rosenthal, *Why Open Orthodoxy Is Not Orthodox*.

38. Shmuly Yanklowitz, "Holy Lies?," *Jewish Journal*, June 1, 2015, https:// jewishjournal.com/opinion/171551/holy-lies-review-of-changing-the -immutable-by-professor-marc-b-shapiro.

39. See Filler, "Stubborn and Rebellious Bible."

40. This essay is original to this volume.

2. CURIOSITY AND INQUISITIVENESS

1. Feiner, *Jewish Enlightenment*, 36.

2. Kogman, "Baruch Lindau's *Rešit Limmudim*," 277–305.

3. Idelson-Shein, *Difference of a Different Kind*, 118–44.

4. Lindau, "Toledot ha-Minim ha-Tiviyim," 211, 212, 218.

5. Marks, "Contemporary Renaissance," 101–2. See Marks, "Naḥman of Bratslav," 751–52.

6. Naḥman of Bratslav, *Likkutei Moharan*, 1:5b (section 1.5).

7. Naḥman of Bratslav, *Likkutei Moharan*, 1:21b–22a (section 1.17). See Dan, *Teachings of Hasidism*, 43–44.

8. Naḥman of Bratslav, *Likkutei Moharan*, 1:101b (section 1.123). See Dan, *Teachings of Hasidism*, 78.

9. See Efron, *Chosen Calling*, 33–35.

10. Gruenberg, *Science*, 5–6, 24–25, 28–29.

11. Dessler, *Mikhtav me-Eliyahu*, 2:142–43, 149.

12. *Avodah zarah*, often translated as "idolatry."

13. Dessler, *Mikhtav me-Eliyahu*, 3:177–79.

14. Hartman, "Halakhic Hero," 253.

15. Soloveitchik, *Halakhic Man*, 5, 17, 20.

16. Heschel, *God in Search of Man*, 51.

17. Heschel, *God in Search of Man*, 43.

18. See Held, *Abraham Joshua Heschel*, 37–45.

19. Heschel, *Man Is Not Alone*, 11. See further discussion in 5–6, 36–37, 68–69.
20. Heschel, *Man Is Not Alone*, 72–73, 76.
21. Ruttenberg, "Hermeneutics of Curiosity," 60.
22. As Ruttenberg notes, the term was coined by Paul Ricoeur, applied to religious feminist thought by Elizabeth Schüssler Fiorenza, and applied to Jewish feminist thought by Ellen Umansky.
23. Ruttenberg, "Hermeneutics of Curiosity," 59–60, 61, 62, 65.
24. As Arnold notes in a footnote to his sermon, he is building on the kabbalistic and Hasidic idea that the numerical values of the Hebrew letters in the words *snake* (*nahash*) and *savior/messiah* (*mashiah*) are the same. Traditional kabbalistic literature, however, promises a "holy serpent" that will destroy the evil serpent from the Garden of Eden; it views that evil serpent as plainly evil, not as redemptive. See Scholem, *Sabbatai Ṣevi*, 308n291.
25. Jamie Arnold, "The Snake, the Skylight, and the Seeker: ReCreating Self with Courageous Curiosity," September 4, 2013, http://tikkunmiddotproject.wikispaces.com/file/detail /erev rosh hashanah sermon on Curiosity 5774.docx. In this sermon Arnold also speaks about the curiosity of the biblical characters Noah (who looks through the skylight on the ark) and Abraham ("the Seeker").
26. See Eilberg, *From Enemy to Friend*, 33–37.
27. *Avot de-Rabbi Natan*, 23. See Eilberg, *From Enemy to Friend*, 1, 260–61.
28. Eilberg, *From Enemy to Friend*, 250–52.
29. Donna Cephas and Sandra Lawson, "Racism in the Jewish Community," 2018, http://evolve.reconstructingjudaism.org/racism-in-the -jewish-community.
30. This essay is original to this volume.

3. HUMILITY

1. Roth, "Towards a Definition," 13–14.
2. Satlow, "They Abused Him," 19–20.
3. Nadler, *Faith*, 165–67.
4. See Nadler, *Faith*, 166–70.
5. See Walzer et al., *Jewish Political Tradition*, 2:149.
6. Pinḥas of Polotsk, *Keter Torah*, 20b, 21b–22a. See Nadler, *Faith*, 167–70; Walzer et al., *Jewish Political Tradition*, 2:142–44.

7. Green, *Tormented Master*, 37–39, 50, 167–70, 179n60.

8. Naḥman of Bratslav, *Likkutei Moharan*, 2.5.

9. Naḥman of Bratslav, *Sefer Hamidot*, 441.

10. Naḥman of Bratslav, *Sefer ha-Middot*, 16a–17a.

11. Tamaret, *Sefer Kenesset Yisrael*, 16–17, 21.

12. Tamaret, *Sefer Kenesset Yisrael*, 63–64.

13. Bamberger, "Are the Jews a Chosen People?," 19.

14. See Kaplan, *Future of the American Jew*, 300.

15. Kaplan, *Future of the American Jew*, 211, 216, 219.

16. *Mekhilta de-Rabbi Yishmael*, Baḥodesh 2.

17. Nissim Gerondi, comment on BT *Nedarim* 30a.

18. Berezovsky, *Netivot Shalom*, 1:19–20.

19. Berezovsky, *Netivot Shalom*, 1:25–26.

20. Berezovsky, *Netivot Shalom*, 1:88–89.

21. Berezovsky, *Netivot Shalom*, 1:126.

22. See Magid, "In Search of a Critical Voice," 206–10.

23. See Claussen, "War," 232–36.

24. See Kahane, *Jewish Idea*, 275–77.

25. Kahane, *Jewish Idea*, 46–47, 53–54, 55, 57.

26. Kahane, *Jewish Idea*, 273–75.

27. Kahane, *Jewish Idea*, 525–27, 530.

28. Butler, "Modern Jewish Thought," 65n45.

29. Alpert, *Like Bread*, 54–55, 57, 58–59, 61–62.

30. Benstein, *Judaism and the Environment*, 102.

31. Benstein, *Judaism and the Environment*, 104.

32. See Benstein, *Judaism and the Environment*, 21–22.

33. Benstein, *Judaism and the Environment*, 23–24.

34. Benstein, *Judaism and the Environment*, 106–7.

35. See Stone, *Responsible Life*, 44.

36. See Stone, *Responsible Life*, xx, 15–16, 188.

37. Stone, *Responsible Life*, 15.

38. Stone, *Responsible Life*, 22.

39. In the elided text, Stone directs his readers to a discussion of pride in Moses Ḥayyim Luzzatto's eighteenth-century musar text *Mesillat Yesharim*; see Luzzatto, *Mesillat Yesharim*, 144–49.

40. Ira F. Stone, "Anavah (Humility)," *Mussar Leadership E-Newsletter* 5, no. 10 (August 4, 2013).

41. See Morinis, *Everyday Holiness*, 45–54.

42. Ruth Abusch-Magder, "Should a Woman Be Humble?," My Jewish Learning, March 6, 2017, http://www.myjewishlearning.com/rabbis -without-borders/should-a-woman-be-humble.

4. COURAGE AND VALOR

1. The phrase is from Peterson and Seligman, *Character Strengths*, 199.

2. See Ravitzky, *Messianism*, 22–25, 47–48, 61–63, 171–73, 211–34.

3. *Tanḥuma*, Toledot 5; cf. *Ester Rabbah* 10:11.

4. Presner, *Muscular Judaism*, 195; Berkowitz, *Western Jewry*, 7.

5. Presner, *Muscular Judaism*, 194.

6. Presner, *Muscular Judaism*, 187–216.

7. Presner, *Muscular Judaism*, 193.

8. Presner, *Muscular Judaism*, 194–95.

9. Erlewine, *Judaism and the West*, 24.

10. Cohen, *Religion of Reason*, 446.

11. Cohen, *Reason and Hope*, 58.

12. Erlewine, *Judaism and the West*, 24, 45.

13. Erlewine, *Judaism and the West*, 35–36; Mittleman, *Hope*, 212–13.

14. Cohen, *Religion of Reason*, 436–40.

15. See Ohana, *Origins*, 53–55.

16. *Tanḥuma*, Toledot 5; *Ester Rabbah* 10:11.

17. Luz, *Wrestling with an Angel*, 43–44.

18. See Shapira, *Land and Power*, 23–24; Luz, *Wrestling with an Angel*, 54–55.

19. Shapira, *Land and Power*, 23; Shapira, "Herzl, Ahad Ha-'Am, and Berdichevsky," 65–66.

20. Berdichevsky, *Ba-Derekh*, 2:58–59.

21. Berdichevsky, *Ba-Derekh*, 2:61–62.

22. A phrase used in a number of locations in the Bible, e.g., Judg. 2:11.

23. Berdichevsky, *Ba-Derekh*, 2:72.

24. The phrase is from Dishon, "Beauty of Yefet," 86. See Garb, "'Alien' Culture," 259–62.

25. See Edrei, "From Orthodoxy," 126*–128*.

26. On the theological underpinnings of Kook's views, see Mirsky, *Rav Kook*, 97–98; Ravitzky, *Messianism*, 101–3; Gelman, "Aesthetics," 204–5.

27. For further discussion of Kook's position on women's suffrage, see Zohar, "Traditional Flexibility," 122–24; Chana Kehat, "Rabbi Abraham

Isaac Kook," https://jwa.org/encyclopedia/article/kook-rabbi-abraham
-isaac.

28. Kook, *Orot*, 1920, 5–6. The final clause uses the language of *Midrash Tehillim* on Psalm 56.

29. Kook, *Orot*, 1920, 7, 11.

30. Kook, *Orot*, 2005, 122–23.

31. Kook, *Abraham Isaac Kook*, 179.

32. Kook, *Ma'amarei ha-Re'ayah*, 1:190, 193.

33. Ravitzky, *Messianism*, 53–57; Inbari, *Jewish Radical Ultra-Orthodoxy*, 182–91.

34. Inbari, *Jewish Radical Ultra-Orthodoxy*, 183–84.

35. Margaliot is here quoting words found in traditional *siddurim* regarding the miracle of Hanukkah.

36. Margaliot, *Ashrei ha-Ish*, 61–65.

37. See Ravitzky, *Messianism*, 79–80, 123–33.

38. Ravitzky, *Messianism*, 132.

39. Kook, *Siḥot*, 1:160.

40. See Eisen, *Peace and Violence*, 151.

41. Kook, *Siḥot*, 1:245–46.

42. E.g., Schwartz, *Ha-Ḥazek ba-Musar*; Schwartz, *Sidrat ha-Middot*. In English, see also Schwartz, *The Ben Torah*, 73–79.

43. Caplan, "Holocaust," 148–49; Caplan, "Ha-Ḥevrah ha-Ḥaredit," 176–208.

44. See Shapira, *Land and Power*, 330–42; Schwartz and Goldstein, *Ha-Shoah*, 180–81.

45. Schwartz and Goldstein, *Ha-Shoah*, 92–93, 198–99.

46. Schwartz and Goldstein, *Ha-Shoah*, 183–84, 192–93.

47. See Wine, *Celebration*, where Wine devotes short chapters to many of these and other virtues.

48. On the centrality of courage, see Wine, *Staying Sane*, xvi–xvii. Courage is also singled out for particular attention throughout Cohn-Sherbok, Cook, and Rowens, *Life of Courage*.

49. See Wine, *Judaism*, 146. See also 124, 259n11.

50. See Wine, *Judaism*, 122, 205.

51. Sherwin Wine, "The Message of Humanistic Judaism," http://www .sherwinwine.com/the-message-of-humanistic-judaism.

52. See, e.g., Wine, *Celebration*, 185–86.

53. See Wine, *Celebration*, 70. An openly gay man, Wine also challenged traditional models of masculine sexuality and affirmed the courage of those who protested against homophobia: see Wine, "Demystifying Family Values," 27.

54. Wine, *Staying Sane*, 152.

55. Wine, *Staying Sane*, 265–66.

56. See Feinstein, *Chutzpah Imperative*, 2–6, 149–52.

57. See Feinstein, *Chutzpah Imperative*, 11–18.

58. The ancient source is *Tanḥuma*, Vayera 23.8. Feinstein is building on a retelling of the story in Wiesel, *Messengers of God*, 92–93.

59. Feinstein, *Chutzpah Imperative*, xix–xx.

60. Feinstein, *Chutzpah Imperative*, 152.

61. Feinstein, *Chutzpah Imperative*, 20–21.

62. Feinstein, *Chutzpah Imperative*, 56, 61.

63. Feinstein, *Chutzpah Imperative*, 77–78.

64. Eilberg, *From Enemy to Friend*, 260–62.

65. This essay is original to this volume.

66. See, e.g., https://www.bendthearc.us/sign_up.

67. "Our Values," https://www.bendthearc.us/values.

68. "Bend the Arc on Donald Trump's Election as the 45th President of the United States," November 9, 2016, https://www.bendthearc.us/bend_the_arc_on _donald_trump_s_election_as_the_45th_president_of_the_united_states.

69. Stosh Cotler, "Are Jews Avoiding Anti-Trump Activism out of Fear, or Moral Failure?," *Haaretz*, November 22, 2017, https://www.haaretz.com /opinion/.premium-1.824297.

5. SELF-RESTRAINT AND TEMPERANCE

1. *Mishnah Avot* 4:1.

2. Rosen-Zvi, *Demonic Desires*.

3. E.g., Maimonides, "Eight Chapters," 79–80.

4. See Rosen-Zvi, *Demonic Desires*, 20–25; Satlow, "Try to Be a Man," 32–33.

5. Satlow, "Try to Be a Man," 27.

6. See Rosen-Zvi, *Demonic Desires*, 121; Satlow, "Try to Be a Man," 28.

7. Satlow, "Try to Be a Man," 28–29.

8. See Biale, *Eros and the Jews*, 33–59. On Jewish law as "sex-positive," see, e.g., Dorff, *Modern Conservative Judaism*, 274. On the polemical nature of such claims, see Epstein-Levi, "Safe, Sane, and Attentive," 92–93.

9. Nahmanides, *Commentary on the Torah: Leviticus*, 282–83 (on Lev. 19:2); see also Maimonides, *Guide of the Perplexed*, 2:606 (3.49).

10. Maimonides, *Guide of the Perplexed*, 2:432 (3.8).

11. See, e.g., Katz, *Tradition and Crisis*, 59; Sacks, *Faith in the Future*, 199.

12. See Diamond, *Holy Men*, 32–33, 70.

13. BT *Ḥagigah* 9b; Diamond, *Holy Men*, 70.

14. Luzzatto, *Mesillat Yesharim*, 172.

15. Many of the authors featured in this chapter have addressed questions of self-restraint in all three of these areas elsewhere in their writings.

16. Biale et al., *Hasidism*, 130–31. Shneur Zalman's writing is clearly gendered and directed at a male audience. See Rapoport-Albert, "From Woman as Hasid," esp. 441–43.

17. Shneur Zalman, *Likkutei Amarim*, 13b–14a (ch. 10).

18. Shneur Zalman, *Likkutei Amarim*, 35b–36a (ch. 27).

19. Shneur Zalman, *Likkutei Amarim*, 37b (ch. 29).

20. Shneur Zalman, *Likkutei Amarim*, 40b (ch. 30).

21. Shneur Zalman, *Likkutei Amarim*, 63b, 65b (ch. 42).

22. See Nadler, *Faith*, 154–59.

23. On Ḥayyim's own asceticism, see Lamm, *Torah Lishmah*, 6–7.

24. See Nadler, *Faith*, 19–20, 24–26.

25. Nadler, *Faith*, 87.

26. This section of the Mishnah concludes by noting that this life of pain will lead to happiness, explaining Ps. 128:2 ("Happy will you be, and it will be good for you") as follows: "Happy will you be" in this world, "and it will be good for you" in the world to come.

27. Ḥayyim of Volozhin, *Ruaḥ ha-Ḥayyim*, 77. The translation of the first two paragraphs is the present author's; the translation of the final paragraph comes from Nadler, *Faith*, 87.

28. Sinkoff, *Out of the Shtetl*, 153–58.

29. See Sinkoff, *Out of the Shtetl*, 114–38, 151–53.

30. Sinkoff, *Out of the Shtetl*, 134–42.

31. Sinkoff, *Out of the Shtetl*, 149, 157–58. See Dynner, *Men of Silk*, 154–55.

32. Lefin, *Ḥeshbon ha-Nefesh*, 3–4 (paragraph 3), 7–8 (paragraph 7), 13 (paragraph 17), 39–40 (paragraph 62).

33. *Ḥokhmah*, *Binah*, and *Da'at*, which form the acronym "Habad" (Chabad), the name of the popular Hasidic movement founded by Shneur Zalman of Liadi.

34. The questions "Who is wise" and "Who is an honored man" are asked in BT *Tamid* 32a and *Mishnah Avot* 4:1. Lefin quotes the answers given in these sources.

35. Lefin, *Ḥeshbon ha-Nefesh*, 62–64 (paragraphs 91–92).

36. Lefin, *Ḥeshbon Ha-Nefesh*, 51.

37. Lefin, *Ḥeshbon Ha-Nefesh*, 74, 76 (paragraph 108).

38. See Brown, "Kedushah," 489. On the factors encouraging such a stringent approach, see 517–22.

39. See Brown, "Kedushah," 488–91.

40. That is, the night (*leil*) of the woman's monthly immersion (*tevilah*) in a *mikveh* after her menstrual period, at which point (according to the tradition that Berezovsky is following) a married couple is obligated to engage in sexual intercourse.

41. Brown, "Kedushah," 492–94.

42. Plaskow draws especially on the work of Audre Lorde and Beverly Harrison. See Plaskow, "Towards a New Theology," 143.

43. See Plaskow, "Towards a New Theology," 144–45.

44. Plaskow, "Towards a New Theology," 141–44, 147–48.

45. Wine, *Staying Sane*, 206–9, 214.

46. Wine, "Our Dietary Laws," 22–23.

47. Borowitz, *Renewing the Covenant*, 164. See Borowitz and Schwartz, *Jewish Moral Virtues*, 175–76, 180–83.

48. Borowitz and Schwartz, *Jewish Moral Virtues*, 9.

49. Borowitz and Schwartz, *Jewish Moral Virtues*, 161, 163, 165–67.

50. Saul J. Berman, Sharon Bloome, Nina Beth Cardin, David Ellenson, Nancy Fuchs Kreimer, Arthur Green, Susannah Heschel, Charles A. Kroloff, Elliot Norse, David Saperstein, Ismar Schorsch, Mitchell Thomashow, and Lawrence Troster.

51. Lawrence Bush, "Jewish Values and Environmental Awareness: The Progressive Use of (Uh-Oh) Religious Metaphor," *Jewish Currents* 59, no. 5 (2005): 20–22.

52. Coalition on the Environment and Jewish Life, "Wonder and Restraint," 67–68, 70–71.

53. Michaelson, "Into Life," 89.

54. Michaelson, "Into Life," 92.

55. Michaelson, "Into Life," 90–91.

56. See the discussion of "loving, accepting, non-judging awareness" in Weinberg, "Leaving Egypt," 158.
57. Weinberg, "Leaving Egypt," 157, 162–63.

6. GRATITUDE

1. See Aberbach, *The European Jews.*
2. Polland and Soyer, *Emerging Metropolis,* 139.
3. Isaacs, "Thanksgiving Sermon," 122.
4. Rabinovitch, "Jews," 40–41, 42–43.
5. Gornick, *Emma Goldman,* 1.
6. See Goldman, *Living My Life,* 1:59–61.
7. Shulman, *Red Emma Speaks,* 64, 243, 244.
8. Goldman, *My Disillusionment in Russia,* xiii–xiv.
9. See Willig, "Gadlut ha-Adam," 157–62.
10. Finkel, *Siḥot,* 1:321–23.
11. *Bereshit Rabbah* 38:9.
12. Finkel, *Siḥot,* 2:543–45.
13. Kushner, *When Bad Things Happen,* 102.
14. Kushner, *When Bad Things Happen,* 99–116.
15. Kushner, *When Bad Things Happen,* 34–35, 38–39, 180, 186–87.
16. Silver, *Plausible God,* 159n1, with reference to the wisdom of John Rawls, Michael Sandel, Socrates, and the Israeli kibbutz movement.
17. Silver, *Plausible God,* 72–75.
18. See Morinis, *Everyday Holiness,* 86.
19. On this sort of difference between the historic Musar movement led in part by Finkel and the revival led in part by Morinis, see Claussen, "American Jewish Revival," 63–69.
20. Following BT *Berachot* 60b.
21. Morinis, *Everyday Holiness,* 68–69, 71.
22. Arush, *Garden of Gratitude,* 112, 217–19, 321–22.
23. Berel Wein, "Implosion," https://www.rabbiwein.com/blog/post-2309.html.
24. See Wolfensohn, *A Global Life,* 417–31; Peter Beinart, "Gaza Myths and Facts: What American Jewish Leaders Won't Tell You," *Haaretz,* July 30, 2014, https://www.haaretz.com/opinion/.premium-gaza-myths-and-facts-what-american-jewish-leaders-won-t-tell-you-1.5257435.

25. Berel Wein, "Saying Thank You," https://www.rabbiwein.com/blog/saying-thank-you-511.html, with reference to BT *Kiddushin* 80b.

26. Berel Wein, "Gratitude," https://www.rabbiwein.com/blog/post-2090.html.

27. Berel Wein, "Gratitude," http://www.rabbiwein.com/blog/gratitude-167.html.

28. The present author has not seen any of Eliyahu's writings that expand on his comment, but Berel Wein's writings make a similar point. As such, Oz's remarks are included out of chronological order in this chapter, following the section on Wein, as if in response to Wein's claims.

29. Oz, *Slopes of Lebanon*, 212–13, 217–18.

30. Lisa Goldstein, "Giving Thanks. Telling the Truth," November 23, 2016, http://www.jewishspirituality.org/november-2016-gratitude-e-letter.

7. FORGIVENESS

1. Newman, "Balancing," 441–45.

2. An expanded version of this formula is found in the "bedtime Shema" liturgy in many prayer books.

3. BT *Rosh Hashanah* 17a; BT *Megillah* 28a; BT *Yoma* 23a; BT *Yoma* 87b.

4. For alternative translations, see: Newman, "Balancing," 444; Levinas, *Nine Talmudic Readings*, 13 (section 7.4 in this chapter).

5. Newman, "Balancing," 450, 453.

6. Newman, "Balancing," 453.

7. *Mishnah Bava Kamma* 8:7, as translated by Newman, "Balancing," 438.

8. *Mishnah Yoma* 8:9, as translated by Levinas, *Nine Talmudic Readings*, 12.

9. See BT *Ketubot* 17a, BT *Sotah* 41b, BT *Kiddushin* 31a–b, BT *Sanhedrin* 19b.

10. *Kohelet Rabbah* 7:25.

11. *Mishnah Avot* 5:18.

12. *Tanḥuma*, Ha'azinu 4.

13. Papo, *Pele Yo'etz*, 2:41b.

14. Papo, *Pele Yo'etz*, 1:11, 1:85, 1:145, 1:167, 2:1a, 2:30b, 2:36a–b, 2:41b .

15. Papo, *Pele Yo'etz*, 2:86a.

16. Papo, *Pele Yo'etz*, 1:7–8.

17. See Biale et al., *Hasidism*, 397–98.

18. Shapira, *Benei Yisakhar*, 2:26–27.

19. Shapira, *Benei Yisakhar*, 2:58.

20. Shapira here cites *Tanḥuma*, Ha'azinu 4, which teaches that God "lifts up [God's] countenance to he who repents. Might this include everyone? [No]—the Torah specifies 'to *you*' [Num. 6:26], and not to another nation."

21. Shapira, *Benei Yisakhar*, 2:107. Shapira expresses similar ideas in 2:51.

22. On Arendt's lack of interest in traditional Jewish sources, see Bernstein, *Hannah Arendt*, 185–86.

23. Arendt discusses forgiving alongside a discussion of promising. She explains that while promises make the world more predictable, forgiveness opens up unexpected possibilities by providing a release from the past. See Arendt, *Human Condition*, 237.

24. See Maier-Katkin, *Stranger from Abroad*, 231–32, 346–48; Erin Carlisle, "How Did She Forgive Heidegger? Hannah Arendt and the Politics of Forgiveness," November 2014, https://tasa.org.au/wp-content/uploads/2014/12/Carlisle.pdf.

25. Arendt, *Human Condition*, 237–38, 240–41.

26. Levinas, *Totality and Infinity*, 283 (emphasis added). See the discussion in Allers, "Undoing," 27–30.

27. Levinas, *Nine Talmudic Readings*, 13.

28. See Hollander, "Contested Forgiveness," 150.

29. Levinas seems to be referring, especially, to BT *Yevamot* 58b–59a.

30. Levinas, *Nine Talmudic Readings*, 19, 24–25, 28–29.

31. Wiesenthal, *Sunflower*, 215–17, 220.

32. Marc Ellis, "This High Holiday Season, Expect Few Words about Palestinians, and Even Less Concern," September 12, 2015, http://mondoweiss.net/2015/09/holiday-revolutionary-justice.

33. Ellis, *Encountering*, 239–40.

34. Ellis, *O, Jerusalem!*, 142–44.

35. "An Interview with Professor Jacques Derrida," January 8, 1998, http://www.yadvashem.org/odot_pdf/Microsoft%20Word%20-%203851.pdf.

36. "Interview with Professor Jacques Derrida."

37. See further discussion in Caputo, Dooley, and Scanlon, "On Forgiveness," 52–72.

38. Derrida, *On Cosmopolitanism*, 34.

39. La Caze, *Wonder*, 151; Derrida, "To Forgive," 30, 46.

40. Derrida, *On Cosmopolitanism*, 41.

41. La Caze, *Wonder*, 152–54.

42. Derrida, *On Cosmopolitanism*, 31–32, 37, 38–39, 45, 58–59.
43. Schnur, "Beyond Forgiveness," 19, 45.
44. Kedar, *Bridge to Forgiveness*, 27–28.
45. Newman, "Balancing," 436–37.
46. Kedar, *Bridge to Forgiveness*, 3, 20, 34.
47. Arush, *Women's Wisdom*, 166.
48. Arush, *Women's Wisdom*, 180.
49. Compare Arush, *Garden of Peace*, 239–40.
50. Arush, *Women's Wisdom*, 161–62.
51. Newman, "Balancing," 436.

8. LOVE, KINDNESS, AND COMPASSION

1. See Van Houten, *The Alien*, 163; Neudecker, "You Shall Love," 499–500.
2. *Sifra*, Kedoshim 4.
3. *Bereshit Rabbah* 54:3.
4. See Green, *Guide*, 43. On the association in classical Rabbinic literature, see *Bereshit Rabbah* 60:2.
5. See Ramon, "Matriarchs," 156–57.
6. *Tanḥuma*, Noaḥ 6.
7. *Midrash Tehillim* 52:6; BT *Sukkah* 49b.
8. For an approach to teaching the diverse perspectives that follow in this chapter, see Claussen, "Teaching Modern Jewish Ethics," 74–93.
9. Mendelssohn, *Netivot ha-Shalom*, 3:347–48.
10. Steinsaltz, *Understanding*, 128 explains: "The goal of existence, of the creation of the worlds, is to arrive at that true 'One into One.'"
11. Shneur Zalman, *Likkutei Amarim*, 3b–4a (chs. 1–2).
12. Shneur Zalman, *Likkutei Amarim*, 43a–44a (ch. 32).
13. See Claussen, *Sharing the Burden*, 109–81.
14. See Claussen, *Sharing the Burden*, 149–50.
15. Cooper, "Maintaining Oppositions," 134–35; Claussen, "Promise," 159–62.
16. *Kitvei ha-Sabba mi-Kelm*, 147–48.
17. Ziv, *Ḥokhmah u-Musar*, 2:7.
18. *Bereshit Rabbah* 82:14.
19. Ziv, *Ḥokhmah u-Musar*, 2:193–95.
20. Ziv, *Ḥokhmah u-Musar*, 1:174.
21. Arendt, *Eichmann in Jerusalem*, 106.

22. Canovan, "Politics as Culture," 633.

23. Canovan, *Hannah Arendt*, 170.

24. Arendt, *On Revolution*, 75–77.

25. Arendt, *Jewish Writings*, 466–68. The editor of *Jewish Writings* notes that the personality referred to "was Golda Meir, then foreign minister and later prime minister of Israel. At Scholem's urging, Arendt deleted Meir's name and changed the feminine pronoun when the letters were first published" (467). See also Kupfer and Turgeman, "Secularization," 188–209.

26. Kearney and Levinas, "Dialogue," 24.

27. Levinas, *Is It Righteous to Be?*, 169, quoting a phrase from Fyodor Dostoyevsky.

28. Gibbs, *Correlations*, 184. See Levinas, *Difficult Freedom*, 17.

29. Levinas, *Of God*, 90–91.

30. See Seeman, "Violence, Ethics," 1017–28; Satherley, "Simple Jew," 57–91; Inbari, *Jewish Fundamentalism*, 131–60; Claussen, "Pinḥas," 483–89.

31. See Magid, "America is No Different," 79–82.

32. See Ginsburgh, *Rectifying*, 176–77.

33. Ginsburgh, *Rectifying*, 75.

34. See Ginsburgh, *Rectifying*, 83–84, 89–95.

35. Ginsburgh, *Rectifying*, 107. See Satherly, "Simple Jew," 77.

36. Quoting the traditional evening (*Ma'ariv*) liturgy.

37. Ginsburgh, *Rectifying*, 75–78.

38. Ramon here cites Adler, "The Jew," 12–18.

39. Ramon notes that, for a critique of the altruistic presentation of the wives of the sages, see Eichenbaum and Orbach, *Understanding Women*, 36–50. On mature mother-daughter relations, see Friedman, *Ba'ah me-Ahavah*, 119–23.

40. Ramon, "Matriarchs," 168, 171–73.

41. Gottlieb, *Trail Guide*, 74.

42. Gottlieb, *Trail Guide*, 75.

43. Levinas, *Beyond the Verse*, 142.

44. Gottlieb, *Trail Guide*, 151.

45. Gottlieb, *Trail Guide*, 94.

46. Gottlieb, *Trail Guide*, 95.

47. Gottlieb, *Trail Guide*, 96.

48. Gottlieb, *Trail Guide*, 128–30.

49. Gottlieb, *Trail Guide*, 152.
50. See, e.g., Yanklowitz, *Soul of Jewish Social Justice*, 406; Yanklowitz, *Post-modern Jewish Ethics*, 95.
51. Shmuly Yanklowitz, "Rabbinic Reflections," *Arizona Jewish Life*, November 1, 2013, https://azjewishlife.com/rabbinic-reflections-351.
52. Shmuly Yanklowitz, "Zionism: The Great Jewish Ethical Project," *Arutz Sheva*, http://www.israelnationalnews.com/Articles/Article.aspx/22022; see Yanklowitz, *Soul of Jewish Social Justice*, 121–24, 395–97.
53. Yanklowitz, *Soul of Jewish Social Justice*, 247.
54. Claussen, "Jewish Virtue Ethics," 210–14.
55. Shmuly Yanklowitz, "Mussar & Loving Animals!" The Times of Israel, March 13, 2018, http://blogs.timesofisrael.com/mussar-loving-animals.
56. Yanklowitz, "Mussar & Loving Animals!"

9. SOLIDARITY AND SOCIAL RESPONSIBILITY

1. See, e.g., Peters, *Solidarity Ethics*, 10–11.
2. A talmudic text parallel to the one referenced here may be found in *Sanhedrin* 27b. On the interpretation of these texts, see Rudman, "Kol Yisrael," 35–49.
3. See Levy, "Edification," 61, 66; Zohar, *Rabbinic Creativity*, 341–45.
4. Farag, "War," 52.
5. Farag, "War," 59.
6. Farag, "War," 54.
7. Farag, "War," 52–55.
8. Stillman, *Jews of Arab Lands*, 229.
9. Levy, "Edification," 66–67.
10. Farag, "War," 49–51.
11. Goldman, *Anarchism*, 149.
12. Goldman, *Anarchism*, 134.
13. Goldman, *Anarchism*, 149.
14. Goldman, "En Route," 353.
15. Goldman, *Anarchism*, 148, 150.
16. Friedman, *Rebbes of Chortkov*, 271, 277, 283.
17. Friedman, *Rebbes of Chortkov*, 295.
18. Kaplan and Dresner, *Abraham Joshua Heschel*, 69.
19. Friedman, *Ginzei Yisrael*, 2:199.

20. Friedman, *Ginzei Yisrael*, 2:90.
21. See Willig, "Gadlut ha-Adam," 313–16.
22. Willig, "Gadlut Ha-Adam," 317.
23. Willig, "Gadlut Ha-Adam," 189–91.
24. See *Bereshit Rabbah* 30.
25. Zohar 1:106a.
26. Finkel, *Or ha-Tzafun*, 2:73–74.
27. Katz, Biderman, and Greenberg, *Wrestling with God*, 173.
28. Katz, Biderman, and Greenberg, *Wrestling with God*, 171.
29. Katz, Biderman, and Greenberg, *Wrestling with God*, 184.
30. Katz, Biderman, and Greenberg, *Wrestling with God*, 174–75.
31. Arendt, *Jewish Writings*, 146.
32. Arendt, *Eichmann in Jerusalem*, 11.
33. Arendt, *Jewish Writings*, 467.
34. Arendt, *Jewish Writings*, 391–92.
35. Arendt, *On Revolution*, 79. See Canovan, *Hannah Arendt*, 171–72.
36. Arendt, *On Revolution*, 79.
37. Arendt, *Jewish Writings*, 391.
38. Canovan, *Hannah Arendt*, 171.
39. Arendt, *Jewish Writings*, 177.
40. A representative Jewish defense organization founded in Paris in 1860. Its Hebrew name was Kol Yisra'el Haverim (All Israel are fellows) and its motto was *Kol Yisra'el arevim zeh la-zeh* (translated here as "All Israel takes care of Israel").
41. Arendt, *Jewish Writings*, 154–56.
42. Arendt, *Jewish Writings*, 263.
43. Arendt, *Jewish Writings*, 168–69.
44. See Ohana, *Political Theologies*, 37.
45. Yanai, "Ben-Gurion's Concept," 154.
46. Kedar, "Ben-Gurion's Mamlakhtiyut," 125–30.
47. Kedar, "Ben-Gurion's Mamlakhtiyut," 129.
48. Ohana, *Political Theologies*, 15.
49. Avi-Hai, *Ben Gurion*, 142–45.
50. Ben-Gurion, *Ḥazon ve-Derekh*, 3:261–63.
51. The organization's founding name was National Emergency Committee of Clergy Concerned About Vietnam.

52. Heschel, "Moral Outrage," 49, 59.

53. Heschel's father grew up in the court of Chortkov, as Friedman's young half-brother. See Kaplan and Dresner, *Abraham Joshua Heschel*, 7–9; Dresner, *Heschel*, 80n36.

54. Heschel, *Man Is Not Alone*, 142.

55. Heschel, *Moral Grandeur*, 238.

56. Heschel, "Moral Outrage," 48–50, 52–53, 55.

57. Levinas, *Is It Righteous to Be?*, 169, quoting a phrase from Fyodor Dostoyevsky.

58. Heschel, *Man Is Not Alone*, 119.

59. Heschel, *Man Is Not Alone*, 142.

60. Britton, *Abraham Heschel*, 243–45.

61. Levinas, *Ethics and Infinity*, 98–99.

62. Levinas, *Levinas Reader*, 224–26.

63. Jaffe, *Changing the World*, 6–11.

64. David Jaffe, "National Jewish Book Award," http://rabbidavidjaffe .com/national-jewish-book-award-win. For another example of Jaffe drawing inspiration from non-Orthodox views of solidarity, see Jaffe, *Changing the World*, 27–29, 245n12.

65. This revised version of Jaffe's essay is original to this volume. The original version is David Jaffe, "MLK Day #TorahForTheResistance: Is Putting One's Life on the Line to Stand Up to Oppression a Jewish Value?," *Jewschool*, January 15, 2018, https://jewschool.com/2018/01 /80805/mlk-day-torahfortheresistance-putting-ones-life-line-stand -oppression-jewish-value.

66. Mbuvi, "Avadim Hayinu," 85–86.

67. Amanda Mbuvi, "Genesis and the Journey from Charlottesville to a New Vision of Community," *The Religion & Culture Forum*, October 20, 2017, https://voices.uchicago.edu/religionculture/2017/10/20/1149. See Mbuvi, *Belonging in Genesis*.

68. For the declaration, see Küng and Kuschel, *Global Ethic*, 13–39.

69. Mbuvi, "Avadim Hayinu," 85–94.

70. Mbuvi notes: "This characterization of Moses should be considered an analogy, not an identification. Race as moderns know it does not exist in the Bible."

71. This essay is original to this volume.

10. JUSTICE AND RIGHTEOUSNESS

1. A number of these aspects are discussed in Newman, *Introduction to Jewish Ethics*, 86–94.
2. See Biale et al., *Hasidism*, 166.
3. *Bereshit Rabbah* 8:5.
4. Biale et al., *Hasidism*, 166.
5. See Jacobs, *Doctrine*; Lamm, *Religious Thought*, 255–70; Biale et al., *Hasidism*, 145–46.
6. Biale et al., *Hasidism*, 146.
7. Biale et al., *Hasidism*, 146, 168.
8. See Zwecker, *Mipeninei Noam Elimelech*, 161.
9. See further discussion in Dynner, *Men of Silk*, 139, 151–52, 154–55; Biale et al., *Hasidism*, 168–69.
10. Elimelekh derives his gendering from descriptions of both men and women in Exod. 35:23–26, but he reads the text as speaking about different types of men and not about actual women.
11. See Scholem, *Messianic Idea*, 200.
12. On Hasidic distancing from women, see Wodziński, "Women and Hasidism," 407–44.
13. *Bereshit Rabbah* 8:5.
14. Weissblum, *No'am Elimelekh*, 22a.
15. Weissblum, *No'am Elimelekh*, 33b.
16. Weissblum, *No'am Elimelekh*, 59a.
17. See Etkes, *Rabbi Israel Salanter*, 197; Claussen, *Sharing the Burden*, 12.
18. See Etkes, *Rabbi Israel Salanter*, 320–22.
19. Etkes, *Rabbi Israel Salanter*, 211–12, 321.
20. In translating *koḥot ha-nefesh* as "soul-force," I follow Goldberg, *Israel Salanter*.
21. See Goldberg, *Israel Salanter*, 119.
22. See Goldberg, *Israel Salanter*, 125–27.
23. See Etkes, *Rabbi Israel Salanter*, 160–62. For a presentation grounded not in Salanter's writings but in stories about his life, see Morinis, *With Heart in Mind*, 180–81.
24. Salanter here cites *Akedat Yitzḥak*, a philosophical commentary on the Torah written by Isaac Arama (Spain, fifteenth century), ch. 10.
25. Salanter, "Or Yisra'el," 87–89.

26. See Ariel, "Christianity," 185; Cohon, *A Living Faith*, 113; Kohler, *Jewish Theology*, 130.

27. See Haberman, "Kaufmann Kohler," 100–101.

28. See Ariel, "Christianity," 186–87.

29. Imhoff, *Masculinity*, 49.

30. See Ariel, "Kaufmann Kohler," 207–23.

31. Kohler, *Hebrew Union College*, 169–72.

32. Kohler, *Jewish Theology*, 120–22.

33. Kohler cites *Sifra* Behar 4 and BT *Bava Metzia* 58b.

34. Kohler, *Jewish Theology*, 485–86.

35. A comprehensive collection of these writings is found in Kook, *Ḥazon*; Kook, *Tzimḥonut*; Rubenstein, "None Shall Hurt."

36. Hertzberg, *Zionist Idea*, 427, 429.

37. Kook, *Ma'amarei ha-Re'ayah*, 1:174.

38. Kook, "Afikim ba-Negev," 656, 658–60, 717–18.

39. See Savvas, "The Other Religion," 1–22.

40. See Stromberg, "Rebellion and Creativity," 12–13.

41. Singer, "Foreword," vii–ix.

42. Singer, "Preface," i.

43. Schnur, "Justice," 331–33.

44. Alpert, *Like Bread*, 34–35, 99–105, 108–9.

45. Alpert, *Like Bread*, 106–7, 110–11.

46. Alpert, "What Is a Jew?," 76–77.

47. Alpert cites Gilligan, *In a Different Voice*.

48. Alpert cites Heyward, *Our Passion for Justice*, 92.

49. Alpert, *Like Bread*, 97–98.

50. On Pruzansky as a teacher of musar, see Alan Brill, "Interview with Rabbi Steven Pruzansky: Country Preacher," October 14, 2015, https:// kavvanah.wordpress.com/2015/10/14/interview-with-rabbi-steven -pruzansky-country-preacher. On Pruzansky's interest in reviving the Musar movement along the lines developed by Salanter, see Steven Pruzansky, "'The Eye Sees, The Ear Hears' (Avot 2:1)," December 3, 2015, https://rabbipruzansky.com/2015/12/03/the-eye-sees-the-ear -hears-avot-21.

51. See Ben Sales, "N.J. Rabbi: Arabs in Israel 'Must Be Vanquished,'" *Jewish Telegraphic Agency*, November 23, 2014, https://www.jta.org/2014 /11/23/news-opinion/united-states/n-j-rabbi-arabs-in-israel-must-be

-vanquished. For another example of controversial remarks, see Uriel Heilman, "Rabbi Pruzansky's Dismissive Comments on Rape Draws Outcry among Jewish Groups," *Haaretz*, April 14, 2016, https://www .haaretz.com/jewish/rabbi-pruzansky-s-comments-on-rape-draws -outcry-1.5432052.

52. Pruzansky, *Judges*, 124–25, 129–30.

53. Steven Pruzansky, "The Tragedy of Shaul," March 6, 2009, https:// rabbipruzansky.com/2009/03/06/the-tragedy-of-shaul.

54. Ellis, *Future of the Prophetic*, 5–6.

55. See Ellis, *Future of the Prophetic*, 10.

56. See Ellis's discussion of Reform Judaism in *Future of the Prophetic*, 252.

57. Ellis, *Future of the Prophetic*, 247–48.

58. Mittleman, "Marc Ellis," 177–90.

59. Mittleman, "Marc Ellis," 183.

60. Mittleman, "Marc Ellis," 182.

61. Ellis, *Future of the Prophetic*, 116–18, 343, 361, 366.

62. See http://en.wikipedia.org/wiki/The_dress and http://en.wikipedia .org/wiki/Yanny_or_Laurel.

63. This essay is original to this volume.

Bibliography

Aberbach, David. *The European Jews, Patriotism and the Liberal State, 1789–1939: A Study of Literature and Social Psychology*. New York: Routledge, 2013.

Adler, Rachel. "The Jew Who Wasn't There: Halakhah and the Jewish Woman." In *On Being a Jewish Feminist: A Reader*, edited by Susannah Heschel, 12–18. New York: Schocken Books, 1983.

Allers, Christopher R. "Undoing What Has Been Done: Arendt and Levinas on Forgiveness." In *Forgiveness in Perspective*, edited by Marieke Smit and Christopher R. Allers, 19–42. Amsterdam: Rodopi, 2010.

Alpert, Rebecca T. *Like Bread on the Seder Plate: Jewish Lesbians and the Transformation of Tradition*. New York: Columbia University Press, 1997.

———. "What Is a Jew? The Meaning of Genetic Disease for Jewish Identity." *The Reconstructionist* 71, no. 2 (2007): 69–84.

Arendt, Hannah. *Eichmann in Jerusalem: A Report on the Banality of Evil*. Rev. ed. New York: Viking, 1964.

———. *On Revolution*. New York: Penguin Books, 2006.

———. *The Human Condition*. Chicago: University of Chicago Press, 1958.

———. *The Jewish Writings*. New York: Schocken Books, 2013.

Ariel, Yaakov. "Christianity through Reform Eyes: Kaufmann Kohler's Scholarship on Christianity." *American Jewish History* 89, no. 2 (2001): 181–91.

———. "Kaufmann Kohler and His Attitude toward Zionism: A Reexamination." *American Jewish Archives* 43, no. 2 (1991): 207–23.

Arush, Shalom. *The Garden of Gratitude*. Translated by Lazer Brody. Jerusalem: Chut Shel Chessed Institutions, 2011.

———. *The Garden of Peace: A Marital Guide for Men Only*. Translated by Lazer Brody. Jerusalem: Chut Shel Chessed Institutions, 2008.

———. *Women's Wisdom: The Garden of Peace for Women Only*. Translated by Lazer Brody. Jerusalem: Chut Shel Chessed Institutions, 2010.

Avi-Hai, Avraham. *Ben Gurion, State-Builder*. New York: Wiley, 1974.

Bamberger, Bernard J. "Are the Jews a Chosen People?" *The Reconstructionist* 11, no. 16 (1945): 16–19.

Ben-Gurion, David. *Ḥazon ve-Derekh*. 2nd ed. 5 vols. Tel Aviv: Mapai, 1953.

Benstein, Jeremy. *The Way into Judaism and the Environment*. Woodstock VT: Jewish Lights, 2006.

Berdichevsky, Mikhah Yosef. *Ba-Derekh*. Vol. 2. Leipzig: Stybel, 1922.

Berezovsky, Shalom Noah. *Sefer Netivot Shalom*. Vol. 1. Jerusalem: Yeshivat Beit Avraham Slonim, 1982.

Berkowitz, Michael. *Western Jewry and the Zionist Project, 1914–1933*. Cambridge: Cambridge University Press, 1997.

Bernstein, Richard J. *Hannah Arendt and the Jewish Question*. Cambridge MA: MIT Press, 1996.

Biale, David. *Eros and the Jews: From Biblical Israel to Contemporary America*. Berkeley: University of California Press, 1997.

Biale, David, David Assaf, Benjamin Brown, Uriel Gellman, Samuel C. Heilman, Murray Jay Rosman, Gad Sagiv, and Marcin Wodziński. *Hasidism: A New History*. Princeton NJ: Princeton University Press, 2018.

Borowitz, Eugene B. *Renewing the Covenant: A Theology for the Postmodern Jew*. Philadelphia: The Jewish Publication Society, 1991.

Borowitz, Eugene B., and Frances Weinman Schwartz. *The Jewish Moral Virtues*. Philadelphia: The Jewish Publication Society, 1999.

Britton, Joseph Harp. *Abraham Heschel and the Phenomenon of Piety*. New York: Bloomsbury, 2013.

Brown, Benjamin. "Jewish Political Theology: The Doctrine of Daat Torah as a Case Study." *Harvard Theological Review* 107, no. 3 (2014): 255–89.

———. "Kedushah: The Sexual Abstinence of Married Men in Gur, Slonim, and Toledot Aharon." *Jewish History* 27, nos. 2–4 (2013): 475–522.

Butler, Deidre. "Modern Jewish Thought and Jewish Feminist Thought: An Uncommon Conversation." *Religion Compass* 6, no. 1 (2012): 51–71.

Canovan, Margaret. *Hannah Arendt: A Reinterpretation of Her Political Thought*. Cambridge: Cambridge University Press, 1992.

———. "Politics as Culture: Hannah Arendt and the Public Realm." *History of Political Thought* 6, no. 3 (1985): 617–42.

Caplan, Kimmy. "Ha-Ḥevrah ha-Ḥaredit be-Yisrael ve-Yaḥasah la-Shoah: Keriah me-Hadash." *Alpayim* 17 (1999): 176–208.

———. "The Holocaust in Contemporary Israeli Haredi Popular Religion." *Modern Judaism* 22, no. 2 (2002): 142–68.

Caputo, John D., Mark Dooley, and Michael J. Scanlon, eds. "On Forgiveness: A Roundtable Discussion with Jacques Derrida." In *Questioning God*, 52–72. Bloomington: Indiana University Press, 2001.

Claussen, Geoffrey D. "The American Jewish Revival of Musar." *Hedgehog Review* 12, no. 2 (2010): 63–72.

———. "Jewish Virtue Ethics and Compassion for Animals: A Model from the Musar Movement." *CrossCurrents* 61, no. 2 (2011): 208–16.

———. "The Legacy of the Kelm School of Musar on Questions of Work, Wealth and Poverty." In *Wealth and Poverty in Jewish Tradition*, edited by Leonard J. Greenspoon, 151–84. West Lafayette IN: Purdue University Press, 2015.

———. "Pinḥas, the Quest for Purity, and the Dangers of Tikkun Olam." In *Tikkun Olam: Judaism, Humanism, and Transcendence*, edited by David Birnbaum and Martin S. Cohen, 475–501. New York: New Paradigm Matrix, 2015.

———. "The Practice of Musar." *Conservative Judaism* 63, no. 2 (2011): 3–26.

———. "The Promise and Limits of R. Simḥah Zissel Ziv's Musar: A Response to Miller, Cooper, Pugh, and Peters." *Journal of Jewish Ethics* 3, no. 1 (2017): 154–77.

———. *Sharing the Burden: Rabbi Simḥah Zissel Ziv and the Path of Musar*. Albany: SUNY Press, 2015.

———. "Teaching Modern Jewish Ethics through Role Play." *Journal of Jewish Ethics* 6, no. 1 (2020): 74–93.

———. "War, Musar, and the Construction of Humility in Modern Jewish Thought." *Interreligious Studies and Interreligious Theology* 3, no. 2 (2019): 216–42.

Coalition on the Environment and Jewish Life. "Wonder and Restraint: A Rabbinical Call to Environmental Action." In *Righteous Indignation: A Jewish Call for Justice*, edited by Or N. Rose, Jo Ellen Green Kaiser, and Margie Klein, 67–75. Woodstock VT: Jewish Lights, 2008.

Cohen, Hermann. *Reason and Hope: Selections from the Jewish Writings of Hermann Cohen*. Translated by Eva Jospe. New York: Norton, 1971.

———. *Religion of Reason out of the Sources of Judaism*. Translated by Simon Kaplan. Atlanta: Scholars Press, 1995.

Cohn-Sherbok, Dan, Harry T. Cook, and Marilyn Rowens, eds. *A Life of Courage: Sherwin Wine and Humanistic Judaism*. Farmington Hills MI: International Institute for Secular Humanistic Judaism, 2003.

Cohon, Samuel S. *A Living Faith: Selected Sermons and Addresses from the Literary Remains of Dr. Kaufmann Kohler*. Cincinnati: Hebrew Union College–Jewish Institute of Religion, 1948.

Cooper, Andrea Dara. "Maintaining Oppositions in Musar." *Journal of Jewish Ethics* 3, no. 1 (2017): 131–37.

Dan, Joseph. "Ethical Literature." In *Encyclopedia Judaica*, 2nd ed., 6:525–31. Detroit: Macmillan Reference, 2007.

———. *Sifrut ha-Musar ve-ha-Derush [Hebrew Ethical and Homiletical Literature]*. Jerusalem: Keter, 1975.

———, ed. *The Teachings of Hasidism*. New York: Behrman House, 1983.

Derrida, Jacques. *On Cosmopolitanism and Forgiveness*. Translated by Michael Hughes and Mark Dooley. London: Routledge, 2001.

———. "To Forgive the Unforgivable and the Imprescriptible." In *Questioning God*, edited by John D. Caputo, Mark Dooley, and Michael J. Scanlon, translated by Elizabeth Rottenberg, 21–51. Bloomington: Indiana University Press, 2001.

Dessler, Elijah Eliezer. *Mikhtav me-Eliyahu*. Edited by Aryeh Carmell and Alter Halpern. London, 1955.

———. *Strive for Truth*. Translated by Aryeh Carmell. 3 vols. Jerusalem; New York: Feldheim, 1978.

Diamond, Eliezer. *Holy Men and Hunger Artists: Fasting and Asceticism in Rabbinic Culture*. Oxford: Oxford University Press, 2004.

Dishon, David. "'The Beauty of Yefet in the Tents of Shem': Gentiles and Jews in the Thought of Rav Kook." *Havruta* 2 (2008): 80–89.

Dorff, Elliot N. *Modern Conservative Judaism: Evolving Thought and Practice*. Lincoln: University of Nebraska Press; Philadelphia: The Jewish Publication Society, 2018.

Dorff, Elliot N., and Jonathan K. Crane, eds. *The Oxford Handbook of Jewish Ethics and Morality*. Oxford: Oxford University Press, 2013.

Dresner, Samuel H. *Heschel, Hasidism and Halakha*. New York: Fordham University Press, 2002.

Dynner, Glenn. *Men of Silk: The Hasidic Conquest of Polish Jewish Society*. New York: Oxford University Press, 2006.

Edrei, Arye. "From Orthodoxy to Religious Zionism: Rabbi Kook and the Sabbatical Year Polemic." *Dine Israel* 26–27 (2010): 45*-145*.

Efron, Noah J. *A Chosen Calling: Jews in Science in the Twentieth Century*. Baltimore: Johns Hopkins University Press, 2014.

Eichenbaum, Louise, and Susie Orbach. *Understanding Women*. London: Penguin, 1992.

Eilberg, Amy. *From Enemy to Friend: Jewish Wisdom and the Pursuit of Peace*. Maryknoll NY: Orbis Books, 2014.

Eisen, Robert. *The Peace and Violence of Judaism: From the Bible to Modern Zionism*. New York: Oxford University Press, 2011.

Elkins, Dov Peretz, and Abigail Treu. *The Bible's Top Fifty Ideas: The Essential Concepts Everyone Should Know*. New York: Specialist Press International, 2005.

Ellis, Marc H. *Encountering the Jewish Future: With Elie Wiesel, Martin Buber, Abraham Joshua Heschel, Hannah Arendt, Emmanuel Levinas*. Minneapolis: Fortress, 2011.

———. *Future of the Prophetic: Israel's Ancient Wisdom Re-Presented*. Minneapolis: Fortress, 2014.

———. *O, Jerusalem! The Contested Future of the Jewish Covenant*. Minneapolis: Fortress, 1999.

Epstein-Levi, Rebecca Jane. "Safe, Sane, and Attentive: Toward a Jewish Ethic of Sex and Public Health." PhD diss., University of Virginia, 2017.

Erlewine, Robert. *Judaism and the West: From Hermann Cohen to Joseph Soloveitchik*. Bloomington: Indiana University Press, 2016.

Etkes, Immanuel. *Rabbi Israel Salanter and the Mussar Movement: Seeking the Torah of Truth*. Translated by Jonathan Chipman. Philadelphia: The Jewish Publication Society, 1993.

Farag, Murād. "The War for Our Nation." Translated by Fuad Saleh. In *Modern Middle Eastern Jewish Thought: Writings on Identity, Politics, and Culture, 1893–1958*, edited by Moshe Behar and Zvi Ben-Dor Benite, 49–61. Waltham MA: Brandeis University Press, 2013.

Feiner, Shmuel. *The Jewish Enlightenment*. Translated by Chaya Naor. Philadelphia: University of Pennsylvania Press, 2004.

Feinstein, Edward. *The Chutzpah Imperative: Empowering Today's Jews for a Life That Matters*. Woodstock VT: Jewish Lights, 2014.

Filler, Emily A. "A Stubborn and Rebellious Bible: Modern Jewish Scripture, Troubling Texts, and the Recovery of Rabbinic Hermeneutics." PhD diss., University of Virginia, 2017.

Finkel, Natan Tzevi. *Or ha-Tzafun*. 3 vols. Jerusalem: Yeshivat Ḥevron, 1959.

———. *Siḥot ha-Sabba mi-Slabodka*. Edited by Yekutiel Cohen. 2 vols. Jerusalem, 2009.

Friedman, Ariella. *Ba'ah me-Ahavah [Annie Oakley Won Twice]*. Tel Aviv: Hakibbutz Hameuchad, 1996.

Friedman, Yisroel of Chortkov. *Ginzei Yisrael*. Vol. 2. Jerusalem: Ezras Yisroel, 1986.

Friedman, Yisroel. *The Rebbes of Chortkov*. Brooklyn: Mesorah, 2003.

Garb, Jonathan. "'Alien' Culture in the Thought of Rabbi Kook's Circle." In *Study and Knowledge in Jewish Thought*, edited by Howard Kreisel, 253–64. Beer Sheva: Ben-Gurion University of the Negev Press, 2006.

Gelman, Yehuda. "Aesthetics." In *The World of Rav Kook's Thought*, edited by Benjamin Ish Shalom and Shalom Rosenberg, translated by Shalom Carmy and Bernard Casper, 195–206. New York: Avi Chai, 1991.

Gibbs, Robert. *Correlations in Rosenzweig and Levinas*. Princeton NJ: Princeton University Press, 1992.

Gilligan, Carol. *In a Different Voice: Psychological Theory and Women's Development*. Cambridge MA: Harvard University Press, 1992.

Ginsburgh, Yitzchak. *Rectifying the State of Israel: A Political Platform Based on Kabbalah*. 2nd ed. Jerusalem: Gal Einai, 2003.

Goldberg, Hillel. *Israel Salanter: Text, Structure, Idea: The Ethics and Theology of an Early Psychologist of the Unconscious*. New York: Ktav, 1982.

Goldman, Emma. *Anarchism and Other Essays*. New York: Mother Earth, 1910.

———. "En Route." *Mother Earth* 3, no. 10 (1908): 351–55.

———. *Living My Life*. 2 vols. London: Duckworth, 1932.

———. *My Disillusionment in Russia*. Garden City NY: Doubleday, Page, 1923.

Gornick, Vivian. *Emma Goldman: Revolution as a Way of Life*. New Haven CT: Yale University Press, 2011.

Gottlieb, Lynn. *Trail Guide to the Torah of Nonviolence*. Paris: Éditions Terre d'Espérance (Earth of Hope Publishing), 2013.

Green, Arthur. *A Guide to the Zohar*. Stanford CA: Stanford University Press, 2004.

―――. *Tormented Master: A Life of Rabbi Nahman of Bratslav*. Tuscaloosa: University of Alabama Press, 1979.

Gruenberg, Benjamin C. *Science and the Public Mind*. New York: McGraw-Hill, 1935.

Haberman, Jacob. "Kaufmann Kohler and His Teacher Samson Raphael Hirsch." *Leo Baeck Institute Yearbook* 43, no. 1 (1998): 73–103.

Harris, Jay Michael. *How Do We Know This? Midrash and the Fragmentation of Modern Judaism*. Albany: SUNY Press, 1995.

Hartman, David. "The Halakhic Hero: Rabbi Joseph Soloveitchik, Halakhic Man." *Modern Judaism* 9, no. 3 (1989): 249–73.

Ḥayyim of Volozhin. *Ruaḥ ha-Ḥayyim: Peirush Rabbi Ḥayyim mi-Volozhin le-Pirkei Avot*. Vilna, 1859.

Held, Shai. *Abraham Joshua Heschel: The Call of Transcendence*. Bloomington: Indiana University Press, 2013.

Hertzberg, Arthur. *The Zionist Idea: A Historical Analysis and Reader*. Philadelphia: The Jewish Publication Society, 1997.

Heschel, Abraham Joshua. *God in Search of Man: A Philosophy of Judaism*. New York: Farrar, Straus & Cudahy, 1955.

―――. *Man Is Not Alone: A Philosophy of Religion*. New York: Farrar, Straus & Young, 1951.

―――. *Moral Grandeur and Spiritual Audacity: Essays*. Edited by Susannah Heschel. New York: Noonday, 1997.

―――. "The Moral Outrage of Vietnam." In *Vietnam: Crisis of Conscience*, edited by Michael Novak, Robert McAfee Brown, and Abraham Joshua Heschel, 48–61. New York: Association Press, Behrman House, Herder & Herder, 1967.

Heyward, Carter. *Our Passion for Justice: Images of Power, Sexuality, and Liberation*. New York: Pilgrim, 1984.

Holdheim, Samuel. *Das Religiöse und Politische im Judenthum*. Schwerin, Germany: C. Kürschner, 1845.

Hollander, Dana. "Contested Forgiveness: Jankélévitch, Levinas, and Derrida at the Colloque Des Intellectuels Juifs." In *Living Together: Jacques Derrida's Communities of Violence and Peace*, edited by Elisabeth Weber, 137–52. New York: Fordham University Press, 2013.

Huff, Dana. "Toward 'Moral Perfection': Integrating Judaic Concepts and Benjamin Franklin's Autobiography." *English Journal* 95, no. 6 (2006): 33–36.

Idelson-Shein, Iris. *Difference of a Different Kind: Jewish Constructions of Race during the Long Eighteenth Century*. Philadelphia: University of Pennsylvania Press, 2014.

Imhoff, Sarah. *Masculinity and the Making of American Judaism*. Bloomington: Indiana University Press, 2017.

Inbari, Motti. *Jewish Fundamentalism and the Temple Mount: Who Will Build the Third Temple?* Translated by Shaul Vardi. Albany: SUNY Press, 2009.

———. *Jewish Radical Ultra-Orthodoxy Confronts Modernity, Zionism and Women's Equality*. Translated by Shaul Vardi. New York: Cambridge University Press, 2016.

Isaacs, Samuel M. "Thanksgiving Sermon." *The Jewish Messenger*, December 3, 1858.

Jacobs, Louis. *The Doctrine of the Zaddik in the Thought of Elimelech of Lizensk*. Cincinnati: Judaic Studies Program, University of Cincinnati, 1978.

Jaffe, David. *Changing the World from the Inside Out: A Jewish Approach to Personal and Social Change*. Boulder CO: Shambhala, 2016.

Kahane, Meir. *Beyond Words: Selected Writings of Rabbi Meir Kahane, 1960–1990*. Edited by David Fein. 7 vols. Brooklyn: Institute for Publication of the Writings of Rabbi Meir Kahane, 2010.

———. *The Jewish Idea*. Translated by Raphael Blumberg. 2 vols. Jerusalem: Institute for Publication of the Writings of Rabbi Meir Kahane, 1996.

Kaplan, Edward K., and Samuel H. Dresner. *Abraham Joshua Heschel: Prophetic Witness*. New Haven CT: Yale University Press, 1998.

Kaplan, Mordecai M. *The Future of the American Jew*. New York: Macmillan, 1948.

Katz, Jacob. *Tradition and Crisis: Jewish Society at the End of the Middle Ages*. Translated by Bernard Dov Cooperman. New York: New York University Press, 1993.

Katz, Steven T., Shlomo Biderman, and Gershon Greenberg, eds. *Wrestling with God: Jewish Theological Responses during and after the Holocaust*. Oxford: Oxford University Press, 2007.

Kearney, Richard, and Emmanuel Levinas. "Dialogue with Emmanuel Levinas." In *Face to Face with Levinas*, edited by Richard A. Cohen, 13–33. Albany: SUNY Press, 1986.

Kedar, Karyn D. *Bridge to Forgiveness: Stories and Prayers for Finding God and Restoring Wholeness*. Woodstock VT: Jewish Lights, 2007.

Kedar, Nir. "Ben-Gurion's Mamlakhtiyut: Etymological and Theoretical Roots." *Israel Studies* 7, no. 3 (2002): 117–33.

Kitvei ha-Sabba mi-Kelm: Inyanei Elul ve-Yamim Nora'im. Benei Berak: Siftei Ḥakhamim, Va'ad le-Hafatzat Torah u-Musar, 1997.

Kogman, Tal. "Baruch Lindau's *Rešit Limmudim* (1788) and Its German Source: A Case Study of the Interaction between the Haskalah and German *Philanthropismus.*" *Aleph: Historical Studies in Science and Judaism* 9 (2009): 277–305.

Kohler, George Y. "Judaism Buried or Revitalised? Wissenschaft Des Judentums in Nineteenth Century Germany–Impact, Actuality, and Applicability Today." In *Jewish Thought and Jewish Belief,* edited by Daniel J. Lasker, *27–*63. Beer Sheva: Ben-Gurion University of the Negev Press, 2012.

Kohler, Kaufmann. *Hebrew Union College and Other Addresses.* Cincinnati: Ark, 1916.

———. *Jewish Theology: Systematically and Historically Considered.* New York: Macmillan, 1918.

Koltun-Fromm, Ken. *Abraham Geiger's Liberal Judaism: Personal Meaning and Religious Authority.* Bloomington: Indiana University Press, 2006.

Kook, Abraham Isaac. *Abraham Isaac Kook: The Lights of Penitence, the Moral Principles, Lights of Holiness, Essays, Letters, and Poems.* Translated by Ben Zion Bokser. New York: Paulist Press, 1978.

———. "Afikim ba-Negev." *Ha-Peles* 3 (1903).

———. *Ḥazon ha-Tzimḥonut ve-ha-Shalom.* Edited by David Cohen. Jerusalem, 1983.

———. *Ma'amarei ha-Re'ayah.* Vol. 1. Jerusalem, 1988.

———. *Orot.* Jerusalem: Degel Yerushalayim, 1920.

———. *Orot.* Jerusalem: Mossad Ha-Rav Kook, 2005.

———. *Tzimḥonut.* Edited by Shlomo Aviner. Jerusalem, 1983.

Kook, Tzevi Yehudah. *Siḥot ha-Rav Tzevi Yehudah.* Edited by Shlomo Aviner. Vol. 1. Jerusalem, 1993.

Küng, Hans, and Karl-Josef Kuschel, eds. *Global Ethic: The Declaration of the Parliament of the World's Religions.* Translated by John Bowden. New York: Continuum, 1993.

Kupfer, Shira, and Asaf Turgeman. "The Secularization of the Idea of Ahavat Israel and Its Illumination of the Scholem–Arendt Correspondence on Eichmann in Jerusalem." *Modern Judaism* 34, no. 2 (2014): 188–209.

Kushner, Harold S. *When Bad Things Happen to Good People.* Twentieth Anniversary Edition. New York: Schocken Books, 2001.

La Caze, Marguerite. *Wonder and Generosity: Their Role in Ethics and Politics*. Albany: SUNY Press, 2013.

Lamm, Norman. *The Religious Thought of Hasidism: Text and Commentary*. New York: Michael Scharf Publication Trust of Yeshiva University Press, 1999.

———. *Torah Lishmah: Torah for Torah's Sake in the Works of Rabbi Hayyim of Volozhin and His Contemporaries*. New York: Yeshiva University Press, 1989.

Lapin, Daniel. *America's Real War*. Sisters OR: Multnomah, 1999.

Lefin, Menaḥem Mendel. *Ḥeshbon ha-Nefesh*. Vilna, 1844.

Levinas, Emmanuel. *Beyond the Verse: Talmudic Readings and Lectures*. Translated by Gary D. Mole. Bloomington: Indiana University Press, 1994.

———. *Difficult Freedom: Essays on Judaism*. Translated by Sean Hand. Baltimore: Johns Hopkins University Press, 1990.

———. *Ethics and Infinity*. Translated by Richard A. Cohen. Pittsburgh: Duquesne University Press, 1985.

———. *Is It Righteous to Be? Interviews with Emmanuel Lévinas*. Edited by Jill Robbins. Stanford CA: Stanford University Press, 2001.

———. *The Levinas Reader*. Edited by Seán Hand. Oxford: Basil Blackwell, 1989.

———. *Nine Talmudic Readings*. Translated by Annette Aronowicz. Bloomington: Indiana University Press, 1990.

———. *Of God Who Comes to Mind*. Translated by Bettina Bergo. 2nd ed. Stanford CA: Stanford University Press, 1998.

———. *Totality and Infinity: An Essay on Exteriority*. Translated by Alphonso Lingis. Pittsburgh: Duquesne University Press, 2013.

Levy, Lital. "Edification between Sect and Nation: Murad Farag and Al-Tahdhib, 1901–1903." In *Intellectuals and Civil Society in the Middle East: Liberalism, Modernity and Political Discourse*, edited by Mohammed A. Bamyeh, 57–78. New York: I. B. Tauris, 2012.

Lindau, Baruch. "Toledot ha-Minim ha-Tiviyim." *Ha-Me'asef* 4 (1788): 211–18.

Luz, Ehud. *Wrestling with an Angel: Power, Morality, and Jewish Identity*. Translated by Michael Swirsky. New Haven CT: Yale University Press, 2003.

Luzzatto, Moses Ḥayyim. *Mesillat Yesharim: The Path of the Upright*. Translated by Mordecai Menahem Kaplan. Commentary by Ira F. Stone. Philadelphia: The Jewish Publication Society, 2010.

Magid, Shaul. "'America Is No Different,' 'America Is Different'—Is There an American Jewish Fundamentalism?" In *Fundamentalism: Perspectives on a Contested History*, edited by Simon A. Wood and David Harrington Watt, 70–107. Columbia: University of South Carolina Press, 2014.

———. "In Search of a Critical Voice in the Jewish Diaspora: Homelessness and Home in Edward Said and Shalom Noah Barzofsky's Netivot Shalom." *Jewish Social Studies* 12 (2006): 193–227.

———. *Meir Kahane: The Public Life and Political Thought of an American Jewish Radical*. Princeton NJ: Princeton University Press, 2021.

Maier-Katkin, Daniel. *Stranger from Abroad: Hannah Arendt, Martin Heidegger, Friendship, and Forgiveness*. New York: Norton, 2010.

Maimonides, Moses. "Eight Chapters." In *Ethical Writings of Maimonides*, translated by Raymond L. Weiss and Charles E. Butterworth, 59–104. New York: New York University Press, 1975.

———. *The Guide of the Perplexed*. Translated by Shlomo Pines. Vol. 2. Chicago: University of Chicago Press, 1963.

Margaliot, Yeshaya Asher Zelig. *Ashrei ha-Ish*. Jerusalem: Breslov, 1921.

Mark, Zvi. "The Contemporary Renaissance of Braslav Hasidism: Ritual, Tiqqun and Messianism." In *Kabbalah and Contemporary Spiritual Revival*, edited by Boaz Huss, 101–16. Beer Sheva: Ben-Gurion University of the Negev Press, 2011.

———. "Naḥman of Bratslav." In *Encyclopedia Judaica*, edited by Michael Berenbaum and Fred Skolnik, 2nd ed., 14:748–53. Detroit: Macmillan Reference, 2007.

Mbuvi, Amanda Beckenstein. "Avadim Hayinu: An Intersectional Jewish Perspective on the Global Ethic of Solidarity." In *Multi-Religious Perspectives on a Global Ethic: In Search of a Common Morality*, edited by Myriam Renaud and William Schweiker, 85–94. New York: Routledge, 2021.

———. *Belonging in Genesis: Biblical Israel and the Politics of Identity Formation*. Waco TX: Baylor University Press, 2016.

Mendelssohn, Moses, ed. *Sefer Netivot ha-Shalom*. Vol. 3. Vilna, 1851.

Meyer, Michael A. "'Most of My Brethren Find Me Unacceptable': The Controversial Career of Rabbi Samuel Holdheim." *Jewish Social Studies* 9, no. 3 (2003): 1–19.

Michaelson, Jay. "Into Life: The Humanism of the Exodus: Parashat Beshalach (Exodus 13:17–17:16)." In *Torah Queeries: Weekly*

Commentaries on the Hebrew Bible, edited by Gregg Drinkwater, Joshua Lesser, and David Shneer, 89–92. New York: New York University Press, 2009.

Mirsky, Yehudah. *Rav Kook: Mystic in a Time of Revolution*. New Haven CT: Yale University Press, 2014.

Mittleman, Alan. *Hope in a Democratic Age: Philosophy, Religion, and Political Theory*. Oxford: Oxford University Press, 2009.

———. "Marc Ellis: The Torah as a Suicide Pact." In *The Jewish Divide over Israel: Accusers and Defenders*, edited by Edward Alexander and Paul Bogdanor, 177–93. New Brunswick NJ: Transaction, 2006.

Morinis, Alan. *Everyday Holiness: The Jewish Spiritual Path of Mussar*. Boston: Trumpeter, 2007.

———. *With Heart in Mind: Mussar Teachings to Transform Your Life*. Boston: Trumpeter, 2014.

Nadler, Allan. *The Faith of the Mithnagdim: Rabbinic Responses to Hasidic Rapture*. Baltimore: Johns Hopkins University Press, 1997.

Naḥman of Bratslav. *Sefer ha-Middot*. Lubavitch, 1821.

———. *Sefer Hamidot: The Book of Traits*. Ebay Hanachal, 2014.

———. *Sefer Likkutei Moharan*. Vol. 1. Jerusalem, 1975.

Nahmanides (Ramban). *Commentary on the Torah: Leviticus*. Translated by Charles B. Chavel. New York: Shilo, 1973.

Neudecker, Reinhard. "'And You Shall Love Your Neighbor as Yourself—I Am the Lord' (Lev 19:18) in Jewish Interpretation." *Biblica* 73, no. 4 (1992): 496–517.

Newman, Louis E. "Balancing Justice and Mercy: Reflections on Forgiveness in Judaism." *Journal of Religious Ethics* 41, no. 3 (2013): 435–56.

———. *An Introduction to Jewish Ethics*. Upper Saddle River NJ: Pearson Prentice Hall, 2005.

———. *Past Imperatives: Studies in the History and Theory of Jewish Ethics*. Albany: SUNY Press, 1998.

———. "Woodchoppers and Respirators: The Problem of Interpretation in Contemporary Jewish Ethics." *Modern Judaism* 10, no. 1 (1990): 17–42.

Ohana, David. *The Origins of Israeli Mythology: Neither Canaanites nor Crusaders*. Translated by David Maisel. Cambridge: Cambridge University Press, 2012.

————. *Political Theologies in the Holy Land: Israeli Messianism and Its Critics.* London: Routledge, 2010.

Oz, Amos. *The Slopes of Lebanon.* Translated by Maurie Goldberg-Bartura. Boston: Mariner Books, 2012.

Padowitz, Joel. "Ḥeshbon ha'Nefesh for the Twenty-First Century." *B'or Ha'Torah* 23 (2015): 110–26.

Papo, Eliezer. *Pele Yo'etz.* Vienna: Joseph Schlesinger, 1876.

Peters, Rebecca Todd. *Solidarity Ethics: Transformation in a Globalized World.* Minneapolis: Fortress, 2014.

Peterson, Christopher, and Martin E. P. Seligman. *Character Strengths and Virtues: A Handbook and Classification.* Washington DC: American Psychological Association; Oxford University Press, 2004.

Pinhas of Polotsk. *Keter Torah.* Jerusalem: Ya'akov Klein, 1896.

Plaskow, Judith. "Preaching against the Text." In *The Coming of Lilith: Essays on Feminism, Judaism, and Sexual Ethics, 1972–2003*, edited by Donna Berman and Judith Plaskow, 152–56. Boston: Beacon, 2005.

————. *Standing Again at Sinai: Judaism from a Feminist Perspective.* New York: HarperSanFrancisco, 1991.

————. "Towards a New Theology of Sexuality." In *Twice Blessed: On Being Lesbian, Gay, and Jewish*, edited by Christie Balka and Andy Rose, 141–51. Boston: Beacon, 1989.

Polland, Annie, and Daniel Soyer. *Emerging Metropolis: New York Jews in the Age of Immigration, 1840–1920.* City of Promises: A History of the Jews of New York 2. New York: New York University Press, 2012.

Presner, Todd Samuel. *Muscular Judaism: The Jewish Body and the Politics of Regeneration.* London: Routledge, 2007.

Pruzansky, Steven. *Judges for Our Time: Contemporary Lessons from the Book of Shoftim.* Jerusalem: Gefen, 2009.

Rabinovich, Shlomo Ha-Kohen. *Sefer Nifla'ot ha-Tiferet Shlomo.* Edited by Avraham Shmu'el Tzevi Hirsch Silberstein. Piotrków, 1923.

Rabinovitch, Simon, ed. *Jews and Diaspora Nationalism: Writings on Jewish Peoplehood in Europe and the United States.* Waltham MA: Brandeis University Press, 2012.

Ramon, Einat. "The Matriarchs and the Torah of Hesed (Loving-Kindness)." *Nashim: A Journal of Jewish Women's Studies & Gender Issues* 10 (2006): 154–77.

Rapoport-Albert, Ada. "From Woman as Hasid to Woman as 'Tsadik' in the Teachings of the Last Two Lubavitcher Rebbes." *Jewish History* 27, nos. 2–4 (2013): 435–73.

Ravitzky, Aviezer. *Messianism, Zionism, and Jewish Religious Radicalism.* Translated by Michael Swirsky and Jonathan Chipman. Chicago: University of Chicago Press, 1996.

Rosen-Zvi, Ishay. *Demonic Desires: Yetzer Hara and the Problem of Evil in Late Antiquity.* Philadelphia: University of Pennsylvania Press, 2011.

Rosenthal, David. *Why Open Orthodoxy Is Not Orthodox.* Yad Yosef Publications, 2016.

Roth, Sol. "Towards a Definition of Humility." *Tradition* 14 (1973): 5–22.

Rubenstein, Jonathan. "None Shall Hurt or Destroy: A Translation of *A Vision of Vegetarianism and Peace* by Rav Avraham Yitzhak Hacohen Cook." Rabbinic thesis, Hebrew Union College-Jewish Institute of Religion, Cincinnati, 1986.

Rudman, Reuben M. "Kol Yisrael Areivim Zeh ba-Zeh." *Tradition* 42, no. 2 (2009): 35–49.

Ruttenberg, Danya. "The Hermeneutics of Curiosity: On Reclamation." In *New Jewish Feminism: Probing the Past, Forging the Future*, edited by Elyse Goldstein, 59–65. Woodstock VT: Jewish Lights, 2009.

Sacks, Jonathan. *Faith in the Future.* Macon GA: Mercer University Press, 1997.

Salanter, Israel. "Or Yisra'el." In *Or Yisra'el*, edited by Isaac Blazer, 41–108. Vilna, 1900.

Satherley, Tessa. "'The Simple Jew': The 'Price Tag' Phenomenon, Vigilantism, and Rabbi Yitzchak Ginsburgh's Political Kabbalah." *Melilah* 10 (2013): 57–91.

Satlow, Michael L. "'They Abused Him like a Woman': Homoeroticism, Gender Blurring, and the Rabbis in Late Antiquity." *Journal of the History of Sexuality* 5, no. 1 (1994): 1–25.

———. "'Try to Be a Man': The Rabbinic Construction of Masculinity." *Harvard Theological Review* 89, no. 1 (1996): 19–40.

Savvas, Theophilus. "The Other Religion of Isaac Bashevis Singer." *Journal of American Studies* 52, no. 3 (2018): 660–81.

Schacter, Jacob J. "Facing the Truths of History." *The Torah U-Madda Journal* 8 (1998): 200–273.

Shneur Zalman of Liadi. *Likkutei Amarim [Tanya].* Shklow, 1806.

Schnur, Susan. "Beyond Forgiveness: Women, Can We Emancipate Our-selves from a Model Meant for Men?" *Lilith Magazine* 25, no. 3 (Fall 2001): 16–19, 45.

———. "Justice." In *Lifecycles: Jewish Women on Biblical Themes in Contemporary Life*, edited by Debra Orenstein and Jane Rachel Litman, 331–33. Woodstock VT: Jewish Lights, 1997.

Scholem, Gershom. *The Messianic Idea in Judaism and Other Essays on Jewish Spirituality*. New York: Schocken Books, 1971.

———. *Sabbatai Ṣevi: The Mystical Messiah, 1626–1676*. Translated by R. J. Zwi Werblowsky. Princeton NJ: Princeton University Press, 1973.

Schwartz, Yoel. *The Ben Torah and His World*. Translated by Yosef Mayer. Jerusalem: Jerusalem Academy, 1990.

———. *Ha-Ḥazek ba-Musar*. Jerusalem: Dvar Yerushalayim, 1982.

———. *Sidrat ha-Middot*. Jerusalem, 1999.

Schwartz, Yoel, and Yitzchak Goldstein. *Ha-Shoah: Leket Devarim be-Nose Ḥurban Yahadut Eiropah 5700–5705 mitokh Aspaklaryah shel Torah*. Jerusalem: Ha-Mosad le-Iddud Limmud ha-Torah, 1988.

Schwarz, Sid. *Judaism and Justice: The Jewish Passion to Repair the World*. Woodstock VT: Jewish Lights, 2006.

Seeman, Don. "Violence, Ethics, and Divine Honor in Modern Jewish Thought." *Journal of the American Academy of Religion* 73, no. 4 (2005): 1015–48.

Shapira, Anita. "Herzl, Ahad Ha-'Am, and Berdichevsky: Comments on Their Nationalist Concepts." *Jewish History* 4, no. 2 (1990): 59–69.

———. *Land and Power: The Zionist Resort to Force, 1881–1948*. New York: Oxford University Press, 1992.

Shapira, Tsevi Elimelekh. *Benei Yisakhar*. Vol. 2. Jerusalem: S. A. Sifrei Kodesh, 2005.

Shapiro, Marc B. *Changing the Immutable: How Orthodox Judaism Rewrites Its History*. Oxford: Littman Library of Jewish Civilization, 2015.

Shulman, Alix Kates, ed. *Red Emma Speaks: An Emma Goldman Reader*. 3rd ed. Amherst NY: Humanity Books, 1998.

Silver, Mitchell. *A Plausible God: Secular Reflections on Liberal Jewish Theology*. New York: Fordham University Press, 2006.

Singer, Isaac Bashevis. "Foreword." In *Vegetarianism: A Way of Life*, by Dudley Giehl, vii–ix. New York: Barnes & Noble, 1979.

————. "Preface." In *Food for the Spirit: Vegetarianism and the World Religions*, by Steven Rosen, i–ii. New York: Bala Books, 1987.

Sinkoff, Nancy. *Out of the Shtetl: Making Jews Modern in the Polish Border- lands*. Providence RI: Brown Judaic Studies, 2004.

Solomon, Esther. "Rabbi Eliyahu Eliezer Dessler: Not Quite the Musar Traditionalist." *Daat: A Journal of Jewish Philosophy & Kabbalah*, no. 82 (2016): cv–cxxxii.

Soloveitchik, Joseph Dov. *Halakhic Man*. Translated by Lawrence Kaplan. Philadelphia: The Jewish Publication Society, 1983.

Steinsaltz, Adin. *Understanding the Tanya: Volume Three in the Definitive Com- mentary on a Classic Work of Kabbalah by the World's Foremost Authority*. Translated by Yaacov David Shulman. San Francisco: Jossey-Bass, 2007.

Stillman, Norman A. *Jews of Arab Lands in Modern Times*. Philadelphia: The Jewish Publication Society, 1991.

Stone, Ira F. "Anavah (Humility)." *Mussar Leadership E-Newsletter* 5, no. 10 (August 4, 2013). Mussar Leadership, Temple Beth Zion–Beth Israel, Philadelphia.

————. *A Responsible Life: The Spiritual Path of Mussar*. New York: Aviv, 2006.

Stromberg, David. "Rebellion and Creativity: Contextualizing Isaac Bashe- vis Singer's 'Author's Note' to *The Penitent*." In *Geveb: A Journal of Yiddish Studies*, June 2016, 1–16.

Tamaret, Aharon Shmuel. *Sefer Kenesset Yisrael u-Milḥamot ha-Goyim*. War- saw, 1920.

Telushkin, Joseph. *A Code of Jewish Ethics*. Vol. 1. New York: Bell Tower, 2006.

Tirosh-Samuelson, Hava. "Judith Plaskow: An Intellectual Portrait." In *Judith Plaskow: Feminism, Theology, and Justice*, edited by Hava Tirosh- Samuelson and Aaron W. Hughes, 1–25. Leiden: Brill, 2014.

Tishby, Isaiah, and Joseph Dan. *Mivḥar Sifrut ha-Musar [Hebrew Ethical Literature: Selected Texts]*. Tel Aviv: M. Newman, 1970.

Van Houten, Christiana. *The Alien in Israelite Law*. Sheffield: JSOT Press, 1991.

Walzer, Michael, Menachem Lorberbaum, Noam Zohar, and Ari Ackerman, eds. *The Jewish Political Tradition*. Vol. 2. New Haven CT: Yale University Press, 2003.

Weinberg, Sheila Peltz. "Leaving Egypt Again: Aging with Awareness." In *Chapters of the Heart: Jewish Women Sharing the Torah of Our Lives*, edited by Sue Levi Elwell and Nancy Fuchs Kreimer, 155–65. Eugene OR: Cascade Books, 2013.

Weissblum, Elimelekh. *Sefer No'am Elimelekh*. Lemberg: A. N. Süss, 1865.

Wiesel, Elie. *Messengers of God*. New York: Simon & Schuster, 1985.

Wiesenthal, Simon. *The Sunflower: On the Possibilities and Limits of Forgiveness*. Rev. and expanded ed. New York: Schocken Books, 1998.

Willig, Simcha. "Gadlut ha-Adam and the Greatness of Humanity: A Textual Analysis of Rabbi Nathan Tzvi Finkel's Psycho-Religious Educational Philosophy." PhD diss., New York University, 2016.

Wine, Sherwin T. *Celebration: A Ceremonial and Philosophic Guide for Humanists and Humanistic Jews*. Amherst NY: Prometheus Books, 2003.

———. "Demystifying Family Values." *Humanistic Judaism* 41, nos. 1–2 (2012–13): 23–27.

———. *Judaism beyond God*. Hoboken NJ: Ktav, Society for Humanistic Judaism, and Milan Press, 1995.

———. "Our Dietary Laws." *Humanistic Judaism* 41, nos. 3–4 (2013): 21–23.

———. *Staying Sane in a Crazy World: A Guide to Rational Living*. Birmingham MI: Center for New Thinking, 1995.

Wodziński, Marcin. "Women and Hasidism: A 'Non-Sectarian' Perspective." *Jewish History* 27 (2013): 399–434.

Wolfensohn, James D. *A Global Life*. New York: PublicAffairs, 2010.

Yanai, Nathan. "Ben-Gurion's Concept of Mamlahtiut and the Forming Reality of the State of Israel." *Jewish Political Studies Review* 1, no. 1–2 (1989): 151–77.

Yanklowitz, Shmuly. *Postmodern Jewish Ethics: Emerging Social Justice Paradigms*. CreateSpace, 2017.

———. *The Soul of Jewish Social Justice*. Jerusalem: Urim, 2014.

Ziv, Simḥah Zissel. *Sefer Ḥokhmah u-Musar*. Vol. 1. New York, 1957.

———. *Sefer Ḥokhmah u-Musar*. Vol. 2. Jerusalem, 1964.

Zohar, Zvi. *Rabbinic Creativity in the Modern Middle East*. London: Bloomsbury, 2013.

———. "Traditional Flexibility and Modern Strictness: Two Halakhic Positions on Women's Suffrage." In *Sephardi and Middle Eastern Jewries: History and Culture in the Modern Era*, edited by Harvey E. Goldberg, 119–33. Bloomington: Indiana University Press, 1996.

Zwecker, Tal Moshe, ed. *Mipeninei Noam Elimelech*. Southfield MI: Targum, 2008.

Subject Index

Aaron (Biblical figure), 244, 282
Abraham (Biblical figure): and courage, 89, 102, 111–13, 115, 121, 123, 132; and curiosity, 376n25; and forgiveness, 222; and humility, 69; and justice, 352; and love, 237, 245, 248–49, 258–59, 264; and solidarity, 284, 285–86, 306, 307, 315
abstinence, sexual, 46, 136, 146, 148–50
Abusch-Magder, Ruth, xxii, 57, 83–86, 87; "Should a Woman Be Humble?," 84–86
activism, 129–32, 267, 305–6, 309–10
Adam (Biblical figure), 39–40, 48, 178–79, 180, 283–84
African Americans, 20, 52–53, 85, 310
Agag, King (Biblical figure), 330, 343
Agudat Israel, 280–81, 287
Akiva, Rabbi, 187–88, 236, 238, 239–40, 254
Alliance Israélite Universelle, 293, 389n39
Alpert, Rebecca, xxii; comparisons with, 77, 79, 83, 235, 346; on humility, 57, 73–76; on justice, 337–40; *Like Bread on the Seder Plate*, 73, 74–76, 337, 339–40
Amalekites, 109, 111, 318, 341, 343–44
America, 18–20, 66–67, 130–31, 160, 172–74, 193–94, 299
America's Real War (Lapin), 18, 19–20
Amidah, 237, 259, 260, 261
Amir, Yagal, 266
anarchism, 177, 279
"Anavah (Humility)" (Stone), 81–83

"and" (concept), 196
angels: and honesty, 11, 12; and humility, 63, 64–65; and justice, 324–25, 325–26; and love, 246, 248; and solidarity, 287, 288
anger, 70, 153–54, 190, 194–96, 203, 204–5, 230, 231
animality of human beings, 56, 58, 70, 77, 138–39, 141, 143–47, 166, 268–70
animals, nonhuman, 56, 77–78, 79, 238, 267–70, 318, 330, 331–35, 341, 343, 353
anthropocentrism, 35, 57, 77–79
antisemitism, 218, 291, 293, 356
apologies, 226, 227
appetites, 35, 38, 40–41, 70, 74, 77, 135–39, 142, 144–47, 163, 164, 168–69
"Are Jews Avoiding Anti-Trump Activism out of Fear, or Moral Failure?" (Cotler), 130–32
Arendt, Hannah: comparisons with, on courage, 117–18, 120; comparisons with, on forgiveness, 211, 215, 217, 218, 219, 220, 222, 225, 229; comparisons with, on love, 253, 257; comparisons with, on solidarity, 295, 306; on compassion, 249–53; *Eichmann in Jerusalem*, 249–50; on forgiveness, 207–10, 385n23; *The Human Condition*, 207, 208–10; *The Jewish Writings*, 292–95, 387n25; Letter for Gershom Scholem, 251–53; on love, 249–53; *On Revolution*, 250, 251–53; on political action, 289–95; on solidarity, 275, 289–95

413

Index of Classical Sources

Mishnah

To order or obtain more information on these or other
Jewish Publication Society titles, visit jps.org.